Popular Culture

Perspectives for Readers and Writers

D1125131

Popular Culture

Perspectives for Readers and Writers

Megan O'Neill

Stetson University

THOMSON
— ✳ — ™
HEINLE

Australia Canada Mexico Singapore Spain United Kingdom United States

THOMSON
TM
HEINLE

Popular Culture
Perspectives for Readers and Writers
Megan O'Neill

Publisher: *Michael Rosenberg*
Development Editor: *Camille Adkins*
Project Manager, Editorial Production: *Barrett Lackey*
Print/Media Buyer: *Marcia Locke*
Permissions Editor: *Beverly Wyatt*
Production Service: *Graphic World Publishing Services*

Photo Researcher: *Cheri Throop*
Cover Images: *(background) The Everett Collection, NY; (front, top) © Reuters Newsmedia, Inc./CORBIS; (front, bottom) © SYGMA/CORBIS; (back, right) © AP Photo/Suzanne Plunkett/AP/Wide World Photos, NY; (back, left) Jim Cornfield/CORBIS*
Cover Printer: *Phoenix Color*
Compositor: *Graphic World, Inc.*
Printer: *Phoenix Color*

Printed in the United States of America
2 3 4 5 6 7 8 9 10   06 05 04 03 02

For more information contact Heinle, 25 Thomson Place, Boston, MA 02210 USA,
or you can visit our Internet site at http://www.heinle.com

ISBN: 0-1550-7113-0

Library of Congress Catalog Card Number: 2001097979

With much appreciation
for her unflagging love and enthusiasm
for anything I ever wanted to do
(no matter how wild it was),
I dedicate this book
to my beloved and much missed grandmother,
Helene Ormonde Edmonds.

PREFACE FOR THE INSTRUCTOR

When I first began teaching college freshmen how to write (I was learning how to teach at the same time), I was encouraged to draw from real life for my writing assignments. Shortly after that, I brought in to class a TV program, which we watched and talked about—and shortly after *that*, I was convinced, like so many other writing faculty have been in the last ten years, that pop culture was the way to go. It was a revelation for everyone in the classroom: the Gen-X teacher was gratified that her obsessions worked as a teaching tool in class, and the students were thrilled that they weren't having to learn "great ideas," even when they were in fact learning about them through the perspective of pop culture. That's the origin of this book: my need to bring in something that everyone, teacher and students, could have a good time with while they were learning from each other in a writing classroom, and my students' need to practice their growing skills at written expression on something they already knew and wouldn't balk at learning more about.

And it's worked for several years. Pop culture in the way this book defines it is a direct application of the everyday filtered through some sort of medium: video, audio, touch, and so forth. Pop culture is the way we talk to each other about issues that matter to us—it's the stories we tell to our children and to our adults, and it's the perspectives of everyone who hears or tells those stories. It's the everyday world and its meanings for us, as Michel de Certeau might say. The freshmen I've been in classrooms with for nearly 10 years seem to agree with me. I'm a better teacher for it, and I still learn something new and valuable every time I walk into class.

Like every writing teacher, I always work to help my students write better and better and better still, and I struggle over writing assignments and I agonize over freshman follies and foibles like the "in conclusion" line or the "in today's world" introduction. We still argue good-naturedly every term about what I think is important for them to learn and what they think is important—naturally, there's some disagreement. In some basic ways, freshmen writers are all alike—some of their writing habits won't change, no matter the text or the teacher. But in some other ways, pop culture gives students a handle on the world. Sometimes they feel completely in control of their lives, and sometimes they feel tossed and buffeted. There's real value in both experiences, because each sheds light on the other. What the average freshman in my courses lacks is a sense of perspective, which I have tried to help them develop.

THE SETUP

The way I chose to help students develop perspective was to introduce them to **one central concept** and then layer it around with **related concepts**, along the way asking questions that would draw out relationships between ideas. An anchor article starts each chapter and lays out some relevant issues and questions. The selections that follow each anchor (articles, images, Internet humor, poetry, interviews, song lyrics) elaborate or illustrate or complement, in some way, that anchor's central idea. This setup allows students to see connections in ways they're often not used to, which encourages them to develop perspective. Looking at each chapter's anchor and related articles through the eyes of the **anthropologist** helps students learn to come to a reading with few prior assumptions about what they might find. Finally, each chapter adds to that layering by suggesting **a different way of reading**—semiotics, reader-response, and so forth. This way, each element of the pedagogy works to reinforce each other element and makes this book work in freshman and sophomore courses as well.

Chapter One, "Listening to Generations," starts from the basics: pop music across the generations, including discussions of money and drugs and the "pop music lifestyle." Chapter Two, "Self Perceptions," asks students to examine the perspectives they have on bodies—and, by extension, on sexuality and gender roles. Chapter Three, "More Than Meets the Eye," examines the role of the image through a semiotic approach, while Chapter Four, "I Believe," explores new territory for pop culture readers by discussing perspectives on spirituality. Chapter Five, "What Comes Next," visits Shakespeare's undiscovered country—the future.

The **writing apparatus** is simple: suggestions for writing, but no assignments *per se*, allow teachers the most freedom and students the most flexibility. Each reading is followed by questions to ensure comprehension and critical thought. Each chapter ends with several ideas for writing in various shapes and forms. Each chapter's introduction includes a one page "extended writing idea," which students can use as a model or as a more detailed writing suggestion, and each chapter's readings conclude with an essay written by a student who worked with these selections and writing ideas.

Instructors can get a lot of **suggestions** for using *Popular Culture: Perspectives for Readers and Writers* well from the *Instructor's Manual*, written by myself and Susan Morris. We wrote it together because we were the ones most familiar with the way the book worked. But more importantly, we wrote it together because Susan and I have virtually nothing in common, no perspective to share, no governing ideology in common—except a love for teaching, for students, for writing, and for good-hearted people like each other. If we can make this book work in our very different class-rooms, we think anyone can make it work. The *Instructor's Manual* takes each chapter in turn and explores the ways to approach each reading, dis-cusses the classroom challenges we met up with, and offers some alterna-tive reading/writing ideas.

I did a lot of research along the path to this book, and I talked to a lot of people from outrider communities as I decided which perspectives to try to include and which ones I was better off leaving out. All the outrider spiri-tual communities, from *santeria* to Wicca to Muslim to orthodox Greek, taught me a lot about what's soul lifting and what isn't. The other outrider communities—practitioners of various sexual orientations and practices, small cults devoted to a single singer, and big fan bases following the Grate-ful Dead, the people who never watch TV but who always have the movie channels on—all talked to me pretty freely. Most of the dozens of people I talked to, from the Old School rap aficionado in Los Angeles to the heavily pierced leather fetishist in New Orleans to the strutting voodoo priest in Miami, all believed in some very basic common things: work on the soul is a good thing. Introspection is a good thing. Making the world healthier spiritually is a good thing. Enjoying sexuality is a good thing. None of them came to their beliefs lightly, and all had read widely and weighed op-tions. All were, in fact, modeling some degree of critical thinking, and the parallel between the kind of writing I teach in my classes and the kind of thinking these not-bound-for-college thinkers were doing was obvious. When the two meet throughout this text, great things can happen.

Popular Culture: Perspectives for Readers and Writers can let a teacher talk about what she finds interesting, and it can let students express what they find interesting. There are opportunities for "great ideas" here—what is Chapter Three but an extended meditation on Plato's allegory of the cave? There are opportunities for silliness too: how much significance is there, re-ally, to how many inches of gold chain Mr. T wears? The selections were chosen so that teachers could take a risky and sexy approach, a conserva-tive and trusted approach, a strictly 18-year-old approach, or a blended classroom approach.

The variety is conscious: short and long, professional and student, witch and "family values" guru, technoliterate and virtually innumerate, newspa-pers and scholarly journals, recognizable authors and brand-new ones, hal-lowed voices and upstarts. I hope you'll find something of value in here, and with any luck, it will be the recognition that any production of any discourse community reflects the tendencies of the group and the preferences of the in-dividual. In other words, this text is both general and specific: it reflects a lot of the artifacts that have made up my world, but it's also inclusive of the ar-tifacts that say "pop culture" to a great many people.

ACKNOWLEDGMENTS

It was a risk to write this text as a solo author, particularly for my first book. Although I was cautioned about doing so (thank you, Dana Elder, Tim Julet, Julie McBurney, and Harriett Prentiss), and now I know why I was cautioned, I'd do it again the same way, gray hairs and five years of ignoring my family notwithstanding. I had great help and support from a lot of people, in both my personal and professional lives. First in my heart are the students on whom I have inflicted this text in a wide variety of formats and revision stages: the freshmen at Eastern Washington University, the University of New Mexico, Creighton University in Omaha, and Stetson University in central Florida never failed to give me useful feedback, unexpected reactions, and questions I'd never thought to ask or answer. Talk about the value of revision: without the students, this wouldn't have been written. Thanks, folks.

Even as a solo textbook author, I had more help than from the students themselves. The faculty and administration at Creighton University and Stetson University gave me a lot of help and useful suggestions. Some even offered to teach from this text to help me get perspective on it. Susan Morris, Bob Churchill, and Nancy Barber each taught all or part of this text over the last few years, which helped me put it all together. In their roles as colleagues, department chairs, and deans, John Pearson; Karen Kaivola; Grady Ballenger; Michael Proterra, S.J.; John Fitzgibbons, S.J.; Bob Whipple; and Greg Zacharias reassured me that the research and scholarship were valuable, and that writing a textbook was a great way to combine teaching and research. They were right.

Most important, though, is to thank the publishing team for this book, because when I started this, I knew nothing about how a book gets published. Permissions, copyediting, typesetting, bargaining, begging . . . I learned, sometimes painfully, how a reader comes out of a press, and I appreciate the teachers who took a chance on a first-timer and were very, very patient with her: Camille Adkins, Senior Development Editor; Barrett Lackey, Production Manager; and Cheri Throop, Permissions Editor. Thanks go also to the reviewers who read version after version and gave me invaluable suggestions and advice:

Linda Brender, McComb College

Beverly Ann Chin, University of Montana

Kathryn Evans, University of San Francisco

Paul Heilker, Virginia Tech

Kathy McClelland, Auburn University

Lou Thompson, Texas Women's University

Even though I mostly ignored my family for five years while writing and revising this text, they never ignored me. My mother, my father and his wife, my sister and her family, and my brother and his wife were sometimes confused, sometimes proud, and sometimes horrified. I'm glad that my part-ner and the love of my life was proud, even when so much time I could have spent with him was spent instead with the book. They were, each of them, always supportive, and I'm glad to say that now that I've emerged from the piles of manuscript and stray scraps of paper, I can have a life again. Can we go to Universal Studios now?

Megan O'Neill

PREFACE FOR STUDENTS

You've probably heard it before, but this isn't your usual pop culture textbook. You've probably come across pop culture readers before, but they never included discussions of body parts and alternative spiritual practices. Good! That way you can be surprised, enlightened, and challenged. This book should get you interested in learning more about what surrounds you every day: pop culture. You already know a lot about it, actually, but this book will help you learn even more about what's going on around you—and what's going on inside your head. I have only a few things to mention before you go on to read the general introduction, so I won't take much of your time.

FIRST OF ALL: DON'T RUSH TO JUDGMENT

There's a whole world of significance out there that you have probably already gotten a glimpse of, some of which you didn't like and some of which you didn't approve of. That's fine. But try to hold off on making final judgments until you've read and discussed and written about things with other people—you might surprise yourself. Certainly the perspectives of others will surprise you. They might also annoy you—but again, be patient with them. Others are being patient with you, too.

Let me tell you how this book happened. I did a lot of research, and I talked to a lot of people from outrider communities, the non-mainstream communities, as I decided which perspectives to try to include and which ones I was better off leaving out. I thought I knew a lot already, but all the spiritual communities, from *santeria* to Wicca to Muslim to orthodox Greek, taught me a lot about what's soul lifting and what isn't. The other outrider communities— practitioners of various sexual orientations and practices, small cults devoted to a single singer and big fanbases following the Grateful Dead, the people who never watch TV but who always have the movie channels on—all talked to me pretty freely. I talked to dozens of people in person and e-mailed even more people.

And oddly, despite all the differences I found, I also found lots of similarities. From the Old School rap aficionado in Los Angeles, who toyed with a gun the entire time we talked, to the heavily pierced leather fetishist in New Orleans (he must have had a pound of metal inserted in his face), to the strutting voodoo priest in Miami (who debunked a *20/20* news report for me), they all believed in some very basic common things: work on the soul is a good thing. Introspection is a good thing. Making the world healthier spiritually is a good thing. Enjoying your own body is a good thing. None of them came to their beliefs lightly, and all had read widely and weighed options. I came to talk to them and discovered I had a lot of preconceived notions I hadn't been aware of. I ask you to remember that you, too, may discover some assumptions you didn't know you had.

SECOND: DRAW ON WHAT YOU KNOW

The trick in college is to turn what you know into a desire to learn more. Any college—technical or liberal arts—wants you to learn how to be a better thinker and a better writer. The way to do that is to remain secure in what you know while at the same time remembering that there's more in the world than you've had a chance to meet yet. Use your own knowledge to objectively assess what you come across. And again, be patient. Learning is hard work, and it takes time.

THIRD: WRITE AS IF YOU WERE THINKING ON THE PAGE

I've heard from a lot of freshmen about how they suffer from a block every time they attempt to write—because they're trying to write perfectly, as the *end result of thinking*. Try instead to think of writing as a way to *record your thought process*. The revision process is where most real "writing" happens— as you work through ideas and make them your own, you'll find yourself making changes in how much you explain things, what kinds of explanation you use, and so forth. In early drafts, you're explaining to yourself; in revisions, you're learning to explain to a larger audience, because you already understand it yourself. Writing your ideas out on the page is a way to separate yourself from them, to see them clearly, to get an objective grasp on them. Writing isn't the enemy here—it's a tool that can be really useful if you learn how to use it.

FOURTH: TAKE THE INITIATIVE

Challenge yourself. Don't sit back and be passive—take charge of your own education and get your hands dirty while you do it. Be involved in discussions, write more than you have to, go the extra mile and bring in outside sources. Do more than you absolutely have to. And then, see what happens. Your writing skill will develop more rapidly, your critical thinking faculties will be sharper faster, and your class will become a lot more involving than you might have thought possible.

FIFTH, AND LAST: ENJOY YOURSELF

Pop culture is fun. Every time you rank on a movie or laugh at a joke, you're responding to pop culture. Have fun with it—this is real life, and you might as well enjoy it. If you can identify the influences on your life, so much the better—but even if you can't, you can still enjoy the readings and the experiences this book will give you. Have a good time with it. I hope you'll let me know what you think of the book. E-mail me at mboneill@stetson.edu with comments, suggestions, or questions.

Megan O'Neill

CONTENTS

CHAPTER 3
MORE THAN MEETS THE EYE: PERSPECTIVES ON POPULAR IMAGES, 129

CHAPTER 4
"I BELIEVE": PERSPECTIVES ON SPIRITUALITY IN POP CULTURE, 215

CHAPTER 5
THE FUTURE: PERSPECTIVES ON WHAT COMES NEXT, 266

Popular Culture

Perspectives for Readers and Writers

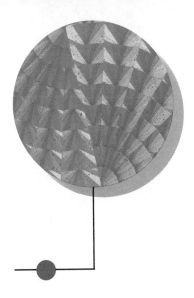

INTRODUCTION

Erica Kane. Darth Vader. The Rock. Barney. The X-Men.

You recognize most if not all of these names. The characters are products or examples of **pop culture**: a culture that develops from the people and that expresses a certain significance or meaning. Characters from soap operas, movies, professional wrestling, popular music, and comic books all participate in pop culture, and when we watch the shows or listen to the music, we're participating in creating that culture. Pop culture is all around you.

You might be most familiar with pop culture as the culture of television and movies. Scholar Barry Brummett defines television as "an immensely rich world" of popular culture, because "nearly everyone watches television and, even if not everyone sees the same shows, they are likely to know in general about the shows that they do not see" (Brummett 20). In other words, the pervasive nature of television (and movies) lets us say that these media are elements of—or perhaps vehicles for—popular culture. For example, soap opera watchers can usually identify a couple of major characters from soaps other than their favorites. Even if someone only watches *General Hospital*, in other words, he'll still be able to tell you what character Susan Lucci plays (Erica Kane) and on what soap (*All My Children*). And nearly everyone in the United States, soap opera fan or not, can describe a soap opera and name a few titles. Try it yourself.

Another example of popular culture is *Star Trek*. One recent study indicated that 53 percent of American citizens consider themselves *Trek* fans, despite demographics that identify *Trek*'s primary audience as young men between ages 18 and 39. The show is everywhere: *Star Trek* has produced five television series, ten movies, an animated series, literally hundreds of novels and comic books, and dozens of conventions every year, both in the United States and abroad. The *Trek* fans have become a phenomenon of pop culture themselves. Even if you've never seen the show, and even if when you saw it you didn't

1

Personalities in pop culture.

like it, you certainly know about *Trek* and may well be able to name the major characters, let alone the starship *Enterprise*. As Brummett says, these things are "part of the everyday experience of most people."

Pop culture is, in many respects, something that all Americans participate in: it's the mass culture *of the people*. And even when we don't actively participate in that culture—if you've never seen *Star Wars*, for instance—it's so pervasive, so inescapable, that you can probably tell us about the Force and even that Darth Vader is Luke Skywalker's father. We're participating in the culture, in other words, even if unconsciously. When we participate in it, even from a distance (for example, through working with a book like this), we're helping to create **popular culture.**

DEFINING CULTURE

Let's back up a few steps. After all, "something that all Americans participate in" could also mean environmental damage, and yet while this topic is often related to pop culture discussion (and is discussed in Chapter 5), not many people would consider the destruction of the ozone layer "pop culture." If the destruction of the ozone layer became the focus of pop songs, however, or if the lead character of a dramatic television series was an environmental activist, we might see things a bit differently. Does that mean that pop culture is what we find on TV or in pop music? Yes, but there's more to it than that.

Feeling the Force of pop culture?

To sort out some of the confusion, we need a working understanding of the term *culture*, which is, according to scholar Raymond Williams, "one of the two or three most complicated words in the English language."

Williams suggests three broad definitions. First of all, he says culture can be used to refer to "a general process of intellectual, spiritual, and aesthetic development" (Williams 90). Note the emphasis here on growth. By definition, culture is like the growth medium scientists use to cultivate bacteria: they grow certain organisms in a medium such as agar, a process that, in fact, is called *culturing*. This definition is rarely what we mean when we speak of *popular culture*, however.

A second use of the word *culture* suggests "a particular way of life, whether of a people, a period, or a group"(Williams 90). If we speak of the cultural development of Western Europe using this definition, we would have in mind, as John Storey points out, "not just intellectual and aesthetic factors, but the development of literacy, holidays, sport, religious festivals" (Storey 2). Thus, the distinction between American culture and Spanish or Uzbeki culture is easy to see—different holidays, different religious practices, different ideas about how to run a country, and so on. In a strictly second-definition sense, then, *culture* is often what makes one group of people collectively different from another group.

Thirdly and lastly, Williams suggests that culture can refer to:

> the works and practices of intellectual and especially artistic activity. In other words, those texts and practices whose principal function is to signify, to produce or to be the occasion for the production of meaning. [. . .] Using this definition, we would probably think of examples such as poetry, the novel, ballet, opera, fine art (91).

In other words, when we express some meaning, the form of our expression helps create an artistic culture of sorts—the culture of jazz music, of stage plays, of bronze sculpture. Music, theater, and sculpture each express some sort of meaning, and when we participate in it (by watching, attending, or admiring), we're helping create that culture of meaning. Note that the word *popular* comes from "the people"—popular culture is the culture of the everyday, created by us, our daily activities, our choices of entertainment, our beliefs, our clothes, and our social life.

To define popular culture in the way this book uses the term, we combine the second and third definitions. The second meaning—*a particular way of life*—gives us examples such as the Super Bowl, the use of piercing and tattooing for body modification, and the traveling road family known as the Deadheads, followers of the late Jerry Garcia and the Grateful Dead. In this book, a "particular way of life" is usually referred to as a particular **perspective**. The second meaning lets us derive the third: some *expression of meaning*. Let's look at it like this: "those texts and practices of a particular people or group, which signify or otherwise intend meaning." There is no single definition of pop culture by any means—in fact, we could argue that every person's pop culture is different than that of every other person. For the purposes of this book, however, pop culture generally refers to **the meaningful productions of a group (or groups) of people, often filtered through mass media and culture.**

A GROUP'S SHARED CHARACTERISTICS AND WAY OF LIFE

Notice how each of these examples of a "way of life" is a group—the Deadheads, the pierced and tattooed, the Super Bowl fanatics. Each group has its own culture: What goes along with football? Beer, the cheerleaders, pretzels, the commentators, the new commercials, the halftime show, pizza, and Monday morning quarterbacking. What "ways of life" go along with the Deadheads? How about the way of life that encourages piercing? We each belong to a lot of groups—you can probably name about a dozen off the top of your head. *Student, child of . . ., athlete, Hispanic, reader, member of the economic middle class, employee of . . ., flirt, X-phile, . . .* the list goes on. Groups can be as small as your family and as big as the whole human species (or bigger—for example, "intelligent life in the universe"), so when you're thinking about groups, don't limit yourself by size. What you want to use are *shared characteristics*, characteristics that members of the group share *and that they produce*.

Whatever is produced by a group is an *artifact* of that group. Artifacts are the "works and practices of intellectual and [. . .] artistic activity," for instance soap operas, pop music, and comics. It might sound odd to consider comic books an example of intellectual activity; after all, they're just comics. And that *is* all they are, if we only read them and don't think about their place in the culture. If we think about them as artifacts of pop culture, however, suddenly several other factors jump in to be considered. Williams suggests that literacy, holidays, sports, and religious practices are part of culture; so are novels, ballet, and fine art. Can we consider comics as an element of cultural literacy? Yes. They are, strictly speaking, *texts*: they tell a story in words and pictures. Can

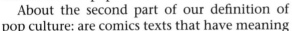

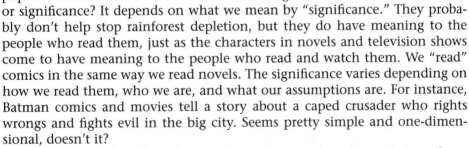

we also consider comics to be an aesthetic production? They offer drawing and color in representative and artistic ways, so again yes. Comics, then, can be seen as artifacts of a mass culture, and although some groups will read them more voraciously than others, all of us know what comics are and most of us have read at least one. Thus, they form and in some ways reproduce parts of the culture. In fact, they're produced in two ways: first, by the collective culture of Americans who participate in the "way of life" of comics, and second, by the culture of the comic artists themselves, the inkers and writers and the rest of the production teams. Comics, then, whether in strips in the Sunday paper or in "graphic novels" in the local Barnes & Noble, are artifacts of pop culture.

About the second part of our definition of pop culture: are comics texts that have meaning or significance? It depends on what we mean by "significance." They probably don't help stop rainforest depletion, but they do have meaning to the people who read them, just as the characters in novels and television shows come to have meaning to the people who read and watch them. We "read" comics in the same way we read novels. The significance varies depending on how we read them, who we are, and what our assumptions are. For instance, Batman comics and movies tell a story about a caped crusader who rights wrongs and fights evil in the big city. Seems pretty simple and one-dimensional, doesn't it?

But when we take a closer look at the context, or the culture, that produces Batman (and there must be one—why else would we have three movies based on the Batman comics?), we see that Batman might arise out of our collective need to see justice done. We hold that sort of ideal very high, culturally speaking. We might have created a fan following for Batman because we identify with him—he's one of our "group," in other words, even if only on the once-removed level of fiction, and he can do things that most of us would probably like to do but will never have the chance to. Batman also has a lot of great toys—the Batmobile is only one of them—and a sense of mystery. Many of us, even if we don't admit it, like to play with or own toys, and many of us find a sense of mystery tantalizing. We claim Batman for our own: he is a fictional representation of many of the importances in life. Once we see him as part of our group, we understand that he's not simple *or* one-dimensional. Quite the reverse, in fact.

Who is this guy Batman, anyway? Where does he come from? What drives him to do good deeds without wanting any recognition? When we find out that his parents were murdered in front of him when he was very young, we start to understand where he's coming from. We begin to identify with his sense of rage and his compulsion to fight evil and punish injustice. We start to agree that spending his considerable fortune in ways that benefit the downtrodden is worthy. In short, we're starting to analyze him, in order to find out what about him fascinates us enough to collectively produce so many Bat-artifacts. But we have to look at Batman's *context* in order to really understand him. Otherwise, he's just a vigilante in a rubber suit. Once we understand his perspective—that he's avenging his parents' murder—we can make sense of him. And we can understand him because we are part of the culture that created him; we share the necessary characteristics, in other words, to understand Batman as a product of his culture. We share enough of the context to understand the perspective. But we have to *look* beneath the random indicators, in this case, the sense of justice and mystery and the fantastical toys.

Batman, then, is one example of the significance of pop culture. He's part of a **mass culture** (nearly everyone in America can tell you who Batman is); he is part of a **text** (the comic book itself in one sense, but also a cultural morality tale about good and evil: our way of life) produced by a particular **group of people** (the team who produce the comics, but also ourselves: we help produce Batman by continuing to support his existence). His significance is a little trickier to see until we place him in context, but it's there once we think about it: justice, evil versus good, and our cultural insistence on doing good works are only three of Batman's meanings. Americans tend to place high value on these characteristics, and our culture thus produces, almost magically, a figure who embodies them (and has a trick rubber suit and a cool car to boot).

From that single example, then, comic book characters are significant: Batman stands for justice. Similarly, the X-Men could stand for an American ideal of unification: as mutants, the X-Men are feared by outsiders even though they use their mutated powers for good. Do all comic book heroes stand for justice? What about the characters in video games? What else might they represent? (It's worth doing some research; you might have a pretty good paper topic.)

Let's take another example of a group culture and look at it more deeply—the culture of science fiction. For the sake of argument, we can divide Americans into two groups: those who enjoy science fiction and those who don't. Regardless of their interest in science fiction, almost everyone knows about it, and it certainly expresses the artistic and aesthetic considerations of a group, so it's a part of pop culture. To some extent, these two groups have similar interests—they're part of American culture, after all.

But in a lot of ways, the two groups are widely divergent. They might read different books, watch different television programs, and pay to see different sorts of movies. People who enjoy science fiction probably went to see the *Alien* movies; people who don't enjoy it probably stayed away, although people who don't like science fiction but like horror movies might have bought tickets. In other words, the group of people who don't like science fiction share some characteristics among themselves that the group of people who have seen *2001: A Space Odyssey* 30 times do not share. These two groups also *produce* different characteristics: some of the members of the second group may write their own science fiction, whereas members of the first group may post to Internet newsgroups arguing that science fiction is a waste of imagination. Some of our best science fiction writers began by creating stop-action short films, so members of the second group may produce filmed versions of science fiction, even while the first group's members are talking with each other about how silly that is (or how bad the films are!).

In other words, each group produces *artifacts of its own culture*. And yet because both groups are fully aware of the presence of science fiction in their lives, we can consider this awareness a shared characteristic of the larger group of people. If we call the first group "anti–sci-fi" and the second group "sci-fi fans," we can call the much larger group of people (to which both of these groups belong) "thinkers about science fiction," and the shared characteristics include short stories, articles, films, conversations, and so on.

The interactions among dozens of groups just like these (comics and science fiction are only two of the possibilities) form a mass culture that expresses the significances and meanings of a way of life. We share ideas about what's important to us; we look for common ground. When we talk about what is and isn't important to us, we're forming and reinforcing a group identity, which looks at the world with a specific perspective: our own.

DISCOURSE AND POP CULTURE

All these modes of communication about our artifacts are forms of discussion, or **discourse**. We usually think of discourse as meaning conversation, but we can also consider a short story, a film, an article, a book, or a section of a book—like this introduction—to be a piece of discourse. Discourse aims to share ideas—it's communication. We have to communicate about ideas in order to share them, improve them, make decisions about them, and so on. So, going back to the sci-fi example, our three groups (the sci-fi fans, the anti–sci-fi fans, and the larger group of people who think about science fiction) form a culture that shares many of the same ideas and disseminates those ideas to other members of the culture; they form a *community of discourse*, and their discourse might not be limited to spoken or written communication.

Because it's a community, they may share other characteristics than just conversation topics; whether the discourse takes the form of gossiping about the next *Star Wars* movie, getting together to bash *A.I.* or to praise *Gattaca*, reading popular physics, making short films, or reading Arthur C. Clarke novels, common interests define the group boundaries. People in any of these groups are interested in how the future is depicted or in how "outer space" is dealt with in literary and nonfictional forms. Those core interests develop into individual tastes, and people having individual tastes then form specific discourse groups that are nonetheless related because of their core interests.

And these groups might interact with other groups in the culture, groups with even more diverse interests and perspectives on how "outer space" is dealt with by pop culture: NASA officials and astronauts, who are actually in the business of making science fiction happen; junior high kids who want to go to Space Camp at Kennedy Space Center; and editors at publishing houses like Harcourt and Pocket. See how the circles of influence and discourse widen and become more and more inclusive, even though they're all still bounded by the same core interests? Altogether, this process fulfills the definition of a discourse community.

You may be part of many, many groups, and you can identify yourself as part of each one because you share some or many of the characteristics of the group. Your gender, race, economic status, education level, preferences for entertainment and employment, choice of friends and lifestyle, and so on can lead you to identify with various groups. In the same way, we can also work backward, identifying a group by its characteristics and interpreting those characteristics. For instance, what group shares the following characteristics:

- short on sleep, long on social life
- a regular schedule of classes to attend
- money worries
- a shared body of knowledge about teachers and courses
- growing away from parents and into who they will be
- experimenting with lifestyles, decisions, and choices

You probably recognize the characteristics. College students all over the country share some or all of them. You can probably identify this group as well:

- they know the first names of Mulder and Scully
- they can name each of the Lone Gunmen
- they seem to either hate or love Chris Carter
- they can knowledgeably discuss alien abductions and government cover-ups

A little more difficult than the first example, perhaps, but you probably came up with the group who watch *The X-Files* (on Fox on Sunday nights and every evening in syndication on cable). After nearly a decade of production, when the names of Mulder and Scully come up in conversation, almost everyone in earshot will know the subject of discussion—*The X-Files* and its labyrinthine mythology and storytelling. The show has become part of mass culture. (One indication of this achievement is when other TV characters refer to Scully and Mulder; when Buffy the Vampire Slayer tells her Watcher, Giles, not to "Scully" her, she means he should take her seriously.) The show connects to several characteristics of American culture: an ongoing paranoia about what the government might be doing and not telling us about, a conviction held by many groups that aliens are currently visiting our planet, and the ongoing reconsideration, through the characters of Mulder and Scully, of the logic of women and the emotionality of men. This is not to say that every single American believes there's a shadow government or has been abducted by aliens, but we find enough points of identification to be able to consider this a shared characteristic.

With these identifications comes a danger, however. Many people bring some additional associations and assumptions to this *X*-phile identification, assumptions that may not be justified: some people automatically assume that someone who watches this program must be the classic "geek," or believes in alien visitation, or believes the government is involved in a massive conspiracy. Parodies of *X-Files* fans often portray them with thick black glasses and other stereotyped attributes of the computer nerd. And some of these assumptions may indeed be true; no doubt at least a few of the people who watch the show do so because they believe that the government is covering up alien abductions. It's a strength to be able to identify (and compensate for) the assumptions you might be bringing to some element of pop culture.

Be careful, however, about the ease of *stereotyping*, reducing a person or group to its various assumed characteristics. It's the idea of *reduction* that's key here: if we say that every person who watches *X-Files* must be a wacko, convinced that the government is covering up contact with aliens, then that's stereotyping; obviously not every watcher of the show fits this description, even if some do. If we say that all college students are lazy, party too much, and never read the course syllabus, that's stereotyping, too. Some of them don't in fact read the syllabus, but what we're doing here is noting that each group has a set of tendencies that some of the members of each group demonstrate and that others don't. Identifying characteristics is stereotyping only if that's all we take into account when we talk about these groups.

INTERPRETATION

We can predict the characteristics that some groups will develop, and we can identify some groups by their characteristics. If someone complains about not having enough time to get her papers done, we can probably deduce that she has too much on her schedule, that she's not managing her time very well, or that she's having too much fun at parties to do her schoolwork. That's a lot to read into a simple complaint. And yet those reasons, and probably a few more, lie underneath the original complaint. This is precisely the same mechanism we used with Batman. What's going on under the surface of the caped crusader? A need to avenge the deaths of his parents. What's going on under the surface of the student who says she can never get her papers done on time? Poor time management or too heavy a work schedule. We perform this sort of interpretation so automatically that we often don't pay attention to it, but we're reading beyond her statements to reveal a deeper significance. Clues must be interpreted in order to be clues. Otherwise, they're just unconnected events.

Anthropologists practice something similar when they look at artifacts of a long-gone culture and deduce something about how that culture lived. Those artifacts might seem irrelevant to us now, but in 500 years, each tiny clue we leave, from restaurant menus to *TV Guide,* will help an anthropologist form a picture of how we live today, just as tribal and cultural artifacts from centuries ago prove revealing to scientists and scholars today. For instance, more than one thousand years ago, a tribe we've named the Anasazi (for Ancient) disappeared from their cliff and desert homes in the American Southwest. Where did they go? How did they leave? Why did they leave? We don't know for sure because the Anasazi didn't leave any writings to tell us. But they *did* leave clues that scientists today are trying to interpret. Seemingly insignificant pieces of broken pot, called *potsherds,* might not seem like much to us—the equivalent perhaps of an old, headless Barbie doll unearthed from someone's backyard—but they're helping some anthropologists form a bigger picture.

The placement, color, and design of painting on those potsherds, for example, is a clue to what the Anasazi thought, just as someone wearing a red and black basketball jersey with the number 23 on it suggests how the wearer feels about Michael Jordan. The shape of the potsherds and what the pots seem to have been used for are other clues to understanding the culture that produced them. Similarly, anthropologists were able to make some pretty good guesses about burial rituals and beliefs when ancient bones were found in what we would consider a very strange place—right underneath the kitchen floor. And yet, this is only odd to us. To the Anasazi, it must have seemed so completely natural that they didn't even think about it, just like we take bagels for granted and don't think that it might seem odd to have a dozen different kinds.

Anthropologists interpret the clues to put together a reasonable picture of what cultural life could have been like. Police officers assemble evidence and rearrange it until a picture of the crime or the criminal emerges. Students read textbooks and get meaning out of those abstract collections of symbols we call *words.* Each group is analyzing culture. Each is "reading" the artifacts of its culture.

WHAT CAN WE CALL TEXT?

The idea of *text* as something other than a book like the one you're holding may be new to you. Think of the term *book,* and what comes to mind? A collection of paper pages, bound together in some sequential order, written by someone or a group of someones. But there's nothing about *book* that automatically means the object you're holding. We've come to accept that the combination of letters that forms *book* means a certain object, and it sets itself apart from, say, a magazine, a world atlas, or a Web site. *Book* has a conventional meaning within certain limitations. In essence, we look at the letters "b-o-o-k" and know what is meant because we have read the text; we've interpreted the symbols in a conventional manner, a manner that each of us has ready to hand, and anyone with the same level of education and exposure will read those same symbols and come up with the same interpretation. We

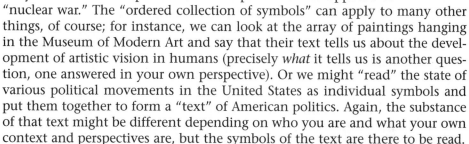

What other kinds of texts do you read?

may not mean the *same* book when we see "b-o-o-k," but we know what it means. We won't, for instance, assume that the symbols "b-o-o-k" mean the object we know as "mountain." We have some shared assumptions that prevent us from getting that meaning.

Text, however, need not mean only the letters that make up a word or the several pages that make up a book. To read *text* in its basic sense means only that we can interpret an ordered collection of symbols to come up with the concept of "cat" as opposed to "nuclear war." The "ordered collection of symbols" can apply to many other things, of course; for instance, we can look at the array of paintings hanging in the Museum of Modern Art and say that their text tells us about the development of artistic vision in humans (precisely *what* it tells us is another question, one answered in your own perspective). Or we might "read" the state of various political movements in the United States as individual symbols and put them together to form a "text" of American politics. Again, the substance of that text might be different depending on who you are and what your own context and perspectives are, but the symbols of the text are there to be read.

From these examples, it's clear that reading is a selective process; the elements we choose to read, in context with what we bring to any given text ourselves, create a meaning that's highly individualized. That is, even the same artifacts create different meanings for different people (because they have different ways of reading). In the academic world, this notion of the reader helping create meaning is called *reader-response theory*, and it means that a symbol gets at least some of its meaning from the reader; in a way, when you read, you're creating the text because you're treating it as a text to be read. If we look at a book as an object that's not necessarily important only to its author, then any meaning we get from it *has* to come from the way we read it. This theory also explains why you might get something different than your neighbor about, say, Batman, or the relative importance of *Star Trek*.

If reading artifacts is selective, however, then obviously reader response has several implications for writing, particularly the kind of writing you'll do in college. If what you write can be—and will be—interpreted in as many different ways as there are readers, how can you ever be sure that your readers will understand what you want them to understand? In some ways, you *can't* be sure. No matter what you do, no matter how carefully you write, some of what you mean will inevitably be lost, just as you, as the reader, will inevitably miss some of what another writer means.

That doesn't mean that it's pointless to write (or to read). Instead, we have to develop ways to make sure—as sure as we can, anyway—that what we mean is what we actually say. And we have to develop ways to read text that give us as much meaning as possible. Readers in college need to read carefully and critically, questioning perspectives and contexts and determining which artifacts (or ideas, or evidence) might be included in a paragraph that someone else, writing that same paragraph, might not include. Asking questions of the reading is the equivalent of examining the contexts of the artifacts you discover in daily life; the meaning is generally more complex than it appears on the surface, so the practice you already have at reading people can be easily transferred to reading a piece of writing.

In contrast to the college reader, college writers have to be sure we're not relying on our readers to dig our meanings out of the words we use. In other words, we have to be as clear as possible, explain a concept in several different ways, use many different kinds of examples, and, most of all, write so that our own perspectives don't get in the way of a reader who has a different perspective. When you write about a subject or an artifact that seems to be one thing but is, in reality, something much different, you've looked under the surface, read the texts, and understood the subtexts. Although this means that every interpretation of a text is going to be subjective, every interpretation will also be guided by the shared assumptions of the groups to which one belongs. A successful writer in college is one who can understand that subjectivity and can write to limit its effect by knowing when a concept needs to be explained and when one kind of example would be better than another.

French cultural theorist Michel de Certeau describes the "supermarket from which readers select the items they want, combine them with those already in their cultural 'pantry' at home, and cook up new meals or new readings according to their own needs and creativities" (Fiske 40). What you make with flour, sugar, chocolate chips, and butter may be an ordinary chocolate chip cookie, but it can also be a double chocolate cupcake—depending on what you want to make with those ingredients. What you get out of Batman may be different than what the person next to you gets from Batman, even if it's the same Batman. He may think Batman is cool because of the toys, but you might like Batman's thirst for vengeance. What's different is not the object or artifact. It's *you*, your assumptions, your beliefs, your preferences—and therefore your perspective.

READING A RECENT TEXT: *SURVIVOR*

An extended example of a recent text should help to clarify what we mean by "reading" a "text" that isn't necessarily a written document. You probably remember the first *Survivor* series, aired during the summer of 2000, when 16 Americans interested in winning a million bucks were drawn from all walks of life in the United States, dumped on a deserted island in the South China Sea (accompanied by a film crew), and told that each week, they would be voting one of their number off the island. They would—as the show's logo put it—have to *outwit, outplay, and outlast,* by fair means or foul: each contestant understood that this was a game.

The rules were simple. At first, the 16 people were divided into two teams, "tribes" named the Tagi and the Pagong, which competed against each other in various challenges. Contestants who won an immunity challenge were safe (for that night) from being voted off the island. If they succeeded in reward challenges, they got a surprise: a gourmet meal, or a phone call from home. Halfway through the series, the remaining contestants merged into one tribe, and the game turned to individual competitions. Whoever was left standing at the end of the series—whoever played the game the best, in other words—would take home the money.

For 39 days, the 16 castaways hunted for food, foraged for firewood, slept in the sand or in slings, and endured insect bites, minor infections, and contests designed to prove their determination. Although nobody would have been seriously injured, the contestants were otherwise on their own. And inexorably, every week, under the watchful eye of the cameras, the castaways voted one of their number off the island and out of the running for the million dollars. All during the summer of 2000, *Survivor* sparked debate, spawned imitators, drew fire from conservatives and liberals alike, was parodied on the late-night talk shows, and had its catch phrases adopted into everyday slang: "voted off the island" became shorthand for any project whose leader was no longer necessary, anyone's plan that was scuttled.

It is perhaps not necessary to state that the show was a ratings success for CBS. "Reality TV" shows have been gaining in popularity (and their numbers are still increasing) ever since *Candid Camera* in the 1960s led to *America's Funniest Home Videos* in the 1980s and *America's Most Wanted*. In recent years, the reality TV trend has spawned everything from *When Animals Attack* to *COPS* to *Judge Judy* to one of the longest-lasting reality shows, MTV's *The Real World*. Reality TV is a highly complex artifact. What do we mean by it? Is "reality" TV meant to be documentary-style, recording the unvarnished truth for its viewers? Perhaps reality TV means TV "based on" reality, just like some movies are based on books. Regardless of how we take the meanings of "reality TV," the sheer proliferation of this kind of programming suggested that *Survivor* might be a hit, but nobody expected it to be as big a success as it was. During the suspenseful final episode, in which the last four castaways were whittled down to two, who then answered questions from a jury of their own voted-off companions, more people watched than watched the 2000 Super Bowl. The episode shattered Nielsen ratings records. Reality draws huge crowds.

How shall we read *Survivor*? It is clearly a text, although one that challenges us to read it. We could put it in several contexts, and look at it from several perspectives. What follows is by no means an exhaustive list of possibilities, but it explains some of the many ways we can understand *Survivor*. As a reality TV program, a morality text, or a question for viewers to answer for themselves, *Survivor* provides insight into our collective conscience. Because the show collected 16 "normal Americans" and put them on TV, we could honestly call this "reality TV." Those people were clearly representative Americans; they spanned our culture almost perfectly, in age, sexual orientation, educational and economic background, and personality. The tribe members were obviously there on the island and were expected to rough it while there. To that extent, this was clearly a "reality" TV show.

To extend the realism, we could note that the endurance and immunity challenges were real and would test legitimate physical abilities, such as being able to hold one's breath underwater for a long time. Instead of providing token contests, *Survivor* asked its castaways to kill and eat a rat, to ingest live beetle larva, to use native materials to build a hut, and to form communities and bonds in order to survive—all challenges we'd have to master if we were in this situation for real. We can read *Survivor* to be what it purports (on the surface) to be: a show in which 16 people are abandoned to survive the best they can, the winner taking home a substantial prize. In this context, the millions of people who watched the show every week might be interested primarily in survival stories; perhaps they would also watch *Titanic* with fascination, or *A Perfect Storm*, or a film about the Donner party resorting to cannibalism to survive. Or people might have tuned in hoping to see death and disaster: sometimes these are the same audience for stock car races, monster truck shows, and daredevil acts. In this reading, is the subtext of *Survivor* the torture of 16 ordinary people for the enjoyment of the watching audience? One begins to think about the lions and the Christians.

On the other hand, those 16 people were picked (from hundreds who applied) by casting agents. An artifact: Casting agents cast actors. Therefore, can we still call *Survivor* "reality" TV? What were the criteria under which each contestant was chosen? Perhaps the casting call read "average American, willing to eat rats and endure bug bites." The fine print might have asked for a blonde, or an athlete, or a specific racial group. No matter what the casting agents were looking for, the fact that they were choosing one contestant over another suggests that that they were helping to create "reality."

Another artifact: Although each castaway could explain his or her vote against a tribe member to the audience via the camera, not every explanation was shown to viewers; it often seemed arbitrary whose explanations were aired. Artifact: The cameras weren't showing us every minute of every day. Viewers got "home movies" of interactions among the castaways, and viewers were shown the various challenges. But we were shown only *selected* footage. Life isn't edited; can we still consider *Survivor* to be reality TV if so many things about it were artificial? In this reading, *Survivor* might be in context with, say, *COPS*, a show following police officers in several cities as they make arrests and counsel the public. Although we see many car chases and gun fights, we know from the police departments themselves that most cops go through their careers never having to shoot anyone—and never getting shot. Who was making the decision about what the viewer would see, and on what basis? Is *COPS* reality? Is *Survivor*? And is the subtext of so much "reality-based TV programming" that we'd rather watch our reality than live it? In this reading, *Survivor* might be the next best thing to doing it ourselves.

For some viewers, *Survivor* was too hokey to take seriously, so "reality TV" became a hoot: the host, Jeff Probst, was given cheesy dialogue to recite, while the castaways carried flaming tiki torches and rang an enormous gong on their way to and from each tribal council meeting. The one voted off the island each week had to watch while his or her torch was ceremonially snuffed out before leaving the island ("the tribe has spoken," Probst would intone dramatically). Finally, the setting of the drama was contrived as well: no desert island would come with the set of the tribal council, and clearly a real survival situation wouldn't involve a well-equipped medical station, film crew camp, or hot showers for a lucky few. In this reading, *Survivor* was no more a serious drama than *Gilligan's Island*, right down to Greg, the young man who spoke into a shell phone. So much for the surface artifacts of what constitutes "reality"—in many ways, it defies definition even as it offers many interpretations.

Reading the show as a morality text, though, lets us see this series much differently. The artifacts we might read from this text were the fairly unpleasant—and yet fascinating to watch—infighting, alliance building, and deception that the viewers saw each week. Some viewers saw the show as an experiment: what values, beliefs, and actions would people take in a do-or-be-poor situation? Aside from questions of ethical behavior, however, are still the more visceral questions of what we'd do for a million dollars. Would we eat live beetle larvae? Would we hunt, kill, and eat a rat? Would we walk over hot coals? And, when it came down to it, would we suffer the indignities of abandoned island conditions? Would you be able, or willing, to vote against people you'd known for several weeks, knowing that they were working for that money as hard as you were?

The text of the show suggests that some people will in fact make the hard decisions, just as they have to in real life. Artifact: When Kelly won the final immunity challenge, she ended up in the position of choosing which of her remaining two companions would leave the island: Rudy, the aging, tough, ex-Navy Seal, or Richard, the corporate trainer. Rudy, although highly conservative, had not made any enemies; Rich had irritated many of the islanders. Rich was in his 40s; Rudy was 72. Although Kelly finally chose to vote Rudy out of the contest, she was clearly conflicted about it, half-trying to retrieve her vote before realizing there was no going back. And yet, she did not win the million dollars. The subtext of her action might be that she chose the wrong person to vote off; or it might be that no choice she made could have been correct. The clues—her facial expression, her half-reach into the voting box, her small shrug, and her obvious exhaustion—could be read either way. How do you read these artifacts?

As a text about American tastes, habits, and preferences, *Survivor* suggests still another reading. On the surface, the final two contestants seemed to be diametrically opposed. Artifacts: Kelly, a young, female, outdoorsy type, versus Rich, a middle-aged, male, white-collar professional. Kelly: heterosexual. Rich: homosexual. Kelly: kept a fairly low profile, lied once, and basically conducted herself with honor. Rich: planned the Tagi alliance that systematically voted off every other person, lied about the existence of the alliance, and was straightforwardly in it to win the game, not to make friends. The text of American preferences would seem to indicate that Kelly would win, particularly when her final statement to the jury asked them to remember that she treated them all decently and was a good person. These are values we respond to. Rich's final statement, on the other hand, stressed that the competition had been a game and he had done things in order to win the game. These too are values we approve of—working hard to win.

Rich Hatch won the million dollars. What might this artifact suggest? A triumph for gay rights, perhaps, or a demonstration that empathetic behavior is not enough. Perhaps it tells us that America's sweethearts can't compete on the tough stuff, or it hints that a corporate trainer can outthink the rest of us. If we apply the text of *Survivor* to "real life," what do we learn about who we are as a culture? If it were one of Aesop's fables, what would the moral be?

No matter the perspective you take, or the context within which you place the *Survivor* series, *Survivor* reached enough of our contemporary beliefs and tastes to incinerate its television competition. If you see the series as a vicious practice akin to the science experiment involving a dozen rats placed in a tiny box, someone else sees it as a game show no worse or better than *Hollywood Squares*. If you're concerned about the moral behavior demonstrated by people on their way to winning a million dollars, someone else is more worried about the rats who were hunted for a ridiculous contest. Each of these positions is valid; each has the artifacts to support it. Clearly a collection of symbols and signs can be read as a text. Again, though, we have to interpret clues. We have to collect evidence, arrange it in meaningful patterns, and interpret it so its significance or significances can be understood. We also have to understand that someone else is likely to read precisely the same artifacts in a much different way.

SUBTEXT AND CONTEXT

If we consider "text" to mean "what appears on the surface and needs to interpreted," we can look at what goes on under the surface as *subtext*. (Subtext is often defined as "reading between the lines.") It's the meaning you get from what isn't said. What goes on around that text can be called *context*, which is simply the bigger picture (or pictures) within which the text appears. The context is what provides the individual symbols, meaningless in themselves, with connections to other symbols.

Survivor's context is everything that's going on around the text of the show. As a game show, it's in context with *The Price is Right, Hollywood Squares*, and *Wheel of Fortune*. As a reality TV show, it's in context with *COPS*, MTV's *The Real World*, and court programs. As a million-dollar show, it's in the same context with that other million-dollar show, *Who Wants to Be a Millionaire?* The context within which we see the show helps determine our reaction to it, its subtext for us, and its interpretation. As another artifact of the reality TV genre, for instance, *Survivor* (along with the other reality TV shows) helps form a text of what reality America will watch, but it adds nothing to an analysis of, say, game shows. And the reverse is true as well: as an artifact of the game show genre, *Survivor* doesn't say much to us about reality TV. The fact that *Survivor* can fit into several genres, or be an artifact of several things at the same time, suggests that the show's existence is more complex than might appear at first glance. Don't be alarmed by the complexity. Think of the possibilities for individual interpretation instead.

A wider context in which *Survivor* might appear would be our cultural interest in extreme sports; we could see it in context with, say, bungee jumping or snowblading. The characteristics in common are their edgy natures. We might also see *Survivor* in context with our tendency to watch rather than get involved; could we read *Survivor* as encouraging passivity rather than activity? We might be able to read *Survivor* as another artifact in the American text of sudden wealth: in context with, say, lottery winners (and hopefuls), *Who Wants to be a Millionaire?*, and all those dot.com CEOs who were millionaires by the time they were thirty years old, *Survivor* becomes another artifact of our cultural desire to be wealthy without having to work at it for fifty years. See how the artifact changes depending on what context we place it in; in many ways, we can say that its significance depends on its location. Reality is what we make it—or rather, where we find it.

Note, however, that each interpretation comes from the perspectives of a different group. Those people worried about the ethical practices of the contestants are probably more interested in the collective mental health of the members of our culture than those fixated on who would win the million. People who wrote outraged letters to newspaper editors about the treatment of animals on the show—remember, they had to hunt, kill, and roast that rat, and it was all shown on TV—were probably disgusted by the entire show and weren't necessarily rooting for any specific contestant to win (or be voted off). Each of us has a set of built-in beliefs and assumptions about the way the world works and should work, and we get those beliefs and assumptions from the groups we associate ourselves with. None of them is necessarily more correct or incorrect than any of the others, but we need to remember that how we see the world is almost certainly not the only way. When you write about pop culture—and certainly when you write for college—you need that awareness.

THE POINT

Our discussion so far has attempted to offer some understanding of the term *popular culture* and how we come to see meaning in it. As a culture, we break apart into separate and yet constituent groups. And each group and combination of groups has its own way of life and its own products, or works of art or intellect. Those products of the group can be called *symbols, artifacts,* or *texts*—and we can read all those separate elements as a larger text, which we can then interpret to mean something. If we only look at the surface of things, we miss a lot of the deeper meaning.

You may remember a commercial for Bud Light about two young men who are faced with a terrible dilemma at the grocery store. They don't have enough money with them for the beer, the toilet paper, and a few other assorted items they'd like to buy. They set aside the nonessentials, but they still don't have enough money. Finally, they're down to a choice between toilet paper and the six-pack of Bud Light. They make their choice—of course, it's the beer—and ask the cashier to put it in a paper bag. Then they grab the receipt—any extra bit of paper is obviously going to be put to good use. The viewer watches this whole sequence and laughs, as expected, at the priority Bud Light wants us to put on buying the product. Beer commercials are, after all, a major artifact of our current pop culture.

But what the viewer cannot see, unless the commercial is recorded and played back slowly, is the headline on a newspaper being read by a man standing in line behind our two hapless heroes. The headline reads, in letters of the size usually used to announce declarations of war, "BIG DUMP PLANNED." Again, it's buried—there's no way for the casual viewer to see it. If you want the punch line, you have to work for it. The point? What you see isn't necessarily all there is. College students are expected to develop and refine analytical skills in order to deal with those deeper meanings. If you look at the things you normally consider insignificant or meaningless and put them in a context, or read their subtext, you can often see meanings that you wouldn't have before. And that's analysis.

INTERPRETING ARTIFACTS

You already know what artifacts are: the *products of a group, an action, or an event*. Eyebrow pierces could be an artifact of a group that at one point wanted to set themselves apart from several other groups. *Star Trek* conventions are artifacts of the phenomenon known as *Star Trek*, which includes all the series and movies as well as the overall philosophy. Even bumps and bruises are artifacts of something: say, a rough game of football, or a beating by the side of an L.A. freeway.

An artifact tells you something, but you have to put the artifact in context to make it mean anything. A bruised arm may indicate a football game, a case of domestic abuse, or a recent shot of insulin, depending on the context. If you mistake the context, though, real trouble can result; if you're a doctor and a child comes in to the emergency room with bruises, you may automatically think "child abuse" and then, because you're legally obligated to report alleged child abuse, you call the police or social services. Perhaps the parent gets arrested or the child is placed in foster care as a result of your interpretation of that bruise.

But what if that child was just trying out her new in-line skates, and her parent didn't know she wasn't wearing her elbow pads? What if the child had been playing a game of basketball with her friends and the bruises were a natural result of a foul? Your interpretation, and your follow-up action, can have serious consequences for a lot of people. (Imagine what could happen if you thought the bruise was evidence of child abuse, but it turned out that the child had just learned how to give herself a shot of insulin to control her diabetes.)

So, as the doctor, you would ask a lot of questions before making any diagnosis. As a student of popular culture, and as a writer in college, you should similarly ask questions of everything before deciding that you know what something means. If you've never known that getting an insulin shot can produce a bruise, what else might you not know that would make a difference? Withholding judgment until you *know* you have the facts is a good practice.

WRITE: Choose three of the following artifacts, and give each two different contexts.

- Footprints on a beach
- Lit candles
- A person wearing a tie-dyed shirt
- A book about world religions
- The cartoon series *Scooby Doo*
- A Tony Bennett album

For instance, a book about world religions could appear in several different contexts. It might be a textbook, in which case we could put it in context with a theology course, a sociology course, or a history course; we could even place it in context with other "world" books—world populations, world economics, world history, world literature. Or perhaps it's a popular book, not meant for study; we could put it in the context of a bookstore or a birthday gift. We could also put it in context with a search for spiritual enlightenment, on our contextual bookshelf right next to the Quoran, the Book of Mormon, and the Bible.

Artifacts need a context in order for us to make any significant meaning out of them. So the next step in this writing exercise is to interpret the artifact and its contexts. What do we do with them? *We read these artifacts and contexts just like they were words in a book.* As John Fiske says:

> The role of the academic critic of popular culture is social as much as, if not more than, textual. As well as tracing the play of meanings within the text, he or she also traces which meanings are generated and put into circulation in which social formation, and how this social play of meaning relates to the social structure at large. (106)

Fiske, a major critic of popular culture and author of several books on the subject, suggests here that the meaning or significance of the text derives at least in part from the culture that produces that text, just as reader-response theory suggests that the meaning of a text derives at least in part from the reader of that text. So while *Star Trek* conventions may seem irrelevant to people who have never heard of *Star Trek*, they reveal something about the culture they spring from. We bring to any artifact the significance that our groups (whatever those groups may be) would give it. That is, we read a text with the assumptions of our group. Again, this is a difference between reading subjectively and objectively: to a certain extent, of course, reading *Survivor* as an artifact of deceit is subjective, but the assumptions that lead to that interpretation can be objectively identified.

Keep thinking about this concept. Look back at the three artifacts and the contexts you gave them. What other elements make up the contexts within which you put your artifacts? Are there associations you can make?

Where else would we find people wearing pointed ears and Klingon costumes?

Do you have preconceived notions about your artifacts and their contexts? Can you identify the groups that hold these notions, and can you understand your artifacts from other perspectives? For instance, would a shelf of books about various religions in a library mean something different than the same set of books in someone's house? They might be old college textbooks or the beginning of a fascination with world religious practices. How would you "read" such a collection of books?

Another collection of stories in a different context would obviously mean something else. As you read this example, keep in mind what you know about artifacts, texts, and "reading" those texts to get meaning. Notice, too, what this examination of pop culture reveals about the culture from which it derives.

In 1992, anthropologist Holly Mathews went to Oaxaca, Mexico, to study the meaning of one specific artifact: the morality tales about a mythic character, La Llorona (the weeping woman). Mathews collected 60 tellings. Here is one telling, which Mathews says is typical:

> La Llorona was a bad woman who married a good man. They had children and all was well. Then one day she went crazy and began to walk the streets. Everyone knew but her husband. When he found out he beat her. She had much shame. The next day she walked into the river and drowned herself. And now she knows no rest and must forever wander the streets wailing in the night. And that is why women must never leave their families to walk the streets looking for men. If they are not careful they will end up like La Llorona. (Mathews, "The directive force of morality tales in a Mexican community." *Human Motives and Cultural Models*. New York: Cambridge, 1992, p 129.)

In each of the La Llorona stories Mathews collected, she found the same artifact: La Llorona kills herself. What meaning does the artifact of suicide have in these stories? Mathews did some research on morality tales in general and observed the community where La Llorona tales were told. She finally concluded that "the morality tale succeeds in shaping people's behavior because the motives of the main characters draw upon cultural shared schemas about gendered human nature" (129). That is, the men and women telling those 60 tales all shared some sets of assumptions, some of the same context about how men and women relate to each other in that community.

(Test yourself here: what are the artifacts Mathews studied? What is the context? Can you tell the subtext? Given what you know of the tales, can you offer some interpretation for why La Llorona kills herself?)

When Mathews read all this information as a text, she got this meaning:

> [In] the cultural model in rural *mestizo* Oaxaca, [men] view women as sexually uncontrolled. Unless they are controlled, or control themselves, their true nature will emerge and they will begin (as the story says) to "walk the streets" in search of sexual gratification. Men, for their part, are viewed by women as sexually insatiable. Men are driven, like animals, to satisfy their desires, even at the expense of family obligations. (130)

The men and women telling these stories, in other words, share certain assumptions but derive something different from them. Whether the assumptions are accurate is beside the point—the groups producing the artifacts believe that the assumptions are accurate. And given those assumptions, the meaning of the stories is that women in rural *mestizo* Oaxaca have no recourse but to kill themselves if their marriages don't work. Given another set of assumptions, the meaning of the stories might change. For instance, we could take an interpretive stance from the perspective of feminists and look at how the patriarchy, or the male-dominated view of reality, affects marriage relationships in Oaxaca.

Notice that Mathews doesn't assume or suggest that this is the only way women and men relate—that would be drawing a faulty generalization. Rather, she looked only at the artifacts and their context, and drew a significant meaning from them. She had a fairly detailed understanding of the context, too: part of her research involved learning how male-female relationships were constructed. For instance, the significance of La Llorona stories might change if in that village men and women never knew each other before they married, if marriages were arranged by the elders in the family, or if young men and women were allowed to fall in love on their own. Each of these contextual elements might change how we read the tales. Mathews discovered during her research that Oaxaca elders traditionally arranged the marriages through a complicated system of shared and exchanged resources like livestock and land, which involved the families in intricate bonds. If the marriage didn't work, it was economically impossible to divorce, so the only way out of an unhappy marriage was for the woman to commit suicide.

Does this mean that in real life women killed themselves to escape unhappy marriages? Is that why the various stories of La Llorona were told? What is the relationship of these morality tales, or any form of popular culture, to real life? These are important questions, as Fiske reminds us. And ultimately, answering these questions is the point of studying and writing about pop culture. You have around you an enormous variety of cultural production, everything from the clothes you wear, to the last movie you laughed at, to the CD you like the best today. Each of these artifacts, in context, suggests something about you and about your culture. How do you fit into your contexts? What is your perspective?

This textbook provides several different perspectives in each chapter, and each reading is a specific individual's take on the topic. Some of the perspectives are dry and scientific, some are relaxed and humorous, and some are risky and controversial; all of them, however, are different from each other, and together they form a kaleidoscope of approaches to this thing called pop culture. If you read them as an anthropologist would read potsherds or folk tales, you'll be forming a pop culture text as you read.

Each chapter has a different *anchor reading*: these readings serve as the anchor of the chapter, providing support and a foundation for the other readings to rest on. Chapter 1, for instance, begins with an anchor article written by a Baby Boomer, focusing on the relentless recycling of classic oldies and rock to sell a younger generation on cars, fast food, and clothes. That anchor provides us with the essential terms we need to make links to every other reading in the chapter: the concept of **recontextualizing** lets us see the conservative perspective on the dangers of rock music, the increasing economic benefit to "selling out" one's artistic vision, a humorous Internet riff on the generations, the influence of pop music on drug use, and the lyrics to the Beatles' famous "Lucy in the Sky with Diamonds," which is often assumed to be about LSD.

The focus of Chapter 2 is on the way we perceive ourselves in terms of sexuality. In the anchor reading, a man "reads" his own body as if someone else were reading it and reflects on the construction of this most personal artifact. The rest of the readings ask you to use these ideas about **reading** to help understand how we construct our self-perceptions. For instance, female sexuality, so long kept under wraps and often considered a threat, contrasts with the reading of the cinematic male body that's developed in response to an increased female audience. And yet, as Dave Barry's column in this chapter suggests, independent women who don't seem to worry about what they look like are in fact still asking that old question: "Do I look fat in this?"

Chapter 3, in contrast to focusing on the body, focuses on reading images, and the anchor provides us with a critical tool called **semiotics**, or the reading of signs. The perspectives on the image in pop culture run from an examination of talk shows to the reasons we watch horror films, reminding you that there's more to an image than meets the eye. That is, images represent something else, and it's in our best interest to be aware of the "something else" if for no other reason than to protect ourselves.

Chapter 4 provides perspectives on the way our spirituality is captured in pop culture—from song lyrics to the use of religious humor in cartoons. The anchor for this chapter comes from the exiled Tibetan religious leader, the Dalai Lama, who proposes religious **tolerance**. The Lama offers us a perspective and attitude to carry through the rest of the readings: the way Charles Schulz worked religion into his *Peanuts* comic strip, the lyrics of a pop song about God, the simple faith that water molecules will hold together, and one woman's look at what it means to walk the path of the Old Religion.

Finally, Chapter 5 offers popular perspectives on the future and what we might expect to see. Each perspective draws from **what's already happened** to build its idea of what will happen next. Legendary science writer Samuel R. Delaney offers his take on what might happen between now and 3000, and each reading that follows the anchor touches on one or more of Delaney's points. First contact with another intelligent species, genetic engineering, and the formation of a software-driven community mesh with the comedy of manners for the year 3000, which we'll need when radioactive mutants knock on the shelter's door. Pop culture will no doubt still be with us then—and we will still be learning from it.

■ Works Cited ■

Allen Robert C., ed. *Channels of Discourse: Television and Contemporary Criticism*. Chapel Hill: University of NC Press, 1987.

Beaudoin, Tom. *Virtual Faith*. San Francisco: Jossey-Bass, 1998.

Bennett, Tony, Colin Mercer, and Janet Woollacott, eds. *Popular Culture and Social Relations*. Philadephia: Open UP, 1986.

Bernard, H. Russell, ed. *Handbook of Methods in Cultural Anthropology*. Walnut Creek: Alta Mira, 1998.

Bernard, H. Russell, and Gery Ryan. "Text Analysis." *Handbook of Methods in Cultural Anthropology*. Walnut Creek: Alta Mira, 1998.

Brecht, Berthold. *On Theatre*. tr John Willett. London: Methuen, 1978.

Brummet, Barry. *Rhetoric in Popular Culture*. New York: St. Martin's, 1994.

Culler, Jonathan. *Pursuit of Signs: Semiotics, Literature, and Deconstruction*. London: Routledge, 1981.

Day, Gary, ed. *Readings in Popular Culture: Trivial Pursuits?* New York: St. Martin's, 1990.

El Guindi, Fadwa. "From Pictorializing to Visual Anthropology." *Handbook of Methods in Cultural Anthropology*. Bernard, H. Russell, ed. Walnut Creek: Alta Mira, 1998.

Farrell, Brenda, and Laura R. Graham. "Discourse-Centered Methods." *Handbook of Methods in Cultural Anthropology*. Bernard, H. Russell, ed. Walnut Creek: Alta Mira, 1998.

Fiske, John. "Popular Discrimination." *Modernity & Mass Culture*. Naremore, James, and Patrick Brantlinger, eds. Bloomington: Indiana University Press, 1991.

____. *Reading the Popular*. Boston: Unwin Hyman, 1989.

Gamson, Joshua. *Freaks Talk Back*. London: University of Chicago Press, 1998.

Garber, Marjorie. *Symptoms of Culture*. London: Routledge, 1998.

George, Nelson. *Hip Hop America*. New York: Viking, 1998.

Leib, Frank B. *Friendly Competitors, Fierce Companions: Men's Ways of Relating*. Pilgrim Press, 1998.

Mandler, Jean. *Stories, Scripts, & Schemes: Aspects of Schema Theory*. Hillsdale, NJ: Laurence Earlbaum, 1984.

Mathews, Holly. "The Directive Force of Morality Tales in a Mexican Community." *Human Motives & Cultural Models*. New York: Cambridge University Press, 1992.

Mukerji, Chandra, and Michael Schudson. *Rethinking Popular Culture: Contemporary Perspectives in Cultural Studies*. Berkeley: University of California Press, 1991.

Naremore, James, and Patrick Brantlinger, eds. *Modernity & Mass Culture*. Bloomington: Indiana University Press, 1991.

Parmentier, Richard J. *Signs in Society: Studies in Semiotic Anthropology*. Bloomington: Indiana University Press, 1994.

Savran, David. *Taking It Like a Man: White Masculinity and Its Constructions*. Princeton: University Press, 1998.

Singer, Irving. *Reality Transformed*. Cambridge: MIT Press, 1998.

Skal, David. *Screams of Reason: Mad Science and Popular Culture*. New York: Norton, 1998.

Smith, Terry. *Visible Touch: Modernism and Masculinity*. Chicago: University of Chicago Press, 1998.

Sperber, Dan. *Explaining Culture: A Naturalistic Approach*. Cambridge: Blackwell, 1996.

Storey, John. *An Introductory Guide to Cultural Theory and Popular Culture*. Athens: University of Georgia Press, 1993.

Willis, Sharon. *High Contrast: Race and Gender in Contemporary Hollywood Film*. Durham: Duke University Press, 1997.

CHAPTER 1

LISTENING TO GENERATIONS: PERSPECTIVES ON MUSIC AND GENERATIONAL IDENTITY

The voice of my generation is:

a. Walter Cronkite

b. Bob Dylan

c. Madonna

d. MTV VJ Kennedy

—Internet humor

Before you start this chapter, identify which generation you belong to. You're probably part of one of the Big Three: the Baby Boomers (born after 1946); Generation X (born after 1966), or the generation after Gen X (that is, born after 1980), which still has not been given a name that's stuck. We've heard that generation referred to as the Information Generation and Generation 2K; in this chapter, they're called Millennials. (Be cautious when dealing with these birthdates, however, because many sources contradict each other by a year or two. Look at these age ranges as general parameters, not as if they're set in concrete.) You can probably name some of the artifacts associated with each of these generations: **Baby Boomers** belong to a specific age range (38 to 50 or so) and have reached a certain socioeconomic

What associations do you have with Woodstock or with the later editions of Woodstock?

standing that seems generally to involve large amounts of disposable income. You can probably name several prominent Boomers without thinking too hard: Bill Clinton, rock singers Tina Turner and Mick Jagger, and Bill Gates, for instance. Boomers are prominent—and dominant—because of their sheer numbers but also because of their place in modern American culture: many of the people we now call Boomers were Hippies in the 1960s and had a distinctly powerful effect on American culture.

The children of the Boomers are often called **Generation X**, from the title of a 1981 book by Douglas Coupland that describes a disillusioned subsection of youth. Just as in algebra, "X" was an undefined variable. When the popular news media began to focus on this group during the early and mid-1990s, these twenty-somethings (actually ranging in age from 24 to 37 or so) were often described as *slackers*, spoiled, or whiny; Gen X was characterized as angry at the Boomers for destroying the planet's environment and not planning for the future. Some of those perceptions have changed, however. Now those twenty-somethings are often called the Lost Generation because they seem to lack a collective unifying force, such as Woodstock and the civil rights protests of the 1960s, which the Boomers all experienced, and which provided a common bond for them.

Past a certain year of birth, Generation X shades into the **Millennials**, who were typically born after 1980. Calling this generation the Millennials is natural because they will "come of age" during the 2000s, but the Millennial generation hasn't been named and studied as much as Generation X or the Boomers; in fact, it's still taking shape. Nonetheless, some media analysts and consumer groups have identified certain characteristics of Millennials. For instance, Millennials tend to be highly optimistic (as opposed to the Boomers' idealism); Millennials are also multicultural, in that its members are the most ethnically diverse the United States has seen. Most readers of this book fall into one of these three generational identities and most likely are members of Generation X or the Millennials. Have you answered the question posed at the beginning of this chapter? What is your **generational identity**?

Like every group, each generation has its artifacts or attributes: they respond to their cultural surroundings, they create their own group identity, and they identify with specific movements or events. They also react against a previous generation's values in the process of forming their own. And each claims its own music: the Boomers are identified with the music of the 60s, specifically the music of Motown and so-called classic rock: The Temptations, the Beatles, and the Rolling Stones, for instance. Generation X's different tastes in music and culture are usually associated with the sounds of Billy Idol and R.E.M. Millennials, with still other tastes, are associated with the sounds of rap (The Notorious B.I.G. or Eminem, for instance), nostalgic remixes of classic hits, and lately with the youth bands like 'N Sync and The Backstreet Boys, who characterize their performances with catchy tunes, careful choreography, and energetic dancing. The 2001 Super Bowl halftime show, as one example, embodied all three: Mary J. Blige, Britney Spears, 'N Sync, and

The
Diana Ross
Story

Joan Baez'
Visit to Hanoi

Jesus Returns
to Jerusalem
as Superstar

The Oldest
Man in the USA

What generational themes do these singers represent?

Aerosmith performed a modernized medley of Aerosmith's huge 1970s hit "Walk This Way." No matter which generation we talk about, though, Robert Knight's adage seems to hold true: Popular music, whether rock or rap, "has perfected the art of inciting the young and irritating their elders" (193).

The musical artifacts of each generation are somewhat different, although as you've already seen, groups and their artifacts can overlap. You may not share all of the musical tastes of your generation, of course, but you probably share some of them. And you may enjoy the music "belonging" to another generation as well—many children of Boomers listen to the Beatles, the Grateful Dead, and the Doors with just as much appreciation as their parents (although parents are often reluctant to extend the same attitude toward the hip-hop or rap that their kids might listen to). What artifacts of your generation's music do you share with other generations?

Music should be:

a.   Melodic and romantic

b.   Annoying to your parents

c.   Annoying to your parents

d.   Annoying to your parents

—Internet humor

There may not seem to be any commonalities between the "sex, drugs, and rock and roll" of the 1960s and the rap and hip-hop culture of the 2000s. The first may be so old and familiar to you that it doesn't rate any closer examination, and the second may be so popular among your group that you don't pay any attention. Or you may, from your context, see nothing but trouble coming from the themes of the 1960s that have generated similar themes in the 1990s. In the student essay in this section, Gina Brazzale writes about getting underneath the common perceptions of each generation's music to see that we are still writing—and singing—about the same things: our thoughts and feelings about events in the culture. In other words, no matter the generation, we create artifacts that reveal our cultural beliefs and attitudes.

And just as many of the ideals of the 1960s are still deeply felt when we speak about freedoms and geopolitical human rights, the issues facing the 2000s—criminal youth, drugs, a kind of neo-racism balanced by a kind of neo-liberalism—are arising in the part of American culture that's slowly coming to mainstream attention. The protest movements of the 1960s are not all that different from the raps about police brutality of the 1990s. Each still provides a text we can read to learn about what's important to the culture. And the authors of each text—the Hippies, the rappers—are telling us a lot about what's important to them. Many of the people we call Baby Boomers (some of whom, as Hippies, scandalized their parents and the rest of the country with their attitudes toward sexuality and human rights issues) are now in positions of power in American culture. In twenty years or less, the rappers will be in that same position and will probably use their formative experiences to shape their own positions of power.

In other words, the patterns of influence are from cultural subtext (what's underneath) to cultural context (what's going on around). As rap and hip-hop move from the margins into the mainstream, "the street" provides new "subtext" from its reaction to "our [mainstream] society's woes" (Nelson George 211), which, as they change, will become the new mainstream. Meanwhile, elements we haven't thought of yet begin to grow in the minority subtexts, and will, in their turn, become the mainstream cultural context. At that point—and probably before that point—how we read our cultural text may be different. The reading will be conditioned by the prevailing tastes of the young, proliferated by

How could we read this face?

their artifacts, and probably abhorred by their parents; how will we react? How do you react now? Music journalist and rapper Nelson George suggests that "at some point they will likely react as teens have always ultimately reacted to the passions of their elders—they'll shout, 'It's boring!' and move on" (212).

Hip-hop beats, dance, art, drugs, music as artifacts—in whose context shall we interpret them? From a politically conservative context, we might be worried that raps about killing cops would encourage that act. But in a liberal context, the artifacts of black street culture indicate the fresh, new approach to an old theme: putting into music the woes of a time period and how to cope with them. Rap can be described as raging against the machine (corporate, white, mainstream, maybe destructive)—as could Bob Dylan's lyrics against the Vietnam war, as Gina Brazzale's essay suggests. We could easily read the 1960s' protest sit-ins as being replaced with 1990s' school shootings. What about reading the new "drugs of choice"—heroin, crack, and ecstasy—as replacing the 1960s' marijuana and the 1980s' cocaine? This process of reading the text involves looking at the artifacts in new contexts.

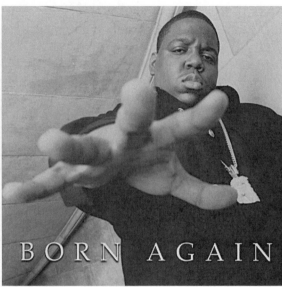

What do R&B and rap have in common with bubblegum pop?

Sex is for:

a. Married couples who want to start families

b. Anyone who wants to start a party

c. Latex-clad partners in a laboratory setting

d. Watching on Jennicam

—Internet humor

As each generational group discovers the artifacts of other generational groups, in other words, each finds something to adopt and to reject. Pop music from America's uproarious 1960s, for instance, is often positively described as encouraging personal freedoms, such as free love, civil rights, and introspection aided by various drugs. This is just one context within which to see pop music from the 60s, of course.

In another context, perhaps an historical one, we might see pop and rock music as encouraging moral laxity in its rejection of traditional sexuality and family relationships. We might even suggest, as Robert Knight does in his article, that pop music is actively Satanic. Parents might listen to the same music that their children do, but they probably hear something entirely different. Depending on the context, the Beatles' "Lucy in the Sky with Diamonds" may be an anthem for LSD or a technical experiment in composing musical imagery. Cypress Hill's song "Something for the Blunted" might be about the sadness of an overstimulated life or it might be about using marijuana. Who is to say which interpretation of the subtext is "correct"? How music creates identity for one generation may not be how another generation's identity is created, of course; and when they overlap, the layers make a rich context.

Writing About Pop Music

We can put pop music into several different contexts, of course, to get different meanings. If, as a writer, you chose to examine sexuality in pop music, you could choose to look at a few different artifacts from different generational perspectives because that approach would give your reader an idea of history. Your essay might start, for instance, by considering Elvis Presley, whose sexuality was clearly indicated by his hip movements; with some research into newspapers and magazines of the 1950s and 1960s, a writer would probably discover that a lot of adults thought Elvis was a hip-wiggling imp of Satan. In the process of that research, you might also discover that the younger folks thought Elvis was the sexiest thing going. Therefore, in your essay you might analyze different reactions. For example, if Presley's hips were the artifact of "sexual threat," too openly sexual to be tolerated by polite society, you could include other examples to offer a contrast: from your perspective, Presley's hips might pale in comparison to Mick Jagger's iconic lips or Michael Jackson's gloved hand grabbing his crotch, the subtext of which is even more overtly sexual than Jagger's mouth. Still another example might be rapper Eminem, who also makes frequent gestures toward his crotch, seemingly in rhythm with the words (which are themselves often blatantly sexual). If you used these various musicians as examples, they'd all be evidence of your ideas about sexuality in pop music. As the writer of the essay, you'd want to do more than just describe

If Mick Jagger is associated with the Rolling Stones, what or who do you associate with a rock band of your choice today?

these performers; to explain why they're significant, you might discuss the function of such sexual references, or analyze the relative sexual freedom of, say, crotch-grabbing as opposed to butt-wiggling.

After a detailed description of the artifacts, a writer would characterize them, or read them. A liberal reading of these texts might suggest that open sexuality is social progress, that we are no longer constrained by older values about propriety. A conservative reading, of course, will be much different, perhaps arguing that the increasingly overt sexuality in music videos and pop lyrics corresponds to a decrease in moral values in American culture. This reading might be supported by one of this chapter's reading selections; rock music, Robert Knight argues, encourages "shedding moral constraints of any kind, leaving the listener in a relativistic universe with a morality of his own making" (203).

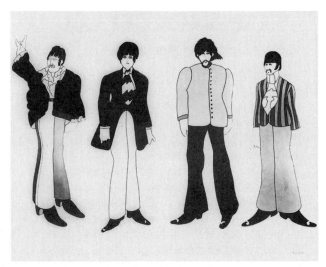

How do these caricatures capture an identity?

The retro culture you see around you is an example of one generational identity overlapping with another. Clothes from the 1970s would be right at home in many closets today; the styles and the shoes clearly recall the fashions of nearly thirty years ago. Swing dancing, popular during the 1950s, is back fifty years later. In the last five or so years, several movies celebrating the 1970s and 1980s appeared, from *54* and *The Last Days of Disco* to *The Wedding Singer* and *Boogie Nights*. In fifteen years, we may see movies that recall events of the 1990s fondly, and we may find ourselves laughing—or furious—to see President Clinton's impeachment recontextualized. In as little as five years, we may look at the current popularity of body piercing as a regrettable fad—or as the precursor to an entirely new way to perceive the body.

Is piercing a tribal rite of passage for some young Americans?

In each film, artifacts of one generation are recaptured and remembered for a new audience. Some members of the audience watching *The Wedding Singer* survived 1986 and laugh to see it recaptured, but other members weren't there firsthand and therefore see something slightly different: *different because the events and ideas are put in a new context.* For instance, as Nelson George mentions in his book *Hip Hop America* (1998), "Rapper's Delight," first released in 1979, celebrated a mainstream emergence of a previously marginalized musical form known as rap. In *The Wedding Singer,*

What indicators of the original meaning remain?

an elderly white woman raps to an audience of wedding guests. The difference between the two raps is obvious: same rap, of course, but different rapper, different situation, different context —in all, a different meaning.

And people who had never heard the rap before its appearance in the movie got a much different idea of what rap was about than those who had heard it on the street in its original form. Some members of some groups read this text of an elderly white female performing a rap and find it funny; some other groups read the same text and find it offensive. (Take a minute or ten and see if you can write about why one group would find humor in something that others find offensive. Can you write in terms of artifact and context?)

When we recontextualize something, we take it out of its original setting and put it somewhere new. So we could just as easily see this wave of nostalgia as a process of recontextualizing the past to get some new meaning out of it. In this chapter's anchor reading, Gary Burns suggests that we call recontextualizing "a constantly widening reclamation project," meaning that we are reclaiming our collective cultural past. Burns gives several examples of musical recontextualizing, for instance using the John Lennon song "Revolution," which muses on the discontents of war, to sell Nike athletic shoes. Or recall the commercial use of Marvin Gaye's "Heard it Through the Grapevine," originally a lament about adultery, as the musical background to dancing raisins —different context, different meaning. In this "recycling" of old music, Gary Burns suggests, the industry "does not at all honor what the song originally meant but rather the sales objective of the moment" (133).

To recontextualize the music of the past to sell the products of the present is to *commodify* that music—to twist its original intention, often past recognition, in order to promote a commercial interest. Advertising is full of examples of commodification, and Burns' article gives us plenty of food for thought. The tunemakers themselves—bands, individual singers, and songwriters—can also commodify their music. This is commonly known as "selling out," as Ryan Theis's article "Popular Music and the Corporate Machine" puts it: "Essentially, if the pursuit of money replaces creative expression as the primary goal in making music, then the musicians involved are considered to have sold out." This may seem a moot point. What does it matter if artistic expression also pays the rent, puts food on the table, and clothes the kids? So what? Does it somehow cheapen musical expression to make a profit from it?

This chapter, then, asks you to look closely at two of the cultures that you're involved in—your generational culture and your musical culture. It might seem odd to be reading articles that talk about a generation you don't belong to, but when examining contexts and reading cultural artifacts for what they reveal, we have to have perspective—and that perspective can only come from an awareness of what else has been important to others. Culture grows as its members do—only those with tunnel vision ignore the impact of one generation on another.

"Popular Music, Television, and Generational Identity" (1996)

Gary Burns

Conventional wisdom has it that popular music is oriented toward *the present*. It is here today and gone tomorrow. It resonates with other current "lifestyle" trends (fashion, dancing, movies) and news events. It celebrates the new, the young, and offbeat deviations from tradition.

While this view is certainly correct in many ways, it is equally true that there is a growing "cult" of the past in popular music. The principal forces driving this phenomenon are demographics and, curiously, technological advancement. New technologies such as the compact disc make it possible to reclaim and "correct" more and more of the past, while hyper-formatted FM radio and satellite cable TV networks such as MTV and VH1 direct this music-of-youth to the Rock Generation, an ever-expanding category that seems to include an age range of about 5-50 (as of 1994). Thus technology and generational narcissism spur the *desire* for a constantly widening reclamation project.

THE ME GENERATION GOES TO HEAVEN

Abbie Hoffman said it shortly before he died: Don't trust anyone under 30. This reversal of the 1960s slogan captures well a certain demographic stereotype that crystallized about the time of the movie *The Big Chill* (1983). At that moment, it became fashionable for Baby Boomers to wallow self-righteously in middle-age angst, to the tune of 1960s hits. The purpose of the music in this case was not to establish diegetic period as in *Shampoo* or *Coming Home*—the action of *The Big Chill* takes place in the present. Rather, the main function of the music is to engender nostalgia and the aforementioned wallowing.

Although previous generations have by no means been disloyal to the popular music of their youth, the tenacious attachment of the Baby Boom to Motown, the Beatles, et al. seems unprecedented. Three main reasons account for this: (1) the Baby Boom has a clearer sense of generational identity than any other generation has had; (2) the Baby Boom generation refuses to let go of childhood and youth; and (3) the mass media, especially in their marketing and advertising functions, encourage (1) and (2).

THE GENERATION THING

Not many generations have names, and certainly no generation has as many names as the Baby Boom-Bulge-Me Generation-Age Wave-Yuppies. While one could argue that these five terms are not exactly synonymous, they are so nearly so that they all apply nicely to the main characters in both *The Big Chill* and the TV series *thirtysomething*.

Having been named so well and so often, Baby Boomers know who they are and that they are distinct from previous generations. They are incessantly studied, written about, renamed, "targeted," and otherwise reminded of their own supposed uniqueness and importance. They are indelibly associated with The Sixties, that most hallowed/wallowed and intensely scrutinized of all decades. The metaphors that bind the generation together, at least according to popular mythology, include Vietnam, protest, and civil rights. Shoved back "in the closet" in such bowdlerized wallowings as the TV series *Family Ties* are the more decisive Big 3 metaphors of the '60s: sex, drugs, and . . . rock and roll. These are arguably even more powerful glue, although drugs are increasingly, and have always been, fairly sharp dividers as well as unifiers—separating those who do from those who don't, and those who used to from those who still do and those who never did. In fact, sex (especially as idealized in the hippie credo of free love) and drugs are mainly "honored" as faded, even discredited, ideologies, whereas music fondly evokes both the idea and experience of youth well wasted. Even one whose youth was "deprived" of profligate sex and drugs can, through music, relive the solidarity that ostensibly united the generation that pioneered the sex-drugs-rock combination.

FOREVER YOUNG

It is not only a sense of generation that causes such interest in 1960s music. The same generation has lived through the 1970s and 1980s, yet there is no consensus of interest in popular music from these periods. Rather, radio stations, for example, play "the music you grew up with," thus directing their format to a specific age group eager to be reminded of a particular stage in their lives.

A poetically appropriate authority in this matter is Timothy Leary, (47-58, esp. 51-52) who theorized that adolescence is a time of heightened neural activity, during which music imprints itself with particular vigor on the nervous system. Barring subsequent "reprogramming," the music of one's adolescence becomes the music of one's life.

But there is more than biology at work in the canonization of 1960s music. Equally fundamental to the longevity of these "oldies" is what Harold Schechter called the myth of the eternal child. As Schechter points out, this myth was especially prevalent in the 1960s. In a sense, World War II ended history and established year Zero. The assassination of John F. Kennedy may have done something similar, so that a Baby Boomer in 1963 was both an adolescent or young adult and also a "child" in the sense of having been psychosocially "reprogrammed" or "wiped clean" by the Kennedy assassination. Thus the Baby Boomer's childhood is detached from history because of World War II, and his or her adolescence or young adulthood is similarly detached because of 11-22-63 (see Hoffman).

Lacking a clear connection to an acceptable history, Baby Boomers tried to create their own substitute through the "counterculture" or "Movement" or "Woodstock Nation." The archaism of these monikers, which were momentarily plausible as synonyms for "Baby Boom," indicates the failure of this generational project and also suggests a societal "wiping clean" of an envisioned page of history. Born three times into worlds without history, the Baby Boom is finally flowing in the mainstream, but some of the ghetto mentality remains from memories of school and other institutional encounters between Them and Us. Childhood having lasted so long, it is a familiar and sometimes comforting frame of mind, transcending, at least temporarily, such barriers as class, occupation, and geography. To the Baby Boom, popular music is history, both personally and generationally. It provides solace from the pains of both the past and present. Old songs are good songs. And as popular culture frequently reminds us, from *Casablanca* to Elton John's "Sad Songs," even if a song was popular during a period of personal strife, the music provided solace then, and it is the solace (qua wallowing) we reexperience when we hear the song today.

RADIO PLAYS THAT FORGOTTEN SONG

Those who run the mass media have been acutely sensitive to these trends. A recent example is the 1989 repackaging of the VH1 video channel into "the first channel for you.'" Who is "you"? Of course, it is "my generation," as one of VH1's recurring segments has been titled. Lest there be any doubt which generation this is, the network has specifically engaged history by airing features such as "Woodstock Minutes," which ran during summer 1989 to commemorate the twentieth anniversary of the Woodstock rock festival. A year later, the network began running a sort of "greatest hits" package of "ABC News reports" about major events from the past 40 years" (Rosenthal 36). As senior vice-president Juli Davidson explained, "We're constantly looking for a kind of programming that's going to say 'Hey 25- to 49-year-old, this is your channel; this is where things you remember are important'" (qtd. in Rosenthal 36).

Thus bite-sized chunks of history cascade along with the rest of the network's "flow," intermingling, in the case of "Woodstock Minutes," a once-transgressive or –transcendent festival with up-to-date videos and commercials. This sort of past-iche is occasionally reinforced via other means such as *VH1 Milestones* (old news footage of Martin Luther King, Robert Kennedy, Muhammad Ali, the 1972 Republican convention, etc.) and compilation-type videos. The latter, including Marvin Gaye's *What's Going On* and Michael Jackson's *Man in the Mirror,* are in a way the ultimate form of historical-regurgitational wallowing, with topical footage decontextualized to serve the soundtrack as almost-abstract imagery. Once-urgent news events become aesthetic spectacle to remind My Generation of pre-couch-potato dialectics.

Of course, "my generation" is also the "me generation," as demonstrated both by the aforementioned pronouns "my" and "you," and also by the focus on convenience in the

pre-couch-potato dialectics · the issues of importance discussed before it became more appealing to be a couch potato.

VH1 slogan "whenever you want it" ("it" casting the tube as metaphor for sex, the breast, and history-as-drug). Some of the promos from 1989 show a couple (and their young child) in bed watching VH1. In a sense, they are watching themselves (a common theme also in music video), since VH1 is you/me—narcissism is neatly combined with idealized imagery of the nuclear family.

The most puzzling ingredient in the VH1 mixture is the insipid vjs, who, with a few exceptions, have not been suitably hippified to address the older-than-MTV generation. In fact, MTV's too-pretty vjs often seem positively articulate by comparison. VH1 seems to have adopted, at least in many of its vj segments, a strategy based on what John Hartley called "paedocracy," which in the present situation means addressing the middle-aged "target" audience as if they were children. Not a bad scheme for dealing with viewers who, despite being adults, are still called the *baby* boom. As VH1's then-president Ed Bennett put it, "We're targeting adults who are still growing up" (qtd. in Grossman 11).

The strategy behind this targeting seems to have changed somewhat in 1994. Whereas in 1993 VH1 defined itself as "the difference between you and your parents," by late 1994 the network was targeting "graduates" of MTV. The aim is still to flatter the viewer into feeling young, but now with music video itself (MTV) as an explicit frame of reference (see Mendoza).

Another example of media exploitation of the musical past, but with a different twist, is the ill-fated song "I Heard It Through the Grapevine." Today it is, unfortunately, best known as the theme song for a group of claymated raisins who appeal to children and presumably to the child in us all. Previously the song was, also unfortunately, best known as the opening theme of *The Big Chill*. The raisin commercial transforms a sinister, on-the-edge love song into a jive sales vehicle, with black-stereotype raisins strutting their good rhythm while ex-counterculture demigod Buddy Miles stands in for the tragically departed Marvin Gaye on the voice track. *The Big Chill* similarly decontextualizes the Gaye recording (not to mention Gladys Knight and even Creedence Clearwater Revival) and reframes the song as very-meaningful-to-white-people.

At a more general level, it is clear that advertising recontextualizes old songs in ways that are disturbing and even shocking. The Nike shoe commercial that cannibalized the Beatles' "Revolution" was a notorious case in point (see Wiener). Whatever John Lennon may have really meant about revolution, he did not mean to be selling shoes. Even more blatantly, a Nissan automobile commercial that aired in 1989 completely inverts the meaning of the O'Jays' song "For the Love of Money." The song condemns avarice. The commercial celebrates it by showing currency erupting from various orifices of a Nissan car, to dramatize how the car supposedly saves the buyer money. The song is changed so that only the refrain "Money money money" is used.

Hit songs are by definition enmeshed in the commercial system through which radio plays records and sells shoes, cars, and practically everything else that can be sold. Thus any hit that criticizes this system is born in irony. Still, hearing an anti-money song on AM radio in 1974 was somehow exhilarating, while hearing it much later on TV as a paean to filthy lucre is infuriating.

Much of advertising's recycling of old music has this same character. Its purpose does not at all honor what the song originally meant but rather the sales objective of the moment. Objections to music video on grounds that the fixed visuals rob viewers' imaginations are misplaced. The real insidiousness lies in the theft of musical-countercultural ideologies of freedom, dissent, and revolution by TV hucksters who feel free to use any piece of music to sell any product. The violation even extends to religious music such as "Carol of the Bells," which has been used in TV commercials for wine and other products.

Similarly, records played unaltered and in their entirety, as on oldies radio, also change meaning as a result of the web of context that develops around them over the years. "Satisfaction" no longer clearly evokes summer 1965, because that evocation is diluted by the dozens of other times one has heard the song—on oldies radio, in concert, in remakes, at the ballpark, in *Apocalypse Now.* And as the listener becomes older and presumably wiser, it is possible one begins to notice that "Satisfaction" is not a very good song. A good performance and recording, yes, brimming with snarl—but as a piece of songwriting, "Satisfaction" is undistinguished. One could excuse this in a hit from summer 1965, if that were all the song is. But after the 500th hearing, the song's flaws become acutely noticeable. One asks, why did I like that song in 1965? Why is it still ubiquitous more than a quarter-century later? Does this song really deserve to be in the Eternal Top 40?

Every time we hear an old song, we hear, and rearrange, its accumulated baggage. Repetition is "dialogic," and when we say a song has or has not "worn well" or "aged well," we are evaluating the original text and all its subsequent "baggage" in light of our present position. Those songs that have "worn well" with the masses, or at least with a demographic subset thereof, are identified by market research and played on radio almost as relentlessly as in their heyday. But the pleasure of oldies radio comes not only from the familiarity of the songs and the predictability of the format. The more interesting moments, actually, are those that violate one's expectation.

"THE MUSIC LASTS FOREVER—THIS OFFER WON'T"

Film theorist Andre Bazin held that the invention of cinema resulted from human beings' psychological impulse toward a "recreation of the world in its own image" (21). In the

Repetition is 'dialogic' • repetition of an old song evokes both old and new contexts, in a continuous cycle like a conversation or dialogue.

case of oldies radio, MTV "Closet Classics," greatest hits albums, and other repackaging ventures, a similar but distinct impulse is at work, namely the desire to preserve and reexperience the "image" (in this case, an acoustic image) that we have produced. The desire for stereo is often conceptualized as a quest to simulate a concert hall with perfect fidelity. But this is no longer the primary function of stereo sound and multitrack recording. The stereo recording is now usually the "original," and a concert performance is often a "reproduction," faithful or otherwise, of the recording (see Attali; see also Goodwin *Dancing*).

Walter Benjamin notwithstanding, the "original" recording has an aura. This aura is based on time, rather than on place as in Benjamin's discussion of statues in temples. The aura of a record arises from its immutability and repeatability. We hear the exact same text (immutability) numerous times (repeatability). Further, the text of "Satisfaction" I heard on radio in Chicago in 1965 is exactly the same as the one someone else heard on a jukebox in Poughkeepsie in 1970.

Oldies radio and similar phenomena depend on our desire to reexperience an exact acoustic image. We want the Rolling Stones' version of "Satisfaction," not Devo's. However, there are cracks in the system that are both interesting and annoying.

If you listen to oldies radio, you are quite likely to hear recordings that differ from the texts originally played on AM radio. Examples include "Let's Hang On!", "Tighter, Tighter," "Cherry, Cherry," "Bend Me, Shape Me," "Penny Lane," "War," "I Can't Turn You Loose," and many others. The stereo mixes used on FM today often sound quite different from the mono and dj versions heard on AM years ago. CD re-releases often involve remixing, re-recording, restoring, and otherwise tampering with the "original."

These alterations disturb the aura of a recording, in much the same way that colorization changes a monochrome movie. Recording engineers reclaim a past we did not even know was there. Suddenly the text, and in a sense the past, is no longer immutable. The new improved past gains relevance but loses authenticity. The past changes not through inversion or denial, but through enhancement.

And so it is that the Columbia CD Club advertised best-of collections by the Who, Doors, and Led Zeppelin on *Postmodern MTV* in 1990. "The music lasts forever—this offer won't." In lasting forever, the music nonetheless changes, both in actual textual substance and in meaning. The Who and The Doors especially were once counter cultural but are now, apparently, postmodern. As audio fidelity becomes clearer and clearer, meaning blurs.

Similarly, as music becomes more intertwined with visual imagery, especially through music video, we see more but know less. More than a decade after MTV's sign-on, there is general agreement that music video is trivial and vapid, yet somehow important. The semiotic slippage often attributed to video clips themselves has spread to MTV as the vehicle of their presentation. What originally was a carefully contrived package of rec-room set, brother/sister-next-door VJs, and New Wave-heavy metal clips in a rotation-format flow has now become something much different.

Gradually and quietly, MTV has taken a turn away from narrowcast-ing and format programming. Its "targeted age group" of 12-34 (MTV Press Release; Russell "MTV in 2nd" 96) reaches into Baby Boom territory and far beyond the pimply teenage range one would expect. Significant programming changes include forays into alleged comedy, game shows, and "real"-life soap operas; expanded roles for VJs and other personali-ties; and increased reliance on titled programs (as distinct from format). As MTV Networks chairman Tom Freston put it, "we found that the ap-plication of proven television-programming techniques—like, you know, shows—gets people to watch longer once they land on the dial" (qtd. in Goldberg 64).

While MTV's publicity as of 1989 maintained that its new programs were on the "cutting edge," many of the changes looked a bit like re-treat into tried-and-true formulas. *Club MTV* merely updated *American Bandstand*, with Tartar-Control Julie Brown in place of Ipana Dick Clark. *Remote Control* was the network's best comedy effort to that point, but mainly because it was a parody of worn-out game-show formulas.

More recently, MTV has taken a lesson from the Fox network in ex-panding its "crossover" appeal, not only along racial lines *(Yo! MTV Raps),* but especially across generations. Like Fox's *The Simpsons,* MTV's *Ren and Stimpy, Beavis and Butt-Head,* and *Speed Racer* are car-toon series that appeal to young people but also "cross over" to an adult audience. *Speed Racer* reminds the older generation of the pro-gram's original run in syndication in 1967. *Beavis and Butt-Head* com-bines timeless "male" bad taste with timeless bad videos from throughout MTV's brief history. The viewers can enjoy the videos on their own terms or can revel in Beavis and Butt-head's voice-over commentary (see Roberts 81-109).

In a sense, *Beavis and Butt-Head* is itself a recycling of MTV's earlier ef-forts at retrospection. These included *Martha's Greatest Hits* (1990), an in-triguing, quasi-historical presentation that dished up a gumbo of past and present videos. The "classics" in this program were disappointingly few and conservatively chosen. Host Martha Quinn was the main link with the past, since she was "one of MTV's original VJs," as an MTV press release proudly noted. In the short period she had been away from MTV, she had grown up and was now a sexy broad rather than a girl-next-door. Originally part of an undistinguished staff of interchangeable, hip-to-be-square presenters, she was in 1990 the major object of promotion in a titled, scheduled slice of format disguised as a program. Ostensibly designed to appeal to people who had watched MTV five years earlier and who perhaps were less inclined to do so in 1990, *Martha's Greatest Hits* was actually extremely soft as a dose of history or nostalgia.

Nonetheless it is significant that MTV repeatedly lays claim to video's past, as it has also done with the past of Baby Boom rock in *Closet Classics*. Late in 1994, VH1 began its own version of *Martha's Greatest Hits*, minus Martha and in fact without any host at all. This flow of old videos, known as *The Big 80's* is identifiable as a program only by virtue of a brief bumper/title sequence and an intrusive logo continuously present in the upper left corner of the screen. Taken together, VH1 and MTV (and possibly their companion network Nickelodeon) seem to be embarked on an ambitious project of engaging the Baby Boom and subsequent generations from "cradle to grave."

CONCLUSION: BECAUSE THE PAST IS JUST A GOODBYE!

"People try to put us down," as pre-corporate Pete Townshend wrote, but sometimes it is hard to see how the process works. The generation gap is a concept as extinct as that of the counterculture, yet Townshend's generation is still put down by virtue of being so often a "targeted" group.

While it may sometimes appear that Baby Boomers have control, directly or indirectly, of much of the television and music industries, the relationship is reciprocal. The control of the Baby Boom depends in large part upon ideological regulation of the contested past, of what are now called "wonder years" and "Woodstock Minutes." Nostalgia is safe. Thinking too seriously about the past and how it led to the present is dangerous.

Ultimately, the successful incorporation of the Baby Boom into the System involves redefinition of some basic terms. When Ed Bennett became President of VH1 in June 1989, he quickly charted a new course for the network: "Now, [Bennett] says, 'the attitude is "having fun with love and work" . . . it's relevant and at times irreverent, and it values experience'" (Grossman 11). Voila—new meanings for "relevant," "irreverent," and "experience." Even more to the point is Bennett's attitude toward "attitude." Woodstock, historical "milestones," and memories of counterculture notwithstanding, present-day love and work are, above all, "fun." Ah—what a relief that our troubles are all behind us!

This is a revised version of a paper presented at the conference of the Central States Communication Association, Detroit, April 6, 1990.

■ *Gary Burns, a professor at Northern Illinois University, is the editor of* Popular Music and Society *and teaches courses in music video, media criticism, and television. Burns is a former President of the American Culture Society. This article originally appeared in the* Journal of Popular Culture.

MAKING SURE OF THE TEXT

1. Do you agree with Burns that American culture seems set on reclaiming its past?
2. What does Burns mean when he refers to the "accumulated baggage" of a particular song?

3. What is meant by "recontextualizing"?
4. How does Burns make the connection between generational narcissism and "generational identity"?
5. What has the role of MTV been, according to Burns?
6. What does Burns find "disturbing and even shocking" about advertising's use of old songs? What does your answer tell you about the context from which Burns writes?

CONSIDERING THE CONTEXT

1. Burns' article appeared in the scholarly publication *Journal of Popular Culture*. Who might the readers of this journal be, and how does Burns establish common ground with these readers?
2. What do you know about Abbie Hoffman, referenced early in Burns' article? What's significant about the reference and the quotation? In other words, what is Burns attempting to do with this reference?
3. Notice the uses of specific terms: the "canonization" of 1960s music; recontextualizing as "disturbing and even shocking"; the "theft" of specific musical ideologies for marketing purposes. Why has Burns chosen "canonization" instead of, for instance, "popularity"? What impact do these word choices have on you?

"Music: Roll Over, Apollo" from *Age of Consent: Moral Relativism in the Age of Popular Culture* **(1998)**

Robert H. Knight

The 1984 movie *Footloose* has a very catchy soundtrack and a typical Hollywood "youth" theme; the kids are not understood by their bewildered parents, but the elders eventually see the light courtesy of their progressive offspring.

What sets *Footloose* apart from other films of this genre is the backhanded respect that it shows religion; even the new kid in town, played by Kevin Bacon, who becomes a sort of clean-cut town rebel, attends church with his mom. And there is a key scene in which the central adult figure, the pastor of the town church, played by John Lithgow, is listening to Bach while writing a sermon. His daughter (Lori Singer) has been campaigning to end the town's ban on dancing, a stricture initiated and sustained by her father's tyrannical influence.

Dad thinks, with plenty of justification, that rock 'n' roll is the devil's music. But he had gone overboard by forbidding dancing via the town council. As it turns out, he went off the deep end because of a terrible tragedy for which he feels responsible. He gets over this by the end of the film, after the rebel quotes a bunch of Bible verses about dancing that the pastor's daughter finds for him. (Who says the devil can't quote Scripture?)

Anyway, the daughter comes in and asks Dad why he doesn't find his own classical music sinful, and he replies that it uplifts the soul because it is harmonious and brilliantly structured. This music appeals to the spirit, he says, unlike other varieties, which bruise the soul by miring it in animalistic urges. This is basically what Allan Bloom said in his famous passages on the dangers of rock 'n' roll in *Closing of the American Mind:*

But rock music has one appeal only, a barbaric appeal, to sexual desire—not love, not *eros,* but sexual desire undeveloped and untutored. It acknowledges the first emanations of children's emerging sensuality and addresses them seriously, eliciting them and legitimating them, not as little sprouts that must be carefully tended in order to grow into gorgeous flowers, but as the real thing. Rock gives children, on a silver platter, with all the public authority of the entertainment industry, everything their parents always used to tell them they had to wait for until they grew up and would understand later.[1]

Rock 'n' roll began as a combination of Afro-American folk music (rhythm and blues) and white country folk music—hillbilly ballads. Elements of jazz, such as horns, abounded, at least early on. Unlike the earlier forms, the spirit of rock was always about rebellion. At first, it was a high-spirited form that celebrated life and

Allan Bloom · American culture critic.

youth. The anthems of Ricky Nelson, the Everly Brothers, and the early Beatles are mostly about love and love lost. During the 1960s, the Beach Boys, along with Jan and Dean, invented a genre of bouncy surf rock that extols the California youth culture. Their sunny lyrics and upbeat stage shows wouldn't have fooled Allan Bloom, however, who insisted that the rock beat is always a musical metaphor for sexual intercourse. Numerous rock stars agree.

Debbie Harry of the eighties group Blondie puts it this way: "I've always thought the main ingredients in rock are sex, really good stage shows, and really sassy music. Sex and sass. I just dance around and shake. Rock 'n' roll is all sex. One hundred percent."[2]

Mick Jagger of the Rolling Stones: "I often want to smash the microphone up because I don't feel the same person on-stage as I am normally. I entice the audience . . . [W]hat I'm doing is a sexual thing. I dance, and all dance is a replacement for sex."[3]

Black music, which white disc jockeys called "race" music in the 1940s, turned the gospel sound into the blues, and rhythm and blues. Artists such as Mahalia Jackson and Aretha Franklin made the crossover into R&B seem almost effortless. Certainly the energy level was the same if the message wasn't. Gospel's power comes from its cathartic ability to take the performer and audience into the heart of Dionysian emotion only to emerge from it, harnessing it for a higher purpose. As Bayles explains, "In gospel, suffering is the path to God, and God will respond to the most agonized cry by turning it into the most jubilant shout. So there's no reason to hold back. Needless to say, the resulting taste for extremes takes on a very different cast when transferred to the realm of sexual pain and pleasure."[4] The switch was exemplified in Marvin Gaye's album, *Let's Get It On,* in whose liner notes Gay proclaimed, "I can't see what's wrong with sex between two consenting anybodies. I think we make far too much of it." Voodoo influenced the music of Screamin' Jay Hawkins, Muddy Waters, Bo Diddley, and later, Jimi Hendrix, who openly sang that he was a "Voodoo Child" in a song by that name.

In terms of impact on the emerging music, the hard-driving Little Richard took it to orgiastic heights in his private life as well as on stage. Fashioning his high-top hair after a homosexual musician named Esquerita who had had sex with him and then taught him to play piano, Little Richard became the inspiration for a whole generation of pop musicians. Combining a driving rock beat and screaming vocals, Little Richard set the standard for rock flamboyance. Among the stars who have cited his work are Elvis Presley, Sam Cook, Otis Redding, John Lennon, Elton John, Janis Joplin, David Bowie, Paul Simon, Marty Balin of Jefferson Airplane, Jon Lord of Deep Purple, and Smokey Robinson, who proclaimed "Little Richard is the beginning of

Dionysian emotion · the Greek god Dionysus represented the wild, sensual, emotional side of our psyche, often but not always connoting a sexual content.

Bayles · Martha Bayles, noted rock music critic.

rock & roll."[5] In fact, it would be hard to find a major rock star who has not at some time cited Little Richard as a major influence. Mick Jagger said it for many when he proclaimed, "Little Richard is the originator and my idol."[6]

The wild antics that Little Richard threw himself into on stage were nothing compared with the orgies he threw backstage or at his hotel rooms. And as pop musicians mimicked his performance style, they also began mimicking his total abandonment of sexual mores—even "clean" bands like the Beatles, who took ample advantage of lovestruck fans before these hapless girls were known as "groupies."

The secularization of black music was also shaped largely by the development of the blues, which Mahalia Jackson said were "songs of despair," as opposed to gospel songs, which are "songs of hope."[7] Blues historian Paul Oliver writes that, "The blues is primarily the song of those who turned their backs on religion."[8] As such, the blues were the perfect vehicle for the emerging white bands from Great Britain and America who wanted to demonstrate their liberation from a Christian-based culture. John Mayall and the Bluesbreakers did their best to sound like American bluesmen and sold a lot of records in the process. Groups like Led Zeppelin appropriated not only the basic blues structure but also some of the seedier lyrics of the more earthy bluesmen. Many of the English blues songs are centered around sexual passion.

If rock is mainly about shedding sexual constraints, it is also about shedding moral constraints of any kind, leaving the listener in a relativistic universe with a morality of his own making. Parental authority was rock's first target, followed by a succession of complaints about "society" in general. From youthful exuberance in the 1950s, albeit an upbeat innocence only in comparison with what was to come, "mainstream" rock gradually began to cease criticizing the culture from within to become a force against civilization itself. Instead of arguing in the parlor, it began throwing rocks at the house from the street.

A major innovation occurred in 1981 when Music Television (MTV) was launched. Originally a twenty-four-hour cable television channel that played music videos, MTV became an all-purpose, electronic youth central, with news programs, situation comedies, game shows, and animated features such as the futuristic "Aeon Flux" and the cynical "Beavis and Butthead." The advent of MTV meant that youth rebellion had its own visual/audio outlet instead of depending on handouts from the established media the way the Beatles had to do on "The Ed Sullivan Show" in 1964 to promote their first big American hit, "I Want to Hold Your Hand."

Meanwhile, another American musical force was rising fast, partly as a reaction to the excesses of rock 'n' roll. Country music had been popular in the South and West since the 1940s, but it broke into the "mainstream" culture after Bob Dylan did his crossover *Nashville Skyline* album in 1969 and novelist Kurt Vonnegut and other celebrities admitted a taste for country music. Manhattan sprouted country music bars, followed by Texas-style chili parlors. Even George Bush, while running for president in 1992, allowed as to how he and his wife Barbara enjoyed country music—and ate pork rinds. It was one thing for the Georgian Jimmy Carter to appear on stage with pony-tailed Willie Nelson; it was another for the hyper-establishment Bushes to own up to a taste for country twang. The music that was despised as the province of the unsophisticated was suddenly in, and the market expanded wildly. In the 1990s, country performers such as Garth Brooks and Dolly Parton achieved star power equal to that of anyone in the television, rock, or film genres. In 1991, for example, Brooks's "Ropin' the Wind" was the top album, with about seven million units sold.

Apart from its catchy tunes and pun-laden lyrics, country music's broader appeal was its reiteration of the themes of family, religion, patriotism, and hard work. Folks who formerly thought of country as hillbilly music found themselves saying, "That stuff speaks to me; it's what my life is all about." While rock 'n' roll careened into nihilism, bloodlust, and sexual explicitness, country borrowed the rock beat and set its homey lyrics to it, spinning tales of real people and real-life situations. Unfortunately, many country bands borrowed liberally from their rock 'n' roll counterparts when creating television videos. Although far more wholesome generally than the fare on MTV or VHS, some of the videos on country music channels feature frenetic pacing and overtly sexual themes. Some of the country bands perform warmed-over, countrified rock tunes, indicating that part of the country music movement is merely rock 'n' roll wearing a cowboy hat and ten years behind the times.

As for rock, its rebellion runs far deeper than the desire to be different. Modernist conceits such as self-absorption as the key to enlightenment or unlimited sexual intrigue are merely the tools by which young minds are seduced away from religion, parents, and individual responsibility. Sex is the prime magnet, but many stars of rock were and are serving another god, to whom sex was just the best possible lure—the occult.

On album cover after album cover of best-selling records of the sixties through the nineties, occultic symbols abound. References to the occult are sprinkled through interviews with stars such as the late Jim Morrison, the self-proclaimed "lizard king" of The Doors. While on stage, Morrison often fell into a shamanic trance, summoning up powers from below. Doors keyboardist Ray Manzarek recalls that he was in awe of Morrison's other-worldly qualities:

When the Siberian shaman gets ready to go into his trance all the villagers get together and shake rattles and blow whistles and play whatever instruments they have to send him off. There is a constant pounding, pounding, pounding. And these sessions last for hours. It was the same way with the Doors when we played in a concert. The sets didn't last that long, but I think our drug experiences let us get

VHS · misprint for VH-1, the pop video channel launched as part of MTV.

into it that much quicker. We knew the symptoms of the State, so that we could try to approximate it. It was like Jim was an electric shaman and we were the electric shaman's band pounding away behind him. Sometimes he wouldn't feel like getting into the state, but the band would keep pounding and pounding, and little by little it would take him over. God, I could send an electric shock through him with the organ. John could do it with his drumbeats. You could see every once in a while—twitch—I could hit a chord and make him twitch . . . And the audience felt it, too.[9]

Heavy metal groups such as Motley Crüe and Black Sabbath openly displayed their loyalty to Satan, as did the Knights in Satan's Service (KISS), which became a mainstream attraction for teenyboppers. Ozzy Osbourne, whose song "Suicide Solution" was cited as the final straw that led at least one young listener to kill himself, wrote often of satanic themes, even penning a tribute to the British Satanist Aleister Crowley entitled *Mr. Crowley.*

Around 1970, Led Zeppelin guitarist Jimmy Page began to shift his focus from songs about sex to songs about the occult after meeting with Church of Satan founding–member Kenneth Anger, a disciple of Aleister Crowley. Album covers, beginning with *Led Zeppelin III,* began to carry Crowley's motto, "Do What Thou Wilt." By the fourth album, the band began identifying openly with Satanic imagery, including a hexagram on the cover that emanates light, an occultic symbol for Satan. The hit song of the album, which has since become a classic of the seventies, "Stairway to Heaven," is a pleasant ballad musically, but it is also a paean to Crowley's secret society of Satanists.

The lyrics were by Robert Plant, who said that as he wrote the song, his pen was moving across the paper almost by itself, as if automatically. In the occult world, "automatic writing" refers to the possession of the writer by a demonic spirit who uses the writer to "channel" the message. It's the principle behind the innocent-seeming Ouija board, another occultic device that has been mainstreamed as a harmless diversion. According to rock historian Mark Spaulding, the line, "There's a feeling I get when I look to the West and my spirit is crying for leaving," is a reference to an initiation rite included in Aleister Crowley's book *MAGICK: In Theory and Practice.* On page thirty-nine, there is this: "After further purification and consecration he [speaking of the initiate] is allowed for one moment to see the Lord of the West, and gains courage to persist." This is an allusion to an initiate being blindfolded, but permitted a moment to gaze at the West. Crowley later states of the initiate that, "In the West he gains energy."[10]

It was the Rolling Stones who first popularized not only references to Satan in rock, but the mixing of sex and violence. Jagger warned his listeners in the *Let It Bleed* album that rape was "just a kiss away" and that the Midnight Rambler wanted "to stick a knife right down your throat, baby, and it hurts." Those lyrics quickly became almost tame compared with the complete embrace of perverse sex and violence by Stones clones such as WASP, which began as the black magic band Sister. Here's a sample of WASP lyrics from their first album:

I am a sinner, I kiss the breast
I am a sadist that RIPS THE FLESH
I take the women, curse those who enter
I am a killer and tormentor

This is still kids' stuff when compared to lyrics from some rap and rock groups in the nineties, such as Getto Boys, 2 Live Crew, Nine-Inch Nails, and others. They freely sing of masturbation, suicide, rape, mutilation, murder, and dismemberment of women (before and after). In November 1997, MTV shattered another barrier by featuring full frontal nudity in the video "Smack the Bitch Up," in which strippers and other women are abused by an unknown assailant, who is revealed to be a woman.

Civil libertines say that such themes are not taken seriously by the youngsters who buy these albums and videos by the millions. All they listen to is the beat, they say. But for a generation brought up on Jungian suggestion and subconscious communication, who spy messages in everything from advertising to soap labels, it is amazing how easily they exempt rock from any mental or moral impact.

But it takes no more than common sense to understand that a constant diet of sleaze makes one more accepting of sleaze, either on one's own part or when it is embraced by others. This is what is known as becoming "jaded." Second, there are troubled people on the margin of sanity who are greatly affected by perverse entreaties from rock idols, and they are usually receiving these messages while in a drugged or drunken state.

Charles Manson, who was rejected in a tryout for the Monkees band and became a rock 'n' roll cult figure in his own California commune, led a group of young people into unspeakable carnage in the Sharon Tate murders in 1969. His hypnotic mixture of personal charisma and a rock-induced drug subculture allowed him to override any decency that was left in his followers. One week after the murders, five hundred thousand people gathered in a New York farm to form "Woodstock Nation."

A heady mix of rock music, politics, drugs, and sex, Woodstock was more than an extended concert. As noted by Rabbi Daniel Lapin of Toward Tradition, Woodstock was a giant "finger in the eye of God," a throwing off of the old moral system. As a cultural landmark, Woodstock was the high point of the New Age of moral relativism that engulfed America. To the mud-soaked, stoned partyers, it all seemed so innocent, so devoid of negative consequences, apart from an overdose here or there. But the Aquarians lost their innocence

Libertines · free thinkers, or people unconstrained by moral considerations.

Sharon Tate murders · the murder of Tate and several others, while Tate was several months' pregnant; the grisly murders were committed by Manson and several of his cult followers.

later that year when a Rolling Stones performance at the Altamont race track in California ended in an orgy of beatings and one killing by blood-crazed Hell's Angels who had been hired as "security" for the concert.

The trouble had begun in the early evening, as the sun went down and the crowd had grown restless. As E. Michael Jones relates: "By the time Jefferson Airplane took the stage, a pattern had been established for the day. The band would bellow out some incitement to revolution, and then stand back in befuddlement as the crowd actually acted on what they were saying. Jefferson Airplane, a group that had always billed itself as front men for the encroaching anarchy and disorder, now seemed at a loss, if not genuinely terrified, as the understanding dawned on them that what they had been preaching in their songs was now happening before their very eyes."[11]

As the Airplane began singing a song about putting people "up against the wall," the Hell's Angels began beating a young black man with lead-filled pool cues. The crowd was both repelled and energized by the blood in the air, and it reached maximum pitch in the middle of the Stones' portion of the concert. Stones insider Tony Sanchez recalled that an unending supply of girls, many in trancelike states, took off their clothes and crawled toward the stage, "impelled as if by some supernatural force, to offer themselves as human sacrifices to these agents of Satan." The Hell's Angels beat the girls senseless, and Jagger began asking the crowd to "cool out now." Violence broke out as soon as the band began the song "Sympathy for the Devil" and continued until a young black man who was carrying a gun was beaten to death by the Hell's Angels. The Stones, who were too frightened to stop playing, finally finished their gig and took off in a helicopter as the beatings began anew, growing to a bloody crescendo. In a film clip of Jagger watching a tape of the carnage, his face is ashen and confused.

The moral restraints that his band had discarded had finally led to murder. As he turned to leave the room, Jagger wore an expression that seemed to indicate he knew that he had been used by something or somebody to bring it about. If God was dead and no longer in control of things, then somebody else was in charge, and it wasn't Jagger.

NOTES

1   Bloom, *The Closing of the American Mind*, p. 73.

2   Mark Spaulding, *The Heartbeat of the Dragon* (Sterling Heights, Michigan: Light Warrior Press, 1992), p. 14.

3   Ibid.

4   Bayles, *Hole in Our Soul*, p. 272.

5   Spaulding, *The Heartbeat of the Dragon*, p. 28.

6   Ibid, pp. 119, 120.

7   Bayles, *Hole in Our Soul*, p. 189.

8   Ibid, p. 189.

9   Jerry Hopkins and Danny Sugerman, *No One Gets Out Alive* (New York: Warner Books, 1980), pp. 158–160.

10   Spaulding, *The Heartbeat of the Dragon,* p. 93.

11   Jones, *Dionysus Rising,* p. 178–179.

■ *Robert H. Knight is the director of cultural studies at the Family Research Council. A leading conservative expert on the issue of public policy and marriage, he regularly appears on national television news programs and is often quoted in the* New York Times, *the* Washington Post, *and other national journals.*

MAKING SURE OF THE TEXT

1. What are Knight's reasons for suggesting that rock music's influence on our culture has been negative? Summarize them.
2. Identify Knight's argument and outline it carefully. How does each piece lead to the next?
3. What gives rock a negative connotation and country music a positive connotation, as Knight describes them?
4. What are "the tools by which young minds are seduced away from religion, parents, and individual responsibility"? How do the tools work?
5. In what ways are Burns and Knight *recontextualizing* when they discuss Marvin Gaye?

CONSIDERING THE CONTEXT

1. The initial reference in Knight's article is to the 1984 movie *Footloose*, a film about a small town whose pastor has denounced music and dancing. Why has Knight used this example, when people who have seen the movie might think it argues against Knight's primary point?
2. Knight is fairly conservative in his views. What language does he use to reinforce this perspective? In other words, how has diction been employed?
3. Knight suggests that a musician's "shamanic trance" relies on "powers from below." Contrast the relationship between spirituality and evil in Knight's article to the relationship discussed in Rose Morrigan's article in Chapter 4.

■ ■ ■

"'da joint!' and beyond," from *HipHop America* (1998)

Nelson George

As for the future of rapping, I think it will become a prerequisite for all black club jocks (and many whites) to be fluent in some form of the language.

—*Nelson George,*
Musician magazine, 1980

I remember when attractive women were simply "fly" and great records were "da joint." Then everything, from laceless sneakers to baseball caps worn sideways, was "fresh." For a while things got "stoopid" and even "stoopid fresh," which could also be "def" when it wasn't "dope." Sometimes, when you really wanted people to believe what you said, "on the strength" certified your commitment, though "word is bond" and, ultimately, "word" could work when you wished to be succinct. "Word" was once a powerful affirmation that you were "droppin' science." When you were "in effect" you were truly "large." A woman or a record always "got me open" but at the moment I write this they both better be "jiggy" if I'm supposed to pay attention.

The language of hip hop, a particularly active subset of the African-American linguistic tradition, marks moments lived and gone. The words go with outdated clothes, closed clubs, and careers startling in their brevity. The distance traveled from the Funky + Plus One's "That's the Joint" to Will Smith's "Gettin' Jiggy with It" spans the history of rap on record and the rapid journey of this culture from cult item to entertainment commodity. That so many of those words and phrases sound ancient and even quaint show we've entered a new era in hip hop, one that embraces cutting-edge and nostalgic artifacts.

On New York radio, Grandmaster Flash and Kool DJ Red Alert host midday old-school radio shows, while in Los Angeles Kurtis Blow has a late-night show and has compiled a three-CD history of rap. As a producer on Chris Rock's HBO comedy show in 1997, I recruited Flash to serve as the musical director and was pleased to see the love Flash received when introduced to the studio crowd. *Wild Style,* both the home video and the CD of the music, were reissued by the archival experts at Rhino, testament to a growing fascination with hip hop's past.

After twenty years of defining the edge, hip hop dances, art, and music are being used as shortcut references to set a mood of the past and to jog memories. "Rapper's Delight," performed by an elderly white woman, is a comic set piece in *The Wedding Singer,* a 1998 film set in 1986. Three-stripe Adidas have become cool fashion statements for off-duty models, and breakers have begun working again in the music videos of Mariah Carey, KRS-One and others, as signs of solidarity with hip hop's roots. Of course, Puff Daddy's magnificent mid-90s hit-making run was based on many riffs taken from earlier hip hop eras, a kind of slightly submerged nostalgia dressed as new music.

Yet hip hop still resists becoming a museum piece as jazz and '60s soul have. Like flesh, it keeps regenerating itself and with each new generation becomes more rooted and builds new alliances. For example, the social schism between buppies and b-boys has been completely smoothed over by the thirst for profit. Sylvia Rhone, product of Pennsylvania's Wharton business school, longtime record biz veteran, and, as president of Elektra, the highest ranking African-American executive in the industry, enjoyed one of her best years in 1997 by aggressively signing and promoting the hip hop—R&B of Missy "Misdemeanor" Elliott. Unlike the previous generation of black executives who missed the boat on hip hop, Rhone has backed this Virginia-based talent with the full commitment of her company, confident that her off-kilter, clean records, lightly spiced with U.K. jungle beats, have as much right to be the sound of young America as fading rock bands and country balladeers.

The buppie–b-boy connection is apparent in other areas as well. Although Quincy Jones conceived *Vibe,* it is Keith Clinkscale, a black Harvard business school grad, who runs the operation on a daily basis. Publishing a hip hop magazine is not exactly what black folks expected from black MBAs when they moved into the business school in the '60s but Clinkscale, who had published his own buppish *Urban Profile* mag before joining *Vibe,* is symbolic of the synergy between African-American street culture and the black upwardly mobile class throughout the industry and the country. There's probably not a college campus in the country in which some of its African-American students are not involved in various entrepreneurial-cultural ventures tied to hip hop.

But, as always, innovations in the culture come straight from the street. Master P (Percy Miller), *ex*–New Orleans street hustler and University of Houston dropout turned country MC and rap mogul, has been selling hundreds of thousands of records since opening his No Limit operation in 1990. His self-promoted and financed *Ice Cream Man* sold 300,000 copies with no visibility outside the South. He has had similar regional success with his signees Mia X, TRU, and Mr. Serv-On, controlling all aspects of their marketing and promotion, and has a distribution deal with that longtime supporter of non–New York rap, Priority.

Master P, who had already made his mark the old-fashioned hip hop way, then made a bold futuristic move. He wanted to make a movie but received nothing but skepticism from the film industry. Working with his protégé, director-writer Moon Jones, Master P created *I Bout It,* a raw tale of the drug life in New Orleans, augmented on a home video-tape by a few music videos and some X-rated action. The tape never made it to theaters, but it was the home video phenomenon of summer 1997. It topped the music video sales chart and challenged

Buppies · slang acronym for *Black Urban Professional.* (Related to 'yuppies'—young urban professionals).

Hollywood products like *Jerry Maguire* for the top spot on *Billboard's* Video Scan chart. While Hollywood blacks moaned about lack of distribution, Master P showed that a gutsy, aggressive black businessman could reach his audience outside the regular distribution channels. Cinematically, *I Bout It* is extremely crude. He's no Spielberg or Scorsese, yet Master P has shown himself to be an-up-by-his-bootstraps Booker T. Washington disciple, which, in this era of corporate control, makes him both a throwback and a visionary.

The crack epidemic that overwhelmed America has abated. Aggressive policing and a major change in how it's sold (clocking on curbs has been replaced by indoor trafficking) have brought crime down all over the country. In response, the tenor of hip hop culture has softened. Rap records with R&B choruses, female vocalists performing over hip hop beats, and dance-oriented records abound. Times are still tough for most black folk during Bill Clinton's second term, yet there is a yearning for a more humanistic, less nihilistic, but still acquisitive future reflected in the current music.

Though hip hop dancers haven't returned to spinning on their heads, movement is again central to the culture with dancers, nasty and otherwise, appearing in videos and stage shows, adding energy and sex appeal. People are sweating in designer clothes (or well-done knockoffs) as dressing down to go out has faded. Where Nike warm-ups once ruled, Dolce & Gabbana T-shirts can now be found. Once high-top fades and, later, bald heads were the official garb of basketball players. Now Allen Iverson's elaborate '70s throwback cornrow hair is the new cutting edge of athletic hair care. Young brothers contemplate whether to follow his lead, while old schoolers wonder, "Where there are men with braided hair, can Afros be far behind?" Out in Cali, young Kobe Bryant is already there with an Afro as fresh (in the old hip hop sense) as his game.

In music, Iverson's stylistic peer is D'Angelo, the soulful crooner who sports cornrows while displaying a falsetto and keyboard touch that recalls uncut soul music. Many feel this singer, who, like Iverson, was born and raised in Virginia, is the future of black music. (Between Iverson, D'Angelo, Timbaland, Missy Elliott, and recent resident Teddy Riley, Virginia, of all places, is looking like the new cutting edge.) While D'Angelo's promise remains to be fulfilled, the anticipation surrounding his career speaks to a quietly insistent question: What will come after hip hop? Since the '60s, musical and cultural trends have risen and burned with blazing speed.

Yet hip hop endures. Despite the vaguely liberal rhetoric of the Clinton presidency, poverty has not receded, the schools have deteriorated, drug addiction has changed—from crack to marijuana and heroin—but hasn't abated, and the class schisms in the country are naked.

Booker T. Washington disciple · reference to someone following in the footsteps of Washington, who was a leader for African-Americans when slavery was illegal but discrimination was not.

This is all terrible for the social fabric of the nation, but it is prime fodder for the makers and consumers of edgy, aggressive culture. The truth is that hip hop—in its many guises—has reflected (and internalized) our society's woes so evocatively that it has grown from minority expression to mainstream appreciation. Our nation's clothes, our language, our standards for entertainment, our sexuality, and our role models are just a few items that have been affected by hip hop's existence. This thing labeled hip hop has simply been in the middle of much, and nothing at the turn of the century has changed that. The allegiance of its true believers is deep and looks to be lifelong. The mainstream—that majority of Americans of all colors for whom culture is a commodity and not a calling—seems far from exhausted by it.

The long-term direction of America, and hip hop's role in it, will be decided by two very different factors. First, the state of America's soul. Will a commitment to social justice, to nonpolarizing politics and old-fashioned community resurface? If so, such a humanist movement would certainly alter the culture, perhaps spawning a musical movement as optimistic as the golden days of Motown. Don't hold your breath.

The second unknowable factor is the taste of twenty-first-century teens. They will find hip hop artifacts everywhere—videos, CDs, Web sites—and what will they think of them? At some point they will likely react as teens have always ultimately reacted to the passions of their elders—they'll shout, "It's boring!" and move on.

One day in the year 2005, 2010, 2020, all this fun and fury will seem as antiquated as spats and big bands do to us. The next generation may reject hip hop for the next sweeping cultural trend. And, by the logic of pop culture, they are actually supposed to.

But, whether they like it or not, they'll know there once was a hip hop America.

Word.

■ *Nelson George is a veteran journalist and a critical fan of African-American musical culture. His previous book,* The Death of Rhythm & Blues *(1991), won several awards for its broad, insightful personality of criticism. This selection is the concluding chapter of his most recent book.*

MAKING SURE OF THE TEXT

1. What, according to George, is the role of hip-hop in American culture?
2. George mentions Will Smith's "Gettin' Jiggy wit' It" and Kobe Bryant's Afro as evidence that hip-hop has moved "from cult item to entertainment commodity." What other examples does he offer?
3. What is important about rap "resist[ing] becoming a museum piece"? What does George suggest is keeping hip-hop alive?
4. What other indications can you think of to support George's claim that "the mainstream—that majority of Americans of all colors for whom culture is a commodity and not a calling—seems far from exhausted" by hip-hop?

CONSIDERING THE CONTEXT

1. George refers to the hip-hop movement as "flesh," in that it "keeps regenerating itself." Do you find other body metaphors? What effect does the physical or bodily metaphor have on George's claims?
2. The "shortcut references" George describes recall or evoke a specific context through the use of a single name; they function as contexts themselves, shortcuts for the readers to "get" much more from the name. What contexts are summoned for you by George's unexplained references to Quincy Jones and Missy Elliott? Are they what George intends?
3. What's the impact of the final one-word sentence? How does it reflect or represent the rest of the article?
4. From your reading of both Knight and George, what would Knight have to say about hip-hop?

■ ■ ■

"Popular Music and the Corporate Machine" (1997)

Ryan Theis

When Green Day signed on to Reprise Records in 1994 and released "Dookie," their first album on a major corporate label, they were denounced by a large segment of the punk rock scene. This west-coast pop-core band had originally released its material on the Berkeley-based Lookout label; now it was doing videos for MTV.

Newsgroups such as alt.punk were plastered with angry rants about the band's corporate complicity. Some went so far as to claim that Green Day was "not punk." While many might disagree with such a statement, one thing was unanimous—Green Day had "sold out."

Of course, punk rock is not the only genre of popular music vulnerable to this phenomenon, and Green Day isn't the only band to have made sacrifices for the big-name scene. Selling out is applicable to any style of music with money-making potential. Any band that dares to approximate the sounds of the MTV generation may hear from the likes of Warner Bros. and Viacom. But what, exactly, does it mean to "sell out"? The term itself highlights the gains that can be made from it—namely, money, and greater audience (which translates into more money). Essentially, if the pursuit of money replaces creative expression as the primary goal in making music, then the musicians involved are considered to have sold out. This statement clearly points to the fact that selling out, or commodification, can occur in not just popular music, but all forms of creative expression. Many people believe that Quentin Tarantino sold out in his transition from *Reservoir Dogs* to *Pulp Fiction*. Popular writers such as Stephen King have been charged with prioritizing money over expression, especially with regard to their roles in the movie-versions of their texts.

That is, in my opinion, an oversimplified answer to a very important question. When confronted with this answer, any critic is justified in stating "so what?" In many cases, bands that sign onto major labels produce music that seems unchanged from their days of local shows and 7" splits. If the output of creative expression remains the same, it becomes difficult to see where the desire for money had any effect upon it.

A more decisive answer lies in the fact that the creative value of a piece of music (or of any work of art for that matter) is not determined by its output alone. To determine whether a group of musicians has sacrificed expression, it becomes necessary to analyze two types of value that apply to expression—intrinsic and extrinsic.

DEFINING THE TERMS

For popular music, and all other forms of creative endeavor, intrinsic value is a direct function of expression. It is determined from the meaning of the music to the musicians themselves—why they chose to express themselves in their particular manner. Intrinsic value deals with the social messages, historical, personal, and cultural significance inherent in the music. For instance, the more music has to say about the culture it originates from, the greater its intrinsic value. Music that has been inspired by the musician's personal tragedies would also have a high intrinsic value. This value-class does not change with time. It is derived from the original, objective meaning of the music, which remains the same since the day it was composed.

Extrinsic value is determined by the audience. The greater the number of people who find meaning and value in a piece of music, the greater its extrinsic value. This value-class is culturally determined. That is, the values of the culture that composes the audience play into it. As these values change through time, so does the extrinsic value of the piece they're being applied to. As an example, the music of Beethoven, having emerged from a less flamboyant scene of Classical composers, originally had a lower extrinsic value. As a transitional form from Classical to Romantic, it did not conform to many Classical standards. But when the Romantic style flourished with the efforts of Schubert and Schumann, these old standards gave way, and Beethoven's music seemed to conform well to an audience's expectations. In this way, the value of Beethoven's music increased extrinsically through time.

Certain standards exist for popular music today, without which a piece of music will have a lower extrinsic value. Among these are the presence of a discernible melody and a uniform time signature—usually 4:4. Key changes, if any, are usually limited to one. Recorded music must have a high sound quality, and include absolutely no mistakes. The quality of vocals differs from genre to genre, but they must be loud enough to be heard, if not understood. And, of course, popular music must meet ideological standards as well. Lyrics that express an ideology that is unacceptable to society as a whole (or to an official representation, as determined by the government, the corporate world, and the media) will bring down the extrinsic value of a piece of music. It is in this way that a band such as Slayer, which includes references to Satanism and horrific slaughter (both being devalued in our society enough to extrinsically decrease the value of the music), produces music with a lower extrinsic value.

Ideological standards are probably the most dynamic of all those I have mentioned, and a great deal of music heard on the radio today would have had a much lower extrinsic value 50 years ago. Jill Sobule, whose music often depicts bisexuality and bi-curiosity, provides a good example of this trend. These themes certainly would not have been featured on MTV had it existed 50 years ago.

APPLYING THE DEFINITIONS

In general, when music is commodified, its intrinsic value decreases. As defined, intrinsic value is fully a function of artistic expression. But of the purposes for commodifying music, expression is not one of them. A musician is free to compose or create regardless of whether carried by an independent or a corporate label. The only purpose for making music a commodity, as stated before, is to make money. This money is made by not just the musicians themselves, but by the major producers, distributors, retailers, and networks which market, sell, and air the music.

It is here where intrinsic value is lost—the fact that other people, whose concerns lie not in creative expression, but in profit alone, are making money off of the music. Thus, citing the critic's example, even if a musician's work remains unchanged in expression from previous, independently released work, and unless the musician had no choice in the matter, anything released into the corporate machine has lost some intrinsic value. In such a situation, the desire for money may not replace creative expression, but it certainly has a negative effect upon the value of that expression.

This is simply an argument for showing how all commodified music loses value. In most concrete examples, however, the amount of intrinsic value lost is much higher, and there is usually a dynamic relationship between the intrinsic and extrinsic values of music sold to corporate America. Such relationships are many and varied, depending upon the circumstances from which they arose. Each of the following bands exemplifies a different intrinsic/extrinsic dynamic.

Green Day

This band illustrates the most common "selling out" scenario—that of music which gains extrinsic value and loses intrinsic value. It illustrates corporate capitalization off of musical "fringe" groups, or "turning rebellion into money", as the Clash put it. When fringe styles of music gain enough popularity (usually among teenagers) to attract the attention of corporate labels, the forerunners of these styles are approached with big-name record deals. Green Day was one such band.

Most fringe styles include musical elements which keep them from becoming mainstream—elements that do not conform to popular standards. In technical jargon, they have a lower extrinsic value than popular radio music. When corporate labels take up a fringe group, the first course of action is to raise the extrinsic value of the music, or "clean it up", as some would put it.

When *Dookie,* Green Day's first Reprise release, is compared with material released on *Lookout,* this musical clean-up becomes evident. The old material, in a word, is raw. Mistakes occasionally occur in the drum line, Billie Joe hits some foul notes, and many of the second vocal lines are distorted or undermiked. All of these elements are negative from the perspective of popular music values, and none of them occur on *Dookie.* The increase in extrinsic value is fairly obvious.

It can be argued, however, that "rawness" is an element inherent to punk rock music. Sloppy drum rhythms and distorted vocals certainly are not major concerns to the musicians, and are sometimes encouraged. In this sense, rawness becomes a defining element of punk rock, and is significant to the punk subculture. When Reprise replaced Green Day's raw sound with a more MTV-friendly sound, it also removed a significant cultural element, thus decreasing its intrinsic value.

The intrinsic loss of value in *Dookie* is most apparent, however, when one considers the fact that punk rock is also traditionally anti-corporate. Anarchist and socialist ideologies have been defining cultural elements for the punk scene since its beginnings, and when such a band yields itself to a profit-driven system, it creates a contradiction that makes a complete farce of the music. These ideologies may not have made their way into Green Day's lyrics, but they are still characteristics of the scene from which Green Day hails. When a corporate label markets any music as "punk," that music has automatically lost some intrinsic value because of it.

Nirvana

Cleaning up the sound of fringe styles for the mass-media seems to be popular among corporate labels these days. The Seattle-based grunge scene has been commodified in the same manner as California pop-core. All one needs to do is listen to Nirvana's first album, *Bleach* (first released on Sub Pop in 1989), and compare the music to that released later on the Geffen labels. Like the material Green Day released on *Lookout, Bleach* contains a certain amount of noise and discordance that are inherent to grunge music. These culturally significant elements are absent on both *Nevermind* and *In Utero* (with the possible exception of "Endless, Nameless," the final track on *Nevermind*), and their absence was fully intentional.

The result was a wave of popular radio music that swept over the international youth culture and became one of Geffen's primary money-making machines. Indeed, the inertia of the Nirvana phenomenon has maintained a scene of commodified "grunge"-like music that continues to dominate MTV and popular radio. Kurt Cobain himself, in his suicide note, seems to have understood the degradation of creativity caused by this corporate scene: ". . . the, shall we say, ethics involved with independence and the embracement of our community has been proven to be very true. I haven't felt the excitement of listening to, as well as creating music, along with really writing something for many years now. I feel guilty beyond words about these things . . ."

Metallica

Bands don't need to sign on to major labels in order to sell out. In many cases, commodification occurs well after a band has been established on a big label. This seems to have been the case for Metallica, which has been carried on the Elektra label since its release of *Master of Puppets* (its third album). It was the fifth album, *Metallica,* that saw a loss in intrinsic value for the band's music. Like Green Day, this loss was accompanied by an increase in extrinsic value. Unlike Green Day, there was no "cleaning up" involved. Any imperfections in the music featured on *Kill Em All,* Metallica's first album, were completely absent by the time their fourth album came out. This album, *And Justice For All,* was, in fact, extremely well orchestrated and produced. In this case, the style of music itself was under attack.

Presumably, Metallica's first style—speed metal, for which they are often credited the inventors—was losing its popularity, its money-making potential. With the release of their first MTV video, "One" (from *And Justice . . .*), Metallica already had one foot in the door for a complete makeover. It was the first video they made and sold to MTV (owned by multi-media giant Viacom) through the Elektra label. Selling any video to MTV through a major label is what I'd call a corporate exchange. The result was a new style—an album of songs that were much more radio-friendly. This style conformed to popular standards more than the traditional speed metal. The songs were shorter, more melodic, and you could dance to them without breaking something (they were slower). It was a change in style that increased the music's extrinsic value.

Intrinsic value was lost solely in the fact that the style change was most certainly made for Elektra. It can be argued that Metallica themselves grew bored of speed metal, and were looking for something new. But in such a case, it seems suspicious that the new style would be so radio-friendly, especially since the change certainly alienated many original Metallica fans. For the corporate machine within which the band had entangled itself, these lost fans were small numbers compared to the revenue increase the new style would bring. It was commodification that depreciated the intrinsic value of Metallica's music, not the style change itself.

Fugazi

Many bands have changed their styles for purely personal reasons, and when such changes are not prompted by the pursuit of money, personal significance keeps the intrinsic value up. This seems to be the case for Fugazi, which has gradually changed its style since the release of *Repeater* (its first album). The independent label Dischord, operated by Fugazi front-man Ian Mackaye, has carried the band for all of its releases, including the last album *Red Medicine*. It was this last album which saw the most dramatic change in style for the band. This style, however, was not accompanied by a significant increase in extrinsic value (you won't hear them on the radio), and based on the fact that no corporate label is involved, no argument can be made for a loss in intrinsic value.

R.E.M.

Bands that have achieved the widest popularity are also the most likely to sign the biggest record deals. These deals are appealing to bands because they involve such large sums of money, and they're appealing to corporate labels because they involve contracts for multiple future albums. Given that a corporate label has adequate marketing resources, this is a way of ensuring a greater chance to profit from a big-name band. Regardless of the quality of material that's being put out, a very popular band, such as R.E.M., will always have a high minimum standard of buyers. The chances of maintaining a profit off each individual album is fairly high, so if the first one doesn't bring in enough revenue, the subsequent productions will. R.E.M.'s relationship with Warner Bros., as of last May, has involved two such deals, and the result has been a mixed-bag. The first contract provided for six albums. It was essentially a promise by the band that they had enough creative inertia to perform such a task. To that promise, the sub-text can be added, "If, at any time, we lose the creative inertia to produce truly expressive work, we'll put out what the listening public wants to hear." For such albums as *Monster* and *Out of Time,* that seems to have been the case—music produced not to satisfy creative urges, but to satisfy the terms of a contract.

These albums lack some of the truly meaningful pieces featured on such albums as *Green* and *Life's Rich Pageant.* Their songs have a high extrinsic value, featuring simple rhythms, coherent lyrics, and catchy choruses suitable for the radio. The albums do not feature anything like "Swan, Swan, Hummingbird" or "The Wrong Child," which have no drum lines (making them extrinsically lower in value), yet express meaningful themes of cultural and literary significance (making them intrinsically higher). These songs indicate that R.E.M. has the capacity to produce intrinsically worthwhile music, and with that in mind, the release of songs like "Bang and Blame" (from *Monster*) require some sort of explanation.

The answer, of course, lies in the Warner Bros. contract, a perfect example of how commodification depreciates intrinsic value. Milking an existing work of expression for as much profit as possible is bad enough; putting capital into the expression even before it is produced is a disaster waiting to happen. R.E.M.'s new contract with Warner Bros., signed last May, provides for five more albums (with $10-million advances for each of them). Whether R.E.M. has the capacity to keep from producing another album like Monster is, for the time, a question to be answered.

■ *Ryan Theis, who wrote this article while a student at the University of Florida, is currently writing freelance for* Perfect Sound Forever, *an online music journal.*

MAKING SURE OF THE TEXT

1. How, according to Theis, has the "corporate machine" changed popular music?
2. How do "intrinsic" and "extrinsic" values relate to a musical group's commercial success or lack of it?
3. What is the relationship between ideological standards and extrinsic values in pop music?
4. What does Theis imply is the spiritual cost to the musician who sells out?

5. Theis suggests that "noise and discordance" in grunge music are "culturally significant elements." What does this mean?

CONSIDERING THE CONTEXT

1. Theis's article was published while he was still a college student. Does his generational identity show through the authorial choices he makes? Consider his diction and his tone; how does Theis establish a common ground with his readers?
2. How does Theis's discussion of Beethoven, Slayer, and Green Day affect you? What is the probable goal of such diverse references?
3. What effect is achieved by Theis's conclusion? How does the conclusion work to tie up the rest of the article?
4. While Burns focuses on one element of commercialization, Theis focuses on another. Compare the two.

■ ■ ■

Which Generation Are You? Internet Humor (2000)

If you answer mostly *A*, you're a pre-Boomer. If you answer mostly *B*, you're a Baby-Boomer. If you answer mostly *C*, you're in Generation X. If you answer mostly *D*, you're in Generation Y.

1. Who is the ideal figure of motherhood?
   A. Eleanor Roosevelt
   B. Donna Reed
   C. Mrs. Brady
   D. Roseanne

2. What did you want to be when you grew up?
   A. Part of a nuclear family
   B. Someone who makes lots of money
   C. Living with your parents
   D. Living with your parents

3. Music should be:
   A. Melodic and romantic
   B. Annoying to your parents
   C. Annoying to your parents
   D. Annoying to your parents

4. Sex is for:
   A. Married couples who want to start families
   B. Anybody who wants to start a party
   C. Latex-clad partners in a laboratory setting
   D. Watching on TV

5. The scariest moment in film history was:
   A. When the mummy rose from his tomb
   B. When the Blob chased Steve McQueen
   C. When the alien burst from the man's chest
   D. When Freddy still would not die

6. The most inspiring American is:
   A. John Wayne
   B. John F. Kennedy
   C. John F. Kennedy Jr
   D. Beavis or Butthead

7. I expect my retirement to be:
   A. The golden years when I can look back on a happy, fulfilling life
   B. An opportunity to finally write my novel
   C. An agonizing slide into abject poverty
   D. A daily struggle to survive in a horribly polluted world

nuclear family · the traditional family structure, in which two parents raise a small number of children close by the grandparents.

8. America is becoming:
   A. More impersonal
   B. More frightening
   C. More expensive
   D. More bogus

9. The American Dream is:
   A. A house with a two-car garage
   B. A healthy family
   C. Winning the lottery
   D. Touring with Metallica

10. My college major was:
    A. Business
    B. Liberal arts
    C. Secondary to my bartending job
    D. Something far, far away

11. A good meal would be:
    A. Meat and potatoes
    B. Vegetarian macrobiotic
    C. From a drive-up window
    D. Microwaveable

12. My favorite footwear is:
    A. Sensible shoes
    B. Earth shoes
    C. Converse high-tops
    D. Doc Martens

13. I learned to drive behind the wheel of a:
    A. '53 Packard
    B. '61 VW
    C. '78 Pinto
    D. Sega

14. The "woman":
    A. Marilyn Monroe
    B. Raquel Welch
    C. Julia Roberts
    D. Sheryl Crow

MAKING SURE OF THE TEXT

1. These answers are revealing artifacts of generational tastes and experiences. Which ones would you pick? Which contexts are they drawn from?
2. Because pop culture moves so quickly, you might have more relevant examples for some categories. How would you update them?
3. Ask your parents and grandparents for their reaction to these questions; would they agree? Disagree? What artifacts would they replace, and with what?
4. B and C answers should, according to the directions, find some parallels in Burns' article because he writes from the Baby Boomer perspective. Read both closely and see what similarities you can find.

CONSIDERING THE CONTEXT

1. This selection has been in Internet circulation for several years. What might be spurring its enduring popularity?

vegetarian macrobiotic · macrobiotic diets, although still in use, hit a fad high during the 70s and 80s as the most effective way to maintain a clean and healthy body.

2. Who are the intended readers of this sort of humor? In other words, who will find it funny and who won't?
3. The selection here is a shortened version of the original. What would you expect to find in the last two pages? Find the complete selection online and see how close you came to predicting accurately.

■ ■ ■

Society's Mixed Messages: How Popular Music Influences Alcohol and Other Drug Use (1998)

Indiana Prevention Resource Center at Indiana University

SONGS WITH APPARENT DRUG REFERENCES

Year	Song Title	Performer	Apparent Drug Reference
1933	*Texas Tea Party*	Benny Goodman & his Orchestra	Marijuana
1938	*Wacky Dust*	Chick Webb & his Orchestra, vocals by Ella Fitzgerald	Cocaine
1938	*If You're a Viper*	Bob Howard & His Boys	Marijuana
1944	*Who Put the Benzedrine in Mrs. Murphy's Ovaltine*	Harry "The Hipster" Gibson	Amphetamines/ Nembutal
1961	*Candy Man*	Sammy Davis Jr.	various*
1963	*Puff (the Magic Dragon)*	Peter, Paul & Mary	Marijuana*
1985	*Puff (the Magic Dragon) [revised]*	Peter Yarrow	anti-smoking
1964(?)	*Rainy Day Women #12 & 35*	Bob Dylan	Marijuana*
1965	*Along Comes Mary*	The Association	Marijuana*
1966	*Mother's Little Helper*	The Rolling Stones	Valium
1967	*Windy*	The Association	LSD*(windowpane)
1967	*White Rabbit*	Jefferson Airplane	Hallucinogens
1967	*Okie from Muskogee*	Merle Haggard	Marijuana (negative)
1967	*Break on Through*	The Doors	psychedelics (unspecified)
1967	*Light My Fire*	The Doors	unspecified*
1967	*Lucy in the Sky with Diamonds*	The Beatles	LSD*
1967	*Hey Jude*	The Beatles	Heroin*
1969	*Bridge Over Troubled Water*	Simon & Garfunkel	Heroin*
1969	*Yellow Submarine*	The Beatles	Nembutal* (yellow-colored "downer")
1971(?)	*Carmelita*	Linda Ronstadt	Heroin
1972	*Speedball Tucker*	Jim Croce	Amphetamines
1975	*Medicine Jar*	Paul McCartney & Wings	various
1977	*Cocaine*	Jackson Browne	Cocaine
1977	*That Smell*	Lynyrd Skynyrd	Whiskey, Cocaine, Quaaludes and Marijuana
1977	*The Joker*	The Steve Miller Band	Marijuana ("mid night toker")
1978	*The Gambler*	Kenny Rogers	Alcohol & Tobacco
1978(?)	*Drinkin' and Drivin'*	Johnny Paycheck	Alcohol

1984	*The Smuggler's Blues*	Glenn Frey	Cocaine & Marijuana
1986	*Fight for Your Right to Party*	Beastie Boys	unspecified
1986	*You Don't Have to Take Your Clothes Off*	Jermaine Stewart	Cherry wine
1986	*Walk Like an Egyptian*	The Bangles	Marijuana(?)*
1986	*Sign of the Times*	Prince	Marijuana & Heroin
1989	*Mr. Brownstone*	Guns 'n Roses	Hashish or Heroin (?)
1989	*Dr. Feelgood*	Motley Crüe	Cocaine, Marijuana, others
1989	*City of Dope*	Too Short	Crack Cocaine, Marijuana
1990	*Ritual de lo Habitual (album)*	Jane's Addiction	unspecified
1991	*If You Don't Start Drinkin'*	George Thorogood & the Destroyers	Alcohol
1992	*Something for the Blunted*	Cypress Hill	Marijuana ("blunts")
1993	*The Chronic*	Dr. Dre	Marijuana
1993	*I Wanna Get High*	Cypress Hill	Marijuana
1996	*This Is a Call*	Foo Fighters	Ritalin

*denotes "indirect reference" either not confirmed or actively disputed by lyricist but often cited by listeners.

■ *The Indiana Prevention Resource Center (IPRC) at Indiana University is a statewide clearinghouse for prevention technical assistance and information about alcohol, tobacco, and other drugs for the State of Indiana. It is Indiana's officially designated RADAR (Regional Alcohol and Drug Awareness Resource) Network State Center.*

■ ■ ■

"Lucy in the Sky with Diamonds" (1967)

John Lennon and Paul McCartney

Picture yourself in a boat on a river,
With tangerine trees and marmalade skies
Somebody calls you, you answer quite slowly,
A girl with kaleidoscope eyes.
Cellophane flowers of yellow and green,
Towering over your head.
Look for the girl with the sun in her eyes,
And she's gone.
Lucy in the sky with diamonds.
Follow her down to a bridge by a fountain
Where rocking horse people eat marshmallow pies,
Everyone smiles as you drift past the flowers,
That grow so incredibly high.
Newspaper taxis appear on the shore,
Waiting to take you away.
Climb in the back with your head in the clouds,
And you're gone.
Lucy in the sky with diamonds.
Picture yourself on a train in a station,
With plasticine porters with looking glass ties,
Suddenly someone is there at the turnstyle,
The girl with the kaleidoscope eyes.

■ *"Lucy in the Sky with Diamonds," cited as part of the IPRC "Mixed Messages" page, was written in 1967 by Paul McCartney and John Lennon.*

MAKING SURE OF THE TEXT

1. From your perspective, which generation is most likely to produce musical artifacts dealing with drug use? Does this drug prevention lesson page support or refute your answer?
2. Are readers of this Web page given a context within which to interpret these listings? That is, are we helped to recontextualize the tunes for reasons other than commercial?
3. What difference do the asterisks indicating "not confirmed or actively disputed by lyricist" make for you? What subtext could be implied by using these markers?
4. After reading Knight's article, what do you think he would say about the influence of alcohol on pop music? Support your answers with carefully chosen quotations from Knight.
5. Read the text of "Lucy in the Sky with Diamonds" carefully. Do you read any words and phrases that appear to be drug references? When they are moved into a lyrical context, does the meaning change with them?

CONSIDERING THE CONTEXT

1. Because the page appears on the Indiana University Web site, who can be

Plasticine · British term for what Americans know as Play-Doh.

assumed to be reading this information? Is this audience the same as the one identified for you?

2. What other uses could this page have if you recontextualized it?

3. What's the effect of presenting the tunes in chronological order? If the list were grouped differently, for instance by drug reference instead of date, would that change the effects? How?

4. How do the song lyrics and the Web page function as artifacts of the same group?

■ ■ ■

I Dare You to Degrade My Music (Student Essay, 2001)

Gina Brazzale

"Music today just is not what it used to be." "Songs in the 60's and 70's had so much more meaning than the superficial lyrics about sex and drugs in the music of the 90's." "Song writers of the past decades are too negative." In many discussions of modern music, participants incessantly utter judgmental comments like these. Many people berate the music of the nineties as unintelligible babble about virtually nothing, while venerating the music of the 60's and 70's as meaningful and thought provoking. Yet, when one takes a closer look at the music and events of both eras, one realizes that these accusations are completely unjustified. Just like the music of the 60's and 70's, songs from the pop genre in the 90's possess deeper meanings, such as tolerance of homosexuality, attacks on apathy and reactions to the new millennium, and are not just about sex, drugs and negativity.

Music adapts to the culture and ideals of the current era. The Prohibition in the 1920's, the Great Depression in the 30's, and World War II in the 40's and 50's affected the music of these generations greatly. Similarly, the music of the 60's and 70's and that of the 90's reflected the history, culture and ideas of their respective eras. Two events were most significant in molding the ideals of youth in the 60's and 70's. The first is the civil rights movement. This ideal continued from the 1950's and altered all concepts of equality. Then, the assassination of Martin Luther King, Jr. on April 4, 1968, sent the movement rushing forward.

The music around this time was greatly affected by this change in perception. For example, Bob Dylan wrote "Blowin' in the Wind," which Peter, Paul and Mary performed, in 1963. At this time, Martin Luther King, Jr.'s lectures and demonstrations were at their peak, forcing America to focus on the Civil Rights movement. Dylan portrayed this by asking, "How many years can some people exist/Before they're allowed to be free? How many times can a man turn his head/And pretend that he just doesn't see?" (Miracle Productions, Inc.) Through these questions, the narrator is accusing the general public in the early 60's of being indifferent to segregation and inequality. Thus, Dylan highlighted the ideals of 1963, and boldly questioned America's standards through this hit.

The second event that shaped the precepts of the Baby Boomer generation is the Vietnam War. Even though direct involvement commenced in 1955 when American advisors were sent to Vietnam, combat troops were not deployed until 1965 and remained in the war until January 1973. Many Americans detested the war, so much so that it is often believed to be the "most unpopular war in which Americans ever fought" (PBS Online).

Due to this opposition Americans did not stand by idly; they demonstrated their dissatisfaction through anti-war protests. However, a common misconception is that Americans protested strongly from the outset of the war in 1955. This is not so. In fact, protest was fairly uncommon until one protest in

Washington, D.C. on November 15, 1969, known as the March on Washington. The March on Washington consisted of three days of marching, rallying and demonstrations, drawing both non-violent and militant protesters. The march down Pennsylvania Avenue to the Washington Monument on November 15 consisted of a crowd of over 300,000 protesters. This massive display of dissatisfaction is considered the turning point of protests during the Vietnam War. After this, the government finally realized America was not pleased with the war (UMI).

In 1967, Simon and Garfunkel censured America's apathy towards the war. The song "Sounds of Silence" boldly confronted Americans about ignoring the fact that 13,000 American soldiers had already been killed in battle ("The Psychedelic Era 1965-1969"). Paul Simon describes a dream, or a supposed dream that is far too close to reality: "And in the naked light I saw,/Ten thousand people, maybe more;/People talking without speaking,/People hearing without listening./People writing songs . . . that voices never shared;/No one dared/Disturb the sound . . . of silence" (Miracle Productions, Inc.). In this dream, the narrator sees a large group of people chatting idly, but not discussing the important issues in their minds; those listening casually, but not thinking about it; and others not sharing their ideas, all because no one wanted to cause an upheaval. There are underlying issues that no one will confront due to apathy and fear. These accusations obviously struck a nerve because just two years later, Americans made the March on Washington.

The 1960's and 70's not only inspired peace, but also a reconsideration of love and sex. Prudish principles of the previous eras, which condemned sex as a dirty weakness, were replaced by openness and unrestrained freedom. In addition, the development of birth control pills allowed sex with lower chances of pregnancy ("The Psychedelic Era 1965-1969"). Also, rebellion ran rampant due to the Civil Rights Movement and anti-war protests. Thus free love became another outlet for defiance, an outlet increased by lowered risks of pregnancy.

The Righteous Brothers emphasized the sexual revolution in 1965 with "Unchained Melody", demonstrating why the world fell so easily into the Summer of Love in '67. The romantic melody accompanies the Righteous Brothers crooning, "Whoa, my love, my darling,/I hunger for your touch./Alone; lonely time . . . I need your love" (Miracle Productions, Inc.). Such words as "hunger" and "need" demonstrate the heightened sexual desire occurring at this time.

One final ideal shaped the musical culture of the 1960's and 70's: the recreational use of drugs. The new ideal of peace inspired a desire to experiment with marijuana for the calming effects it produced. In addition, the experiments of Timothy Leary kindled the use of LSD. A practicing psychologist who emphasized human interaction, Leary discovered psychedelics in 1960 and began studying these "chemical brain-changers" and their effects on the human nervous system. Even after LSD became illegal, Leary released instructions for its safe use, pushing respect for the drug and educating the public on avoiding "bad trips." Leary's philosophy of "Tune in, Turn on, Drop out" encourages people to begin thinking—turn on—connect to the exterior world and "interact harmoniously"—tune in—and to detach from unnecessary and useless commitments—drop out (Graves). America listened, and the popularity of LSD and other drugs peaked in 1967 when Paul McCartney admitted to taking LSD and two Rolling Stones were in jail for drug charges ("The Psychedelic Era 1965-1969").

One song that depicts the developing open attitude toward drugs is the Beatles' "Lucy in the Sky with Diamonds." Not surprisingly, the Beatles fell in line with other music artists and depicted the ideals of the era. Yet this time, an LSD trip is the focus. The psychedelic adventure begins with an invitation to experience the trip: "Picture yourself in a boat on a river/With tangerine trees and marmalade skies/Somebody calls you, you answer quite slowly/A girl with kaleidoscope eyes" (Pannell). The images resembling hallucinations and the delayed response to a call from a girl with the appearance of also being stoned definitely suggests some type of hallucinogenic drug experience. Since LSD was popular at the time and Paul McCartney confessed to his use of LSD in the same year this song was released ("The Psychedelic Era 1965-1969"), assuming LSD is the drug depicted in this experience is logical.

The major events of the 1960's and 70's shaped the ideals of the Baby Boom generation. The devastation of the country during Vietnam, the deaths of President John F. Kennedy and Martin Luther King, Jr., the potential for tolerance inspired by the Civil Rights Movement, and the acceptance of peace, sex and drugs changed the way the generation of the 60's and 70's looked at the world. Music took advantage of this change in principles and depicted the new axioms through lyrics. Thus, one can view the music of the 1960's and 70's as meaningful and thought provoking.

Just like the music of the previous eras, songs of the 1990's are also shaped by our culture. True, a controversial war did not consume the ideals of our era. However, the Sexual Revolution of the 1960's has also left its effects on the 1990's. Yet, now the lyrics are bolder and the topics more controversial. In the 60's the Beatles released the hit, "I Wanna Hold Your Hand". The 90's equivalent of this song, "I Wanna Sex You Up" by Color Me Badd, released in 1991, told the world that open sexual references were replacing feigned innocence.

Along with open discussion of sex comes open portrayal of sex as well. Madonna's music and videos in the 1980's are a good example. Her album "Like a Virgin" brought Madonna fame as a sex symbol: not only was the title racy but also the video "Material Girl," where she dressed as Marilyn Monroe. Then the video "Like a Prayer" secured her association with sex while she danced provocatively in front of burning crosses and kissed black saints. She went on to confront teenage pregnancy in the song "Papa Don't Preach." Madonna's controversial display of sexual references in the 1980's carried over into the 90's; through her career, she influenced other artists, such as Mariah Carey. Flaunting sexuality through supremely risqué clothing, Mariah Carey struts across every stage in a skin-tight minidress. Yet physical exhibition of sexuality is just the beginning. Explicit lyrics depicting sexual experimentation ooze from the music of the 90's. Madonna's song "Erotica", for example, released in 1992, discusses sexual domination. "If I'm in charge and I treat you like a child/Will you let yourself go wild/Let my mouth go where it wants to/Give it up, do as I say/Give it up and let me have my way . . . put your hands all over my body" (Zalewski). These statements are self-explanatory, utterly depicting the boldness of sexuality in 1990's music.

The Sexual Revolution is not the only aspect of the 1960's and 70's that carried over into the 90's. Drug use is still a major part of 90's culture. Marijuana is still smoked regularly and people still drop acid, but heroin is added to the list of major drugs in the '90's. On May of 1993, the lead singer of Nirvana, Kurt Cobain, overdosed on Heroin (Bastone and Green). Then just one year later, in March of 1994, Cobain shot himself with a twenty-gauge shotgun after fleeing from a Drug Rehabilitation Center in California. Rumors on the internet cannot be confirmed by confidential medical records, but the belief persists that Cobain had injected himself with 250mg of heroin immediately prior to pulling the trigger. Drug paraphernalia found in a cigar box next to his body could confirm this theory (Flashpoint). For another example, the lead singer of the band Sublime, Bradley James Nowell, died May 25, 1996 from a heroin overdose. The song "Garden Grove", released in 1996, covers the band's acceptance of drug use through the lyrics, "if you only knew the love I found/its hard to keep my soul on the ground . . . sticking needles in your arm . . . I'm happy when I'm not finding roaches in the pot/all these things I do/they're waiting para tu". In this excerpt, Sublime also openly admits to marijuana and heroin use and informs listeners that these experiences are available to them as well—"para tu" means "for you" in Spanish (Sublime).

However, not all of the music in the 1990's centers solely around drugs and sex. The Gay Rights Movement parallels the Civil Rights Movement. Left over from the 1960's and 70's, the Gay Rights Movement has achieved much in the 1990's. The Gay and Lesbian Alliance Against Defamation (GLAAD), founded in 1985, made great strides in the 90's. For example, in 1990, the Los Angeles school district approved GLAAD's Anti-Homophobic program and the Anti-Defamation League's program, "A World of Difference". In 1993, GLAAD pushed the military to accept the "Don't ask, don't tell" policy. And the world was shocked when Ellen DeGeneres' character on her sitcom "Ellen" (and DeGeneres herself) came out as lesbian in 1997 (GLAAD).

Music of the 1990's depicts the change in the view of homosexuality. Lesbian artists such as Melissa Etheridge, kd lang, and the Indigo Girls join together in festivals like the Lilith Fair. Boy George came out as "Absolutely Queer" on his record in 1991, and depicted his struggle with admitting to homosexuality: "When I was young/They poisoned my mind/They told me to fight/But I'm just not that kind" in "If I Could Fly" (Feedland). In this excerpt, the speaker is being pressured by the society of the 80's, represented as "they," to fight his homosexual tendencies. Yet he just cannot lie forever, so he admits his sexual preference. Later in the decade, George Michael also admitted to being homosexual in April of 1998 when he was arrested for performing a homosexual act in a Los Angeles public restroom (Spaulding). These examples remind us that homosexual issues including privacy and tolerance needed to be addressed more openly.

Not surprisingly, grunge and alternative rock provide another parallel to the meaningful topics of the 1960's and 70's. Just as Simon and Garfunkel confronted America's indifference to the Vietnam War, Nirvana censured the generation of the 1990's for their apathy as well. The song "Smells Like Teen Spirit," off the album "Nevermind" (1991), soared up the charts after challenging the listeners: "I'm worse at what I do best/And for this gift I feel blessed/Our little group has always been/And always will until the end . . . And I forgot/Just why I taste/Oh yeah, I guess it made me smile/I found it hard/It was hard to find/Oh well, whatever, nevermind" (Millar and Karle). Cobain, accusing teens of a pre-occupation with personal interest and taking pleasures for granted, charges them with self-pity in the first two lines, ending with the sarcastic comment that the narrator feels "blessed" for his or her inadequacies. This egotistical focus then renders the narrator unable to identify why he or she partakes in tasting, which would give most people pleasure. Then the narrator apathetically dismisses the potential search within his or her mind with the comment, "nevermind." Through this representation of an apathetic teen, Cobain shows youths the danger of carelessness and pushes them to find deeper meanings.

Yet in every generation, there is one event that shapes music immeasurably. In the 1990's, the anticipation and fear of the upcoming millenium controls the ideals and thus the music just as much as Vietnam ruled those of the 60's and 70's. The new millenium is coming fast, and the world is anticipating some huge event. No matter what view is portrayed, the premonitions of the millennium are not pleasant. Most involve mass chaos and destruction, ultimately resulting in "the end of the world as we know it," so precisely summarized by R.E.M. For example, the band Tool portrays the apocalypse in their song "Aenema" on the album "Aenima" released in 1997. The lyrics:

Some say a comet will fall from the sky/Followed by meteor showers and tidal waves/Followed by fault lines that cannot sit still . . . Some say the end is near/Some say we'll see Armageddon soon . . . Here is this hopeless . . . hole we call L.A./The only way to fix it is to flush it all away/Any . . . time/Any . . . day/Learn to swim,/I'll see you down in Arizona Bay . . . Fret for your figure and/Fret for your latte and/Fret for your hairpiece and/Fret for your lawsuit and/Fret for your prozac and/Fret for your pilot and/Fret for your contract and/Fret for your car./It's a Bullshit three ring circus sideshow of Freaks . . . Fuck all these gun-toting/Hip gangster wannabees . . . Fuck all you junkies and/Fuck your short memory . . . Fuck smiley glad-hands/With hidden agendas. (Keenan)

These lyrics graphically express Tool's belief that due to a natural disaster, involving comets and earthquakes, California will fall into the ocean. Yet there is reason behind this negativity, which does inevitably feed into the music of the 1990's. Tool feels that the apocalypse will come as a result of the apathy discussed by Nirvana, materialism, and intolerance. By mocking people in Los Angeles, Tool suggests that worrying about material objects is close-minded and will bring about the ruin of California.

However, this negativity does not completely control the ideals of the 90's. Just like in the 1960's, pessimism gives rise to other concepts. Tool provides a solution to these vices of the 90's: lachrymology. This philosophy is supposedly based on the novel "The Joyful Guide to Lachrymology" by Donald P. Vincent. Since neither the book nor the author can be found anywhere, the philosophy is attributed to Tool. Lachrymology focuses on abolishing apathy and admitting one's pain. By observing and analyzing pain, one can evolve one's self and become a better being. Satisfaction with one's self then results in both tolerance and lack of materialism. Since lachrymology teaches one to listen to oneself in order to interact more harmoniously with the outside world, it provides an obvious parallel to Leary's "Tune in, Turn on, and Drop out," which preached the same end with different means. Suddenly the superficiality of 90's music is melting into hidden profoundness (Smith).

Yes, in the music of the 60s, 70s, and 90s, supposedly superficial topics such as sex and drugs are discussed at length. However, these subjects are a part of each generation's culture and help define its ideals. Yet more meaningful and thought-provoking themes are represented in music as well. So, I invite those people claiming that music of the nineties has no meaning or is not thought provoking to distance themselves from the emotional attachment to the Vietnam War and music of the 1960's. True, war is not an issue for the musicians of the nineties, but many other important topics are. People who are so infatuated with the 60's that they slap harsh judgments on aspects of other eras need to open up their horizons and take an objective look at the philosophies and searching that appears in the music of the nineties. They will find themselves questioning whether they made a justified judgment in saying that today's music just is not as deep as that of the 1960's.

■ ■ ■

■ **Works Cited** ■

Bastone, William and Daniel Green. "The Smoking Gun: Kurt and Courtney: No Nirvana." *The Smoking Gun.* Apr. 2001. Online. Internet. 7 Apr. 2001. Available http://www.thesmokinggun.com/kurt/kurt/shtml.

Flashpoint. "Details on Kurt Cobain's Death." *Flashpoint On-line.* 15 Mar. 1999. Online. Internet. 7 Apr. 2001. Available http://www.mosquitonet.com/~chuck/music.htm.

Feedland, Jonathan. "The Boy is Back . . . and Crying All the Way to the Bank." *The Washington Post* 21 Mar. 1993: n. pag. Online. Internet. 28 Mar. 1999. Available http://www-personal.umich.edu/~geena/ktbcstuff/articles/washpost.html.

GLAAD. *Welcome to GLAAD Online . . .* 1994. Online. Internet. 28 Mar. 1999. Available http://www.glaad.org/.

Graves, Christopher. *Timothy Leary's Home Page.* 18 Feb. 1999. Online. Internet. 26 Mar. 1999. Available http://www.leary.com/.

Keenan, Maynard James. "Aenima." 13 Mar. 1997. Online. Internet. 26 Mar. 1999. Available http://toolshed.down.net.

Kowalczyk, Edward. "Lyrics-Merica: 'Pillar of Davidson'." *Live-Merica.* Online. Internet. 26 Mar. 1999. Available http://www.geocities.com/SunsetStrip/Palms/1070/tc_lyrics.html#pillar.

Millar, Grant and Jeff Karle. *Peace, Love and Empathy, The Nirvana Homepage.* 12 Jan. 1997. Online. Internet. Available http://www.escape.ca/~grsd/.

Miracle Productions, Inc. *Baby Boomers HeadQuarters: The Sixties Section.* 15 Mar. 1999. Online. Internet. 26 Mar. 1999. Available http://www.bbhq.com/lyrics.htm.

Pannell, Dana. *Karaoke Beatles Page: "Lucy in the Sky with Diamonds."* 8 Feb. 1999. Online. Internet. 26 Mar. 1999. Available http://wsp3.wspice.com/~dpannell/beatles/lucy.htm.

PBS Online. *The American Experience/Vietnam.* 1997. Online. Internet. 26 Mar. 1999. Available http://www.pbs.org/wgbh/pages/amex/vietnam/intro.html.

"The Psychedelic Era 1965-1969" rockhall.com. Online. Internet. 26 Mar. 1999. Available http://www.rockhall.com/exhibits/featured/psychedelic.html.

Smith, Ralph E. "The Joy of Lachrymology." *Innuendo Cornecopria: Sagacious Interpretations of Tool.* 2001. Online. Internet. 5 Apr. 2001. Available http://innuendo-cornecopria.com/LACH.htm.

Spaulding, Captain. "Careless Whispers from the Vox Populi." *Pandemonium Online.* Online. Internet. 9 Apr. 1999. Available http://seattlesquare.com/pandemonium/columns/24HoorayForMe.htm.

Sublime. *Sublime.* Online. Internet. 28 Mar. 1999. Available http://www.hallucinet.com/sublime/main.html.

UMI. "Great Events VI: Anti-Vietnam War Demonstrations 1969." *The New York Times* n. dat.: n. pag. Online. Internet. 26 Mar. 1999. Available http://www.umi.com/hp/Support/K12/GreatEvents/Vietnam.html.

Zalewski, Kenny. *Madonna Song Lyrics.* 4 Mar. 1998. Online. Internet. 28 Mar. 1999. Available http://www.cs.rpi.edu/~kennyz/madonna_lyrics/erotica.html#erotica.

■ Ideas for Writing ■

Journal

1. Reflect on a particular hit song that's important to your generation or group. What is important about it? Consider the differences between the song itself and the video that probably accompanies it.

2. How does Burns use the phrase "accumulated baggage"? Identify possible accumulated baggage in religious contexts, or in the context of beauty, using Chapters 4 and 2 to help you.

3. Aside from music, what helps develop generational identity? For instance, clothing styles and television viewing habits might be read as distinct for each generation.

4. Nelson George suggests in his article that hip-hop reinvents itself; in Chapter 4, Rose Morrigan discusses reinventing her spirituality. Many of the Hippies reinvented themselves as Baby Boomers. What role has "reinventing" played in your life?

Response

1. What music did the older generation around you listen to? Provide some specific examples, reading the text of the lyrics for evidence that a piece of music might be significant across generational identities.
2. Do you currently have a favorite piece of music (rap, rock, country, R&B) that you think a younger generation might also adopt as its own? What would they find valuable about it, given their context and yours? Or will they, as Nelson George suggests, "shout 'It's boring!' and move on"?
3. What do you think about Ryan Theis's ideas of extrinsic and intrinsic value? Is there a time when you've said to yourself, "they sold out!" How might Ani DiFranco's letter, in Chapter 2, help you explain this reaction?

Analysis

1. Identify your generation's or other specific group's tastes in music, providing plenty of examples. As artifacts of musical taste, what do your examples tell you about your place in current culture, your age group, and your political and/or sexual preferences?
2. Robert Knight agrees with Martha Bayles that "What is wrong with most modern music is that it no longer satisfies the soul." Contrast this perspective with Nelson George's, who writes that "the future of hip hop will be partly determined by the state of America's soul. Will a commitment to social justice [. . .] and old-fashioned community resurface?" How do these contrasting viewpoints grow from each writer's perspective?
3. Each of the readings in this chapter is an artifact of pop culture itself. What perspective does the collection of readings suggest? In other words, read the artifacts in this chapter and analyze the significance. Remember to maintain the anthropological perspective.

Argument

1. Ryan Theis and Chapter 2's Ani DiFranco provide two different contexts for "popular music." Would they argue with each other about the commercialization of musical tastes? Where do you stand on this issue? From which perspectives might you be able to draw support for your stance?
2. The song lyrics on the Indiana Parents' Resource Center Web page are characterized as drug references. Do you agree that models of drug use promote drug use? Do we ape what we see? You might consider, as additional evidence for this dynamic, Knight's article, Chapter 4's religious cartooning, Chapter 5's dismal visions of the future, and so forth.
3. Knight suggests that a musician's "shamanic trance" relies on "powers from below." Contrast the relationship between spirituality and evil in Knight's article to Rose Morrigan's article in Chapter 4 and illustrate what you see as the contrasts between prevailing belief systems.

Research

1. Research the social contexts of the Beatles' "Revolution" or "Happiness is a Warm Gun." What significances might those songs have had to their listeners,

remembering that contexts are highly malleable? If you have heard these tunes in other contexts (advertising, for instance), how were they presented?

2. Knight claims that several noted rock artists were occultist, whether by practice or by association. Research this position's validity by looking for interviews, biographies, lyrics, and discographies from the artists in question.

3. Go through each of the readings in this chapter and list names and references you didn't fully understand. Check to see if these references were annotated. Then, go to the library or to your computer and look up these unknowns. How does this research provide a context for your list? How does annotation provide a context?

CHAPTER 2

SELF-PERCEPTIONS: PERSPECTIVES ON MEN, WOMEN, AND SEX

"A garment that squeezes the testicles makes a man think differently."
—UMBERTO ECO

In 2000, the Academy Award for Best Actress went to Hilary Swank for her performance in the film *Boys Don't Cry*. In this true story, Teena Brandon (re-creating herself as Brandon Teena) lived as a man in rural Nebraska for several years, preparing for sex-change surgery and falling in love, before two disapproving local men took brutal and permanent action. When interviewed about the role, Swank described the challenging process of transforming herself: for instance, for several weeks before filming, to begin the transition, she ran errands dressed as a man. She was helped in this transformation by the film's direction and production team as well; most movies are filmed out of sequence, but *Boys Don't Cry* was filmed chronologically so that Swank could develop a believable progression from self-identified female to self-identified male. Recalling the gradual transition on film, Swank said that by the end of filming, she had taken on so many male characteristics that she was having trouble maintaining her perception of herself as female. (In this context, it's worth mentioning that when she accepted her Oscar, her watching husband wept, a fact reported widely in the entertainment news the next day.)

We probably each have ideas about the behaviors we consider "masculine" or "feminine." We probably also have ideas about sexuality—our own and that of others, how (and if) we practice it, and how (and if) others should practice it. How much of the way we perceive our gender is constructed for us by our unconscious reading of the social text about sexuality? And exactly what *is* the social text about sexuality? Although the sexual differences between men and women are obvious, the way we read those differences changes depending on our perspective. If, as anthropologists would, we examined the social text around bodies and gender, we might read some interesting stories.

It's easy to look around and see that the body has been "read" as a text for years. Our anthropologist would be able to identify the female body, specifically, being used as a popular advertising gimmick since the mid-1940s, when advertisers realized that a woman draped provocatively across the hood of a car sold more of those cars. The subtext of those ads was easily read: buy this car, and this sexuality can be yours. In advertising, when you buy the product, you get the image as well. Looking from a broad perspective, the marketing of the female body as an enticement for men (in the 1940s, men were the primary purchasers of cars) might suggest a larger marketing of female sexuality; the economic use of the female body is, of course, one of the issues raised by gender studies and feminism.

The male body can be read as a text as well: to a body builder, the artifacts of a well-built masculine figure might be virility, sex appeal, and/or health, whereas a thinner male might be read as scrawny. To someone who spends a lot of money on clothes, a well-dressed man might signify a reader of *GQ* or *Maxim*; or he might suggest effeminacy. If some of the traditional artifacts of "masculinity" are well-developed muscles, thick short hair, or broad shoulders, some of the traditional artifacts of "femininity" are a curved waist and hips, long hair, and large breasts. Sometimes these artifacts are interpreted differently—for instance, the man who spends a great deal of time developing rippling muscles might be read as homosexual (from the perspective that gay men are obsessed with body image) or, equally easily, as modern (from the perspective of the hetero man who goes shopping for clothes as casually

Are these bodies more sexual, less sexual, or just right?

as he might go to a sports bar). Women, too, can be read in many ways: a woman with short hair, little if any makeup, and no particular concerns about how she dresses might be read as lesbian by someone who identifies those artifacts in a sexual context—or she might be read as too busy to care about surface concerns.

As in the case of nearly every artifact in our popular culture, the perspective from which one sees it and the context within which one encounters it affect its meaning. When it comes to perceiving our own gender, we hold in our minds the cultural and societal images of what that gender means. Our own images of ourselves fit, more or less perfectly, within that perception, depending on several variable influences.

We could relate nearly everything in our personal lives to our bodies. The text of clothes, for example, makes a specific contribution to our self-perceptions. Tight jeans and t-shirts might be suggestive of confidence, whereas baggy pants and a workout tank top might suggest a certain diffidence—or nonchalance— about appearances. If you're feeling good about yourself, you might wear bright colors; if you're depressed about something, you might be wearing black. (Black clothes don't necessarily mean depression, of course; from some perspectives, black clothing is essentially a uniform, reinforcing a group identity.) Clothes as a part of self-perception go beyond appearance, however; what about sensation? In one reading in this chapter, philosopher Umberto Eco says that tight jeans reinforce his feeling of masculinity. What clothes might reinforce a feeling of femininity?

The constructed social texts of masculinity and femininity are interesting examples, too. Professional female athletes such as Michelle Timms (basketball), Brandi Chastain (soccer), and Gabrielle Reece (volleyball), for instance, are common now, but few young men and women remember the time when female athletes were the rare exception to the norm. In the late 1970s, a federal entitlement program known as Title IX guaranteed (among other things) girls the same access to athletic programs that boys had always enjoyed; a whole generation of women and men has now grown up taking that experience for granted. As a result, we have successful organizations that would have been impossible before Title IX: the U.S. women's soccer team, the women's Olympic softball team, and the Women's National Basketball Association. Thus the text of "female athlete" has been constructed from increased access to athletics and greater respect for women in general.

But despite the shifts in gender roles and expectations, some of us hold on to certain beliefs about gender behavior in general and, by extension, our own. When someone else's perspective contradicts our own, we have the opportunity to reexamine our self-constructions. Chastain, ripping off her shirt after the winning goal in the World Cup Soccer match, garnered worldwide attention, not because she showed any unusual amount of skin, but because traditionally that has been a victory gesture performed by men in the moment of triumph. Was the media attention negative or positive? You might want to do some research to find out; newspapers and sports journals covered

Who wears these items? What is their sexual nature?

the soccer games and Chastain specifically at some length.

Obviously, we're influenced in our self-perceptions by the combined texts of role models, advertising, parental expectations, our spiritual beliefs, the news and entertainment media, and a host of other influences. The cultural anthropologist might be able to tell, then, that our self-perceptions are a result of *social constructionism*—the ways that we are socialized to behave and think come largely from those around us. We can think of it in this way: as we read the texts surrounding us, we take certain things and not others, and build ourselves. This process isn't necessarily conscious, but in a very real way, we're constructed by our surroundings. Our self-perceptions are a text, built from outside influences. Recalling our definition of pop culture, then,

How is this image one of power?

we can say that *the texts about (and practices of) human bodies are significant.*

What are the texts and practices of bodies? More generally, what are the textual practices of sexuality?

The perspectives in this chapter cover a wide range of approaches, from the wearing of clothes, to the gaze with which one looks at another, to the unexpected reactions we get from others about ourselves. For instance, the anchor essay in this chapter, Phillip Lopate's "reading" of his own body, suggests that how he feels about the way he looks (and how that translates to his sexuality) depends in part on how his body is read by others. Ex- and current sex partners, clerks in clothing stores, his students, and his sister all read his body differently, depending on their perspective and their relationship to Lopate himself. "What a wonder to be so misread!" he writes in response. As an example of social constructionism, Lopate's reading of his own body derives in part from the readings of others.

A second example of social construction derives from how we look at other people. For instance, while women are usually allowed to look at other women and comment on their figures, men are often constrained from observing each other and may feel threatened by doing so. One of the unwritten rules of the men's bathroom, for instance, is that one does not look at someone else's body. Clearly, the social dynamic around intimacy and sexuality determines a lot of what we perceive as "normal" and, by extension, "abnormal." That is, American culture places restrictions on how men may look at each other. What's the origin of this reluctance? Philip Culbertson offers several reasons in his article, including a fear of being considered homosexual. Michael Gilkes, the student writer in this chapter, points out in his response essay that young men are conditioned by their environments and their cultures not to gaze at other men; despite the intellectual understanding that a gaze need not mean anything negative, straight men avoid the objectifying gaze at other men in favor of directing it at the more socially acceptable target—women.

How we represent our bodies can also tell us something about our culture. You've probably seen photos of the ancient, small, carved figurines of women with large breasts, stomachs, and hips; they're collectively known as Willendorf figures, or the Venus of Willendorf. Those figurines, taken in context with other carven items, are often assumed to be religious artifacts, expressing a cultural respect for what the figure symbolizes: fertility, life, and so forth. In this perspective, the representations of the human body take on a new significance for us to read. The Barbie doll may not be that much different from the Venus of Willendorf. The photo essay in this chapter offers several different ways to look at how we represent the human body.

As Margaret Atwood suggests, Ken and Barbie are problematic: Barbie "gives a young girl a false notion of beauty," whereas Ken is "the one with the underwear glued on" (42). Despite the variety of possible readings, it's undeniable that Barbie pulls in more money than virtually any other doll, and this adds additional evidence to our anthropologists' view that the female body is a highly marketable thing. In one subtext of this reading, recalling the discussion of commodification from Chapter 1, Atwood suggests that The Female Body is worth a lot of money—and is simultaneously worthless because it can be replaced so easily with another female's body. As Atwood puts it, "Is *this* the face that launched a thousand products? You bet it is, but don't get any funny big ideas, honey, that smile is a dime a dozen" (43). How does this fit with your perception of the female body? Or your own? If dolls are a legitimate artifact of our cultural habits, what does it mean that we have dozens of Barbies and yet only one Ken?

If we read the text of these dolls looking for a reading on sexuality, then, we would deduce, as the anthropologist probably would, that Barbie's obvious orientation is heterosexual. After all, when she has a man around, it's either Ken or G.I. Joe. Is the subtext that little girls should want to be with little boys? What would the subtext of a gay doll be? Billy, the world's "first out and proud gay doll," was originally designed to be sold within the gay community for the benefit of AIDS charities. The impressively anatomically correct Billy doll was, however, so successful that Billy now has two doll friends: Hispanic Carlos and African-American Tyson. Billy's Web site (www.billyworld.com) includes discussions and photos of Billy's friends, opinions, fashion statements, and political platforms. If you search the Web, you'll find dolls representing an enormous diversity of perspectives.

If we project our fears, dreams, and values onto something apart from ourselves, we can use those representations to "read" ourselves and others. Just as anthropologists would, we can examine dolls and other figures and

Writing About Self-Perceptions

Writing about self-perception might seem to require that you write personally, about yourself, revealingly. Although Phillip Lopate's essay does in fact offer what might seem highly personal observations, student writers don't have to unless they want to. Instead, writing about self-perceptions might simply involve looking at the social text and reading the signs. Let's take one example: the ubiquitous, shapely, popular, highly adaptable Barbie doll. According to our definition of pop culture, Barbie is a text of great significance, but she can be read in so many ways that identifying her "significance" depends on your perspective. What does the artifact of Barbie say about our perceptions of our sexuality, our gender, our social roles . . . in short, what does she say to us about our self-perceptions?

A writer could begin by researching the doll's origin. After some reading, the writer would have some interesting information to begin the analysis with. According to author M. G. Lord, Barbie is in fact the American model of a European prostitute. For a writer, this might put a whole different spin on how much money Barbie earns for Mattel; a daring writer might suggest that Mattel is acting as a pimp, for example, and reflect further on what that might indicate for Americans who collect the various costumed Barbies. A writer interested in another perspective might read Barbie in the context of child psychology, where she's been a target of social criticism for some time. An astute writer, having done some reading on this subject, might read the question in several ways: if Barbie's improbable figure is what young girls aspire to, a writer might suggest that this is a dangerously inaccurate model for a healthy female body. On the other hand, a writer might examine Barbie's astonishing breadth of careers, from cheerleader to CEO, and suggest that Barbie might be a positive influence, because she tells little girls not to settle.

Both readings of Barbie's social significance to little girls have been offered and argued many times over, but an interesting and challenging approach to the diverse readings might be for a writer to see both readings themselves as artifacts. What might it mean that we can come up with such radically different readings of the same doll? Barbie is Barbie. Isn't she? Nothing about her changes except her context—and the perspective we take on her.

For example, a writer placing Barbie in context with other dolls, like Ken, would then be able to compare and perhaps identify some of our cultural beliefs about how men and women interact. You've probably heard the arguments, and you could easily repeat them in an essay before examining them in depth: Ken isn't anatomically correct, but neither is Barbie, being endowed with breasts far larger than the norm. Therefore, a writer might argue, little boys are encouraged to look for a woman with Barbie's measurements, whereas little girls are taught to settle for sexless men. What other artifacts would support this sort of reading? Some of the raunchier television programs might help you out here, for instance. Elsewhere in this chapter, you'll see other readings of Barbie that will help you write about her.

figurines to see what they mean to us. This chapter's photo essay shows representations of the human body that are significant to a variety of American cultures: the human figures included represent Hispanic, Navajo, educational, comedic, and African-American interests. When we look at a young American Indian girl playing with her doll on the red sand in Utah, are we really seeing anything different than when we look at Rachel with her collection of Barbies? What would the anthropologist make of the late Frank Zappa, equal-opportunity offender and musical satirist, bringing an inflatable woman onstage, or of the variety of small plastic couples one can find to stand on top of wedding cakes, in a representation of the pair being married? Each representation of the human figure might mean something different; some might indicate hope for the future, or perhaps scorn at what's past. Some might have religious significance, some a more secular importance. It's up to you to determine why these representations are important to their cultures. What artifacts would you include were you collecting "representations of American bodies"?

The social text about sexuality goes beyond our bodies and our representations of those bodies, of course. The social text also includes popular perceptions about the interactions between men and women. When a man hears "How do I look?" from a woman, he's in big trouble, or so columnist Dave Barry says. And as he points out, the man is in big trouble because there's no good answer to the question. A woman might ask this question when she means "tell me I'm attractive," or when she means "do you think this suit is too dressy for my business meeting?" In other words, women sometimes mean one thing and say another, just as men sometimes say one thing and mean another. Nobody's necessarily lying; it's just the way we communicate about sensitive matters like sexuality and attractiveness. We trust—sometimes we desperately hope—that the other person will know what we really mean. The stuff of sitcoms provides plenty of other popular perceptions of male-female interaction: any sitcom starring a married couple or any dating situation relies on the predictable sallies from each gender about the other's foibles for its laughs.

When she's on stage, why does it matter how much money she makes?

One perception of female sexuality is only possible after the sort of sexual revolution that redefines our perspectives for us. One of feminism's early platforms was about treating women as objects, not intelligent wage earners in their own right. The battle became, in part, about ensuring that women could earn an equal wage to men, that they could be valued just the same. When a woman was "successful," it meant her work earned good money. Forty years of American feminism, however, has changed the various platforms in response to social changes. While 1960s feminism worked against the oppression of women, for example, 1990s and 2000s feminism often denies that women are oppressed; while early feminism often raised barriers between men and women, modern feminism tends to build coalitions among the genders.

Now, feminism has led our culture collectively to the point where calling a woman "successful" because of her income might be objectionable. When *Ms.* magazine included folk singer Ani DiFranco in its salute to successful women, it was because of her financial success; DiFranco, however, resisted that perception of success because of its narrow definition. "Imagine how strange it must be," she writes, "for a girl who has spent 10 years fighting as hard as she could against the lure of the corporate carrot [. . .] to be eventually recognized by the power structure as a business pioneer." She feels like a success *despite* having made money, not because of it. How does her perception of herself as "female" differ from the magazine's perception of her? What influences helped create her definition of success?

What does our social text about sexuality suggest to you? You should notice the contradictions, especially the ones you embody yourself. We are perhaps most attached to the contradictions surrounding what it means to be male and to be female; read the texts of the various perspectives offered in this chapter and see what self-perceptions you can identify.

"Portrait of My Body," from *Portrait of My Body* (1996)

Phillip Lopate

I am a man who tilts. When I am sitting, my head slants to the right; when walking, the upper part of my body reaches forward to catch a sneak preview of the street. One way or another, I seem to be off-center— or "uncentered," to use the jargon of holism. My lousy posture, a tendency to slump or put myself into lazy, contorted misalignments, undoubtedly contributes to lower back pain. For a while I correct my bad habits, do morning exercises, sit straight, breathe deeply, but always an inner demon that insists on approaching the world askew resists perpendicularity.

I think if I had broader shoulders I would be more squarely anchored. But my shoulders are narrow, barely wider than my hips. This has always made shopping for suits an embarrassing business. (Francoise Gilot's *Life with Picasso* tells how Picasso was so touchy about his disproportionate body—in his case all shoulders, no legs—that he insisted the tailor fit him at home.) When I was growing up in Brooklyn, my hero was Sandy Koufax, the Dodgers' Jewish pitcher. In the doldrums of Hebrew choir practice at Feigenbaum's Mansion & Catering Hall, I would fantasize striking out the side, even whiffing twenty-seven batters in a row. Lack of shoulder development put an end to this identification; I became a writer instead of a Koufax.

It occurs to me that the restless angling of my head is an attempt to distract viewers' attention from its paltry base. I want people to look at my head, partly because I live in my head most of the time. My sister, a trained masseuse, often warns me of the penalties, like neck tension, that may arise from failing to integrate body and mind. Once, about ten years ago, she and I were at the beach and she was scrutinizing my body with a sister's critical eye. "You're getting flabby," she said. "You should exercise every day. I do—look at me, not an ounce of fat." She pulled at her midriff, celebrating (as is her wont) her physical attributes with the third-person enthusiasm of a carnival barker.

"But"—she threw me a bone—"you do have a powerful head. There's an intensity . . ." A graduate student of mine (who was slightly loony) told someone that she regularly saw an aura around my head in class. One reason I like to teach is that it focuses fifteen or so dependent gazes on me with such paranoiac intensity as cannot help but generate an aura in my behalf.

I also have a commanding stare, large sad brown eyes that can be read as either gentle or severe. Once I watched several hours of myself on videotape. I discovered to my horror that my face moved at different rates: sometimes my mouth would be laughing, eyebrows circumflexed in mirth, while my eyes

Francoise Gilot · biographer.

coolly gauged the interviewer to see what effect I was making. I am something of an actor. And, as with many performers, the mood I sense most in myself is that of energy-conserving watchfulness; but this expression is often mistaken (perhaps because of the way brown eyes are read in our culture) for sympathy. I see myself as determined to the point of stubbornness, selfish, even a bit cruel—in any case, I am all too aware of the limits of my compassion, so that it puzzles me when people report a first impression of me as gentle, kind, solicitous. In my youth I felt obliged to come across as dynamic, arrogant, intimidating, the life of the party; now, surer of myself, I hold back some energy, thereby winning time to gather information and make better judgments. This results sometimes in a misimpression of my being mildly depressed. Of course, the simple truth is that I have less energy than I once did, and that accumulated experiences have made me, almost against my will, kinder and sadder.

Sometimes I can feel my mouth arching downward in an ironic smile, which, at its best, reassures others that we need not take everything so seriously—because we are all in the same comedy together—and, at its worst, expresses a superior skepticism. This smile, which can be charming when not supercilious, has elements of the bashful that mesh with the worldly—the shyness, let us say, of a cultivated man who is often embarrassed for others by their willful shallowness or self-deception. Many times, however, my ironic smile is nothing more than a neutral stall among people who do not seem to appreciate my "contribution." I hate that pain-in-the-ass half-smile of mine; I want to jump in, participate, be loud, thoughtless, vulgar.

Often I give off a sort of psychic stench to myself, I do not like myself at all, but out of stubborn pride I act like a man who does. I appear for all the world poised, contented, sanguine when inside I may be feeling self-revulsion bordering on the suicidal. What a wonder to be so misread! Of course, if in the beginning I had thought I was coming across accurately, I never would have bothered to become a writer. And the truth is I am not misread, because another part of me is never less than fully contented with myself.

I am vain about these parts of my body: my eyes, my fingers, my legs. It is true that my legs are long and not unshapely, but my vanity about them has less to do with their comeliness than with their contribution to my height. Montaigne, a man who was himself on the short side, wrote that "the beauty of stature is the only beauty of men." But even if Montaigne had never said it, I would continue to attribute a good deal of my self-worth and benevolent liberalism to being tall. When I go out into the street, I feel well-disposed toward the (mostly shorter) swarms of humanity; crowds not only do not dismay, they enliven me; and I am tempted to think that my passion for urbanism is linked to my height. By no means am I suggesting that only tall people love cities; merely that, in my case, part of the pleasure I derive from walking in crowded streets issues from a confidence that I can see above the heads of others, and cut a fairly impressive, elevated figure as I saunter along the sidewalk.

Some of my best friends have been—short. Brilliant men, brimming with poetic and worldly ideas, they deserved all of my and the world's respect. Yet at times I have had to master an impulse to rumple their heads; and I suspect they have developed manners of a more formal, *noli me tangere* nature, largely in response to this petting impulse of taller others.

The accident of my tallness has inclined me to both a seemingly egalitarian informality and a desire to lead. Had I not been a writer, I would surely have become a politician; I was even headed in that direction in my teens. Ever since I shot up to a little over six feet, I have had at my command what feels like a natural, Gregory Peck authority when addressing an audience. Far from experiencing stage fright, I have actually sought out situations in which I could make speeches, give readings, sit on panel discussions, and generally tower over everyone else onstage. To be tall is to look down on the world and meet its eyes on your terms. But this topic, the noblesse oblige of tall men, is a dangerously provoking one, and so let us say no more about it.

The mental image of one's body changes slower than one's body. Mine was for a long while arrested in my early twenties, when I was tall and thin (165 pounds) and gobbled down whatever I felt like. I ate food that was cheap and filling, cheeseburgers, pizza, without any thought to putting on weight. But a young person's metabolism is more dietetically forgiving. To compound the problem, the older you get, the more cultivated your palate grows—and the more life's setbacks make you inclined to fill the hollowness of disappointment with the pleasures of the table.

Between the age of thirty and forty I put on ten pounds, mostly around the midsection. Since then my gut has suffered another expansion, and I tip the scales at over 180. That I took a while to notice the change may be shown by my continuing to purchase clothes at my primordial adult size (33 waist, 15½ collar), until a girlfriend started pointing out that all my clothes were too tight. I rationalized this circumstance as the result of changing fashions (thinking myself still subconsciously loyal to the sixties' penchant for skintight fits) and laundry shrinkage rather than anything to do with my own body. She began buying me larger replacements for birthdays or holidays, and I found I enjoyed this "baggier" style, which allowed me to button my trousers comfortably, or to wear a tie and, for the first time in years, close my top shirt button. But it took even longer before I was able to enter a clothing store myself and give the salesman realistically enlarged size numbers.

Clothes can disguise the defects of one's body, up to a point. I get dressed with great optimism, adding

noli me tangere · Latin, "touch me not."

one color to another, mixing my favorite Japanese and Italian designers, matching the patterns and textures, selecting ties, then proceed to the bathroom mirror to judge the result. There is an ideal in my mind of the effect I am essaying by wearing a particular choice of garments, based, no doubt, on male models in fashion ads—and I fall so far short of this insouciant gigolo handsomeness that I cannot help but be a little disappointed when I turn up so depressingly myself, narrow-shouldered, Talmudic, that grim, set mouth, that long, narrow face, those appraising eyes, the Semitic hooked nose, all of which express both the strain of intellectual overachieving and the tabula rasa of immaturity . . . for it is still, underneath, a boy in the mirror. A boy with a rapidly receding hairline.

How is it that I've remained a boy all this time, into my late forties? I remember, at seventeen, drawing a self-portrait of myself as I looked in the mirror. I was so appalled at the weak chin and pleading eyes that I ended up focusing on the neckline of the cotton T-shirt. Ever since then I have tried to toughen myself up, but I still encounter in the glass that haunted uncertainty—shielded by a bluffing shell of cynicism, perhaps, but untouched by wisdom. So I approach the mirror warily, without lighting up as much as I would for the least of my acquaintances; I go one-on-one with that frowning schmuck.

And yet, it would be insulting to those who labor under the burden of true ugliness to palm myself off as an unattractive man. I'm at times almost handsome, if you squinted your eyes and rounded me off to the nearest *beau idéal*. I lack even a shred of cowboy virility, true, but I believe I fall into a category of adorable nerd or absentminded professor that awakens the amorous curiosity of some women. "Cute" is a word often applied to me by those I've been fortunate enough to attract. Then again, I attract only women of a certain lopsided prettiness: the head-turning, professional beauties never fall for me. They seem to look right through me, in fact. Their utter lack of interest in my appeal has always fascinated me. Can it be so simple an explanation as that beauty calls to beauty, as wealth to wealth?

I think of poor (though not in his writing gifts) Cesare Pavese, who kept chasing after starlets, models, and ballerinas—exquisite lovelies who couldn't appreciate his morose coffeehouse charm. Before he killed himself, he wrote a poem addressed to one of them, "Death Will Come Bearing Your Eyes"—thereby unfairly promoting her from rejecting lover to unwitting executioner. Perhaps he believed that only beautiful women (not literary critics, who kept awarding him prestigious prizes) saw him clearly, with twenty-twenty vision, and had the right to judge him. Had I been more headstrong, if masochistic, I might have followed his path and chased some beauty until she was forced to tell me, like an oracle, what it was about me, physically, that so failed to excite her. Then I might know something crucial about my body, before I passed into my next reincarnation.

Cesare Pavese · Italian-born poet.

Jung says somewhere that we pay dearly over many years to learn about ourselves what a stranger can see at a glance. This is the way I feel about my back. Fitting rooms aside, we none of us know what we look like from the back. It is the area of ourselves whose presentation we can least control, and which therefore may be the most honest part of us.

I divide backs into two kinds: my own and everyone else's. The others' backs are often mysterious, exquisite, and uncannily sympathetic. I have always loved backs. To walk behind a pretty woman in a backless dress and savor how a good pair of shoulder blades, heightened by shadow, has the same power to pierce the heart as chiseled cheekbones!. . . I wonder what it says about me that I worship a part of the body that signals a turning away. Does it mean I'm a glutton for being abandoned, or a timid voyeur who prefers a surreptitious gaze that will not be met and challenged? I only know I have often felt the deepest love at just that moment when the beloved turns her back to me to get some sleep.

I have no autoerotic feelings about my own back. I cannot even picture it; visually it is a stranger to me. I know it only as an annoyance, which came into my consciousness twenty years ago, when I started getting lower back pain. Yes, we all know that homo sapiens is constructed incorrectly; our erect posture puts too much pressure on the base of the spine; more workdays are lost because of lower back pain than any other cause. Being a writer, I sit all day, compounding the problem. My back is the enemy of my writing life: if I don't do exercises daily, I immediately ache; and if I do, I am still not spared. I could say more, but there is nothing duller than lower back pain. So common, mundane an ailment brings no credit to the sufferer. One has to dramatize it somehow, as in the phrase "I threw my back out."

Here is a gossip column about my body: my eyebrows grow quite bushy across my forehead, and whenever I get my hair cut, the barber asks me diplomatically if I want them trimmed or not. (I generally say no, associating bushy eyebrows with Balzackian virility, *élan vital;* but sometimes I acquiesce, to soothe his fastidiousness). . . . My belly button is a modest, embedded slit, not a jaunty swirl like my father's. Still, I like to sniff the odor that comes from jabbing my finger in it: a very ripe, underground smell, impossible to describe, but let us say a combination of old gym socks and stuffed derma (the Yiddish word for this oniony dish of ground intestines, is, fittingly, *kishkas*). . . . I have a scar on my tongue from childhood, which I can only surmise I received by landing it on a sharp object, somehow. Or perhaps I bit it hard. I have the habit of sticking my tongue out like a dog when exerting myself physically, as though to urge my muscles on; and maybe I accidentally chomped into it at such a moment. . . . I gnash my teeth, sleeping or waking. Awake, the sensation makes me feel alert and in

Jung · Carl Jung, psychologist who studied the forms of consciousness such as archetypes.

Élan vital · the stuff of life.

contact with the world when I start to drift off in a daydream. Another way of grounding myself is to pinch my cheek—drawing a pocket of flesh downward and squeezing it—as I once saw JFK do in a filmed motorcade. I do this cheek-pinching especially when I am trying to keep mentally focused during teaching or other public situations. I also scratch the nape of my neck under public stress, so much so that I raise welts or sores which then eventually grow scabs; and I take great delight in secretly picking the scabs off. . . . My nose itches whenever I think about it, and I scratch it often, especially lying in bed trying to fall asleep (maybe because I am conscious of my breathing then). I also pick my nose with formidable thoroughness when no one, I hope, is looking. . . . There is a white scar about the size of a quarter on the juicy part of my knee; I got it as a boy running into a car fender, and I can still remember staring with detached calm at the blood that gushed from it like a pretty, half-eaten peach. Otherwise, the sight of my own blood makes me awfully nervous. I used to faint dead away when a blood sample was taken, and now I can control the impulse to do so only by biting the insides of my cheeks while steadfastly looking away from the needle's action. . . . I like to clean out my ear wax as often as possible (the smell is curiously sulfurous; I associate it with the bodies of dead insects). I refuse to listen to warnings that it is dangerous to stick cleaning objects into your ears. I love Q-Tips immoderately; I buy them in huge quantities and store them the way a former refugee will stock canned foodstuffs. . . . My toes are long and apelike; I have very little fellow feeling for them; they are so far away, they may as well belong to someone else. . . . My flattish buttocks are not offensively large, but neither do they have the "dream" configuration one sees in jeans ads. Perhaps for this reason, it disturbed me puritanically when asses started to be treated by Madison Avenue, around the seventies, as crucial sexual equipment, and I began to receive compositions from teenage girl students declaring that they liked some boy because he had "a cute butt." It confused me; I had thought the action was elsewhere.

About my penis there is nothing, I think, unusual. It has a brown stem, and a pink mushroom head where the foreskin is pulled back. Like most heterosexual males, I have little comparative knowledge to go by, so that I always feel like an outsider when I am around women or gay men who talk zestfully about differences in penises. I am afraid that they might judge me harshly, ridicule me like the boys who stripped me of my bathing suit in summer camp when I was ten. But perhaps they would simply declare it an ordinary penis, which changes size with the stimulus or weather or time of day. Actually, my penis does have a peculiarity: it has two peeing holes. They are very close to each other, so that usually only one stream of urine issues, but sometimes a hair gets caught across them, or some such contretemps, and they squirt out in two directions at once.

This part of me, which is so synecdochically identified with the male body (as the term "male member" indicates), has given me both too little, and too much, information about what it means to be a man. It has a personality like a cat's. I have prayed to it to behave better, to be less frisky, or more; I have followed its nose in matters of love, ignoring good sense, and paid the price; but I have also come to appreciate that it has its own specialized form of intelligence which must be listened to, or another price will be extracted.

Even to say the word "impotence" aloud makes me nervous. I used to tremble when I saw it in print, and its close relation, "importance," if hastily scanned, had the same effect, as if they were publishing a secret about me. But why should it be *my* secret, when my penis has regularly given me erections lo these many years—except for about a dozen times, mostly when I was younger? Because, even if it has not been that big a problem for me, it has dominated my thinking as an adult male. I've no sooner to go to bed with a woman than I'm in suspense. The power of the flaccid penis's statement, "I don't want you," is so stark, so cruelly direct, that it continues to exert a fascination out of all proportion to its actual incidence. Those few times when I was unable to function were like a wall forcing me to take another path—just as, after I tried to kill myself at seventeen, I was obliged to give up pessimism for a time. Each had instructed me by its too painful manner that I could not handle the world as I had previously construed it, that my confusion and rage were being found out. I would have to get more wily or else grow up.

Yet for the very reason that I was compelled to leave them behind, these two options of my youth, impotence and suicide, continue to command an underground loyalty, as though they were more "honest" than the devious strategies of potency and survival which I adopted. Put it this way: sometimes we encounter a person who has had a nervous breakdown years before and who seems cemented over sloppily, his vulnerability ruthlessly guarded against as dangerous; we sense he left a crucial part of himself back in the chaos of breakdown, and has since grown rigidly jovial. So suicide and impotence became for me "the roads not taken," the paths I had repressed.

Whenever I hear an anecdote about impotence—a woman who successfully coaxed an ex-priest who had been celibate and unable to make love, first by lying next to him for six months without any touching, then by cuddling for six more months, then by easing him slowly into a sexual embrace—I think they are talking about me. I identify completely: this, in spite of the fact, which I promise not to repeat again, that I have generally been able to do it whenever called upon. Believe it or not, I am not boasting when I say that: a part of me is contemptuous of this virility, as though it were merely a mechanical trick that violated my true nature, that of an impotent man absolutely frightened of women, absolutely secluded, cut off.

I now see the way I have idealized impotence: I've connected it with pushing the world away, as a kind of integrity, as in Molière's *The Misanthrope*—connected it with that part of me which, gregarious socializer that I am, continues to insist that I am a recluse, too good for this life. Of course, it is not true that I am terrified of women. I exaggerate my terror of them for dramatic effect, or for the purposes of a good scare.

My final word about impotence: Once, in a period when I was going out with many women, as though purposely trying to ignore my hypersensitive side and force it to grow callous by thrusting myself into foreign situations (not only sexual) and seeing if I was able to "rise to the occasion," I dated a woman who was attractive, tall and blond, named Susan. She had something to do with the pop music business, was a follower of the visionary religious futurist Teilhard de Chardin, and considered herself a religious pacifist. In fact, she told me her telephone number in the form of the anagram, N-O-T-O-W-A-R. I thought she was joking and laughed aloud, but she gave me a solemn look. In passing, I should say that all the women with whom I was impotent or close to it had solemn natures. The sex act has always seemed to me in many ways ridiculous, and I am most comfortable when a woman who enters the sheets with me shares that sense of the comic pomposity behind such a grandiloquently rhetorical use of the flesh. It is as though the prose of the body were being drastically squeezed into metrical verse. I would not have known how to stop guffawing had I been D. H. Lawrence's lover, and I am sure he would have been pretty annoyed at me. But a smile saying "All this will pass" has an erotic effect on me like nothing else.

They claim that men who have long, long fingers also have lengthy penises. I can tell you with a surety that my fingers are long and sensitive, the most perfect, elegant, handsome part of my anatomy. They are not entirely perfect—the last knuckle of my right middle finger is twisted permanently, broken in a softball game when I was trying to block the plate—but even this slight disfigurement, harbinger of mortality, adds to the pleasure I take in my hands' rugged beauty. My penis does not excite in me nearly the same contemplative delight when I look at it as do my fingers. Pianists' hands, I have been told often; and though I do not play the piano, I derive an aesthetic satisfaction from them that is as pure and Apollonian as any I am capable of. I can stare at my fingers for hours. No wonder I have them so often in my mouth, biting my fingernails to bring them closer. When I write, I almost feel that they, and not my

Molière's *The Misanthrope* · seventeenth-century stage play in which the star loathes humanity to such an extent that he actively avoids personal contact.

Teilhard de Chardin · paleontologist, Jesuit priest, and philosopher. Today Teilhard is best known for his unique evolutionary cosmology, which supporters believe predicted the arrival of a global "internet" more than half a century before its creation.

intellect, are the clever progenitors of the text. Whatever narcissism, fetishism, and proud sense of masculinity I possess about my body must begin and end with my fingers.

■ *Phillip Lopate, author of several books and articles, is a recipient of the Guggenheim Fellowship. Nationally recognized for his personal essays, Lopate lives in New York and teaches at Hofstra University.*

MAKING SURE OF THE TEXT:

1. What is Lopate's point in this personal essay?
2. Summarize the reactions of the people Lopate mentions. How does each of them see his body? How do their differing perspectives contribute to their readings?
3. In what ways does Lopate discuss "reading" the body?
4. Identify two passages that surprise you with their detail or honesty. How has your culture constructed your reaction?

CONSIDERING THE CONTEXT

1. How does Lopate organize this essay so that the reader reads his body along with his description of it?
2. Lopate and Culbertson seem to be discussing different aspects of the same thing—reading the body. How might Lopate respond to Culbertson's claim that men are reluctant to look at their own bodies?
3. What's the effect of Lopate's references to Koufax, Picasso, and Pavese? In what ways do the references help to illustrate Lopate's portrait of his own body?

■ ■ ■

"Designing Men: Reading the Male Body as Text" from *Textual Reasoning* (1998)

Philip Culbertson

The study of the human body as a metaphorical vehicle is sometimes called "Human Social Anatomy." Dutton describes it as follows:

> The human body, in this view, can be understood only in the context of the social construction of reality; indeed, the body itself is seen as a social construct, a means of social expression or performance by which our identity and value—for ourselves and others—are created, tested, and validated.[1]

The human body is not simply a blank page upon which words have not yet been written. It is, more aptly, a textless text whose meaning is read by many readers, whether they are invited to read or not. It is a text which is almost always read from the outside (the reader introjecting meaning), but which always has the potential to be read from the inside, in that the body-bearer may at any point choose to wrest control over the text to interpret it as his or her own, making unique meanings and giving them primacy of place.

OBJECTIFICATION, THE MALE GAZE, AND HOMOSOCIALITY

To read indicates "to objectify." We maintain the comfortable fiction that encountering a text is an I-Thou relationship, though the history of religious literalism and fundamentalism indicates it is mostly an I-It relationship. In fact, we can't read into a subject because it won't sit still for us to do that. We have to objectify in order to interpret and then meaning-make.[2] In the same way, we objectify the body texts around us. At present, the way that men look at women is the most commonly studied form of objectification within the field of gender studies.

The term "the male gaze" seems to have been first used by Laura Mulvey, who argued that within the classical structure of cinema, men possess the gaze and women are its object.[3] As Schehr explains:

> it is the gaze, the defining mode of operation of masculist discourse, that constructs the "woman" as textual object, prevents the woman from being herself—from "being," from "Being," from having a "self" separate from or prior to the sociovisual construct imposed by the male gaze and its/his discourse.[4]

A gaze turns a subject into an object. The male gaze values—when turned toward a woman, it desires; when turned toward a gay man, it often despises. In either case, it seizes control from the other. The other may experience the male gaze as a violation, a rape; the object of the gaze is no longer another person, but someone to be possessed or disposed of. Within the world of texts, the male gaze might be described as

I-Thou relationship · the assumption that when one reads a text, the "I"—the reader—encounters only one other: the text.

"one-handed reading," in that its purpose is clearly one of self-stimulation and erotic satisfaction.[5]

Homosociality is a term coined by Eve Kosofsky Sedgwick to describe the basic structure of patriarchy: men pleasing other men via the medium of women.[6] Sedgwick describes the process whereby men attempt to establish some intimacy with each other, usually in a triangulated relationship with a woman who functions to disguise the gestures between the men, as "homosociality":

"Homosocial" is a word occasionally used in history and the social sciences, where it describes social bonds between persons of the same sex; it is a neologism, obviously formed by analogy with "homosexual," and just as obviously meant to be distinguished from "homosexual."[7]

Sedgwick's theory is directly related to family systems theory, presuming that human beings relate to each other within triangular structures.[8] In the triangle of two men and a woman, the attraction between the two men must be taken at least as seriously as the attraction between each man and the woman. The attraction is heightened when either man realizes that he can accumulate further power and influence by forming an alliance with another of the two members of the triangle. Since women rarely have power, the obvious choice with whom to form the alliance is the other man. The alliance may take the form of cooperation or competition or even aggression. Whatever its form, the alliance as power-brokering cannot be denied. This desire to unite powers with another man is one possible non-genital form of Eros, this desire and attraction creating the exaggerated impulse to homosociality. Sedgwick even describes the attraction as "intense and potent." Most men operate this way on occasion, though few are aware of it.

The male gaze not only objectifies, but must objectify for homosociality to work. Ironically, the homosocial system can be maintained only when men avert their gaze from each other; the gaze, however figuratively, must remain focused on a woman. When the male gaze turns toward another man, homosociality threatens to disintegrate into homoeroticism, as the novels of D. H. Lawrence illustrate.[9] Thus patriarchy is built upon the assumption that a male body is a text which will reject all attempts by other men to read it. To accept such an attempt would be to destroy the basis of power and control.

Thinking about writing this essay, I decided to poll a group of men I spend a lot of time with. Sitting in a corner at a party, I asked them, "When a woman walks into the room, what's the first thing you notice about her?" They answered variously: "Her breasts; I'm a tit man." "Her legs." "Her hair." "Her ass." Each man had a quick and clear answer. I continued: "So when a man walks into the room, what's the first thing you notice about him?" "The whole package," they seemed to answer in one voice. Not satisfied, I asked my question about men again, and got the same univocal answer again. In fact, the guys wouldn't budge. They would not name a male body part that attracted their attention, would not name any aspect of a male that they read first as an entry point into the larger text. They were willing to engage the text as a whole, but not to do the sort of close reading which is now assumed within the field of textual criticism.

AVERTING THE GAZE, REFUSING TO READ

Why is it so difficult for men to direct their heterosexual male gaze toward another man? Why is it apparently even more difficult for them to turn the gaze upon their own male bodies? The complexity of the answer may help explain why the subject is almost completely ignored in the exploding literature on masculinity. Let me explore five different reasons.

Reading is Dangerous

To read is to risk making one's self vulnerable, to risk encountering what Wayne Booth has called "the otherness that bites."[10] Most people are highly selective about what they read, and will avoid texts which threaten their comfortability or security. A man may not be consciously aware that to read another man's body is dangerous, but subconsciously he is aware. He is also aware that to read another man's body raises the possibility that another man may attempt to read his, and perhaps in the reading find him wanting.

Reading Re-Positions the Reader

As I have claimed elsewhere, masculinity as a gender construction in virtually every society is fragile and must be constantly defended.[11] Michael Satlow makes the same claim in relation to the rabbinic understanding of masculinity: "For the rabbis, therefore, manliness is never secure; it is achieved through the constant exercise of discipline in pursuit of virtue, and vanishes the moment a male ceases to exercise that discipline."[12] To gaze at another man re-positions a straight man as a gay man, thereby shattering his fragile masculinity. Reading affects the reader much more deeply than it affects the text; gazing affects the gazer much more deeply than the one toward whom the gaze is directed. Susan Bordo points out that the male gaze has the power not only to objectify, but to feminize:

What exposure is most feared in the shower? Not the scrutiny of the penis (although this prospect may indeed make a heterosexual men uncomfortable), but the moment when one bends down to pick up the soap which has slipped from one's hands. It is in the imagination of this moment that the orthodox male is most undone by the consciousness that there may be homosexuals in the shower, whose gaze will define him as a passive receptacle of their sexuality, and thus as "woman." There is a certain paradox here. For although it is the imagined effeminacy of homosexual men that makes them objects of heterosexual derision, here it is their imagined masculinity (that is, the consciousness of them as active, evaluating sexual subjects, with a defining and "penetrating" sexual gaze) that makes them the objects of heterosexual fear.[13]

Men's fear of the male gaze, ultimately, is the fear of becoming, feeling, or representing female desire within the phallocentric order. In the shower, the homosexual body is the same as the heterosexual body, the only difference being in the desirer.[14]

Reading a Text Which Won't Focus

As if the male body were not already a difficult enough text to read, it seems to disappear altogether when a man is unclothed. In a patriarchal system, the penis cues masculinity, and once that occurs, the body, "the being" disappears and the person becomes a function, the form becomes the essence, the masculinity, the "doing." The part overwhelms the whole, so that the whole fades into insignificance, leaving us to attempt to read a part or "member" which is, at best, dissociative.

The penis will not behave: now a penis, now a phallus, the one when we wish the other, it is itself a text that we can barely read, even with double-vision. It seems not one thing but two. The phallus is haunted by the penis and vice versa. It has no unified social identity, but is fragmented by ideologies of race and ethnicity. "Rather than exhibiting constancy of form, it is perhaps the most visibly mutable of bodily parts; it evokes the temporal not the eternal. And far from maintaining a steady will and purpose, it is mercurial, temperamental, unpredictable."[15] It is this unpredictability which fascinates, frustrates, and ultimately offends many readers of male bodies.

Because it is two and not one, we do not even know how to count the male body parts. Girls are made of indiscrete amounts of stuff: "sugar and spice and everything nice." No quantities are given, nor do they need to be. But boys are made of countable things: "snips and snails and puppy dog tails ...." Countable, if not to say detachable, things, metonymies of their always castrated penises.[16] But do we count the penis as one and the phallus as another? Or is the penis simply a potential text, a text which seems to self-create at will? St. Augustine claimed it was two: the penis, which is the "logical extension" of all rational men, created in the image of the divine logos, and the phallus, which as rationally uncontrollable, must simply be the handiwork of the Not-God, Satan. The phallus for Augustine is the wily serpent in the garden[17] and, as the only body part which refuses to submit to the brain, the constant reminder of our fallenness. Augustine despised the phallus, the conveyer of original sin. And yet even so great a saint could be overcome by his phallicly-inflated male ego, declaring that in heaven, women will receive their penises back. Perhaps he would have been happier if the penis really had been detachable, to be awarded, or not, like a prize for good behavior.

Source of pride, seat of shame, many men cannot figure out how

mercurial · changeable, as in mercury responding to temperature changes.

to read their own penises realistically, and refuse to read the penises of others. Judaism attempted to resolve the textual dilemma with the cry "Off with its hat!" Christianity responded more adamantly: "Off with its head," creating a culture of either symbolic or literal castration. The Christian male body was symbolically castrated through body-denial, the circumscription of sexual activity to heterosexual intercourse within marriage for the sole purpose of procreation, and the forbidding of *jouissance*.[18] For some of the saints, this was not enough. Origen in the 3rd century, and Peter Abelard in the 12th century, are two who excised altogether any genital text from their body.[19]

Reading a Text Which Does Not Belong To Us

Those who have the greatest investment in reading interpretive meanings into textless texts are those whose power is most easily promoted by the interpretation. The entire subject of identifying readings, of deconstructing the construction of the heterosexual male body, is so inherently elusive that I had repeatedly to struggle to keep any sense of objectivity while writing this essay.

Those with the greatest investment in reading meaning into the male body are governments and politico-military authorities which need men to conceive themselves in certain ways in order to retain their present positions of power. In other words, the primary reader who inserts meaning into the male textless text is the government structure of the society in which these men live. In his essay "Consuming Manhood," Michael Kimmel points out that in order for a man in nineteenth-century puritanical America to become a real man, a "Marketplace Man," governments realized it would be necessary to control the flows of desire and of fluids filling his body.[20] Certain flows of desire would need to be deemed morally repugnant because they were economically counterproductive; undesirable or counterproductive flows of desire would henceforth be deemed pathological. In *The History of Sexuality,* Michel Foucault stresses the development of such discourses of biopolitics, those official discourses that seek to regulate the individual through a series of proscriptions, admonitions, and recommendations. The discourses of biopolitics involve the identification of the individual with his (and not "his or her") political self as a citizen. The individual was to act so as best to fulfill the functions of a member of society. In order to produce Marketplace Men, bodies would need to be owned, men would have to be read as both heterosexual and "manly," and the siring of children would be understood as mandatory. These were the responsibility of every good citizen.[21]

Jouissance · French term referring to the joyous creative urge of humans.

Origen and Peter Abelard · men who voluntarily castrated themselves.

Male bodies are textless texts into which governments read self-securing values and expectations, giving the lie to the myth of genuine concern or human rights. Heterosexuality is read onto men's bodies, which is why, in the present debate on the genesis of sexual orientation, gay men can usually chart the development of their sexual self-awareness, while straight men believe they have "always been that way." Heterosexuality is a government-designed and -controlled process of breeding, of animal husbandry. Masturbation, voluntary celibacy, homosexuality, and any other alternative sexual expression has to be controlled and even anathematized, for only through heterosexual marriage and the procreation of children can a phallic political power assure its own authority into the future.[22] The heterosexual male gaze is the ultimate sign of capitulation to an imposed external meaning, an abandonment of human *jouissance*.

Reading Unmasks the Divine Ambiguity

An additional difficulty in reading men's bodies confronts Jewish and Christian men, whether gay or straight. Danna Nolan Fewell and David Gunn,[23] and Howard Eilberg-Schwartz,[24] have explored extensively the central gender problem of scripture: how can men and women understand themselves as created in God's image when God apparently has no body? Eilberg-Schwartz writes:

Does God have genitals and, if so, of which sex? It is interesting that interpreters have generally avoided this question. This seems a particularly important lacuna for interpreters who understand Genesis 1:26-27 to mean that the human body is made in the image of the deity. By avoiding the question of God's sex, they skirt a fundamental question: how can male and female bodies both resemble the divine form? Since God's sex is veiled, however, any conclusions have to be inferred indirectly from statements about God's gender. But however this question is answered poses a problem for human embodiment generally and sexuality in particular. If God is asexual, as many interpreters would have it, then only part of the human body is made in the image of God.[25]

The part of a man's body which is obviously not made in God's image is the penis. To read another man's body is to read the Divine Ambiguity. And this ambiguity, too, is read into men's penises—into the penises of others, and into one's own.

Given how daunting all this is, no wonder that the heterosexual male gaze is never directed toward other heterosexual men. No wonder "the guys" only wanted to look at the whole package, if even that! If a man cannot read the body of another, what then is the effect when he turns his male gaze upon himself, upon his own body with all its strengths and weaknesses?

NOTES

1. Kenneth Dutton, *The Perfectible Body: The Western Ideal of Male Physical Development* (New York: Continuum, 1995), 13.

2. Many authors develop this idea. Among the foundational texts are J. L. Austin, *How To Do Things With Words,* 2nd edition, ed. by J. O. Urmson and Marina Sbisa (Cambridge: Harvard University Press, 1975); Stanley Fish, *Is There a Text in This Class? The Authority of Interpretive Communities* (Cambridge: Harvard University Press, 1980); and Mikhail Mikhailovich Bakhtin, *The Dialogic Imagination: Four Essays,* edited by Michael Holquist, translated by Caryl Emerson and Michael Holquist (Austin: University of Texas Press, 1981).

3. Laura Mulvey, "Visual Pleasure and the Narrative Cinema," *Screen* 16:3 (1975), 6–18: see also the analysis of Peter Lehman, *Running Scared: Masculinity and the Representation of the Male Body* (Philadelphia: Temple University Press, 1993). 2–3.

4. Lawrence Schehr, *Parts of an Andrology: on Representations of Men's Bodies* (Stanford: Stanford University Press, 1997), 82–83.

5. See Jean-Jacques Rousseau (*Confessions*) and Jean Marie Goulemot (*Ces livres qu'on ne lit que d'une main*); see also Schehr, 113.

6. Eve Kosofsky Sedgwick, *Between Men: English Literature and Male Homosocial Desire,* (New York: Columbia, 1985); see also Gayle Rubin, "The Traffic in Women: Notes on the `Political Economy' of Sex," in *Toward an Anthropology of Women,* ed. by Rayna Reiter (New York: Monthly Review Press, 1975). Sherry Ortner, in *Making Gender: The Politics and Erotics of Culture* (Boston: Beacon Press, 1996), describes Polynesian cultures as homosocial, in that powerful men retain their position by bartering young virgins in order to form political alliances. Such a social structure appears to make women important, but in fact their value is only in their agency as "negotiable tender." Mark George, in "Assuming the Body of the Heir Apparent: David's Lament," in Timothy Beal and David Gunn, eds., *Reading Bibles, Writing Bodies: Identity and the Book* (London: Routledge, 1996), 164–174, describes the relation between David and Jonathan as sitting at the homosexual end of the homosocial spectrum.

7. Sedgwick, 1.

8. See Murray Bowen, *Family Therapy in Clinical Practice* (Northvale: Jason Aronson, 1985); and Philip Guerin, Thomas Fogarty, Leo Fay, and Judith Gilbert Kautto, *Working with Relationship Triangles: The One-Two-Three of Psychotherapy* (New York: Guilford, 1996), for cogent explanations of this theory.

9. See, for example, the relationship between Maurice and Bertie in his short story "The Blind Man," or between Gerald Crich and Rupert Birkin in *Women in Love.*

10. "I embrace the pursuit of the Other as among the grandest of hunts we are invited to;...But surely no beast that will prove genuinely other will fail to bite, and the otherness that bites, the otherness that changes us, must have sufficient definition, sufficient identity, to threaten us where we live." Wayne C. Booth, *The Company We Keep: An Ethics of Fiction* (Berkeley: University of California Press, 1990), 70.

11. Philip Culbertson, *New Adam: The Future of Male Spirituality* (Minneapolis: Fortress Press, 1992); *Counseling Men* (Minneapolis: Fortress Press, 1994); "Men's Quest for Wholeness: The Changing Counseling Needs of Pakeha Males" (in press).

12. Michael Satlow, "'Try to Be a Man': The Rabbinic Construction of Masculinity," *Harvard Theological Review* 89:1 (1996), 27.

13. Susan Bordo, "Reading the Male Body," in Goldstein, 287.

14. Schehr, 151.

15. Phillip Lopate, "Portrait of My Body," in Goldstein, 211.

16. Schehr, 80.

17. See the excellent comments by Ilona Rashkow, "Daughters and Fathers in Genesis . . . Or, What is Wrong with this Picture," in Athalya Brenner, ed., *A Feminist Companion to Exodus to Deuteronomy* (Sheffield: Sheffield Academic Press, 1994), 32 n.32. For a vivid picture of adolescent revulsion at phallic erection, see Stephen Fry's novel *The Hippopotamus* (London: Arrow Books, 1994), 88–89.

18. See, among various sources, Uta Ranke-Heinemann, *Eunuchs for the Kingdom of Heaven: Women, Sexuality, and the Catholic Church* (New York: Penguin, 1990).

19. See Peter Brown, *The Body and Society: Men, Women, and Sexual Renunciation in Early Christianity* (New York: Columbia University Press, 1988), 117, 168–169. I believe there are deeper psychological implications of male castration which are not yet adequately explored. For example, is Christian castration a form of despair masquerading as discipline? Is it a early form of mental illness like the forms of self-mutilation we know today, where a patient will bang her head against a wall repeatedly, creating a controlled external pain which distracts from the uncontrollable internal psychiatric pain? Unfortunately, the subject of voluntary castration in Christian tradition is little written-about; one of the few texts is Peter Browe, *Zur Geschichte der Entmannung: Eine religions- und rechtsgeschichtliche Studie* (Breslau: Muller, 1936).

20. Michael Kimmel, "Consuming Manhood: The Feminization of American Culture and the Recreation of the Male Body, 1832–1920," in Goldstein, 12–41.

21. In Jim Thompson's novel *The Nothing Man*, protagonist Clint Brown returns from World War II having had his genitals blown off by a landmine. He describes himself as having "given his penis for his country" (New York: Mysterious Press, [1954], 1988, 3).

22. *The Hite Report on Male Sexuality* (1981) concluded that sexual intercourse for men was satisfying not only because of their attraction to their sexual partner "but also from the deeply ingraved cultural meaning of the act. Through intercourse a man participates in the cultural symbolism of patriarchy and gains a sense of belonging to society with status/identity of 'male'." See Marianne Walters, Betty Carter, Peggy Papp, and Olga Silverstein, *The Invisible Web: Gender Patterns in Family Relationships* (New York: Guilford, 1988), 215.

23. Danna Nolan Fewell and David Gunn, "Shifting the Blame: God in the Garden," in Beal and Gunn, eds., 16-33.

24. Howard Eilberg-Schwartz, "The Problem of the Body for the People of the Book," in Beal and Gunn, eds., 34–55; see also his *God's Phallus, and other problems for men and monotheism* (Boston: Beacon, 1994).

25. Eilberg-Schwartz, "The Problem....," 47.

■ *Philip Culbertson is Director of Pastoral Studies at St. John the Evangelist in Auckland, New Zealand. The author of several books exploring theology and masculinity, Culbertson combines the two in this article.*

MAKING SURE OF THE TEXT

1. Culbertson offers several reasons why men seem to find it "so difficult [. . .] to direct their heterosexual gaze" at anyone other than women. Summarize each of these reasons.
2. Can you think of examples to support Culbertson's suggestion that people tend to avoid reading texts that "threaten their comfortability or security"? What "texts" do you instinctively back away from?
3. What patterns of development does Culbertson use to support his claims?
4. What is meant by "homosociality," and how is it distinct from "homosexuality"?

CONSIDERING THE CONTEXT

1. This essay was published in an online journal whose contributors are mainly theologians. What assumptions do you have about what interests rabbis and priests? Does the subject matter seem out of context?
2. Why is it important whether God has gender? What religious context do you bring to this question, and how might it contribute to your reading?
3. Culbertson spends progressively more time on each of his explanations of the male reluctance to look at other men. What effect does this sequence have for you?
4. Culbertson's final question seems to be answered in Lopate's essay. How would you characterize that answer?

■ ■ ■

"Open Letter to the Editors of *Ms.*," from *Perfect Sound Forever* (1998)

Ani DiFranco

An open letter from Ani Difranco to the editors of *Ms.* . . . So I'm poring through the 25th anniversary issue of *Ms.* (on some airplane going somewhere in the amorphous blur that amounts to my life) and I'm finding it endlessly enlightening and stimulating as always, when, whaddaya know, I come across a little picture of little me. I was flattered to be included in that issue's "21 feminists for the 21st century" thingybob. I think ya'll are runnin the most bold and babe-olishious magazine around, after all.

Problem is, I couldn't help but be a little weirded out by the paragraph next to my head that summed up her me-ness and my relationship to the feminist continuum. What got me was that it largely detailed my financial successes and sales statistics. My achievements were represented by the fact that I "make more money per album sold than Hootie and the Blowfish," and that my catalogue sales exceed ¾ of a million. It was specified that I don't just have my own record company but my own "profitable" record company. Still, the ironic conclusion of the aforementioned blurb is a quote from me insisting "it's not about the money." Why then, I ask myself, must "the money" be the focus of so much of the media that surrounds me? Why can't I escape it, even in the hallowed pages of *Ms.*?

Firstly, this "Hootie and the Blowfish" business was not my doing. The *LA Times* financial section wrote an article about my record label, Righteous Babe Records, in which they raved about the business savvy of a singer (me) who thwarted the corporate overhead by choosing to remain independent thereby pocketing $4.25 per unit, as opposed to the $1.25 made by Hootie or the $2.00 made by Michael Jackson. This story was then picked up and reprinted by *The New York Times, Forbes,* the Financial News Network, and (lo and behold) *Ms.*

So here I am, publicly morphing into some kinda Fortune 500-young-entrepreneur-from-hell, and all along I thought I was just a folksinger!

OK, it's true. I do make a much larger profit (percentage-wise) than the Hootster. What's even more astounding is that there are thousands of musicians out there who make an even higher profit percentage than me! How many local musicians are there in your community who play gigs in bars and coffee shops about town? I bet lots of them have made cassettes or CDs which they'll happily sell to you with a personal smile from the edge of the stage or back at the bar after their set. Would you believe these shrewd, profit-minded wheeler-dealers are pocketing a whopping 100% of the profits on the sales of those puppies?! Wait till the Financial News Network gets a whiff of them!

I sell approximately 2.5% of the albums that a Joan Jewelanis Morrisette sells and get about .05% of the airplay royalties, so obviously if it all comes down to dollars and cents, I've led a wholly unremarkable life. Yet I choose relative statistical mediocrity over fame and fortune because I have a bigger purpose in mind. Imagine how strange it must be for a girl who has spent 10 years fighting as hard as she could against the lure of the corporate carrot and the almighty forces of capital, only to be eventually recognized by the power structure as a business pioneer.

I have indeed sold enough records to open a small office on the half-abandoned main street in the dilapidated urban center of my hometown, Buffalo. I am able to hire 15 or so folks to run and constantly reinvent the place while I drive around and play music for people. I am able to give stimulating business to local printers and manufacturers and to employ the services of independent distributors, promoters, booking agents and publicists. I was able to quit my day job and devote myself to what I love. And yes, we are enjoying modest profits these days, affording us the opportunity to reinvest in innumerable political and artistic endeavors. RBR is no Warner Bros. But it is a going concern, and for me, it is a vehicle for redefining the relationship between art and commerce in my own life. It is a record company which is the product not just of my own imagination, but that of my friend and manager Scott Fisher and of all the people who work there. People who incorporate and coordinate politics, art and media every day into a people-friendly, sub-corporate, woman-informed, queer-happy small business that puts music before rock stardom and ideology before profit.

And me, I'm just a folksinger, not an entrepreneur. My hope is that my music and poetry will be enjoyable and/or meaningful to someone, somewhere, not that I maximize my profit margins. It was 15 years and 11 albums getting to this place of notoriety and, if anything, I think I was happier way back when. Not that I regret any of my decisions, mind you. I'm glad I didn't sign on to the corporate army. I mourn the commodification and homogenization of music by the music industry, and I fear the manufacture of consent by the corporately-controlled media. Last thing I want to do is feed the machine.

I was recently mortified while waiting in the dressing room before one of my own shows. Some putz suddenly takes the stage to announce me and exclaim excitedly that this was my "largest sold-out crowd to date!" "Oh, really?," I'm thinking to myself, "that's interesting . . . too bad it's not the point." All of my achievements are artistic, as are all of my failures. That's just the way I see it. Statistical plateau or no. I'll bust ass for 60 people, or 6,000, watch me.

I have so much respect for *Ms. Magazine*. If I couldn't pick it up at newsstands my brain probably would've atrophied by now on some trans-Atlantic flight and I would be lying limp and twitchy in a bed of constant travel, staring blankly into the abyss of the gossip magazines. *Ms.* is a structure of media wherein women are able to define themselves, and articulate for themselves those definitions. We wouldn't point to 21 of the feminists moving into the 21st century and define them in terms of "Here's Becky Ballbuster from Iowa City, she's got a great ass and a cute little button nose . . ." No ma'am. We've gone beyond the limited perceptions of sexism and so we should move beyond the language and perspective of the corporate patriarchy. The Financial News Network may be ultimately impressed with me now that I've proven to them that there's a life beyond the auspices of papa Sony, but do I really have to prove this to you?

We have the ability and the opportunity to recognize women not just for the financial successes of their work but for the work itself. We have the facility to judge each other by entirely different criteria than those imposed upon us by the superstructure of society. We have a view which reaches beyond profit margins into poetry, and a vocabulary to articulate the difference.

Thanks for including me, *Ms.*, really. But just promise me one thing; if I drop dead tomorrow, tell me my grave stone won't read: "ani d., CEO."

Please let it read: songwriter, musicmaker, storyteller, freak.

■ *Ani DiFranco, noted (and financially successful) folk singer and self-identified "freak," started performing professionally when she was 15. She began her own record label, Righteous Babe Records, so that she would be able to control her music. This letter to* Ms. *appeared in January 1998.*

MAKING SURE OF THE TEXT

1. What seems to have prompted DiFranco's letter to *Ms.*?
2. DiFranco lists her primary "who I am" traits at the close of the letter: "songwriter, musicmaker, storyteller, freak." She is quite explicit earlier in the letter that she is "just a folksinger, not an entrepreneur." How does her own self-perception vary from *Ms.* magazine's perception of her?
3. Do the math DiFranco describes: how much money is she referring to? How does that make a difference in her reaction to *Ms.'s* feature article?
4. What sort of context does DiFranco see herself being placed in by her inclusion in *Ms.*? Read how she describes the magazine and how she describes herself.

CONSIDERING THE CONTEXT

1. DiFranco incorporates a subtext about her art and the "commodification and homogenization of music." How would you describe the relationship between "art and commerce"? You might draw on Theis, Chapter 1, to help you.
2. What effect does DiFranco achieve when she describes *Ms.* as "the most bold and babe-olicious magazine around"? How does this support or refute her reference to *Ms.* as "hallowed"?
3. What sort of criteria does DiFranco seem to have in mind when she suggests that "we have the facility to judge each other by entirely different criteria than those imposed upon us by the superstructure of society"?

Photo Essay: Dolls and Other Human Representations

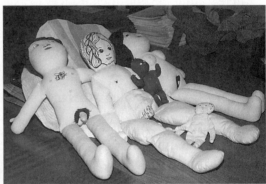

MAKING SURE OF THE TEXT

1. In what ways are these representations employed? See if you can identify a primary function for each.
2. What kinds of self-perceptions are represented here? For example, what dolls depict "humor" or "future roles"?
3. What reading can you apply to the bodies and the clothing of these dolls? How might they affect our perceptions of ourselves?

CONSIDERING THE CONTEXT

1. What dolls would you add to this collection of "self-perceptions"? Why?
2. These images are recontextualized by appearing in this book. What other contexts might the collection appear in?
3. Contrast "real" depictions of sexuality with "idealized" or "representational" depictions. What do you notice about your own perspectives?

■ ■ ■

"The Female Body" *Michigan Quarterly Review* (1990)

Margaret Atwood

'. . . entirely devoted to the subject of "The Female Body." Knowing how well you have written on this topic . . . this capacious topic . . .'
—LETTER FROM THE *MICHIGAN QUARTERLY REVIEW*

1.

I agree, it's a hot topic. But only one? Look around, there's a wide range. Take my own, for instance.

I get up in the morning. My topic feels like hell. I sprinkle it with water, brush parts of it, rub it with towels, powder it, add lubricant. I dump in the fuel and away goes my topic, my topical topic, my controversial topic, my capacious topic, my limping topic, my nearsighted topic, my topic with back problems, my badly behaved topic, my vulgar topic, my outrageous topic, my ageing topic, my topic that is out of the question and anyway still can't spell, in its oversized coat and worn winter boots, scuttling along the sidewalk as if it were flesh and blood, hunting for what's out there, an avocado, an alderman, an adjective, hungry as ever.

2.

The basic Female Body comes with the following accessories: garter-belt, panty-girdle, crinoline, camisole, bustle, brassiere, stomacher, chemise, virgin zone, spike heels, nose-ring, veil, kid gloves, fishnet stockings, fichu, bandeau, Merry Widow, weepers, chokers, barrettes, bangles, beads, lorgnette, feather boa, basic black, compact, Lycra stretch one-piece with modesty panel, designer peignoir, flannel nightie, lace teddy, bed, head.

3.

The Female Body is made of transparent plastic and lights up when you plug it in. You press a button to illuminate the different systems. The Circulatory System is red, for the heart and arteries, purple for the veins; the Respiratory System is blue, the Lymphatic System is yellow, the Digestive System is green, with liver and kidneys in aqua. The nerves are done in orange and the brain is pink. The skeleton, as you might expect, is white.

The Reproductive System is optional, and can be removed. It comes with or without a miniature embryo. Parental judgement can thereby be exercised. We do not wish to frighten or offend.

4.

He said, I won't have one of those things in the house. It gives a young girl a false notion of beauty, not to mention anatomy. If a real woman was built like that she'd fall on her face.

She said, If we don't let her have one like all the other girls she'll feel singled out. It'll become an issue. She'll long for one and she'll long to turn into one. Repression breeds sublimation. You know that.

He said, It's not just the pointy plastic tits, it's the wardrobes. The wardrobes and that stupid male doll, what's his name, the one with the underwear glued on.

She said, Better to get it over with when she's young. He said, All right but don't let me see it.

She came whizzing down the stairs, thrown like a dart. She was stark naked. Her hair had been chopped off, her head was turned back to front, she was missing some toes and she'd been tattooed all over her body with purple ink, in a scroll-work design. She hit the potted azalea, trembled there for a moment like a botched angel, and fell.

He said, I guess we're safe.

5.

The Female Body has many uses. It's been used as a door-knocker, a bottle-opener, as a clock with a ticking belly, as something to hold up lampshades, as a nutcracker, just squeeze the brass legs together and out comes your nut. It bears torches, lifts victorious wreaths, grows copper wings and raises aloft a ring of neon stars; whole buildings rest on its marble heads.

It sells cars, beer, shaving lotion, cigarettes, hard liquor; it sells diet plans and diamonds, and desire in tiny crystal bottles. Is this the face that launched a thousand products? You bet it is, but don't get any funny big ideas, honey, that smile is a dime a dozen.

It does not merely sell, it is sold. Money flows into this country or that country, flies in, practically crawls in, suitful after suitful, lured by all those hairless pre-teen legs. Listen, you want to reduce the national debt, don't you? Aren't you patriotic? That's the spirit. That's my girl.

She's a natural resource, a renewable one luckily, because those things wear out so quickly. They don't make 'em like they used to. Shoddy goods.

6.

One and one equals another one. Pleasure in the female is not a requirement. Pair-bonding is stronger in geese. We're not talking about love, we're talking about biology. That's how we all got here, daughter.

Snails do it differently. They're hermaphrodites, and work in threes.

7.

Each female body contains a female brain. Handy. Makes things work. Stick pins in it and you get amazing results. Old popular songs. Short circuits. Bad dreams.

Anyway: each of these brains has two halves. They're joined together by a thick cord; neural pathways flow from one to the other, sparkles of electric information washing to and fro. Like light on waves. Like a conversation. How does a woman know? She listens. She listens in.

The male brain, now, that's a different matter. Only a thin connection. Space over here, time over there, music and arithmetic in their own sealed compartments. The right brain doesn't know what the left brain is doing. Good for aiming though, for hitting the target when you pull the trigger. What's the target? Who's the target? Who cares? What matters is hitting it. That's the male brain for you. Objective.

This is why men are so sad, why they feel so cut off, why they think of themselves as orphans cast adrift, footloose and stringless in the deep void. What void? she says. What are you talking about? The void of the Universe, he says, and she says Oh and looks out the window and tries to get a handle on it, but it's no use, there's too much going on, too many rustlings in the leaves, too many voices, so she says, Would you like a cheese sandwich, a piece of cake, a cup of tea? And he grinds his teeth because she doesn't understand, and wanders off, not just alone but Alone, lost in the dark, lost in the skull, searching for the other half, the twin who could complete him.

Then it comes to him: he's lost the Female Body! Look, it shines in the gloom, far ahead, a vision of wholeness, ripeness, like a giant melon, like an apple, like a metaphor for breast in a bad sex novel; it shines like a balloon, like a foggy noon, a watery moon, shimmering in its egg of light.

Catch it. Put it in a pumpkin, in a high tower, in a compound, in a chamber, in a house, in a room. Quick, stick a leash on it, a lock, a chain, some pain, settle it down, so it can never get away from you again.

■ *Highly regarded Canadian novelist Margaret Atwood has published dozens of articles and poems, in addition to several highly praised novels. A feminist author, Atwood writes primarily about the stories of women in the present, past, and possible future.*

MAKING SURE OF THE TEXT

1. Whose voices does Atwood include to help make her points? How are those voices related to the female body?
2. What are the differences, in this reading, between the female brain and the male brain?
3. What can you add to this reading? Can you identify other contexts in which you've seen or placed the female body?

CONSIDERING THE CONTEXT

1. Atwood places the female body in multiple different contexts in this reading, without expressly identifying any of them. For instance, the second section describes "accessories" as if a female body were sold like a doll in a toy store. Can you identify the other contexts Atwood writes from?

2. What structural changes govern Atwood's use of numbered sections? What pattern is being set up for the reader?
3. Atwood uses many food metaphors to describe the female body—apples, melons, eggs, pumpkins. What effect does this have on the reader? What is the intended effect?

■ ■ ■

"Men, Women See Themselves Differently,"
The Miami Herald (1998)

Dave Barry

If you're a man, at some point a woman will ask you how she looks.

"How do I look?" she'll ask.

You must be careful how you answer this question. The best technique is to form an honest yet sensitive opinion, then collapse on the floor with some kind of fatal seizure. Trust me, this is the easiest way out. Because you will never come up with the right answer.

The problem is that women generally do not think of their looks in the same way that men do. Most men form an opinion of how they look in seventh grade, and they stick to it for the rest of their lives. Some men form the opinion that they are irresistible stud muffins, and they do not change this opinion even when their faces sag and their noses bloat to the size of eggplants and their eyebrows grow together to form what appears to be a giant forehead-dwelling tropical caterpillar.

Most men, I believe, think of themselves as average-looking. Men will think this even if their faces cause heart failure in cattle at a range of 300 yards. Being average does not bother them: average is fine, for men. This is why men never ask anybody how they look. Their primary form of beauty care is to shave themselves, which is essentially the same form of beauty care that they give to their lawns. If, at the end of his four-minute daily beauty regimen, a man has managed to wipe most of the shaving cream out of his hair and is not bleeding too badly, he feels that he has done all he can, so he stops thinking about his appearance and devotes his mind to more critical issues, such as the Super Bowl.

Women do not look at themselves this way. If I had to express, in three words, what I believe most women think about their appearance, those words would be: "not good enough." No matter how attractive a woman may appear to be to others, when she looks at herself in the mirror, she thinks *woof.* She thinks that at any moment a municipal animal-control officer is going to throw a net over her and haul her off to the shelter.

Why do women have such low self-esteem? There are many complex psychological and societal reasons, by which I mean Barbie. Girls grow up playing with a doll proportioned such that, if it were a human, it would be seven feet tall and weigh 81 pounds, of which 53 pounds would be bosoms. This is a difficult appearance standard to live up to, especially when you contrast it with the standard set for little boys by their dolls . . . excuse me, by their action figures. Most of the action figures that my son played with when he was little were hideous-looking. For example, he was very fond of an action figure (part of the He-Man series) called "Buzz-Off," who was part human, part flying insect. Buzz-Off was not a looker. But he was extremely self-confident. You could not imagine Buzz-Off saying to the other action figures: "Do you think these wings make my hips look big?"

But women grow up thinking they need to look like Barbie, which for most women is impossible, although there is a multibillion-dollar beauty industry devoted to convincing women that they must try. I once saw an *Oprah* show wherein supermodel Cindy Crawford dispensed makeup tips to the studio audience. Cindy had all these middle-aged women applying beauty products to their faces; she stressed how important it was to apply them in a certain way, using the tips of their fingers. All the women dutifully did this, even though it was obvious to any sane observer that, no matter how carefully they applied these products, they would never look remotely like Cindy Crawford, who is some kind of genetic mutation.

I'm not saying that men are superior. I'm just saying that you're not going to get a group of middle-aged men to sit in a room and apply cosmetics to themselves under the instruction of Brad Pitt, in hopes of looking more like him. Men would realize that this task was pointless and demeaning. They would find some way to bolster their self-esteem that did not require looking like Brad Pitt. They would say to Brad: "Oh YEAH? Well what do you know about LAWN CARE, pretty boy?"

Of course many women will argue that the reason they become obsessed with trying to look like Cindy Crawford is that men, being as shallow as a drop of spit, WANT women to look that way. To which I have two responses:

1. Hey, just because WE'RE idiots, that doesn't mean YOU have to be; and
2. Men don't even notice 97 percent of the beauty efforts you make anyway. Take fingernails. The average woman spends 5,000 hours per year worrying about her fingernails; I have never once, in more than 40 years of listening to men talk about women, heard a man say, "She has a nice set of fingernails!" Many men would not notice if a woman had upward of four hands.

Anyway, to get back to my original point: If you're a man, and a woman asks you how she looks, you're in big trouble. Obviously, you can't say she looks bad. But you also can't say that she looks great, because she'll think you're lying, because she has spent countless hours, with the help of the multibillion-dollar beauty industry, obsessing about the differences between herself and Cindy Crawford. Also, she suspects that you're not qualified to judge anybody's appearance. This is because you have shaving cream in your hair.

■ *Dave Barry, Pulitzer Prize–winning columnist, lives in Miami. His column is syndicated in most of the country's newspapers, and he has won the Pulitzer Prize for "Distinguished Social Commentary" in a series of columns. He often writes about the interactions between men and women.*

MAKING SURE OF THE TEXT

1. In the guise of humor, Dave Barry suggests that men and women differ in their self-perceptions in some specific ways. What are they?
2. What roles do gender-specific toys have for Barry? What impact does Barbie or He-Man have, and how does it work?
3. Examine your own assumptions. If you're male, ask yourself whether, as Barry suggests, you "don't even notice 97 percent of the beauty efforts" made by women. If you're female, ask yourself if you really believe that "men, being as shallow as a drop of spit, want women to look" like Cindy Crawford.
4. Barry's column begins with a question: how a man can answer a woman who asks him how she looks. Barry also provides the entire social context within which his answer lies. Identify the elements of the context.

CONSIDERING THE CONTEXT

1. How does Barry avoid being considered sexist? How do his choices of examples, diction, and presentation contribute to his nonsexist stance?
2. How does the structure of Barry's column contribute to the effect? For instance, how do the introduction and conclusion echo each other?
3. Barry purposely employs a logical fallacy known as "begging the question" when he asks why women have such low self-esteem rather than questioning *if* they do. What is the effect? How does this help the reader move through the article?

■ ■ ■

"Lumbar Thought," from *Travels in Hyperreality* (1995)

Umberto Eco

A few weeks ago, Luca Goldoni wrote an amusing report from the Adriatic coast about the mishaps of those who wear blue jeans for reasons of fashion, and no longer know how to sit down or arrange the external reproductive apparatus. I believe the problem broached by Goldoni is rich in philosophical reflections, which I would like to pursue on my own and with the maximum seriousness, because no everyday experience is too base for the thinking man, and it is time to make philosophy proceed, not only on its own two feet, but also with its own loins.

I began wearing blue jeans in the days when very few people did, but always on vacation. I found—and still find—them very comfortable, especially when I travel, because there are no problems of creases, tearing, spots. Today they are worn also for looks, but primarily they are very utilitarian. It's only in the past few years that I've had to renounce this pleasure because I've put on weight. True, if you search thoroughly you can find an extra large (Macy's could fit even Oliver Hardy with blue jeans), but they are large not only around the waist, but also around the legs, and they are not a pretty sight.

Recently, cutting down on drink, I shed the number of pounds necessary for me to try again some *almost* normal jeans. I underwent the calvary described by Luca Goldoni, as the saleswoman said, "Pull it tight, it'll stretch a bit"; and I emerged, not having to suck in my belly (I refuse to accept such compromises). And so, after a long time, I was enjoying the sensation of wearing pants that, instead of clutching the waist, held the hips, because it is a characteristic of jeans to grip the lumbar-sacral region and stay up thanks not to suspension but to adherence.

After such a long time, the sensation was new. The jeans didn't pinch, but they made their presence felt. Elastic though they were, I sensed a kind of sheath around the lower half of my body. Even if I had wished, I couldn't turn or wiggle my belly *inside* my pants; if anything, I had to turn it or wiggle it *together with* my pants. Which subdivides so to speak one's body into two independent zones, one free of clothing, above the belt, and the other organically identified with the clothing, from immediately below the belt to the anklebones. I discovered that my movements, my way of walking, turning, sitting, hurrying, were *different*. Not more difficult, or less difficult, but certainly different.

As a result, I lived in the knowledge that I had jeans on, whereas normally we live forgetting that we're wearing undershorts or trousers. I lived for my jeans, and as a result I assumed the exterior behavior of one who wears jeans. In any case, I assumed a *demeanor*. It's strange that the traditionally most informal and anti-etiquette garment should be the one that so strongly imposes an etiquette. As a rule I am boisterous, I sprawl in

Luca Goldoni · Italian journalist.

a chair, I slump wherever I please, with no claim to elegance: my blue jeans checked these actions, made me more polite and mature. I discussed it at length, especially with consultants of the opposite sex, from whom I learned what, for that matter, I had already suspected: that for women experiences of this kind are familiar because all their garments are conceived to impose a demeanor—high heels, girdles, brassieres, pantyhose, tight sweaters.

I thought then about how much, in the history of civilization, dress as armor has influenced behavior and, in consequence, exterior morality. The Victorian bourgeois was stiff and formal because of stiff collars; the nineteenth-century gentleman was constrained by his tight redingotes, boots, and top hats that didn't allow brusque movements of the head. If Vienna had been on the equator and its bourgeoisie had gone around in Bermuda shorts, would Freud have described the same neurotic symptoms, the same Oedipal triangles? And would he have described them in the same way if he, the doctor, had been a Scot, in a kilt (under which, as everyone knows, the rule is to wear nothing)?

A garment that squeezes the testicles makes a man think differently. Women during menstruation; people suffering from orchitis, victims of hemorrhoids, urethritis, prostate and similar ailments know to what extent pressures or obstacles in the sacroiliac area influence one's mood and mental agility. But the same can be said (perhaps to a lesser degree) of the neck, the back, the head, the feet. A human race that has learned to move about in shoes has oriented its thought differently from the way it would have done if the race had gone barefoot. It is sad, especially for philosophers in the idealistic tradition, to think that the Spirit originates from these conditions; yet not only is this true, but the great thing is that Hegel knew it also, and therefore studied the cranial bumps indicated by phrenologists, and in a book actually entitled *Phenomenology of Mind*. But the problem of my jeans led me to other observations. Not only did the garment impose a demeanor on me; by focusing my attention on demeanor, it obliged me to *live towards the exterior world*. It reduced, in other words, the exercise of my interior-ness. For people in my profession it is normal to walk along with your mind on other things: the article you have to write, the lecture you must give, the relationship between the One and the Many, the Andreotti government, how to deal with the problem of the Redemption, whether there is life on Mars, the latest song of Celentano, the paradox of Epimenides. In our line this is called "the interior life." Well, with my new jeans my life was

Hegel • German metaphysician interested in the workings of the mind.

Andreotti • Giulio Andreotti, Italian statesman, held the position of Premier three separate times before being tried for corruption. Cleared of the charges in 1999.

Celentano • Adriano Celentano, popular Italian Singer of pop, rock, and rap.

Epimenides • Cretan prophet. The paradox refers to Epimenides' claim that he was lying. If he was lying when he said he was lying, then he would be telling the truth. If he were telling the truth, of course, then he couldn't be lying.

entirely exterior: I thought about the relationship between me and my pants, and the relationship between my pants and me and the society we lived in. I had achieved heteroconsciousness, that is to say, an epidemic self-awareness.

I realized then that thinkers, over the centuries, have fought to free themselves of armor. Warriors lived an exterior life, all enclosed in cuirasses and tunics; but monks had invented a habit that, while fulfilling, *on its own,* the requirements of demeanor (majestic, flowing, all of a piece, so that it fell in statuesque folds), it left the body (inside, underneath) completely free and unaware of itself. Monks were rich in interior life and very dirty, because the body, protected by a habit that, ennobling it, released it, was free to think, and to forget about itself. The idea was not only ecclesiastic; you have to think only of the beautiful mantles Erasmus wore. And when even the intellectual must dress in lay armor (wigs, waistcoats, knee breeches) we see that when he retires to think, he swaggers in rich dressing-gowns, or in Balzac's loose, *drôlatique* blouses. Thought abhors tights.

But if armor obliges its wearer to live the exterior life, then the age-old female spell is due also to the fact that society has imposed armors on women, forcing them to neglect the exercise of thought. Woman has been enslaved by fashion not only because, in obliging her to be attractive, to maintain an ethereal demeanor, to be pretty and stimulating, it made her a sex object; she has been enslaved chiefly because the clothing counseled for her forced her psychologically to live for the exterior. And this makes us realize how intellectually gifted and heroic a girl had to be before she could become, in those clothes, Madame de Sévigné, Vittoria Colonna, Madame Curie, or Rosa Luxemburg. The reflection has some value because it leads us to discover that, apparent symbol of liberation and equality with men, the blue jeans that fashion today imposes on women are a trap of Domination; for they don't free the body, but subject it to another label and imprison it in other armors that don't seem to be armors because they apparently are not "feminine."

A final reflection—in imposing an exterior demeanor, clothes are semiotic devices, machines for communicating. This was known, but there had been no attempt to illustrate the parallel with the syntactic structures of language, which, in the opinion of many people, influence our view of the world. The syntactic structures of fashions also influence our view of the world, and in a far more physical way than the *consecutio temporum* or the existence of the subjunctive. You see how many mysterious paths the dialectic between oppression and liberation must follow, and the struggle to bring light.

Even via the groin.

Balzac · Honoré de Balzac, author.

Madame de Sevigne · 1626–1696, French woman of letters.

Vittoria Colonna · 1492–1547, Italian poet.

Rosa Luxemburg · 1871–1919, German revolutionary.

■ *Umberto Eco is an Italian-born philosopher and social critic. After a beginning in journalism, Eco became a professor of semiotics and has now earned honorary degrees from more than 25 countries. His development of semiotics contributes to his essay in this text.*

MAKING SURE OF THE TEXT

1. What has Eco discovered about clothes and the way he wears them?
2. Does Eco seem to you to wear jeans for fashion or comfort?
3. What other clothing contexts does Eco offer here? Where do his jeans fit in with those contexts?
4. Eco writes that "A garment that squeezes the testicles makes a man think differently." Can you offer a feminine parallel to this statement? Would a different hair cut have the same effect on someone? What about shoes?
5. What effect do the clothes you are wearing right this minute have on the way you walk or sit?

CONSIDERING THE CONTEXT

1. Part of the context Eco provides is historical: Victorian, Viennese, and so forth. What does this contribute to his discussion?
2. The discussion throughout this short essay hinges on the distinctions between interior and external life, suggesting that clothing helps one to achieve one or the other. How is the metaphor of interior and external carried through the essay? In other words, can you identify compositional elements that could be related to interior and external?
3. What is the effect of the short, single-sentence paragraph at the conclusion? How does it contribute to the tone of the essay?

■ ■ ■

The Man in the Mirror (Student Response Essay, 2000)

Michael Gilkes

For young men of many cultures around the world, becoming a man is a matter of passing a test, a rite of passage into manhood that certifies and proclaims their metamorphosis from boyhood to manhood. For me, it has been more like a journey, a quest for the secret of manhood. This quest has forced me to engage in self-evaluation in which I have questioned and explored those things that have defined me as a person. The question then is, "When I look in the mirror, who and/or what do I see? Do I see a man because it is what I am or what I think I am?" In his article, "Designing Men: Reading the Male Body as Text," Philip Culbertson discusses how the perception of a man's body defines and maintains what it means to be a man. Culbertson's article expands on some of the issues that I face as a man today.

Just a few weeks from my twentieth birthday, I have realized that there are many definitions of "a man." Even after someone believes he has become a man, his manhood can be challenged and then he must defend it. Why is this so? Does a man have to be a certain way, act a certain way, look a certain way? Our society seems to be confused and at the same time obsessed with defining what a man should be. This dilemma is directly related to Culbertson's argument. Culbertson, speaking about how the male body is read and interpreted, focuses on the point that men look at a woman's body differently than at that of a man. The "male gaze", as he calls it, "has the power not only to objectify, but to feminize." This becomes a problem for men when a man 'gazes' upon another man. Therefore the existence and persistence of homosexuality (even the less threatening "homosociality") threatens the very definition of what it means to be a man.

As children, we were socially molded to distinguish between a boy and a girl and also between a boy and a man. As a boy, I wanted so much to be a man. I wanted to be big, strong and fearless, like my father. I wanted to be respected and independent, and I wanted facial hair! In order to be a man, I realized that I had to be more like a boy and less like a girl. This involved not acting "like a girl" and not doing the same things that they did. This involved not liking other boys. Thus, from an early age I was a devout student of what Culbertson calls "Social Constructionism." "Social Constructionism creates each of us... by teaching us how to see; what to value; and how to respond once we have seen and valued" (Culbertson 1). In a recent discussion with one of my former English professors, the issue of same sex attraction came up. When this happens to boys at an early age, it can be very confusing because usually the attraction is unexpected. The boys do not understand why they are attracted to another boy when their teachings say that they should not. For most boys, involuntary same sex attraction threatens their goal to be a man because, in their social mindset, 'men don't gaze at other men'. Even in this example of young boys, it is clear that Culbertson's conclusion about the "male gaze" is true: it is threatening.

The onset of puberty brings on a whole new set of rules and perceptions about "manhood." In the section "Reading a Text Which Won't Focus," Culbertson says that "In a patriarchal system, the penis cues masculinity, and once that occurs, the body, "the being" disappears and the person becomes a function...The part overwhelms the whole, so that the whole fades into insignificance." In retrospect, this is exactly what happened to me at puberty. I started to get pubic hair, my penis grew and all of a sudden It became the issue. I got uncontrollable and sometimes embarrassing erections. I had nocturnal emissions that came with explicit, and again uncontrollable, dreams. Suddenly, how I dressed was an issue in that it did not look 'right' for my penis to bulge from my pants. Initially, for me this was really strange to say the least. The message that I was getting was that I was becoming a man and so had to act accordingly.

Along with these changes came the intense liking of girls, the training ground for the development of Culbertson's "male gaze." At this point I started to notice particular things about girls that I liked. Certain parts of their body attracted me. I began to "objectify" the female body. It gave the adolescent me a sense of becoming a man, but I knew that I was not a man yet. Even when I thought I was a man, my ego would be shot down by my parents, other adults, or even from girls who all reinforced that I was still a boy. In other words, who I was became a function of the new changes to my body. I felt more masculine and in charge, but my newfound freedom was extinguished when I realized that being a man was not just about my maturing body; at the same time, if you did not have these physical qualities, then you were not considered a man.

Being Christian brought another dimension into my quest for manhood. Being a man now seemed to include being honest, following God's will, and abstaining from sex before marriage. Compared to what most other young men my age believed, these attributes were not masculine, but ridiculous. In addition to that, most Christian churches teach that you should run from temptation. This includes temptations to lie, cheat, steal, engage in premarital sex, and be homosexual. So at that point in my life, although I liked girls and was around them all the time, I had to 'control' myself. My mind had now been conditioned by reason of my social and religious influences.

In the year 2000, I can say that I see myself as a man. This conclusion is not based solely on any on the above-mentioned reasons or because of any particular age or even because of some form of approval. Rather, for me it is based on the presence of not only physical maturity, but also mental and social maturity. I definitely have the ability to make wise decisions and stand up for what I believe it. In spite of what I believe to be my achievements as a man, I am still faced with the issues of sexual orientation and masculinity. Although I consider myself a man from my level of maturity, it still seems as though, as a man, I must address and continually defend my masculinity and sexual orientation.

Ironically enough, although these qualities did not make me a man, they seem to be what makes others, and paradoxically myself, think that I am still a man. Culbertson used the term "Reader Response" to describe what I mean. Reader response puts "as much of the responsibility for meaning-making upon the reader as upon the text itself." Inherently, the male body is analogous to a textless text, meaning that it is a book in and of itself. How the male body is viewed and perceived can either strangle or re-enforce what it is to be a man. More clearly, there are boundaries to my masculinity, which were set by establishing a socially constructed heterosexual orientation. Anything that threatens my orientation threatens my masculinity.

A half-naked man with a sleek toned body, ripped muscles, and glossy skin was looking straight at me singing in a sexual and sensual tone. I saw this in a music video a few months ago. For obvious reasons, I could not stand to watch it for more than thirty seconds. The musical artist was D'Angelo and the title of the music video was "Untitled." This music video alone embodies Philip Culbertson's essay. The title itself is a testament to the body being a textless text. D'Angelo's body was, truthfully, an excellent example of a strong (if I dare say), sexy, and masculine man. Despite this truth, I was turned off by the appearance of this sexually appealing body. D'Angelo's intent was to sexually appeal to women, to present the male body as having the potential to be exotic and erotic. The problem was how I saw it as a male. As Culbertson states, "reading affects the reader much more deeply then it affects the text." Keeping in mind that the male gaze has the power to feminize, the possibility that looking on D'Angelo's body might feminize it was a risk that I was not consciously willing to take. As Culbertson put it: "patriarchy is built upon the assumption that a male body is a text which will reject all attempts by other men to read it. To accept such an attempt would be to destroy the basis of power and control."

Another example that relates to what Culbertson states involves my relationship to my fellow man. Unless it is my father or brothers, I would not hug any man in a loving, careful way. Any time a male apart from my family hugs me that way, I feel uncomfortable. If a male gets too close in terms of touch and expression, I feel uncomfortable. This, I agree, is a fear of getting close to other men, and a means of keeping the power of "manhood" sacred. This form of fear appears to maintain the strength of a patriarchal society. As Culbertson points out, a man does not want to receive the gaze of another male for then he will become the "passive receptacle of their sexuality, and thus [be] 'woman.'" "Men's fear of the male gaze, ultimately, is the fear of becoming, feeling, or representing female desire within the phallocentric order."

Unlike a rite of passage, my journey to manhood was long but worthwhile. Being a man in this century presents new challenges. As the definition and boundaries of who and what a man is considered change, each man must therefore defend what his rite to manhood is and represents. Nevertheless, to maintain the power and control of men in our patriarchal society it is imperative for each man's perspective on being a man to reflect one main idea. Isn't it?

■ Ideas for Writing ■

Journal

1. Have you ever felt an "objectifying gaze" from someone else? That is, have you ever felt as though someone was looking at you as a thing rather than as a person? What was that experience like?
2. What are you wearing today? How does your clothing affect your sense of yourself?
3. Think back to the toys and dolls you played with as a child. Did they help to form your perceptions of your body and/or your sexuality? How?

Response

1. DiFranco's *Open Letter to Ms.* refers to some of the same issues that Ryan Theis brings up in his article in Chapter 1. Do you think DiFranco would agree or disagree with Theis?
2. What relationships do you see between Lopate's and Culbertson's articles in this chapter and Graham Ward's in Chapter 3?
3. Culbertson's discussion of the "divine ambiguity" of the male body could stir up a heated reaction from a reader. Drawing from your reading of the selections in Chapter 4, what is your reaction to the idea of modeling the human body after a divine figure?

Analysis

1. Eco's article describes the impact his jeans have on how he feels "masculine," whereas Culbertson points out that the male body "seems to disappear altogether when a man is unclothed." Do these points of view seem contradictory to you? Analyze the different contexts from which each author presents his perspective.
2. Drawing on Chapter 1's emphasis on music and Chapter 3's on image, develop a perspective on your own body's text as it has resulted from these two influences. Model the analysis after Lopate, if you wish.
3. Contrast the dolls in the photo essay with other popular toys: the X Men, Transformers, the Cabbage Patch Kids, Pokémon, and so forth. Read the text of these toys for their function in American culture.
4. Choose one of the readings in this section to read closely. As you read, consider these points: What is the author's position? What are the author's qualifications for writing about this subject? How does the author signal transitions in ideas? From these questions, develop an analysis of one of the following: the author's perspective on the issue; the way the author has structured the article for the reader; who the intended audience is for the reading.

Argument

1. Culbertson suggests that the American government and the military have a specific interest in maintaining a certain masculine stance. Would you agree or disagree with his reading of the artifacts? What alternative artifacts can you identify?

2. Robert Knight's article from Chapter 1 suggests that sexuality—specifically male sexuality—is susceptible to the evils of rock music. What would Knight, or another conservative author of your choice, say about female sexuality?
3. Our self-perceptions are usually based on genetic reality. For instance, we might be able to alter our hair or eye color, but we can't alter our genetic predisposition to dwarfism or obesity. What might genetic engineering do to our self-perceptions? Read Ralph Brave's article in Chapter 5 to help you.
4. Ani DiFranco's letter to *Ms.* magazine might be considered ungracious, a feminist rant, or completely appropriate. Take a position on this question and support your perspective with material from DiFranco's letter and past issues of *Ms.* magazine.

Research
1. Religions and spiritual practices differ in their attitudes toward sexuality. Christianity, for example, treats sex much differently than does the Craft. Research the perspectives of at least two or three different religions on sexual practices. How does each religion contextualize sexuality?
2. Poll your classmates, teachers, and friends about what influences they've felt as they've grown up; how do they characterize their own development as human beings?
3. Research the clothing customs of other cultures, for example European or African. What do you learn about how others wear their hair or other body ornaments? Can you apply Burns's idea of recontextualizing to, for instance, how some cultures practice piercing or remove body hair?

CHAPTER 3

MORE THAN MEETS THE EYE: PERSPECTIVES ON POPULAR IMAGES

Blink and you'll miss it.
            —CLICHÉ ABOUT SMALL TOWNS

People who watch the long-running Fox animated series *The Simpsons* are often treated to a surprise when they record an episode and then replay it

frame by frame. You probably know that when baby Maggie is accidentally checked out at the supermarket in the opening credits, her "price" flashes too quickly for you to see, but you may not know that Maggie's "scan" price often reads "TILT." The producers of *The Simpsons* weave subtle bonus jokes into every episode, but viewers can't see them unless they record the episode and then play it back: the funny frame is buried in a string of images that go by too quickly to register. And in fact, each episode is designed so that you *must* dig for meaning if you want to find it. The jokes are there but hidden beneath the surface, and you have to be looking from the right perspective to see more than meets the eye.

Why is Bart aiming his slingshot at the viewer?

129

Images, these days, are worth more than a thousand words, if they were ever worth only that. Because they move so swiftly, because they represent so much, and because they are ubiquitous, images are perhaps the single most accessible element of pop culture—and the element most debated. A thousand years from now, anthropologists poring over image archives from the late twentieth and early twenty-first centuries for some understanding of our culture will have their work cut out for them. Imagine what they might find in a pop cultural cross section of photos, film, and video clips.

- Michael Jordan, wearing a suit instead of a uniform
- *Jerry Springer* audience member
- *the Starship Enterprise* hanging in the Smithsonian
- a *Matrix* movie poster
- a black robe and fright mask from *Scream* as a Halloween costume

Each of these images represents something specific about our current culture—our attitudes, our beliefs, our preferences, and our dislikes. In fact, while each image is an artifact in itself, the collection of images is another artifact, and we are all part of the culture that created it. If we read the images properly, therefore, they tell us a lot about ourselves. Imagine anthropologists in the future, studying these artifacts. What would they need to know to understand the images?

Anthropologists probably wouldn't start out knowing that the silver ship suspended on wires from the Smithsonian's ceiling had a Russian in a command position (during the height of American paranoia about the Soviet Union); they certainly wouldn't know that the black robe and fright mask were vital to not one but three enormously successful slasher films. Without the context we have by virtue of being surrounded by the culture that produces these images, the anthropologists would have to reconstruct the culture carefully. We have to do the same thing when we examine the image in pop culture; when we aren't instinctively aware of the contexts and meanings, we need some way to figure out the ways to reconstruct.

Images can be read two ways, as Ellen Seiter's "Semiotics, Structuralism, and Television" points out. We can look at images as a representation of something else or we can put those representations in a structure that provides meaning. Any image isn't actually the thing it's an image of; it's a *representation* of that thing. Similarly, a frown on someone's face represents, or stands for, unhappiness or anger. But signs like frowns are meaningless until we put them into a context, a system of related things, which gives us a way to look at them and find meaning in them.

In other words, reading the signs lets us understand that there really is more than meets the eye. The photo of the teen queen on the cover of *Details* is only one artifact, but when we put it in context with a system of similar images of the female body, and we see that many, many magazines' cover photos are of young and attractive women, that single artifact begins to suggest the others; as an indexical sign, it's taking on meaning from what's

What cultures produce these artifacts?

Writing About Images

Let's take a single example. Under the right lights, with the right makeup and the right photographer, an awkward, lanky 12-year-old girl suddenly appears to be a poised and beautiful 20-year-old Cover Girl. If, as a student writer, you examined several of the images of these women further, you might see a definite tendency toward the very slim, the very blonde, the very young; you might argue that this is how the image of "beauty" comes to suggest young, blonde, and slim. This image of beauty is reinforced for us on billboards and in commercials—to say nothing of television programs—and each of these images would be additional evidence in your essay about the artifacts of beauty. If you read these images as an indicator of our interest in beauty, you might argue that Americans tend to prioritize youth and beauty; the billboards and commercials and television shows would all be individual artifacts of our cultural belief in this beauty mystique.

This text—beauty—is one thing on the surface and something different underneath, as a writer might explain. If a writer looked at enough of the images, and then enough of the culture that produced them, the essay might reveal a causal connection between these images and the thousands of young women convinced, perhaps subliminally, that they aren't beautiful, that they're too fat or have the wrong color hair. The essay might observe that we see otherwise healthy teens starving themselves to be "beautiful," which means "thin." In this way, beautiful becomes one of the signs of thin, just as smoke becomes one of the signs of fire.

Once the writer took apart the image and explained how it works to summon other images, readers would be able to look at a photograph of *Ally McBeal*'s Calista Flockhart and see not a successful, somewhat flighty lawyer but another in a long television lineup of painfully thin blondes, perhaps reinforcing the stereotype of blonde beauty and perhaps contributing to yet another teenage girl going on an unnecessary diet. (Or, from another perspective, a writer might look at Ally McBeal herself and reveal to a reader that female lawyers are so commonplace now that they need not be held up as role models for behavior.)

around it. Seiter's analytical process, *semiotics* and *structuralism*, gives us a way to study the image that many cultural scientists use when studying the world around them.

The photos of models and young beauties are artifacts of several industries, including fashion, which would crash without the clotheshorse models on the runways; advertising, whose commercials so often focus on the beautiful; and cosmetics, without which the illusion of perfection would be destroyed. Photos of models and other young beauties are also artifacts of desirability for young women and drag queens, who duplicate the waxed eyebrows of one model and the collagen-injected lips of another. The images are also artifacts of our reverence for youth, our desire to attain the unattainable, the association of beauty

Our future anthropologists, discovering in the image archives hundreds of magazine cover images of made-up, stylized female faces, thin figures, and perfect hair (and comparatively few images of men, no matter how they look), might conclude that American culture in this age idealizes the youthful allure of the female body. They might not be too far wrong. What other images can you identify whose prevalence suggests something about the way we live?

Why do TV lawyers look different from real-life lawyers?

with popularity and success, and our love of buying clothes (and in fact, buying nearly anything).

Would the anthropologists studying our culture get all this from one perfectly made-up face on one perfect, young, sexy body on the cover of *Cosmopolitan* or *Maxim*? Perhaps not, but we can, if we read the texts carefully. We have an advantage they don't: we *live* in this culture. We have inside information. We already know the contexts and the connections. We just need to learn to see more than first meets the eye.

What should we make of a poster from *The Matrix*, showing a body closely encased all in black leather except where it reveals the pale, hairless skin of a young hero? We, the audience, know this is the body of a hero, because we know the role Keanu Reeves plays in the film. People studying our culture, though, might not see "heroic"—not when so many other representations of the heroic figure include the bulging biceps, the strong jaw, and the well-muscled torso of, say, Arnold Schwarzenegger or Jean Claude van Damme. (Heroic figures wearing black are also in contrast to the traditional white garb.) We can identify the contrast between muscled brawn and pale leanness as significant because when a traditional expectation changes, it means something. If we know enough to identify the tradition that's changing, we can tell that the image of "the heroic male" seems to be evolving from the muscle guy to the intelligent guy. In his article, Graham Ward has his own ideas about why that image is gradually shifting; as the cultural scientist, you'll have ideas of your own, once you look around and see how the signs of the "heroic male" are represented. This might be another good paper topic: What are the signs of "heroism"? What does it look like, who embodies it, and what can we say about the contexts in which heroism's artifacts appear?

What would someone studying the images of our popular culture make of the persistent images of

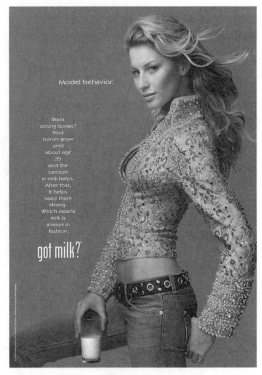

Is the connection between healthy eating and beauty recent or well-established?

How is heroism constructed from average bodies?

young men and women, often white and usually middle or lower class, chastising people on a stage while being encouraged by an emcee? We'd know the signs—this is a talk show, which encourages people to confront and surprise each other, telling hidden truths about shocking conduct in the guise of "truth" and "honesty." The shows mimic therapy by asking people to share their feelings, but when one young woman in an audience shouts her disgust to the people on stage, is it therapy or is it entertainment? From some perspectives, our cultural scientists might see a therapeutic parallel, but if we put these particular artifacts in context with, say, game shows, we see a different significance. In the same way, these indexical signs might suggest that Jerry Springer attempts to help people solve their problems or that he encourages mayhem. Drawing a connotative parallel between the signs of "therapy" and the signs of a degenerating culture of violence, Vickie Abt and Leonard Mustazza put the talk show into yet a third context, a provocative morality tale that reveals a lot about who we are to an onlooker.

An image of a bald, African-American male wearing a business suit and a big smile might also be an isolated image to an observer—until we ask what it represents. By itself, it might not represent much; perhaps the quickest, easiest analysis is that the man is an executive, which we know because executives dress like that. People who recognize Michael Jordan would associate that suit not just with business but with multimillion-dollar endorsement deals for batteries and hotdogs. Some people would also associate this image with the poignancy of a hand poised in the air as, for the last time, the basketball touched "nothing but net." While future social scientists might not have all that additional contextual information, our inside information tells us how to read that image: perhaps with satisfaction for one of the richest product endorsers, with sorrow for Jordan's retirement from basketball, with envy to "be like Mike," or a combination of all these.

When taken altogether by someone who's read the signs and the contexts, the image of Michael Jordan stands for a great deal more than "basketball player." As Nelson George reads the signs, Jordan represents the dynamic family man, the internationally worshipped sex symbol, and the casual guy who happens to wear Hanes. To thousands—perhaps millions—of kids, Jordan connotes the ultimate athlete; to George, Jordan evokes "the flip side of the crack dealers," the guy who offers "a welcome alternative to the you-know-what-I'm-sayin' syndrome." How you read Jordan depends on what you know about him and what artifacts you're looking at; if you've never watched him play basketball, you lack that first-hand understanding of his athleticism. If you've only seen him acting as the General Manager for the Washington Wizards or hawking hot dogs in the commercial limelight, you've gotten a much different idea of what Michael Jordan is all about. When George writes about Jordan, he considers the variety of images that together form a full Michael rather than focusing on just one facet; student writers can use this technique to their advantage because a single artifact rarely means only one thing.

An image of the Starship *Enterprise* hanging in the National Air and Space Museum might be anomalous by itself, for instance, but if we look around, we

Do the warp nacelles signify the freedom of flight?

learn that it isn't anomalous at all. It fits in context with advances in aerospace technology, for example with the first airplane, the *Hindenburg*, and the Mars *Rover*. By placing the ship into a different context—the history of ships named *Enterprise*—we get a different reading: the name *Enterprise* has been a tradition behind which generations of military men and women have been proud to stand. In this context, the Starship suggests that humanity will survive long enough to establish a tradition of space-going ships—and that one of them will inevitably be named for history. Astute observers, looking at other aerospace vehicles, will learn that NASA's first space shuttle was, by nearly unanimous vote, named *Enterprise*. Is this an artifact of the naval tradition of the name or of the tv series' popularity? What sort of indexical— or iconic—sign is this? The *Enterprise* is usually seen in the same context with aliens, humans, and racial tolerance. Our anthropologist observer might suggest—as one of the producers of *Star Trek* does—that the ship and the series stand for the American cultural ideal of "retaining your pride in your heritage" at the same time that "you're also supposed to live within the broader value system" (Greenwald 136). What other ways can you read the *Enterprise*? What does it stand for? If you put all the readings together and write about them, *Star Trek* might reveal itself to be a complex, multifaceted event in television history, one loaded and layered with meaning; and if you wrote about several of those layers, you might be able to identify more meanings than have been described here.

Examining the horror film genre reveals the same complexity. By now, most people reading this book probably recognize the black robe and fright mask from the *Scream* slasher trilogy, simply because we've seen the two together so often that we make an automatic association. It might not occur to us, though, to wonder why the horror film is so popular in the first place. There's apparently something compelling about watching young people get killed in gory ways. If you saw a dozen or so similar images of pretty girls being tortured, strung up, raped, or beaten, what would you make of it? Our anthropologists might think there was a systemic hatred of the young, beautiful girl because she is so often the victim of horrible crimes—on film at least, and perhaps in real life. Would we watch someone being murdered if we knew it was real? Clark McCauley poses this question in his article: Why do we watch violence with such gusto? The student writer in this section, drawing on McCauley's ideas, analyzes how she watches two violent films, *The Matrix* and *The Cube*, pointing out that knowing a film is fiction makes a big difference. The anthropologist might not be able to tell the difference between reality and fiction, but we have the advantage of living in this culture—we can draw out the meaning of the artifacts of violent images without having to guess.

And when we put all these images together—what then? What does the compound image of talk shows, starships, basketball players, and horror films tell us about ourselves? The images we find around us are literally our world—a world nearly every one of us shares—and realizing that there's much more going on behind the image than we might think is an ongoing process.

The point is that we are surrounded by the image. We can ignore it, or we can pay attention and learn from it. Sometimes the payoff is a funny line, but sometimes the payoff is a much more useful bit of intelligence about the way the world works, particularly the world of the image artifact, which is where we live. Unless you live in a plastic bubble, with absolutely no contact whatsoever with the world, you live in an image-filled world. How you read it (as pointless, overanalyzed, revealing, or shocking) is up to you.

"Semiotics, Structuralism, and Television," from *Channels of Discourse* (1996)

Ellen Seiter

Semiotics is the study of everything that can be used for communication: words, images, traffic signs, flowers, music, medical symptoms, and much more. Semiotics studies the way such "signs" communicate and the rules that govern their use. As a tool for the study of culture, semiotics represents a radical break from traditional criticism, in which the first order of business is the interpretation of an aesthetic object or text in terms of its immanent meaning. Semiotics first asks *how* meaning is created, rather than *what* the meaning is. In order to do this, semiotics uses a specialized vocabulary to describe signs and how they function. Often this vocabulary smacks of scientism to the newcomer and clashes with our assumptions about what criticism and the humanities are. But the special terminology of semiotics and its attempt to compare the production of meaning in a diverse set of mediums—aesthetic signs being only one of many objects of study—have allowed us to describe the workings of cultural communication with greater accuracy and enlarged our recognition of the conventions that characterize our culture.

Structuralism stresses that each element within a cultural system derives its meaning from its relationship to every other element in the system: there are no independent meanings, but rather many meanings produced by their difference from other elements in the system. Beginning in the 1960s, some leading European intellectuals applied semiotics and structuralism to many different sign systems. Roland Barthes carefully analyzed fashion, French popular culture from wrestling to wine drinking, and a novella by Balzac. Umberto Eco turned his attention to Superman comic strips and James Bond novels. Christian Metz set out to describe the style of Hollywood cinema as a semiotic system. By addressing the symbolic and communicative capacity of humans in general, semiotics and structuralism help us see connections between fields of study that are normally divided among different academic departments in the university. Thus they are specially suited to the study of television.

THE SIGN

The smallest unit of meaning in semiotics is called the *sign*. Semiotics begins with this smallest unit and builds rules for the combination of signs. Fredric Jameson has pointed out that this concern with discerning the smallest unit of meaning is something that semiotics shares with other major intellectual movements of the twentieth century, including linguistics and nuclear physics, but it is an unusual starting point for criticism, which has

Frederic Jameson · literary critic who focuses on the interplay between linguistic meaning and form.

tended to discuss works as organic wholes. Taking the definition of the smallest unit as a starting point indicates a shift in the sciences from perception to models: "where the first task of a science henceforth seems the establishment of a method, or a model, such that the basic conceptual units are given from the outset and organize the data (the atom, the phoneme)."[1] Saussure conceptualized the sign as composed of two distinct parts, although these parts are separable only in theory, not in actual communication. Every sign is composed of a *signifier,* that is, the image, object, or sound itself—the part of the sign that has a material form—and the *signified,* the concept it represents.

In written language, the sign *rain* is composed of the grouping of four letters on this page (the signifier) and the idea or concept of rain (the signified)—that is, the category of phenomena we reserve for water falling from the sky. Saussure stressed that the relationship between the signifier and the signified in verbal language was entirely conventional, completely arbitrary. There is no natural or necessary connection between *rain* and the concept for which it stands. Furthermore, words have no positive value. A word's meaning derives entirely from its difference from other words in the sign system of language. On the level of signifier, we recognize *rain* through its distinguishability from *brain* or *sprain* or *rail* or *Braille* or *roan* or *reign.* The signified is meaningful because of its difference from *sprinkle, drizzle, downpour, monsoon,* or from *hail, sleet,* or *snow.* Other words could be invented, such as *raim* or *sain,* that use the same alphabet and are pronounceable, but because these "words" do not enter into relationships with other signs in the system in a meaningful way, they remain at the level of nonsense.

Saussure was interested in studying the structure of language as a system, and he bracketed off the real objects to which language refers: its *referents.* Semiotics does not concern itself with the referent of the sign rain, that is, actual water falling from the sky on a particular day at a particular place. The concept of rain is independent of any given occurrence of the actual event. Moreover, both Saussure and Peirce recognized that some signs have no "real" object to which they refer: abstractions (truth, freedom) or products of the imagination (mermaids, unicorns). More important, they wished to argue that all signs are cultural constructs that have taken on meaning through repeated, learned, collective use. Peirce emphasized that even when we try to define a sign, we are always forced to use another sign to translate it; he labeled the sign that we use to describe another sign the *interpretant.*

In this book, for example, we will be describing television's audiovisual sign systems using linguistic signs (words on these pages) and

Saussure · Ferdinand de Saussure shares credit for inventing the field of semiotics (or semiology) with **Peirce**.

Charles S. Peirce · American philosopher who shares credit with linguist **Saussure** for creating field of semiotics.

black-and-white still photographs that are in many ways quite distant and different from the original object. To take another example, when an image on the television news is identified as "Corazon Aquino," a sign produced by an electronic image is translated into another sign system—that of proper nouns. Proper names are a special class of signs that seem to have a real, easily agreed-upon referent. But our understanding of persons (especially those represented frequently on television) is filtered through sign systems: we don't "know" anything or anyone (even ourselves) except through language.

Images do not have an unmediated relationship with their referents. The image of Aquino could be understood in terms of general categories ranging from "world leaders" to Filipino women. The referent of Aquino's image will vary greatly depending on the cultural context—for example from the United States to Japan. The proper name could refer to another interpretant, such as "president of the Philippines." Even if we were in the same room with Aquino and used our index fingers to point to her and say, "*There* is Corazon Aquino" we would have used another set of signs, gestural and verbal ones. Charles S. Peirce saw the process of communication as an unending chain of sign production, which he dubbed "unlimited semiosis." Peirce's concept of the sign forces the realization that no communication takes place outside of sign systems—we are always translating signs into other signs. The conventions of the sign system control the ways we are able to communicate (that is, produce signifiers) and limit the range of meanings available (that is, what signifieds can be produced).

Umberto Eco defines a sign as "everything that, on the grounds of a previously established social convention, can be taken as something standing for something else."[2] Surprisingly, Eco means to include in this definition even those signs that at first glance seem to be more "natural" than linguistic ones. It is through social convention and cultural appropriation that a dark, cloudy sky becomes a sign for "impending storm." Those same dark clouds could be used to signify bad luck, or nature responding in kind to one's own gloomy mood (as in the literary convention of pathetic fallacy). The meaning of rain can vary greatly from one culture to another: in some Polynesian societies, a rainstorm is taken to mean that the sky is crying for the death of a child.

Eco's conception of the sign is adapted from the work of Peirce, who did not limit himself to symbolic signs (language), as Saussure did, but attempted to account for all types of signs, including pictorial ones. To do so, he introduced specific definitions of the terms *icon* and *index*. The categories *symbolic, iconic,* and *indexical* are not mutually exclusive. Television constantly uses all three types of signs simultaneously. Television images are both

Corazon Aquino · in the 1980s, Aquino was elected Philippine president after the assassination of her husband.

Umberto Eco · Italian philosopher also excerpted in Chapter 2.

iconic and indexical, and programs often use words (symbolic signs) on the screen and the soundtrack.

In the iconic sign, the signifier structurally resembles its signified. We must "learn" to recognize this resemblance just as we learn to read maps or to draw. The correspondence between a drawing of a dog, for example, and the signified "dog" (which might be a particular specimen of dog or the concept of dog in general) could take many different forms. The drawing could be skeletal or anatomical, in which case it might take a trained veterinarian or zoologist to recognize any structural similarity between the drawing and the signified "dog." The iconic sign could be a child's drawing, in which case another kind of expert decoder, for instance the child's parent or teacher, might be required to detect the structural resemblance. Most drawings rely on rules that dictate point of view and scale; an "aerial view" of a dog, a head-on angle, or a drawing done twenty times larger than scale would be much harder for most of us to recognize than the conventional side-angle view in which two legs, a tail, a pointed ear, and whiskers will do the job, even if no attempt is made at coloration and the drawing appears only as an outline in black. Most of these admonitions about the conventionality of drawings hold true for video images as well, even though we think of television as more lifelike.

Indexical signs are different from iconic ones because they rely on a material connection between signifier and signified: smoke means fire, pawprints mean the presence of a cat; a particular set of fingerprints signifies "Richard Nixon"; red spots signify "measles." Most images produced by cameras belong to Peirce's class of "indexical signs" because they require the physical presence of the referent before the camera lens at some point in time for their production. This fact about an image is, however, virtually impossible to verify without being present at the time the image was made. Stand-ins and look-alikes, trick photographs, special effects, computer-generated graphics, multiple exposures, and animated images can all be used to lie to the camera. Even images that we treat as particularly unique because they have as their signified an individual living creature may be dictated by convention. Throughout Lassie's career as a television character, many different dogs (most of them male) have been used in the part, often within the same episode. Although many individual Lassies have now died, the iconic sign "Lassie" lives on, thanks to the skills of the various production crews and the animal trainers who find new dogs whenever a new version of the Lassie series is produced. It may be a blow to our faith in physiognomy, but we can be fooled by pictures of persons almost as easily.

Indexical signs are also established through social convention. Animals have left pawprints for as long as they have roamed the earth, but their pawprints became a sign only when people began to use them for tracking. As Umberto Eco explains: "The first doctor who discovered a sort of constant relationship between an array of red spots on a patient's face and a given disease (measles) made an inference: but insofar as this relationship has been made conventional and has been registered as such in medical treatises a *semiotic convention* has been established. There is a sign every time a human group decides to use and recognize something as the vehicle for something else."[3] Indexical signs are no less tainted by human intervention than symbolic or iconic ones; they require the same accumulation of use and the same reinforcement and perpetuation by a social group to be understood as signs in the first place.

To understand television images, we must learn to recognize many conventions of representation. One of the characteristics of such representational codes is that we become so accustomed to them that we may not recognize their use; they become as "natural" to us as the symbolic signs of language, and we think of iconic signs as the most logical—sometimes as the only possible—way to signify aspects of our world. We can watch this learning taking place when infants and toddlers begin to watch television. Toddlers, for example, like to touch the screen frequently as they struggle to understand the two-dimensional nature of television's iconic signs. Conventional expectations of scale, perspective, camera angle, color, lighting, lens focal length, and subject-to-camera distance (that is, nonrepresentational aspects of the image) are acquired through exposure to television; if a camera operator violates too many of these conventions, we may not be able to "recognize" the image at all.

To engage in fantasy for a moment, consider producing a newsbreak about a completely fictional event for broadcast on network TV. If we gave some careful thought to the way newsbreaks are written and the topics usually covered in them, we could script and storyboard a newsbreak that exactly conformed to the mode or presentation typical of U.S. network newscasting. If we had access to the facilities, technicians, equipment, supplies, and personnel of one of the networks, and if we could coerce an anchor to violate professional ethics (or find a convincing impostor) and read our script, we could produce a newsbreak, complete with "live action" reports, that would be indistinguishable from the authentic item. Semiotics reminds us that with nonfictional television, no less than with its fictional counterpart, we are dealing not with referents but with signs. In the end, it is impossible to verify the referent from television's sounds and images. Perhaps this is why, as Margaret Morse argues, the person of the news anchor, in his or her "ceremonial role," has become increasingly important in securing our belief in the news and our sense of its authenticity.[4] In this and many other ways, television relies heavily on the figure of the unique individual, the television personality. Most of television's signs are easily copied because they are based in convention, but the on-camera talking head of a known television personality is still one of the more difficult aspects of the image to fake.

DENOTATION AND CONNOTATION

So far we have been discussing the sign in terms of denotative meaning. Connotative meanings land us squarely in the domain of ideology: the worldview (including the model of social relations and their causes) portrayed from a particular position and set of interests in society. Roland Barthes devoted much of his work to the distinction between *denotation* and *connotation* in aesthetic texts. In images, denotation is the first order of signification: the signifier is the image itself and the signified is the idea or concept—what it is a picture of. Connotation is a second-order signifying system that uses the first sign (signifier and signified), as its signifier and attaches an additional meaning, another signified, to it. Barthes thought of connotation as fixing or freezing the meaning of the denotation; it impoverishes the first sign by ascribing a single and usually ideological signified to it.[5] This is why it takes many words to describe the signifier at the first level—we must include camera angle, color, size, lighting, composition, and so on. But connotations can often be described in just one word (noble, romantic, gritty, patriotic, humorous). Sometimes the difference between connotation and denotation seems rather mechanical in television criticism because television's signs are nearly already complex messages or *texts,* making it difficult to isolate the difference between the two levels of signification. Perhaps it is best to think of connotation as a parasite attaching itself to a prior signification.

To begin with a simple denotation, the fade to black has as its signifier the gradual disappearance of the picture on the screen and, as its signified, simply "black." This sign has been strongly conventionalized in motion pictures and television so that it exists as the following connotative sign: the signifier is "fade to black" and the signified is "ending" of a scene or a program. Television production texts insist that students must always use the fade to black at the end of every program and before any commercial breaks.[6] The fade to black has become part of a very stable signification. But connotations may eventually change through repetition. On *Knots Landing,* a CBS prime-time soap opera that has cultivated an image as a "quality program," each segment ends with a fade to black that lasts several beats longer than in most programs. This "fade to black" is part of the tone of *Knots Landing;* it is used for the connotation "serious drama" or "high-class show" (suggesting that the audience needs a moment to collect itself emotionally, to think over the scene before going on to the commercial). The longer fade to black now appears on many shows that aspire to such a connotation, including *thirtysomething* and *L.A. Law.* Connotations fix the meaning of a sign, but in other

Barthes · Roland Barthes, noted philosopher concerned with ideology and signification.

kinds of texts—those not of broadcast television—the denotation "fade to black" could take on other meanings as well. In a student production, frequent use of the fade to black could connote "rank amateur direction"; in an art video, it could connote "experimental, modernist style."

Some aspects of the image and soundtrack that we think of as non-representational actually function as symbolic signs and often carry connotative meanings; examples may include the color of light (pink for femaleness, white for goodness); music (minor chords and slow tempos signifying melancholy, solo instrumentals signifying loneliness); or photographic technique (soft focus signifying romance, hand-held cameras signifying on-the-spot documentary). Television is not completely different from written language in this respect. Printed words are inseparable from their nonrepresentational form in terms of typeface, size of type, boldness, color of paper, and so forth. These signs are all established through convention and repeated use. Such nonrepresentational signs have not been studied as thoroughly by semioticians as have representational ones.[7] One of the goals of semiotic analysis of television is to make us conscious of the use of connotation on television, so that we realize how much of what appears naturally meaningful on TV is actually historical, changeable, and culturally specific.

Barthes argued that connotation is the primary way in which the mass media communicate ideological meanings. A dramatic example of the operation of "myth," as Barthes called such connotations, and of television's rapid elaboration of new meanings is explosion of the space shuttle *Challenger.* The sign consisted of a signifier—the TV image itself—that was coded in certain ways (symmetrical composition, long shot of shuttle on launching pad, daylight, blue sky background) and the denoted meaning or signified "space shuttle." On the connotative level, the space shuttle was used as a signifier for a set of ideological signifieds including "scientific progress," "manifest destiny in space," and "U.S. superiority over the Soviet Union in the cold war."

On 28 January 1986, these connotations were radically displaced. On that day, all three commercial networks repeatedly broadcast videotape of the space shuttle exploding. This footage was accompanied first by a stunned silence, then by an abundance of speech by newscasters, by expert interviewees, by press agents, and by President Reagan (who canceled his State of the Union address to speak about the explosion), much of which primarily expressed shock. The connotation of the sign "space shuttle" was destabilized; it became once again subject—as denotation—to an unpredictable number of individual meanings or competing ideological interpretations. It was as if the explosion restored the sign's original signified, which could then lead to a series of questions and interpretations of the space shuttle relating to its status as a material object, its design, what it was made out of, who owned it, who had paid for it, who had built it, what it was actually going to do on the mission, how much control the crew or others at NASA had over it. At such a moment, the potential exists for the production of counterideological connotations. Rather than scientific progress, the connotation "fallibility of scientific bureaucracy" might have been attached to the space shuttle; "manifest destiny in space" might have been replaced by "waste of human life"; and "U.S. superiority over the U.S.S.R." by "basic human needs sacrificed to technocracy."

Television played a powerful role in stabilizing the meaning of the space shuttle. The networks, following the lead of the White House, almost immediately fixed on a connotation compatible with the state ideology. This connotative meaning is readable in the graphic, devised by television production staffs, that appeared in the frame with newscasters when they introduced further reports on the *Challenger:* an image of the space shuttle with a U.S. flag at half mast in the left foreground. This image helped to fix the connotation "tragic loss for a noble and patriotic cause" to the sign "space shuttle." Television produced this new connotation within hours of the event. Some of its force comes from its association with cultural and ideological codes that already enjoy wide circulation: the genre of war films, the TV news formula for reporting military casualties, the history of national heroes and martyrs. Later interpretations of the *Challenger* explosion or the space shuttle program had to compete with this one.

The study of connotation indicates the importance of understanding television signs as a historical system—one that is subject to change. Semiotics allows us to describe the process of connotation, the relationship of signs within a system, and the nature of signs themselves. But the study of connotation also directs us outside the television text and beyond the field of semiotics. We might want to study the producers of television messages (television networks, NASA, the White House press corps), the receivers of messages (the U.S. public), and the context in which signification takes place (the object of study of economics, sociology, political science, philosophy). Semiotics often leads us to questions about these things, but it cannot help us answer the questions because the study of the referent is outside its domain.

COMBINATIONS AND CODES

In language a small set of distinctive units—letters and sounds (phonemes)—are used to create more complex significations: words, sentences, paragraphs. Unlike language, television does not conveniently break down into discrete elements or building blocks of meaning; it has no equivalent of an alphabet. The closest we can come to a smallest unit is the technological definition of the frame from Herbert Zettl's widely used textbook: "A complete scanning cycle of the electron beam, which occurs every $\frac{1}{30}$ second. It represents the smallest complete television picture unit." But images already are combinations of several different signs at once and involve a complex set of denotations and connotations. Furthermore, if we use the frame as the smallest unit of meaning, we ignore the soundtrack, where $\frac{1}{30}$ second would not necessarily capture a meaningful sound and where speech, sound effects, and music may be occurring simultaneously. Christian Metz had given painstaking attention to this problem as it exists for the cinema. When he wrote his semiotics of the cinema, he identified five channels of communication: image, written language, voice, music, and sound effects. In borrowing these categories, I substitute the term *graphics* for *written materials* so as to include the logos, borders, frames, diagrams, and computer-animated images that appear so often on our television screens. In *Cinema and Language,* Metz concluded that television and cinema were 'two neighboring language systems" characterized by an unusual degree of closeness.

From a semiotic viewpoint, one of the most important characteristics of television in general (and one that is shared by many genres) might be its tendency to use all five channels simultaneously, as television commercials typically do. This might also explain television's low status as an aesthetic text: on TV too much goes on at once and there is too much redundancy among sound and image elements for it to be "artistic." The primacy of the soundtrack violates conventional notions in cinema aesthetics about the necessity of subordinating soundtrack to image.

The high degree of repetition that exists between soundtrack and image track and between segments is mirrored at the generic level of the series, which is television's definitive form. As Umberto Eco explains the debased aesthetic status of TV: "This excess of pleasurability, repetition, lack of innovation was felt as a commercial trick (the product had to meet the expectations of its audience), not as the provocative proposal of a new (and difficult to accept) world vision. The products of mass media were equated with the products of industry insofar as they were produced *in series,* and the 'serial' production was considered as alien to the artistic invention."[8]

Because semiotics recognizes the role of combination in all verbal and visual sign production—including aesthetic production—it tends to take a less condemning view of television and therefore may have more to say about TV as a communication system than have more traditional approaches in the humanities, which tend to dismiss TV as a vulgarity. Other kinds of performances that rely on just one channel at a time (music only, or images only, or printed words only) enjoy a higher and more serious aesthetic status. In comparison to novels or silent films or oil paintings, television is a messy thing. But this is precisely why it has been of interest to semioticians: simply describing its signs presents a formidable challenge. Indeed, semiotics and structuralism have played a polemical role in universities by presenting television as a complex experience worthy of serious analysis.

STRUCTURALISM

Structuralism has proven a very useful tool in studying television be-cause, as a method, it characteristically sets aside questions of aesthetic worth or value to concentrate on the internal rules for the production of television meaning. As developed in linguistics and anthropology, structuralism sought to understand a language or a culture on its own terms and urged the analyst to put aside judgment and evaluation. Journalistic television criticism has often been so interested in critical dismissal that careless generalizations and faulty descriptions have been the rule rather than the exception. The application of structuralist methods has made television criticism more rigorous, more accurate in describing its object, and less evaluative. As do semioticians, structural-ists study things synchronically and are interested in the system as a whole more than in particular manifestations of it. Rather than study-ing forms of language, as semioticians normally do, structuralists study the way that a cultural system produces a set of texts or signs, which could be anything from folktales to kinship relations to dietary rules. Characteristically, a structuralist analysis proposes binary oppositions such as individual/community, male/female, nature/culture, or mind/matter and argues that every element within the system derives its meaning from its relationship to these categories. A structuralist analysis often leads to a description of the worldview of a culture—its organizing principles for making sense of relationships among people who live in the same society and between people and their material en-vironments.

The work of Robert Hodge and David Tripp on children's animated series provides a good example of the usefulness of semiotics and structuralism in the analysis of television, as well as the problems and further questions raised by such methods. Hodge and Tripp argue that cartoons—widely considered one of the lowest forms of television—are surprisingly complex. The reason children are fascinated by car-toons is not because they have been turned into television zombies but because they are understandably engaged by the complex blend of aesthetic, narrative, visual, verbal, and ideological codes at work in them. Though cartoons are characterized by a great deal of repetition and redundancy, Hodge and Tripp argue that their subject matter and their way of conveying it is complicated stuff. Children use cartoons to decipher the most important structures in their culture. To make this point, Hodge and Tripp analyze the titles sequence of the unex-ceptional 1978 cartoon *Fangface,* an animated series about the adven-tures of werewolf Sherman Fangsworth and his teenage companions Kim, Biff, and Pugsie. Generically, the series was based primarily on a comedy-mystery type of story (sometimes called the "Let's get out of here" adventure formula) found in many examples of cartoons from *Scooby Doo* (1969–80) to *Slimer and the Real Ghostbusters* (1986–).

Hodge and Tripp base their analysis on a single twenty-minute cartoon. This starting point is significant in that it is the typical founding gesture of the semiotician to gather a small, manageable, and synchronic (contemporaneous) text or set of texts for analysis and, using the text as a basis, try to establish the conventions governing the larger system (in this case the series *Fangface* and the larger system of children's animated television). Compared with other studies of children's television, Hodge and Tripp's work seems startlingly new. For, in fact, cartoons have only occasionally been subjected to any kind of literary analysis, and never to the painstaking detail Hodge and Tripp expend on *Fangface*. Instead, child psychologists and media sociologists have tended to use the methods of quantitative content analysis to "measure" the children's cartoon during a fixed block of hours in the broadcasting schedule.

Content analysts count how many acts of violence occur, how many male and female characters there are, how many minority characters appear, how often villains speak with a foreign accent, and so on. The virtue of a structuralist/semiotic analysis in this case, then, is that it focuses on both syntagmatic and paradigmatic relations. These combinations and structures are usually lost in content analysis, in which the meanings of discrete units of information within a television program are not thought to depend on the context in which they appear. This is another important principle of structuralism: the meaning of each sign within a text derives from its relationship to other signs in the same system. As Terry Eagleton puts it: "Structuralism proper contains a distinctive doctrine . . . the belief that the individual units of any system have meaning only by virtue of their relations to one another. . . . [Y]ou become a card-carrying structuralist only when you claim that the meaning of each image is wholly a matter of its relation to the other[s]."[9]

In this essay, I will limit myself to recounting Hodge and Tripp's discussion of the fifty-second opening of *Fangface,* which they describe as "highly compressed, using rapid, small-scale syntagms." In most cases, these openings will be "the most salient memory children will have" of a program and its characters. In the first image, Fangface appears wearing a red hat. He licks his lips and smiles. Hodge and Tripp analyze the image this way:

Syntagm and paradigm · syntagm, the order in which elements in a system appear; paradigm, the choices in a particular system (e.g., a television **syntagm** [commercial, initial teaser for program, introduction credits, commercial] makes choices between which commercials are shown [the **paradigm** of commercials]). "Fangface" is a paradigm choice among several other children's television shows.

The picture itself is a syntagm, consisting of a face of an animal with a hat. How do we categorize the two elements, to make up a meaning? Or what categories are implied by meanings that we assign it? The hat looks odd, on Fangface's head. To express the oddness, we can point to the animal nature of Fangface, and the human, cultural quality of the hat. . . . In the paradigmatic dimension the options are a pair of categories *nature/culture* (or *animal/human,* which is a more specific instance of the broader pair), which is the source of the image's meaning. We can translate this meaning into words—Fangface is both animal and human, both nature and culture. This meaning, of course, also underlies the concept of a werewolf. Fangface's hat is odd in another way: it faces backwards. Here one set of paradigmatic categories concerns the position of a hat. This pair backwards/ forwards constitutes a single structure. Forwards signals, among other things, conformity, normality; backwards therefore, signals the opposite: abnormality, non-conformity.[10]

In this passage, Hodge and Tripp have introduced the binary opposition (nature/culture) and proceeded to organize the elements of the television image into paradigmatic sets. Even at this early point, they acknowledge that their description of this one image is partial and incomplete. They have not discussed Fangface's tooth (single like a baby tooth, but big and powerful like adult permanent teeth), or the color of his hat (red, contrasting with other primary colors and with brown, a secondary color).

Hodge and Tripp continue with a description of the next three shots, which follow a bolt of lightning and the title "Fangface":

The sequence is clearly organized by a movement from outside to inside, from nature (as a dangerous threatening force) to culture, the house and the bassinet and the baby protected within by both, . . . starting with a shot of the moon (outside, nature) then showing the baby at the window (not threatened by nature). The baby spins rapidly, like a whirlwind (nature) or like a machine (culture), and turns into a baby werewolf (nature). However, this werewolf is not a threatening figure. It has a cute expression, and wears a nappy (human culture). Then, with the soundtrack saying "only the sun (nature) can change him back to normal," we see a picture of the sun with alongside it the words "Sunshine Laundry."[11]

A zoom-out reveals that the sun that changes Fangface back into Sherman Fangsworth is not the real sun but a picture of the sun on a box of laundry detergent in the kitchen. To Hodge and Tripp, this signals another ambiguous rendering of the nature/culture split, in this case between the sun belonging to nature—one of the stars— and the sun used for the purposes of a commercial trademark and located in the domestic sphere (culture). So far, Hodge and Tripp have covered only the first nine shots of the title sequence. This is one of the perennial problems plaguing the semiotician, especially the semiotician of television, in which each segment, each image, can produce an enormous (some would say preposterous) amount of analytical text.

Hodge and Tripp's analysis of the verbal track is more concise. The voice-over in this opening sequence explains: "Every 400 years a baby werewolf is born into the Fangsworth family, and so when the moon shined on little Sherman Fangsworth he changed into Fangface.

A werewolf! Only the sun can change him back to normal. And so little Fangs grew up and teamed with three daring teenagers, Kim, Biff, and Pugsie, and together they find danger, excitement and adventure." The verbal track is used for conveying time, causal relationships, and exposition—for example, the tale of Fangface's origins. Following Barthes, Hodge and Tripp find that the verbal channel anchors the meaning of the visual. But Hodge and Tripp note that even the verbal track offers some "interesting illogicalities." They focus on the use of "so" to suggest a causality where none logically exists between being a werewolf and growing up and teaming up with "three daring teenagers." However, most viewers would never notice this contradiction unless the words of the *Fangface* opening were printed out for them to read. The words alone do not reveal the strong parodic connotation of the "voice of God" style in which the opening is read and the announcer's voice—deep, booming, masculine, and middle-aged.

Despite the length and detail of many structuralist analyses, critics of the method have accused structuralists of ignoring stray meanings in the text and of closing off potential interpretations. The organization of all the various elements here into one class or the other, nature or culture, is an example of this flaw. But Hodge and Tripp do not impose a singular, unifying meaning in the television opening: "The pattern throughout this sequence is built up of different arrangements of primary opposition: nature-culture; human-animal. The result is not a single consistent message about the relations between the two. Sometimes nature is seen as threatening, sometimes as compatible with culture. Fangface is the focus of both ambiguity and ambivalence."[12]

Is Hodge and Tripp's analysis relevant to other cartoon examples? Does it have a usefulness beyond the specific example of *Fangface?* It may be helpful to attempt to extend this kind of analysis to a more recent example of the television animated series, *Teenage Mutant Ninja Turtles.* In the series opening sequence, the main characters are revealed to be a group of four teenagers, as in *Fangface.* The turtles do not undergo any physical transformations (from human to werewolf); rather, they personify the combination of nature and culture. The turtles are green amphibians "in a half-shell" (nature), but they are also mutants who speak, walk on two feet, bear the names of Renaissance painters, and wear clothing (culture). Each of them wears a masklike scarf over his eyes (in blue, red, orange, and purple) and matching sweatbands around his knees, wrists, and ankles. Each also wears a belt around the waist that secures different martial arts weapons (threatening), and the theme song informs us that they are a "fearsome fighting team" against the evil Shredder. Yet they have big cute eyes and are not yet grown up (safe). The theme song repeatedly offers the combination of *Ninja* and *teenager* (as in the line, "Splinter taught them to be Ninja teens"), a paradox that emphasizes the oppositions of old/young, discipline/rebellion. *Teenage Mutant Ninja Turtles* seems to reinterpret the nature/culture split as freewheeling, nonconformist American adolescence (nature) versus strict, conformist Japanese adulthood (culture).

Hodge and Tripp find that the nature/culture axis is a highly significant one in the world of *Fangface,* and our brief analysis suggests that it might be applied to *Teenage Mutant Ninja Turtles* as well. Lévi-Strauss found that the same binary opposition underlay the mythological systems of South American tribal cultures. Is nature/culture a binary opposition so basic to narrative that it will always figure in the structuralist's findings? Are structuralism's categories predetermined for the critic by the body of work that has gone before? Or are they so general that the same categories will be found everywhere, in all kinds of texts, thus becoming too general to be valuable as a critical tool? The answers to these questions seem to be both yes and no.

There is a suspicious resemblance between Lévi-Strauss's findings and those of Hodge and Tripp, despite a great divergence in historical and cultural settings. But one can also look at the larger field of children's literature, animated television, and commercial culture and find that the nature/culture division, or the blurring of the two, is a central characteristic of children's media. Animal characters who dress in clothes, talk, and walk on two feet have appeared with ever greater frequency in children's literature throughout the twentieth century: all of them can be seen as negotiating in some ways the nature/culture, animal/human oppositions. Television animation is especially fond of such characters, and they are often treated by journalists and experts on childhood as a new, bizarre, and grossly commercialized example of collusion between toy manufacturers and the television industry. Teenage Mutant Ninja Turtles are just the most recent example.

Many of the licensed characters that proliferated in children's television in the 1980s lend themselves to a structuralist analysis using the nature/culture pair: My Little Ponies (horses in pastel colors and makeup); Thundercats (tigers, lions, and cheetahs operating high-tech spacecraft); Ghostbusters (the spirit world tamed by the technical gadgetry of ectoblasters and proton packs). But how do we explain specific manifestations of the binary opposition? The figures of the werewolf in *Fangface* and Splinter (who is simultaneously a Japanese Ninja master and a rat) in *Teenage Mutant Ninja Turtles* are products of different historical moments and different racial ideologies. Does the use of the binary opposition nature/culture to analyze these cartoons obscure important differences by being too universalist?

Terry Eagleton has remarked that one of the primary drawbacks to structuralist research is that it is "hair-raisingly unhistorical." To take just one example, the history of children's television and animation lend some important information for an understanding of *Fangface,* although Hodge and Tripp, like most structuralists, do not concern themselves with this context. The animated television series found on Saturday morning television and throughout syndication today are very different from "cartoons" in the sense of animated motion picture shorts by Disney and Hanna Barbera—Donald Duck, Bugs Bunny, or Tom and Jerry. A historical approach could trace these important changes: "limited" animation techniques (fixed backdrops and restricted character movement) were developed in the 1950s for animated television series like *Fangface* in an effort to cut time and costs; these new series then adapted storytelling conventions from the television series and the comic book. Interviews with children suggest how important it is to understand television in such "intertextual" frames. Many children, on seeing *Fangface* for the first time, whispered "Scooby Doo" and "Incredible Hulk" to one another during the opening sequence—they immediately recognized the show's similarity to other television texts.

A historical approach to the animated television series would also allow us to contextualize and explain the kinds of changes that can be observed in different series from the 1970s to the 1990s, between series like *Fangface* and *Scooby Doo* and contemporary examples like *Teenage Mutant Ninja Turtles.* In the 1970s, the groups of four adventurers were usually made up primarily of human beings, with a token female making one of the four. By the 1990s, many programs had few humans and no females among the group. The settings changed from the small town and the countryside to Manhattan and Tokyo. The villains have been transformed from the cold war's mad scientists, complete with Russian or German accents, into Japanese technocrats; the generic references are no longer to the mystery story and horror film but to the martial arts movie, although both the series discussed here retain many of the conventions of science fiction. All of these comparisons need to be pursued by someone studying the cartoon from the perspective of genre criticism or narrative or ideological analysis. If we pursue a structuralist analysis alone, we might simply arrange the different elements in *Fangface* and *Teenage Mutant Ninja Turtles* into nature/culture oppositions and conclude that they are very similar, whereas a critic better versed in the history of the animated series and the different cultural and political contexts in which they were made might see the differences between the types of series and be better able to explain these differences.

In society various discourses about television compete with one another; each is informed by and represents a specific set of interests. For example, in writing about children's television, competing and contradictory discourses are produced by industry producers, such consumer protection groups as Action for Children's Television, and academic "childhood professionals" such as educators, pediatricians, psychologists, and social workers. Each of these groups contributes to a discourse that allows certain things to be said and rules out other things—or makes them unimaginable. The discourse of child experts usually assumes a certain normative view of what children are like (naive, impressionable, uncritical), of what television should do (help children learn to read and to understand math and science), of what is an appropriate way to spend leisure time (being physically and mentally active, *doing* things), and of what television viewing is (passive and mindless). These ideas derive from larger medical, religious, and social science bodies of thought.[13]

Discourse is not "free speech." It is not a perfect expression of the speaker's intentions. Indeed, we cannot think of communicative intentions as predating the constraints of language at all. When Hodge and Tripp interviewed children about *Fangface* and other television shows, they found, in analyzing videotapes and transcripts of the discussion, that in many instances boys silenced girls, adults silenced children, and interviewers silenced subjects—through nonverbal censure of some remarks (glances, laughter, grimacing), by wording questions and responses in certain ways, or by failures to comprehend each other's terms. We can never think about the meaning of television outside of these contexts. As Hodge and Tripp put it, "Verbal language is also the main mediator of meaning. It is the form in which meanings gain public and social form, and through discussion are affected by the meanings of others."[14] They remind us that the entire topic of children and television is circumscribed by spoken and written discourse. No matter how complete the textual analysis of television, no matter how well designed the audience study, it "would still be partial because it would still be located in particular social and historical circumstances."[15]

Perhaps the best way to think of semiotics and structuralism is as a kind of useful exercise for making sure that we know our object before venturing out into other models of study. As a descriptive method, it makes sure we have spent sufficient time with a text before moving on to a series of questions regarding audience activity and the play of television as discourse.

Semiotics is extremely useful in its attempt to describe precisely how television produces meaning and its insistence on the conventionality of the signs. For if signs are conventional, they are also changeable. But semiotics remains silent on the question of how to change a sign system. Stubbornly restricting itself to the text, it cannot explain television economics, production, history, or the audience. Still, semiotics and structuralism, even with their liabilities, have raised questions about theories of gender, of the subject, of psychoanalysis, of ideology—and about the practice of all cultural criticism—that have been usefully applied to television.

■ *Ellen Seiter is a Professor of Communications at the University of California at San Diego. Nationally recognized for her work in media studies, she has recently published* Television and New Media Audiences *(2000). She has published widely on such topics as soap opera, Saturday morning children's television, women filmmakers, and ethnographic approaches to media consumption.*

NOTES

1. Fredric Jameson, *The Prison House of Language: A Critical Account of Structuralism and Russian Formalism* (Princeton, N.J.: Princeton University Press, 1972). p. 105. In a similar vein, Raymond Williams discusses the borrowing of the term *structural* from the sciences and the problems this created (*Keywords* [New York: Oxford University Press, 1976], pp. 254–55).

2. Umberto Eco, *A Theory of Semiotics* (Bloomington: Indiana University Press, 1976), p. 16.

3. Ibid., p. 17 (Eco's italics).

4. Margaret Morse, "The Television News Personality and Credibility," in *Studies in Entertainment: Critical Approaches to Mass Culture,* ed. Tania Modleski (Bloomington: Indiana University Press, 1986), pp. 55–79.

5. Roland Barthes, "Myth Today," in *The Barthes Reader,* ed. Susan Sontag (New York: Hill and Wang, 1982), pp. 93–149.

6. Herbert Zettl, *Television Production Handbook* (Belmont, Calif.: Wadsworth Publishing Company, 1984), p. 596.

7. Richard Dyer makes this point in "Entertainment and Utopia," in *Movies and Methods II,* ed. Bill Nichols (Berkeley: University of California Press, 1987), pp. 226–27.

8. Umberto Eco, "Innovation and Repetition: Between Modern and Post-Modern Aesthetics," *Daedalus* 114 (Fall 1985): 162.

9. Eagleton, *Literary Theory,* p. 94.

10. Robert Hodge and David Tripp, *Children and Television: A Semiotic Approach,* pp. 26–27.

11. Ibid., pp. 26–27.

12. Ibid., p. 28.

13. See Ellen Seiter, "Sold Separately: Aspects of Children's Consumer Culture" (tentative title), publication forthcoming.

14. Hodge and Tripp, *Children and Television,* p. 71.

15. Ibid., p. 27.

MAKING SURE OF THE TEXT

1. Be sure that you can define and identify examples of each term in the following list: *semiotics, structuralism, sign, referent, denotation, connotation, iconic sign, indexical sign,* and *binary opposition.* You might find it useful to paraphrase what Seiter writes about each one and then find examples of your own to support the paraphrases.

2. How does semiotics parallel the activity of anthropologists?
3. How would you apply Metz's five channels of communication to, for instance, the latest Mitsubishi or Sprite advertising campaign?
4. Identify indexical and iconic signs in *The Simpsons* or *The Montel Williams Show*.

CONSIDERING THE CONTEXT

1. Seiter refers to the 1986 *Challenger* explosion as "displacing" several established connotations. What more recent event can you identify that displaced connotations in the same way? What is that event an artifact of?
2. What effect is achieved by the extended example of *Fangface*?
3. Note how many references in Seiter's article might need to be explained in footnotes; what does this level of reference suggest to you about her intended audience?

■ ■ ■

"Hung Like a Horse: Male Stripping in Recent Films," *Textual Reasoning* (1998)

Graham Ward

The male body has been a cinematic fetish for many years. This is not to deny that women have featured as erotic objects throughout cinematic history. It is simply to observe that from the late fifties there has been an awareness of the female gaze such that the physiques (or at least naked torsos) of Burt Lancaster, Kirk Douglas, Charlton Heston and (since 1964 and *A Fistful of Dollars*) Clint Eastwood have constructed what one film studies scholar has termed "masculinity as a spectacle."[1]

In the early 70s Burt Reynolds was the first of many male film stars to pose nude for the centerfold of a women's magazine (*Cosmopolitan*) and with the appearance of Gibson, Ford, Stallone and Schwarzenegger we have moved into another generation of male icon. The presentation of this female gaze can present problems in the form of erotic sub-currents. For quite frequently the kind of action films in which these iconized bodies feature are orientated towards a male audience; the *Mad Max, Rambo, Die Hard* and *Terminator* series, for example.

A homoerotic gaze plays about these screenings of the male body. Hollywood has become more frank about this gaze and its appeal. Several of its younger stars have submitted their bodies to such a construction: River Phoenix in *My Own Private Idaho,* Brad Pitt in *Interview with a Vampire,* Leonardo DiCaprio in *Total Eclipse.*

Each of these presentations of the male body in cinema reinforces the ideology of masculine potency. The bodies are shaped to elicit audience desire. Whether what is screened is the muscular, hirsute and toned physique of Bruce Willis (in *Twelve Monkey*) or the lean, pale and hairless body of Brad Pitt (in *Thelma and Louise*), both, in their different ways, are representations of phallic power—though the more toned and muscular, the more the body consciously and visibly presents itself as one great hard-on.

What is interesting and significant, therefore, is a series of recent films where the male body is stripped and exposed to the erotic gaze in a way that expresses not its potency but its vulnerability. Rather than figuring male erection, these representations critique phallocentrism and, in their frank shots of the male penis, show that for the majority of the time, that penis is detumescent.

Three films, in particular, point the way towards a different scripting of the male

cinematic fetish · literally, an object by which deep significance is evoked, whether religious or sexual.

homoerotic gaze · a mutual sexual tension recognized between members of the same gender, in this case the gaze of the male audience on the iconized male body.

body: *The Pillow Book* (Peter Greenaway), *Boogie Nights* (Paul Thomas Anderson), and *The Full Monty* (Peter Canttaneo). In the first of these films, Jerome (Ewan McGregor), an English translator living in Japan, allows his body to be written upon so that a woman poet might enable her work to be read by an important, exploitative homosexual publisher.

The camera lovingly films, in close-up, the calligraphic movement of the pen upon the male body. Jerome then delivers himself into the hands of the publisher and strips before him in such a way that we are conscious of how both Jerome's body and the homoerotic desire and gaze are scripted. The flesh becomes text—quite literally, for Jerome's body is finally skinned and made into a book.

The plot of *Boogie Nights* follows the rise, fall and resurrection of Eddie Adam alias Dirk Diggler's (Mark Wahlberg) enormous cock in the pornography industry. In the final scene, Dirk stands before a mirror, just prior to the shooting of his comeback film (all sexual innuendoes are intended by the film), unzips his pants and pulls out for his gaze and the audience's, the instrument which has been concealed (and yet foregrounded in dialogue) throughout the film.

In a long take, while Dirk pumps up his ego before the mirror, the camera dwells on the length and impotence of this ridiculous member. Dirk's dick is no more than a kitsch accessory in a film which plays *a la* Tarantino with the dramatic as the banal.

The Full Monty narrates the story of a group of steel workers rendered socially, politically and physically impotent by unemployment. Inspired by Gaz (Robert Carlyle), who observes the impact that the Chippendale male strippers have on the local women and his own lack of cash, the group get together and train to take the stage at the local pub for one night.

The significant difference between the Chippendale version and their own act is that the Chippendales all present the tanned and toned-up bodies of the masculine sex-icon, and (to keep sexual illusion constantly in play) they keep their jockstraps on; this group of emaciated, pale, unmuscular (but for one), overweight and aged male bodies are determined to go all the way, revealing the inner sanctum of masculinity, the cock behind the jockstrap—for one night only.

In each of these films there is a staging of the self-conscious spectacle of the male body. The exposure of the genitals receives an audience within the film itself, and this audience is significant for the naming of the ostensive gaze and desire. Jerome is caught between the gaze of the female poet and the male homoerotic gaze of the publisher; his body functions as a screen for the projection of their parallel desires. Dirk gazes at himself, but it is a gaze without desire. His narcissism is fragile; it is required so that he can give himself an erection, because without an erection he will not be able to perform for the cameras which await him. But the dick remains limp as he folds it away and bursts out of his dressing room door determined to conquer.

The audience in the pub who have come to see Gaz and his friends perform, is mixed, but it is the female desire and gaze which is foregrounded. There is an exuberance displayed by the men, an ecstasy of final unveiling, concomitant with the ecstasy on the faces of the women, as the strippers approach, hands on the police hats covering their genitals, ready for the climax. Both performers and audiences, men and women, share a sense of triumph, release, even giftedness, when the hats are tossed aside. But the cinema audience is withheld from that final participation. The camera views the men from behind and then freezes the frame before the credits roll.

In each film, though much more so in *Boogie Nights* and *The Full Monty,* the audience is interloper, voyeur; we are never (or only momentarily in *The Pillow Book*) directly invited to be excited by what we see. The male bodies are not fetishized; they are presented as vulnerable organic forms caught up in a play of social, political, economic and sexual scriptings which plot for them the possible modes of action.

How do we read these scriptings of the male body? Certainly they announce a new consciousness by men (each film is directed by a man) of their vulnerability; of the way their bodies have been written upon (by the film industry, by pornography, by commercial advertising). These bodies are no longer in charge, no longer wielders of phallocentric power.

In *Boogie Nights* and *The Full Monty* being hung like a horse is viewed, on one level, as a certain advantage. But the advantage is economic; if money cannot be earned by the sweat of the worker's brow then the male worker has to find other assets. When a young, good-looking and Greek-figured man auditions for Gaz, he displays the size of his dick as his only qualification for joining the troupe. Gaz immediately remarks that the man has become their "walking lunch-box."

In *The Pillow Book* and *Boogie Nights* there appears no way of escaping this scripting; both men are sacrificed for the sake of productions that far exceed their importance. Jerome's body being turned into a book in a way parallels Dirk's cashing the bank cheque that his body has become in order to live well, materially. Both bodies, in these films, men—now on the other side of phallocentrism—are reduced to flesh bought, sold and exchanged.

In *The Full Monty,* on the other hand, both the men and the women join together in resisting the sex-icon scriptings for the male body. There is a celebration of the male body in a manner which does not exalt itself at the expense of the female body. As the credits roll, Hot Chocolate sing "I believe in miracles." There is a resurrection of the male body; a salvation. From the despair and failure with which the film opens, there emerges an affirmation. The affirmation has required self-exertion, but it does not depend upon self-assertion (and the subsequent denigration of others).

Read eschatologically, that is, read in terms of the movement of the body of Christ in and through cultural history towards full redemption: these films announce new images of male possibility beyond the hung-like-a-horse power-play of the phallus. Expressed is a desire for a new openness and honesty, an examination (at last) of the gendering of men: with *The Full Monty,* the promise of a new affirmation of male embodiment in a multigendered society; with *The Pillow Book,* the castrating fears that new vulnerability brings; and with *Boogie Nights* the cynical comment that now men's bodies too, as women's bodies previously, are both used and users.

■ *Graham Ward is dean of Peterhouse College in Cambridge, England, and a lecturer at the University in Christian theology, philosophy and critical theory. His books include* Theology and Contemporary Critical Theory *(Macmillan, 1996), and* The Postmodern God *(Blackwells, 1997). He is senior editor of the journal* Literature and Theology *(OUP).*

NOTES

1. "Masculinity as Spectacle: Reflections on Men and Masculinity," in Steve Neale and Ina Rae Mark, eds., *Screening the Male: Exploring Masculinities in Hollywood Cinema* (London: Routledge, 1993), 9–20.

MAKING SURE OF THE TEXT

1. In the first two films Ward mentions, *The Pillow Book* and *Boogie Nights,* "men—now on the other side of phallocentrism—are reduced to flesh bought, sold, and exchanged." How is *The Full Monty* different?
2. What signs of male sexuality has Ward identified? List them.
3. What do "potency" and "vulnerability" mean in the context of male and female sexuality? You might find it useful to paraphrase Ward on the subject of male sex icons; from there, you may be able to extrapolate the female counterpart.
4. Rephrase Ward's argument in terms of sign, referent, connotation, and denotation (from Seiter's article).

CONSIDERING THE CONTEXT

1. Why does Ward find it important to examine the three films in his article? What do these films reveal about the phallocentric culture that surrounds filmed male bodies?
2. Some of Ward's diction might surprise or shock a reader; what do his slang references for male genitalia suggest to you about his intended readers?
3. Ward's and Culbertson's articles appear in the same issue of *Textual Reasoning,* an online journal practicing close and analytical reading of various texts. In what other contexts would you be able to find both men's articles?
4. What larger significance might Ward's observations reveal about the female viewing audience and the male heroic figure? In other words, why does it matter if the heroic figure changes in response to viewers?

■ ■ ■

**"Entertaining Sin: The Rules of the Game,"
from *Coming After Oprah* (1997)**

Vickie Abt and Leonard Mustazza

*Self-restraint seems almost sacrilege in a society that depends on the
dogma of economic materialism . . . [t]he excitement of demands for
more . . . and the almost infinite extension of the market. . . . Instead
of [materialism] being regarded as a means to an end . . . it has become the supreme end of individuals and society alike. . . . Thereupon
the appetites thus excited have become freed of any limiting authority.*
     —EMILE DURKHEIM
     SUICIDE (1897)

*A society that insists on stressing self-expression over self-control gener-
ally gets exactly what it deserves.*
     —CHARLES SYKES,
     A NATION OF VICTIMS (1992)

*Who needs meaning, after all, if you can have constant sensation? . . .
Thinking limits one's commercial possibilities.*
     —TOM GRIMES,
     CITY OF GOD (1995)

Montel: The music is uncharacteristically slow and serious to fit the gravity of
the subject: the reunion of mothers and their runaway teenaged daughters. Like
the theme music added to movies it's there to put the audience in the right
frame of mind, to set the tone and mood, but in this case, it does more. The music helps to bridge the gap between familiar entertainment devices and the slice
of reality portrayed, making them one and the same. It also helps those listening to forget that their diversion derives from spying on spectacles of pain, suffering, social and psychological dysfunction, and family disintegration. The
audience is reassured that they are not voyeurs eavesdropping on what ought to
be private conversations . . . not really. After all, it's just a show that they're
watching, and they're taking the subject as seriously as the music tells them to
take it, just the way it works in a sad movie.

JuJu, fifteen, has tattoos running up most of the surface of her arms and legs.
She cries a lot during the brief time she's allotted to be a media attraction. So
does her mother, who is occasionally photographed sitting backstage with two
other mothers in the same predicament. All three have the eyes of frightened
deer paralyzed by the headlights of an approaching death engine.

By contrast, the host's eyes on camera look self-confident but concerned.
From time to time, he joins his guests on stage and speaks in low tones, as if no
one else is listening to him elicit information from these troubled girls and to
dispense soothing dollops of "advice." Before one commercial break, he tells the
audience that these young women and their mothers have been brought here
to be helped, not to air their dirty laundry; before another, he issues a similar
disclaimer, promising to "give them things," to offer help and follow up, to

track them as they put their lives back together as a result of this appearance. "Aftercare," some call it. He wants the girls—and, ultimately, the world—to see just how serious he's taking all of these proceedings, and the performance is fairly convincing, except when the camera's eye catches him looking away, probably getting his cues from the director.

Through her crying, JuJu says that she sincerely wants to put her life in order, and it's easy enough to believe that. But when Montel asks the high-school dropout what she wants to do, JuJu replies that she wants to be a "pioneer brain surgeon." He doesn't ask what she means by that curious phrase. He doesn't ask how she expects to achieve this goal realistically, given her academic record, her family circumstances, and her lack of financial resources. He simply nods his head in supportive understanding. The statement takes its place on the stage with the other props in this theatre of the absurd.

The best drama is saved for last. First, Montel brings out Dr. Joy Browne, who's identified as a radio psychologist with a program that is syndicated to over 200 stations, and then JuJu's teary-eyed mother, Julie. After Montel admonishes JuJu repeatedly to "look at your mom," as if the girl hasn't seen her mother's desperation before, the psychologist can begin her healing work. "When you give advice," she asks Julie, "does the word 'sermon' come to mind?" "You're the mom." "We don't hit, no matter what. Can you promise you won't hit JuJu?" His hired healer having "saved" mother and daughter with these therapeutic words, Montel has a surprise. He brings out JuJu's sister, Chrissie, whom she hasn't seen in six months. Now there are three women crying and hugging on stage.

The camera comes in for a tight shot before the commercial break, after which we will hear from Brandi, an obese thirteen-year-old who looks far older than her years. A red bow is tied in her hair, making a mockery of the childhood Brandi has probably been denied. But there's hope . . . always hope. The promised subject flashes on the screen before the break: "Coming Up—Overweight Girl Makes Peace with Mom." Everything is going to be all right. (August 1995)

In our information age it's especially true that the messages we receive from the various media we are exposed to require constant questioning. If we passively sit back and receive unexamined messages, failing or refusing to consider not only *what* is said to us but *how* and *why,* we are open to the grossest kinds of manipulation, passing itself off as "entertainment." In that case, Jefferson's "wholesome discretion" becomes impossible.

Perhaps more than any other brand of media message that we receive, television talk programs deliberately use such gross manipulation in their attempt to entertain and supposedly "inform" us. While they employ a deceptive, game-like atmosphere, the information they provide about "real life," claiming that it's just a "reflection" of reality, is worse than useless. It's dangerous to play with and at deviance, for it puts us in the habit of "entertaining sin" in both senses of that phrase—using the moral errors and deviance of others for our entertainment and tolerating such behavior as a normal part of life. As we've noted, games

deviance · other than the societal or expected norm; most often sexual deviance.

are supposed to be played for fun, but this one isn't so much fun when it threatens to spill over into the nonplaying world. Here we look at the nature of the deceptive pseudogame, the techniques that are used to blur the distinction between play and the everyday world. (Later, we will consider the behind-the-scenes players and the business interests that make the game possible and profitable.)

THE PLAYERS

Like all sporting contests and board games, the pseudogame of talk TV first requires players, willing participants who agree to leave the real world for a while and to enter the play world, abiding by its contrived laws, suspending belief in the rules of life as we know it, climbing into the game frame. This particular game has three main players: the host, the guests, and the studio audience. Of course, beyond the last of these, there is the television-viewing audience, but this group, although numerically vast, is passive in terms of the actual play, something like the television viewer of professional sports. As we shall see, however, the home audience is really not passive at all in the last analysis since it is they who will carry the value projections of the game into the real world, thus breaking the play frame.

As in all entertainment programs, we begin with the star of the show, and, in our time, star quality is critically important to the success of any theatrical enterprise. Movies, theater, concerts, recordings, and television programs that feature stars draw crowds, and the bigger the star, the bigger the box office. To be sure, talk-show stars are big box office for the little box. Geraldo and Donahue and Oprah are recognizable "one-name" celebrities, who like their counterparts in sports and show business, are photographed wherever they go, are hounded for autographs, and are venerated by our culture, whose fascination with celebrity is seemingly endless.

Like other theatrical actors talk-show stars are performers, and in this capacity they have assumed in their work roles personas that differ from their real-life selves. We know nothing about stage and screen actors or singers just by watching their staged work except that they can carry the role off. But a big difference exists between the talk-show celebrity and the theatrical star. While we fully expect actors to step out of their roles once they are off the stage, we have no such expectation for the talk-show performer.[1] (We tend to regard newscasters in the same way, incidentally.) We expect that what we see on "stage" in terms of care, concern, intelligence, and sensitivity is what we get off the little screen as well, and if the star player can make us believe just that, then he or she is playing the role well.

The specific role that these individuals are called upon to play is that of *host*. That term has a very specific meaning and very clear connotation in our culture. A host is a person who receives and entertains guests in a familiar, nonthreatening setting, often his or her home. The host is responsible for seeing to it that the guests are made comfortable and that they are at ease interacting with other invited guests. On the surface, the talk-show host operates in much the same way. He or she represents a reassuring familiar face welcoming into a familiar place guests who think they "know" the host. (In fact, if the hosts changed every day, it would not work at all.) Everyone present is on a first-name basis, everyone is made comfortable at the start of play: we're all friends here, we're all in this together.

Acting in the role of enabler, the host is there to put the guest and audience at their ease and to facilitate easy discussion—regardless of how bizarre, heinous, or cruel the topic or the player's behavior may be—thus providing a stable basis for the game. Accordingly, unlike the guest, who will be changed by this game, the host's real life is not unduly affected by the nature of the talk; all is of a piece, and the show goes on day after day. Whether the guest is an unwed mother trying to pull her life together or a serial rapist claiming to be a victim of society, the host always begins the game in the very same way—politely welcoming guests, making sure they feel comfortable and prepared to speak about their "problems," often expressing, at least in the hosts' welcoming remarks, nonjudgmental concern and objectivity, ensuring what will take place during the next hour (minus commercials) is just some friendly, societally useful conversation among equals. If the guest is a teenaged drug addict wearing torn clothing and living on the street and the host is a man wearing a $1,200 suit and living on Fifth Avenue, no matter. The host's role is to make them look all the same.

The guests, on the other hand, seem to have an easier role than the host's. Whereas the host has a number of professional tasks to carry out in order to keep the game going, guests principally have one role—to talk provocatively, to confess, to express their feelings. As the center of attention (and often of controversy), guests must stick to the prescribed subject, whether or not it fully represents the contexts in which they live their lives. Let's say that the guest is a dentist with a predilection for child molesting. He must speak only of that topic, not about his practice of dentistry or his golf score. Although not a professional actor like the host, the guest, too, must fit into a role that may have comparatively little to do with his real life, and the audience (in this case, both the studio and home viewers) must believe that they "know" him just as they "know" the host. By contrast, the audience, who are really no different from the guests in real life, are made to believe that they are somehow different from and superior to the guest in this game, owing primarily to the fact that the guests have something to confess and the audience has the right to hear, judge, and counsel.

The studio audience's role is the easiest of the three. Like the ancient Greek chorus they comment on the action. They function much like the fans at a ball game or the spectators at the crap tables in Atlantic City or, unfortunately, like participants in a new-age therapy group. Initially brought together to see their favorite television star, the host, they are free to sit there, observe, and possibly participate in the interrogation of the guests. Of these audience "roles," however, this last "role" is the most disturbing and potentially socially problematic one. Let's bear in mind that they are usually a crowd of people who have stood in line to see a show, knowing neither the subject of the program nor the guests in advance. After only a few minutes of listening to the guests' stories, the audience is coached and encouraged to feel free enough to give advice on intimate subjects to people who will enter and leave their lives in a matter of an hour at best. The complicated social and personal lives of people are distilled and commented upon by total strangers in the course of a brief meeting.

Needless to say, the whole thing is patently ridiculous. Even old-time gossips usually confined their talk to those in their own communities, people they had some personal knowledge of, and contact with, in everyday life. In real life, moreover, the "confessant" and the listener would probably never meet in public and begin this kind of interaction. Why, then, do we accept it when we see it on TV? Or, turning that question around, if the TV version of reality is "valid" and everyone is an "open book" to be read in a four-minute encounter, why bother to spend the time and energy it takes to get to know people? In fact, taking our cues from television, many people might think that such social "interaction" is transferable to real life, and that's a worrisome thought indeed.

The studio audience's main role, though, is cheering and jeering, adding emotional intensity and an air of authenticity and immediacy to the proceedings. Without their presence, the dynamic of the game would be vastly different, resembling more a tabloid-television show (e.g., *A Current Affair, Inside Edition*) than a "useful" and "practical" discussion of everyday American life. Imagine a sporting event played in silence, without a crowd of reactive fans. That's what the talk-show game would look like without the studio players.

Apart from their role as cheering/jeering fans, moreover, they are there for a variety of other purposes, and while admission to the game may be free, there are expectations imposed on them, too. Individually, they come forward to ask questions, share anecdotes, offer therapeutic advice, express opinions, challenge interpretations, even physically confront at times. Collectively, they must react "appropriately" to the juicy revelations and heartfelt confessions. Their reactions are expected to be visible and often audible. Apart from the host, whose celebrity status brings the home viewers in, the studio audience is most crucial for connecting the program content to the millions of television viewers out there. Indeed, the guests themselves do not seem to differ from the studio audience, which further solidifies the connection. Home viewers are comforted by, and identify with, the presence and reactions of these "everyday" people, thus bringing the people from the TV audience into the game, regardless of their physical distance from the playing field.

THE RULES OF PLAY

All games have rules, and these rules must be understood by all players. Formal game rules are typically codified and, in professional games, invariable. (In informal games among friends, rules are sometimes altered on the spot by agreement, but hardly ever are they changed enough to create an entirely new game.) At times prospective players learn these rules simply by reading them on a game box or in a manual, but more often they learn them through observation and instruction by the initiated. In that way, a common game experience is transmitted to all players, and the games can be perpetuated by imitation.

The rules of the talk-television game are not codified in quite the same way as are the game rules that come with Monopoly. Rather, they are transmitted by observation, imitation, and coaching by the program producers. The fact that these shows are highly produced (to "manage shocks," among other things) is often overlooked. The salaried producers are largely responsible for choosing topics, getting and screening guests, making guests comfortable enough to open up, and scripting the proceedings, which participants can often read right off the rolling TelePrompters. These behind-the-scenes people are, in effect, the "brains" of the shows. (Later we will discuss the larger "brains" behind the scenes, the equity of the owners/producers and syndicators.) Interestingly, many of the personnel on the talk shows move to competitors' programs, a fact that may explain in part the similarities among all of the shows in this genre. Unlike the major corporate players, these lesser sharks also tend to view themselves as "politically correct liberals," people who privately disavow the shows and argue that, if they didn't produce them, others would. "I only work here" is the general refrain that allows them to displace responsibility back to the audiences who supposedly want this stuff, the prospective participants who write or call their idea in, and the free market system in general. One industry insider, Lora Wiley, who has worked for both Jerry Springer and Geraldo Rivera, has said, "Some people contend that we contribute to the degeneration of society. . . . But I maintain we're not the cause of it, we're the result" (Stasio 253). Our point is, however, that they do *contribute* to society's degeneration regardless of the original "cause" of this social breakdown. A drug dealer can't excuse his activity by claiming not to have been the inventor of the drugs or the cause of the abuser's addiction. Such arguments all turn out to be very self-righteous and deliberately confusing.

As for the rules of the game they play, there are ten common ones although there are some small variations among the talk shows:

1. The guest must talk provocatively about the prescribed subject to the exclusion of all other "irrelevant" aspects of his or her life.

2. The guest must confess all and is not encouraged to remain silent, assert that a topic is one of the host's and studio audience's business, or leave the stage.

3. The guest must appear to be an understandable and representative American regardless of appearance and the nature of confession. At the same time, however, the guest's actions, words, and/or appearance must be bizarre enough to be entertaining and to allow the audience to feel "smug" about not being like him or her.

4. The guest need not be informed in advance of surprise guests, unexpected personal information to be disclosed publicly about him or her, forced "outings," and other revelations.

5. The host must welcome and continuously interact with the guest in a familiar manner, often using his or her first name, regardless of the nature of the subject for discussion or the character of the guest.

6. The host must appear at all times interested, knowledgeable, concerned, sensitive and "appropriately upset," carrying the game forward regardless of how silly or scandalous the revelations may be.

7. The host cannot reveal the true nature (goal) of the game by telling guests that they are interesting or boring, important or insignificant, only in terms of the show's ratings for the day.

8. Neither the host nor the guest must regard any subject as taboo or inappropriate for public discourse. The object of disclosure is to let the guest speak without immediate dismissal.

9. The studio audience must act as participants by reacting visibly and audibly to the guest's revelations in response to the host's interrogation of the guest.

10. All players—the host, the studio audience, and other guests—are encouraged to provide advice, counsel, observations, therapy, praise, and censure of the guest under consideration.

WINNING STRATEGIES

So much for the rules, but how is the game won? As is the case with all games, winning this particular sport requires strategy and cunning. Let's say a National League baseball team is narrowly losing a game, and they manage to load the bases in the seventh inning with two outs and the pitcher batting next. Although the National League's official rules of play do not allow for a designated hitter, neither do they prevent the manager from suddenly deciding on a pitching change so that he can use a pinch hitter in this crucial situation. So it is with all games. While some spell out strategies for success, most do not codify such information. Rather, the successful players are the ones who devise ways to manipulate the rules in order to win. The television-talk game has its own winning strategies, but since we are dealing here not with sporting competition but the "magical" and primarily fictional world of television art, we prefer to see strategies as the illusions created to promote and sustain interest.

LIFE IMITATES ART

The first illusion concerns the milieu—the mood, setting, assumptions, and point of view—created through the technical manipulation of the medium. These involve things like the careful and artistic use of selective editing, graphics, camera angles, and music. Before looking at the way in which talk shows play with these techniques, however, let's consider some of the assumptions we make when we consume art.

It is true that, at some level, all art imitates life, but it is also true that this particular brand of imitation takes a very distinct form within a context which we are calling a "frame." Art is actually a controlled conspiracy between imagination and real life. In their imaginative construction of fictional stories, writers typically select their materials from everyday reality and arrange them in an orderly fashion so that they make artistic sense to readers, who agree to enter the frame world of the fiction. These readers know that, unlike real life—which is alternatively spontaneous and routine, messy and orderly, predictable and exciting, boring and interesting—the successful narrative world is always tightly controlled, fascinating, and orderly. It has a clear beginning, middle, and end. Moreover, simple solutions to complex problems are not hard to bring about in art because the magician behind the machine controls all things. Solutions in life, of course, are another matter altogether, but we can easily understand and accept the differences between our lives and our fictions because the frames are different. As a sage person once noted, "[T]he very notion of resolution is a sentimental deception."

A specific kind of narrative art—indeed, before television, the kind from which most people in our society received their fictions—is film. While the narrative frame is comparable to the one we find in prose fiction, the medium itself is different because of the manner in which the story is told. Added to the idea of artistic selection and imposition of order are the audio-visual techniques used to tell the story, and again, by knowing the frame, we know the rules of the game and can distinguish it from everyday life. In real-life situations, for instance, we expect stimuli to come at us from all directions, and even solemn moments can be broken by uncontrolled and spontaneous stimuli—say, a person sneezing loudly during a funeral eulogy. On the other hand, although film narratives create illusions of life, true spontaneity is not permissible. Dramatic twists and turns that appear shockingly spontaneous are actually scripted, and true spontaneous events like a ladder falling onto the set are edited out. Moreover, it is not your eye that finds what is interesting to look at from among the available stimuli, but the camera's eye. Careful editing of the images in that eye then ensures viewer fascination. To heighten dramatic effect even more and to efficiently establish mood, appropriate music accompanies the edited image we finally see. Sad music doesn't usually play during life's heartbreaking events, but it usually does during a heartbreaking scene in a movie. That's just the way things work, and we accept all of them as long as we understand the fictional vs. the real frames in which they (and we) are meant to operate.

Television uses comparable techniques, and we accept them there, too. But television—by far the most pervasive and invasive medium in our daily lives—goes much farther, for it often employs the materials of fiction in its presentation of real-life situations (mixing frames). News programs represent a prime example. Like dramatic fiction, all of them begin and end with "appropriate" theme music. All of them also present the news using a narrative (often dramatic) structure—selecting, arranging, and editing details—much as fiction writers do to create credible, coherent stories. Finally, all of them use the camera's eye to focus our attention. The television coverage of the O. J. Simpson trial was a good case in point. Ponderous, almost Wagnerian theme music was used to set a tone of gravity for this real-life drama. The camera continually focused on "interesting" scenes. If the coroner provided a graphic interpretation of the brutal murders of Nicole Simpson and Ronald Goldman, the camera found O. J.'s face, looking for a reactive shot. Although real trials (this one included) have a large number of boring moments in which legal procedural business is conducted, news programs give us only the juicy stuff from this slice of life—precisely what a fiction writer does. The confusion of messy, boring life and neat riveting drama is inevitable. And since most Americans get their news today from television rather than newspapers, it can be downright dangerous, especially in light of the fact that we are going about the business of our own real lives as we consume these images.[2] Whereas the darkened theater and the printed page represent frames in themselves, the images on the TV playing in the family room are a part of the everyday life going on around them.

Talk television, which is also supposed to be concerned with real life, uses the same techniques and because it's dealing with everyday people talking about private matters in a game format, it's more disconcerting. The deceptive techniques for winning the "game" (in this case, the ratings game) also begin with theme music—familiar sounds that are employed at the beginning, before commercial breaks, and the end, providing a stable and familiar base from which to proceed. The music is sometimes slowed or accelerated in the course of the program in accordance with the topic generally and the dramatic moments of the program specifically.

The camera is also used to provide riveting drama. Unlike the human eye which follows random stimuli, the camera's eye is strictly trained on the stars-for-a-day, the guests, alternating between long shots of the panel on stage and close-ups of the individual confessants. Close-up shots of the real star, the host, are also frequent, and this technique showcases the host's performance skills as he or she shows appropriately registered objectivity, concern, outrage, disbelief, sympathetic support, and so on. The studio audience also appears on camera periodically, but they are, as a group, more problematical and unpredictable than the other "stars." They are, after all, just people who have stood in line to see a theatrical exhibition starring their favorite daytime personality. Although the producers promise to provide the illusion of unscripted real-life drama, they are not about to tell the studio audience that the program is highly controlled, with guests often given instructions on what to say, how explicitly to say it, even what to wear. Nevertheless, there are some unpredictable theatrical lapses. The audience members may appear restless or self-conscious or adjust their clothing or look at their watches or get up and head for the bathroom. In that case, random shots would break the fictional frame, and so the producers must take only reactive shots of the audience as they register shock, amusement, anger, and other emotions.

Finally, of course, the whole is carefully edited to get rid of the boring stuff, to fit the material within the program's time limits, and to achieve maximum (even threatening) dramatic tension. In much the same way that hundreds of hours of theatrical film are edited into a tight ninety-minute movie, so several hours of videotape become forty-five minutes of television entertainment. Even the commercials, which ought to break the dramatic mood (imagine a movie with commercials between scenes), are brilliantly integrated, used for a timeout or a break from the story and bringing another kind of contrived "real life" into our homes along with the images seen on the talk shows. The realistic frame, in short, is deceptive, and this particular fiction is passed off as a slice of real life—life as art.

JUST THE "FACTS"

To say the least, the human mind is complex, and even people who are troubled in one particular area can live relatively normal lives in every other respect. To recycle the example we used earlier, a man may have a predilection for child abuse and still be an excellent dentist, a golfer with an enviable handicap, a loving husband and father, and a contributing member of society. This particular man would probably not look, act, or smell like a monster—not in real life anyway.

However, that sort of rounded projection of human life won't pass muster in the ratings game, and the winning strategy here involves focusing the entire portrayal of this person on his desire to receive and inflict pain. If that means ignoring the entire context in which his life is lived, then so be it. This is, after all, a game, and games have every right to be selective in their enactments of reality. Here are several highly effective techniques:

- Captions or subtitles known as chyrons are used to "define" the guest. If the chyron beneath the close-up shot of the dentist says "child abuser," then that is what he *is*, why he's there, and all other information about him becomes either irrelevant or interesting only in the context of his confession. If a show is about "out-of-control teenagers," the weight of an obese mother sitting there would not be an issue, whereas her weight would be highlighted if the show were about "obese mothers." In other words, the chyron tells one what to focus on.
- Each show is focused on a particular theme, and the guests are treated as variations on that theme rather than as individuals with unique biographies.
- Although the full biographical context of the guest's life is basically extraneous material, the audience must be made to feel as if they "know" the guest. This knowledge is basically the result of what little we are told about him and/or what he himself confesses. The credibility of his story, particularly in light of the limited time in which it is told, must not be questioned too closely, and if it is, the guest's truthfulness is to be measured by how sympathetic he appears and how forthcoming he has been with confession.
- Dramatic turns are most effective in focusing the game. Surprise guests hidden from the participants' view, outings, shocking public revelations, and other such devices ensure dramatic tension and corroboration of the singular program theme.

FLATTENING THE ROUND

For better or worse, we carry all of our cultural biases into our encounters with people, especially brief encounters. If an attractive woman in a business suit were to approach you in a crowded place during daylight hours to ask directions, you'd be more likely to stop and help than you would if any of the delimiters mentioned were altered—appearance, setting, time of day, perhaps even gender. (Not incidentally, successful con artists know how to exploit all of these biases.) By contrast, when we know a person well, all of these variables become far less important, even completely insignificant.

In literary analysis, characters are sometimes studied using the concepts of "roundness" and "flatness." Round (or dynamic) characters are multi-faceted, presented as three-dimensional people with strengths and flaws; flat (or static) characters, on the other hand, are those whom the author leaves one-dimensional, showing us only a particular side of his or her personality. If we apply this way of looking at characters to television talk shows, we find something very interesting—and very deceptive—taking place. Because of the genre's time and deliberate thematic limitations, guests (the characters of this particular fiction) are flattened and one-dimensional, like comic-book characters complete with talking balloons over their heads. However, at the same time, the audience is given the illusion that they "know" these people and are therefore in a position to judge and advise them. (Actually, by the time they come forward with advice, audience members have only heard from these strangers for about three minutes.) Likewise, the audience also has the illusion that they "know" the real star of the show, the host, even better since he or she is a familiar "friend" who appears on television every day and acts the same during each friendly encounter: concerned, helpful, knowing, wise, objective, sensitive, and unflappable. In reality, though, the host is a character in a real-life fiction, and for all of his or her seeming familiarity, this individual is even more "flat" than the guest since the persona that he or she reveals to us is more tightly scripted than that of the guest.

The effective creation of this illusion of familiarity is crucial to the success of the talk game. The audience's implied trust in the host and snap judgments of the contestants must occur efficiently if the game is to work, and to carry this process off, these programs must use our cultural biases, our "blueprints," against us. How is it done?

First and foremost, those guests who are the most likable and sympathetic are considered to be the most truthful. In fact, regardless of how odious the confession is, guests will be congratulated for their honesty and bravery if they maintain a pleasant and polite persona. By contrast, those who are contemptuous of the audience and/or of society at large are rejected, even if their judgments are valid. Such guests are typically chided for telling tales or gossiping irresponsibly or violating confidences.

Regardless of how flagrant the guests' confessions are, moreover, the host is always asking the audience to let them tell their side of the story (as if all admissions were formal arguments) and saying to the guests things like "We need to hear what you have to say" and "My audience wants to know your story." An illusion is thus created that the host is really a friend when in actuality he or she is only enabling the guests to strip themselves for public amusement. The overall effect is to make the host look reasonable to the audience and the confessant often more bizarre in his tastes, opinions, attitudes, and the like. Despite this, however, the ongoing discussion manages to give the illusion that these guests are representative members of society rather than an extremely biased and self-selected sampling of people desperate enough for attention or unstable enough to allow themselves to be made public spectacles. They feel cared about and thus drop whatever social guards they possess against public humiliation and stigma. This game is analogous to the gambling practice of "comping" losers in order to make them feel important and appreciated. In this way, television becomes a "safe place," giving them a sense that they are somehow beyond the bounds of normal public consequences.

Although, at least at the beginning of play, the host is supposedly objective and protective toward the guests, "on their side," they are often left to tell their stories alone onstage, unprotected, while the host wanders among the audience. This is more often the case on the newer and more successful programs (Jerry Springer, Ricki Lake, Jenny Jones), than on the earlier shows, in which Oprah Winfrey and Phil Donohue would usually sit on stage with their guests. The effect of leaving them alone is to isolate them while the host, however objective he or she may claim to be, is physically and intellectually *with* the audience, thereby increasing, without any real cause, his or her own credibility with them. Hosts tend to return to sit or stand near guests who are in danger of "breaking frame" or leaving the "game" (stage). They may even try to comfort them by physically holding them, touching them, or offering them a tissue. If all of this fails, they go to station break, and after the break, the guest has usually been cajoled into returning. Few leave for the duration of the broadcast. Eventually, some hosts (especially Geraldo and Montel) actually turn on the guests, attacking them personally for their disclosures, without which, ironically, the program would fail.

In turn, the audience, many of whom we've implied resemble the guests in condition, educational level, and some other factors, attack the guests too, for the audience members are given the illusion that they are somehow different from, better than, those telling their tales. All audience members appear equally credible in this populist, egalitarian, democratic world, and because of that illusion, they can feel good about what would normally be considered despicable behavior—eavesdropping on private matters, giggling at titillating disclosures, egging on the guests to provide more lurid detail. In general, the message is that the entire microcosm of the talk show (guests, hosts, producers, audience members in the studio and at home, advertisers) and the societal macrocosm are *all in this together.* In fact, the main problem is that, at some level, we are!

The seeming "normality" of these proceedings is important for maintaining conversation. If the confession were to appear beyond the pale of normal, useful talk, people would reject as outlandish what they were hearing. To the contrary, such talk often leads to requests for even more graphic description, which is gladly provided. The illusion created is that this talk is socially necessary and practical and that it can take place anywhere at any time and with anyone without social repercussion. Imagine being in a supermarket when a stranger comes up and says, "I think it's important that you know that my wife just ran off with my best friend." At that point, you'd probably run, too. But watching the talk-show game is different. Nothing is outrageous, including surprise guests with information about the contestant and public outings. Few revelations, however shocking, are met with "that's none of our business." No one is supposed to say, "How dare you ask such an inappropriate question?" as one likely would in real life. No one feels threatened enough to run for the hills or call the cops. Less drastically but no less effective, one rarely walks out of the studio or even turns the television set off. But we have evidence to suggest that people do consider these confessions outrageous in real life. When many guests return home, they find that they are indeed shunned and hated by their *real* friends and neighbors, looked upon as embarrassing pariahs.

THERAPY IN THE ARENA

Therapy, like surgery, is not a spectator sport carried out for our entertainment. And yet, one of the chief strategies of the talk shows is to present the illusion that since confession is supposedly good for both the individual and collective social souls, the advice offered to troubled confessants by hosts, audience members, call-in viewers, and pop psychologists can help to heal both the guest and the greater society whose "problem" he or she supposedly represents. None of us is privy to the training (or lack thereof), theories, track records, or biases of these particular "therapists." Legitimate therapists, needless to say, do not practice in televised soundbites, and talk-show performers and their audiences are not in a position to "heal" anyone. In *Tuning in Trouble,* the authors, Jeanne Heaton and Nona Wilson, who interviewed Abt, agree that "the shows make a mockery of the mental health profession" and indicate their own concern when therapy is reduced to "the level of sound-bite sensation" (5).

Of course, the purpose of the confessants' disclosures is entertainment, not therapy, and that entertainment has been known to go to bizarre lengths. For a while Oprah and others were devoting shows to hair-raising stories by "adult children" who suddenly remembered repressed memories of childhood incest and other parental abuses. These people would appear to tell their shocking tales on television, often with their own or the resident "therapist" and sometimes their horrified aging parents trying to defend themselves. Because many of these parents have brought legal actions against such therapists for "brainwashing" troubled people into believing they remembered things that never actually happened, there are virtually no shows devoted to this topic any longer. So much for the social usefulness of these therapeutic programs. This is not to say that all repressed memories are false, only that they are not easily validated phenomena and, more important, that talk shows are not able to deal with the complexities of human memory, disturbed familial relationships, and complicated interactions and emotions.

Rather, they treat all subjects briefly (between frequent commercial breaks) and in black and white terms with easy answers and quick fixes. This approach, which is more

pariahs · exiles, people outcast.

appropriate for entertainment than for healing, is responsible for generating a variety of socially dangerous illusions:

- That quick fixes to complex problems are possible in a public airing, working out with a few minutes of "advice" the difficulties of a lifetime, as if coming clean were enough
- That appearing on the show is "therapy" in itself and, if really necessary, that people will follow up the quick-fix therapy with more traditional long-term therapy, though the hosts and producers rarely provide systematic evidence of such follow-up or its efficacy
- That all therapy is equally useful or, indeed, that it works at all most of the time (criminologists today pretty much agree that verbal therapy for sex offenders, for instance, doesn't usually work)
- That the personal revelations of troubled people will help to heal comparable problems within society itself (e.g., teenage pregnancy), since their problems, insights, and solutions are assumed to be universal
- That pop "psychobabble" or trite homilies or generalized panaceas (e.g., developing self-esteem) will repair the failures brought about by illness, economic deprivation, educational inadequacy, and other cultural conditions
- That audience members, hosts, and "legitimate" therapists are in a position to give therapeutic advice or reject as "freaks" those beyond the help of two-minute healing sessions
- That large social forces—economic, political, historical, bureaucratic— are subordinate to pop concepts like "hugging your inner child," "getting in touch with your higher power," "self-esteem," "communication," and getting away from "co-dependency" and "enabling"
- That emotional moments like forgiving reunions, replete with close-up shots of crying participants who are "sorry" for their past actions, are anything more than the stuff of fiction applied to real-world problems
- That people who have engaged in or have been victims of such serious offenses as incest or rape can be rapidly rehabilitated, or at the very least helped by confession, advice, or "finding God" and that there need be no irrevocable consequences (emotional pain, stigma) of these actions.

Knowing how a magician manages to perform a sleight-of-hand illusion may wreck the entertainment value of the trick, but the sleight-of-hand illusions performed by talk shows, although seemingly mere entertainment, may be contributing to the wrecking of our common civil culture. Only by understanding the game, the players, and strategies does the viewer—and the culture—have a better chance to win.

■ *Vickie Abt and Leonard Mustazza are professors at Penn State Abington in suburban Philadelphia. Abt has written numerous scholarly articles and is co-author of a landmark book on gambling,* The Business of Risk: Commercial Gambling in Mainstream America. *Mustazza, a professor of English and American studies, is the author of many articles on literature and popular culture, as well as two books about writer Kurt Vonnegut and one about singer Frank Sinatra.*

NOTES

1. Montel Williams's nonexploitative persona may have been undermined by June 1996 stories that some female employees have accused him of sexual harassment and that he reportedly held production staff meetings while he was dressed in his underwear (Speers F2).
2. This troubling blurring of news and entertainment has been widely discussed. See especially Ken Auletta, *Three Blind Mice: How the TV Networks Lost Their Way* (New York: Random House, 1991); and Neil Postman and Steve Powers, *How to Watch TV News* (New York: Penguin, 1992).

MAKING SURE OF THE TEXT

1. Who are the players and what are their roles in daytime talk shows such as *The Oprah Winfrey Show, Maury,* and *The Jerry Springer Show*?
2. Why is talk television particularly deceptive in its "realistic frame"? What happens when you look behind the frame?
3. Identify elements of the talk show that correspond to Seiter's *sign, referent, connotation,* and *denotation.*
4. In what ways are our cultural biases used against us by "the talk game"?

CONSIDERING THE CONTEXT

1. What effect is achieved by contextualizing the talk show as a game? Why might Abt and Mustazza have chosen to pursue this analogy?
2. Look at another genre of television (the soap opera, the reality TV show, the courtroom or hospital drama) and identify the rules by which it works. Is it a game, like the talk TV show, or do the rules you identify apply to something different?
3. What other reading might you give of the talk show genre? What artifacts would you choose to support this reading?

■ ■ ■

"Rare Jordan," from *Essence* (1996)

Nelson George

A few seasons ago, in the now-defunct Chicago Stadium, Michael Jordan was being guarded by the eager but over-matched John Starks. I sat fifteen rows behind them, wearing my Knicks cap amid a sea of Bulls red and black. I'd flown in the day before and scalped tickets, determined to see Starks and the rest of my beloved New York team finally dethrone the Bulls.

What a joke.

Sometime during the second half, Jordan rises, the No. 23 on his chest suspended in air as Starks elevates. The Knick, who earlier in the series jammed in Jordan's face, has hopes, but no one is Jordan. Starks begins his journey back to earth, but Jordan continues to hang, defying gravity. He releases the ball and, like a bird of prey, the potential three-pointer soars toward the hoop. The shot is good. The crowd explodes. I cringe and of course the Knicks lose. Of the fifty-four points Jordan scores that night, it is this single shot that lingers in my mind.

This is my Jordan moment. You probably have your own. Built one by one, they have lifted him to the enviable, extraordinary and undoubtedly taxing position of African-American hero—with equal emphasis placed on the African and the American. His achievement comes in an era when unqualified Black male heroism is rare and thus particularly precious. While White-chosen heroes (Christopher Darden,[1] Clarence Thomas[2]), flawed icons (Tupac Shakur, Mike Tyson) and polarizing forces (Marion Barry,[3] Louis Farrakhan[4]) proliferate, Jordan has universal respect from women and men, Blacks and Whites and children of all ages.

That's not to say the ride has always been smooth. There have been failures, eccentric choices and profound tragedies in his otherwise charmed life. These trials, along with the triumphs, have shaped him into something of a living, breathing Rorschach test.[5] When this country looks at Jordan, it sees its dreams, obsessions—even its fears.

After all, there are many Michael Jordans. There is Jordan the star. Jordan the athlete. Jordan the family man. Jordan the sex symbol. Jordan the commodity. Jordan the role model. And Jordan the personification of Black masculinity. By that I mean that Michael embodies some of the deepest fantasies Black men have of themselves. Like those of Jack Johnson, Joe Louis, "Sugar" Ray Robinson, Jackie Robinson, Willie Mays, Muhammad Ali, Julius Erving and a handful of

---

[1]Christopher Darden: An attorney for the prosecution in the O. J. Simpson case.
[2]Clarence Thomas: Supreme Court justice who was cleared of sexual harassment charges in the Anita Hill investigation.
[3]Marion Barry: Former mayor of Washington, D.C., who was convicted on drug charges.
[4]Louis Farrakhan: Radical black leader of the Nation of Islam.
[5]Rorschach test: Diagnostic test used by psychologists in which patients are asked to interpret ink blots.

others, Michael Jordan's movements, boldness and skill allow African-American men to see the best of themselves projected in the symbolic war of sports.

In every culture the warrior plays the role of elemental icon of a community's spirit. In America our history of enslavement sometimes makes us nervous about how much emotion we should invest in these athletes. Are they not just well-paid studs? Do they not entertain at the whim of wealthy White men? No doubt both observations have some merit.

But to negate the individual will of these men, to ignore the power and glory of their prowess, is to deny ourselves access to the purity and strength they display. There is a thrill, a kinetic quality of life that a Louis, a Mays, a Jordan taps into that we need. Now African-Americans need other things too. (An emphasis on literacy would be a great start.) Yet Michael's brand of Black masculinity—explosive, graceful, yet grounded in work and morality—is quite simply beautiful and essential.

Jordan, of course, consistently transcends his role as mere player. Through a series of megabuck endorsement deals, he hovers above the game as a commercial staple, a Black face with the mass appeal to sell goods (and himself), rivaled only by prime time's favorite sepia pitchman, Bill Cosby. Plying the media with his cool southern charm, while playing the game spectacularly, Jordan defies the stereotypes of the street-hardened, inner-city athlete. He grew up in the Sunbelt state of North Carolina in a solid nuclear family.

Religious, well-spoken and with none of the wariness of Whites that hampers many African-American men, Michael Jordan represents the flip side of the crack dealers who populate the local news broadcasts of big cities. With the exception of Julius Erving, no previous African-American basketball hero has had the same balance of tremendous talent, public poise and personal charisma. But it's the late tennis great Arthur Ashe whom, because of his southern background, charm and crossover appeal, Jordan calls to mind. While Ashe was the real-life Sidney Poitier[6] amid the country-club set, Jordan, with his clean-cut, starched shirt on Sunday morning, epitomizes Black masculinity—without the rough edges of so many Generation X players.

More than any other contemporary African-American athlete, he thrives in the pressure cooker of corporate commitments—appearances at charitable events, golf tournaments and commercial shoots—while never making any embarrassing "I'm not Black, I'm universal" comments and without selling his soul. He works in the system while retaining his Black identity, and he has arrived without a nose job or a White wife.

---

[6]Sidney Poitier: Suave African American actor who starred in the movie *Guess Who's Coming to Dinner* and *To Sir, With Love.*

Just as he succeeded Erving on the court, Jordan followed the elegant Dr. J as the preeminent Black athletic sex symbol. And Jordan's smooth, chocolate handsomeness has made it easier for brothers to get dates when the Bulls come to town. His wagging tongue, baggy (now standard issue) shorts and 800-watt smile reflect a stylish, idiosyncratic and confident man. By coolly accepting his baldness, he made his glistening Black dome the defining African-American hairstyle of the era, chasing out the seemingly entrenched high-top fade. At the same time Jordan's public-speaking style grew increasingly polished, a welcome alternative to the you-know-what-I'm-sayin' syndrome that too many other brothers display.

When I ask women what they like about Jordan, the answer is often, "He married the mother of his children," which they felt spoke to his morality and class. Unlike many other Black sports superstars of this era, Michael never let himself be perceived as a dog. He married Juanita Vanoy in September 1989, within a year of the birth of their first child, Jeffrey Michael. Two more children, Marcus and Jasmine, followed. Though Jordan wisely guards his home life with his wife and children, it's clear that his professional accomplishments are made possible by the solid foundation he and Juanita have created at home.

The credit for Jordan's character goes back to the steadying influence of his parents. During his childhood, they set the kind of hardworking example so many Black men lack. His late father, James, a smallish, relaxed southern man, worked his way up from forklift operator to a supervisor at Wilmington's General Electric plant. His mother, Deloris, who recently authored a book on child rearing and was the stern disciplinarian, worked as a clerical supervisor at United Carolina Bank. On occasions when Michael had misbehaved, she wasn't averse to taking him along to sit beside her and do his homework.

But Jordan's loving childhood and his astute decision making haven't immunized him against the violence that rocks our community. Which brings me to my next Jordan moment, one that is sure to linger in my mind long after he retires. In fact, for anyone who saw it, it helped redefine the man. The moment came right after the Bulls knocked out the Seattle Supersonics in game six last June, when Jordan snatched the game ball and fell to the floor, clutching it as teammates and fans began celebrating around him.

Then, seeking privacy, he sprinted to the locker room, where despite all the frivolity, he sought a moment of solitude. Of course he didn't get it. Cameras, a constant in his life, dogged his steps, and with them came the eyes of the whole world. We watched as he lay on the floor, crying for the man who could not be there. It was Father's Day, and the basketball great grieved anew for his father, who had been murdered three years before.

Unlike so many contemporary public figures, Michael never used his tragedy to gain sympathy for himself. No cheap sentimentality. No playing the victim. No sobbing on Oprah. He has handled the entire matter with a dignity as heroic as any jump shot. And yet, in a moment of profound public triumph, he gave in to private pain. The journey Jordan has taken in recent years—retirement, baseball career, the difficult comeback—arguably had as its catalyst his father's death. So it was only fitting that James Jordan's presence loom large in that championship locker room.

Over time, the lesson of Michael's career may be to illustrate how even the great can be humbled. Steeled by fire, he returned to basketball with heightened appreciation for the game and his role within it. Moreover he has made peace with aging. These days, his atmospheric forays to the hoop are far less frequent. Instead he attacks with a pump fake, turning a defender's legs into jelly and then burying a jump shot. No more a sprinter, he, like a canny distance runner, paces himself until the crucial third and fourth quarters.

Ultimately, history will not judge Jordan's greatness by his vicious slam dunks or clever ad campaigns. Rather it will judge him as a father and a son, and as a man, a Black man—one of the best we've ever had.

■ *Nelson George is a veteran journalist and a critical fan of African-American musical culture. His previous book,* The Death of Rhythm & Blues *(1991), won several awards for its broad, insightful personality of criticism.*

MAKING SURE OF THE TEXT

1. How does Jordan "epitomize Black masculinity"? Contrast this statement with George's comment about the "you-know-what-I'm-sayin'" types.
2. How does George describe the moment in the Bulls locker room when Jordan "sought a moment of solitude" that the cameras prevented? Does his writing about that moment suggest a second invasion of privacy or does he have another purpose in mind?
3. Examine the image of Michael Jordan carefully. If you found this image in a heap of other images (choose a variety to give this question some weight), how would you compare it to the others? On what grounds?

CONSIDERING THE CONTEXT

1. What signs of greatness does George see in Jordan? How would you read those same signs in another person?
2. What is the context of the image George describes at the beginning of his article? How does that context affect his reading of the scene? Consider, for instance, George's own emotional investment in seeing the Bulls play, the location of the game, and the opposing team.
3. What is the effect of contrasting the various Michaels? What other Michaels would you identify?

■ ■ ■

Future Perfect: How Star Trek Conquered Planet Earth (1998)

Jeff Greenwald

PATRICK STEWART, "CAPTAIN PICARD"

"What is it about the show," I ask, "that speaks to villagers in Bangladesh, Croatia, or even Mongolia?"

"Storytelling is international," Stewart unzips his parka; Beavis and Butt-head leer beneath the fleece. "All cultures use it as the basis of their literature, their drama, their legends, their mythology. And *Star Trek* tells very good stories. I think that's something we've done very well. Then," he pauses reflectively, "there's a broader, perhaps more philosophical aspect to *The Next Generation.* One of the things that kept my interest high was the fact that the program was about *ideas* as well as stories."

Another explanation for the show's global popularity, Stewart theorizes, is that it coincided with an octave shift in the tenor of international relations. "Human rights" was becoming a familiar phrase, and skillful diplomacy was gaining ground against aggression and hostility.

"During the lifetime of our show, look what happened in the world! During the seven years that we were doing *The Next Generation,* the Berlin Wall came down, and the repressive, authoritarian Communist regimes were overthrown in most countries. In Northern Ireland, the IRA and the British government began to talk to one another. In South Africa, apartheid ended, and Nelson Mandela came out of jail.

"It was simply extraordinary," Stewart says, his voice impassioned. "Things changed in the world that I did not expect to see changed in my lifetime. And a lot of those things changed because people sat down and talked. They said, 'There have been sins in the past, but we must put them aside. We must be able to talk with one another, otherwise we will never move forward.' And that," he slaps the arm of his chair, "is fundamental of *The Next Generation.* It's absolutely Captain Picard's main thrust as a negotiator. You talk and talk and talk . . . you talk until you don't have any breath left. There's always something that can be negotiated. And you do it with respect. You try to see the other person's point of view, to put yourself in their shoes.

"Of course," he recalls, reining himself in, "TNG also spanned the Gulf War, and the beginning of the nightmare in the Balkans. And Rwanda, yes, and the increasing repression in China."

> **Apartheid** · the national policy of discrimination against black Africans.
> **Nelson Mandela** · jailed political leader of South Africa; when released after 25 years, he was elected to the highest political position in the country.
> **"the nightmare in the Balkans," Rwanda** · references to policies of genocide, or "ethnic cleansing."

MICHAEL DORN, "WORF"

The conversation turns toward my travels and my perception of *Star Trek* as a real time international myth. When I ask Dorn about the gap the show might be filling in the collective psyche, though, he snorts in dismissal. "*Baywatch* is filling a bigger space than . . ."

"Yeah," I counter, "but *Baywatch* hasn't lasted for thirty years."

"But in terms of it being global, *Baywatch* is a bigger show. Look." Dorn turns up his hands. "I think that people who are obsessed with *Star Trek* would like to attach some importance to it—more than what it is. But I think Gene [Roddenberry] would be the first person to tell you, it's a *people* show. He was just doing great television."

"Well, it certainly transcends the medium for a lot of the people I've spoken with."

But Dorn's not having any. "I've heard," he says, "that people think [*Star Trek*] really shows the future that we hope for. God, I hope not! I hope our future's a lot better than this one!" He tilts his head toward the darkened set. "They also say, 'Oh, the stories are moralistic, they're all morality plays!'

"But me?" He shrugs. "I think that if somebody cures cancer by watching this show, if they're inspired to go beyond their physical limitations or abilities, that's great. But if you're asking honestly, I think it's great television—and that's just about it. It's something everybody can relate to. You can sit down and escape, after eight hours of fighting all day."

"Still," I insist, "the show is one of the only programs with a consistently positive ethical premise. Meanwhile, the rest of television is dumbing off into vaudeville-type comedy, hospital dramas, cop shows . . ."

Dorn stares at me; his eyes are unblinking and intense. "This is a bone of contention for me. Television is entertainment. It's great if it educates; I'm all for that. But I don't think you can educate through sitcoms, or even through dramatic shows, because they're written for a particular reason. It's *entertainment*. Same with this movie. If you want an education, you should go to PBS, or a library, and read about real heroes. Otherwise, I think entertainers should entertain—and TV should be television."

GATES MCFADDEN, "DR. CRUSHER"

I ask McFadden if she has any specific thoughts about why the *Star Trek* mythology has penetrated so deeply into the global psyche.

She has; and her observation revolves around one of Campbell's theories. The mythologist, she recalls, once wrote about early nomadic codes: commandments stating that one must never kill or steal within one's own group. Limited as they were, such codes recognized that, to ensure survival, the members of a vulnerable society must be mutually supportive.

That ideal is breaking down in modern society. The world is shrinking, groups are dispersing, and a free-for-all mentality is in vogue. *Star Trek,* McFadden explains, reaffirms the nomadic code—on a planetwide scale. The *Enterprise* is a metaphor, a microcosm of what Buckminster Fuller called "Spaceship Earth."

"You see that people can encounter the unknown—the fears, the lawlessness, the new worlds—and get along with each other. They can work together and still maintain control. Rather than dissolve and get completely overwhelmed—which is, of course, a huge and primal fear."

Another reason *Star Trek* is universally appealing, McFadden believes, is that it offers an antidote to the isolation that new technologies—laser disc players, the Web, Walkmans—are pressing upon us. "Even though electronic communication is much faster and more frequent, one-on-one communication seems more difficult than it used to be. The computer gives us information, and we have more things to digest. More is expected of us, because everything is so compressed.

"But the *Star Trek* people don't let technology control them. The computer is just another character, and they know how to coexist with it. That is *very* reassuring: We've worked technology into the myth. You see it very clearly in *First Contact.* There's the Borg, who use technology to destroy, and there's Starfleet, which uses technology to prevail over those evil forces."

Listening to this, I'm reminded again of how far a leap *Star Trek* is from "traditional" science fiction—and classic mythology. *First Contact* would have a much different slant if the aliens summoned by the *Phoenix's* warp drive had chained Zefram Cochrane to a rock and let vultures pick at his liver.

"Have you studied religion," I ask McFadden, "as deeply as you've studied mythology?"

"I haven't studied it, yet I am fascinated by it." She waves to Jonathan Frakes, who waves back and signals "five minutes" with splayed fingers. "I loved the Mass in Latin. I loved the *mystery* of it. The power of ritual was something I remember very much growing up. And I think that's what attracts me to ritual in theater."

Patrick Stewart and Marina Sirtis appear on the set, followed by James Cromwell, Alfre Woodard, and LeVar Burton. Everyone but Michael Dorn and Brent Spiner will be in this final scene, in which the *Enterprise* away-team witnesses first contact before warping back to the 24th century.

McFadden watches them arrive, surveying the players with a critical eye. "I've also studied mask theater," she remarks, "and it's striking how there are always similar characters in every major culture."

"Do you collect masks?"

"I do. I've made about sixty myself. They're all in trunks, in New York. It's a

Buckminster Fuller · visionary and religious leader.

The Borg · race of beings who are half-humanoid and half-machine.

Zefram Cochrane · *Star Trek's* inventor of warp (faster than light) drive.

whole part of my life that's been stashed away. I have beautiful masks from Europe, Japan, India, Bali . . ."

"Whereas in Bali," I laugh, "they're probably collecting vintage *Star Trek* episodes."

"That's because *Star Trek,* too, is a morality play." Gates stands up, tosses her hair, and prepares to join her famous clan. "It's a science fiction *parable* that's seen all over the world. And yet, there is not this sense—as you get in a lot of science fiction—that, 'there is no light in the world anymore. All is darkness.' You get the fact that there is indeed light. There is the possibility of redemption—and we are there to do it."

RON MOORE, EXECUTIVE PRODUCER, AND JOE MENOSKY, WRITER

"I don't think the show has broken a lot of new ground as far as the technology of the future goes—the way people think of Asimov or Jules Verne—but it *is* unique, and it *has* broken ground, in what it says about what we want to be as a people. As human beings." Ron [Moore] splays his hand, and starts ticking off his fingers. "We want to have gotten rid of racism. We want to have solved crime. We want to have beaten poverty. We want to be out there in the galaxy, bringing our idealistic view to other people. And we want to be nonjudgmental."

I think this over. It's true enough that Gene Roddenberry was a great believer in multiculturalism. But that didn't prevent a democratic chauvinism from dominating, at least in the original series. Captain Kirk was forever making speeches, pointing out how primitive or deluded various other civilizations were.

"That's the difference," Moore confirms, "between the '60s and the '90s."

"What's most revealing to me," I add, "is that *Star Trek* assumes that humanity's highest good, our best and brightest attribute, is *curiosity.* It's a heroic view of science."

"Yeah." Ron's heard this one before. "The quest for knowledge. *To boldly go.* It's right in the prologue; that's always driven the show."

"*Star Trek* translates," I observe, "precisely because humans *are* curious. And because we're so easy to entertain." I tell Moore about a group of rickshaw drivers I saw in Bali, watching *CHiPs* on the village television. They were laughing and shouting, reacting just as they would during a traditional shadow-puppet play.

Moore smiles, and rocks back in his chair. "It makes me feel better, to hear things like that. When we talk about the global reach of what we do, it sometimes makes me uncomfortable. But if people in Indonesia are watching *CHiPs* . . ." he snorts, "I *know* we're not doing any more damage than that."

I reach over to Moore's desk and pick up a die-cast replica of the *Enterprise.* Someday, baffled archeologists will dig this stuff out of the rubble—assuming California doesn't cleave off into the sea. "What strikes me," I comment, "is the irony of all this. *Star Trek* posits a future in which the Earth is basically one nation. But getting to that point, to the point of Starfleet and the United Federation of Planets, requires that everyone on the planet ultimately buy into the same value system: ours."

"Yeah." Menosky gives an abbreviated laugh. "That's terrible, isn't it?"

"That's the comforting, frightening thought of the future," Moore pronounces. "That we'll all become one."

"Just look at America," I remark. "Are we actually consolidating? Or are we shattering into a zillion different ethnic and interest groups, each with its own agenda?"

"In TNG, we were fighting that battle too." Moore bat his thumb on the desk. "We were trying to draw the lines between the unique cultural identities of our characters, yet they all had to service the Federation philosophy together."

"Even *Voyager* may still reflect this a little bit," Menosky concedes. "When you think about Chakotay [the Native American first officer of *Voyager*], there is an emphasis on retaining his ethnicity, ancient beliefs and world view, but *within a given value system*. We do assume that everyone has a Starfleet view. Things like fundamentalist Islam are just not compatible in this system. We seem," he concludes wryly, "to disallow absolute incompatibilities in the *Star Trek* universe."

"Again, like America," Moore observes. "America wants you to retain your pride in your heritage. But you're also supposed to live within the broader value system that we have chosen to run this country by."

He shakes his head. "We've always said, amongst ourselves, that there is profoundly more diversity on the planet Earth than we have ever portrayed in the galaxy. The aliens we meet on the show are pretty tame," he quips, "compared to the Bushmen of the Kalahari."

"What we *really* are," Menosky adds, "is a reflection of late-20th-century *California* culture. The original series is an amazing time capsule of the 1960s. The colors, the music—everything. And I guess *The Next Generation* will do the same for the 1980s. When people look back on *Next Gen,* the single thing that will date the show most is *Counselor Troi on the bridge.* That was the embodiment of how far therapy went in the '80s. A therapist was so important, she had to sit next to the captain!"

Moore stands up. His stomach growls. "Determining what the '60s were like as opposed to the '80s is already an archeological project," he muses. "Other shows that came out of that time are also about the '60s— *Love American Style* is about relationships, on some strange level—but *Star Trek* tells you about the New Frontier, and JFK, and what we wanted to be. Why we were going to the moon in the first place."

"It's Camelot." I nod. "In space."

"Camelot in space." Moore likes the taste of the words. "Which was a noble goal. And that goal still drives us, to a certain extent. We're the ones they passed that torch to."

KATE MULGREW, "CAPTAIN JANEWAY"

But what does she, the woman charged with carrying the mythos forward, make of all this?

"It *is* a family drama. But would it be a drama of such compelling proportions if we were not lost in space in the 24th century? I don't think so. It also comes from an unbelievably exciting extension of the imagination that can put us into the future—with hope and with curiosity. That's the glue. That's the attraction. It triggers everything that's exciting about human nature." She frowns. "But I frankly do not understand the global proportions. I don't *get* the phenomenal aspect of it, because I'm so subjectively involved. And we don't hear about all that in Hollywood. We've been low man on the totem pole around here."

"I guess that's why Paramount brought in a Borg babe with big tits. They're looking for something that will sell the show to their assumed audience: boys between the ages of eighteen and thirty."

She offers a pained smile. "If that's their main thing, all I can say to you is, *Why did they hire a female captain in the first place?* A middle-aged female captain is not going to appeal to their demographic! A man would; or I might, as a first officer. So they're going to have to readjust their thinking a little . . . along with me. I can bend a little bit; they've got to bend a little bit. They have to understand that it's *adult* women and men who find this captain appealing. And girls, all over the world.

"As for young boys, between eighteen and thirty—" her voice tightens with conviction. "They want a good story more than anybody else. They need the mythology more than any other faction or demographic group. They don't need any more tits and ass than they already see in every hour of their day." Mulgrew shakes her head. "Maybe I'm wrong. I hope I'm not wrong."

LEONARD NIMOY, "SPOCK"

As Nimoy speaks, I find myself stealing glances at his ears. They are large, beautifully shaped, and, for the moment, perfectly human. They may be, I realize, the most notorious ears in history. Nearly every book about the making of *Star Trek* describes in exquisite detail the agonies these poor ears have suffered: the endless plaster castings, the rubber molds, the fittings with foam rubber and glue; month after month of trial and error, culminating at last in the otherworldly appendages familiar to everyone from Dennis Rodman to the Dalai Lama. Seeing those famous ears this way—in their natural, unguarded state—is vaguely shocking, like seeing God without his beard.

"You know," I say, "what you've done may be unique in the history of entertainment. You've created a mythological character as compelling as any in world literature. But have you given any thought as to *why* Spock strikes such a universal chord? What is it about Spock himself that resonates so deeply with people?"

"I think it operates on a lot of levels," he reflects. "Early on, when the show first went on the air, I was receiving mounds and mounds of fan mail from little kids. They couldn't have had any concept of what Spock was about, except that he was a strange and interesting-looking man, one who didn't *frighten* them."

The children sent him thousands of drawings, all of Spock. Something about the Vulcan's image—the ears, the eyebrows, the bowl-cut hair—was tremendously compelling to them.

"Which was very interesting, because NBC was very trepidant about the ears and the eyebrows." Nimoy leans back, his arm draped casually behind his head. "They especially thought Spock might be problematic in the Bible Belt, where people would see him as a devilish character." He smiles faintly. "It was quite the contrary, of course."

Nimoy swivels slowly in his chair. I peer around the office, noticing a 1951 pulp poster from *Kid Monk Baroni*. This was Nimoy's first starring role; he was twenty. Like Spock, this character had an odd appearance. The "Monk" was a slightly disfigured Italian boxer, a forceps baby from New York's Lower East Side.

"And then there's the aspect of Spock's distance, Spock's *coolness*," Nimoy continues. "Which played well in the sixties, when 'cool' was important. I've also read pieces by women, that describe Spock as someone whom women wanted to nurture, as he seemed to need the warmth that a woman can offer. There was also the challenge of, 'Could I be the one to "awaken" Spock? Could I be the one who can help him get in touch with his sexuality, and with intimacy?'"

I was hooked on Spock at twelve—but it obviously wasn't about sex, or nurturing. And although I never trotted out my Vulcan Green Crayola, he definitely got under my skin. He's there still—and I admit as much to Nimoy. He nods sympathetically.

"That's because there is also a sensitive side to Spock, to which a lot of people, male *and* female, responded. Also very important—at least *I* thought it was, because it was what I was constantly playing—is the yin/yang balance between our right and left brains. How do you get through life as a feeling person, without letting emotions rule you? How do you balance the intellectual and emotional sides of your being? I think people identified with that and understood that, in that sense, Spock is a very *human* character. He chooses to downplay, ignore, deny, his emotions—but he *has* them."

"I think Spock was a proud alien," Nimoy concludes. "Proudly alienated. And kids still identify with that. I see kids today with strange hair, strange piercings, tattoos; this is all about alienation, and establishing a separate identity. 'I am *not* one of the crowd. I am different. I am special.' And Spock always *was* different and special. Jokingly, to Dr. McCoy [DeForest Kelley], he would say, 'This is the way I am, and I don't have a problem with it. If you do, it's *your* problem.' I think that resonates for young people. Teenagers, adolescents, who are trying to play out their own identity in the world, without getting sucked into the mass culture."

When all is said and done, though, no one—with the exception of Gene Roddenberry himself—has had a longer, more vital, or more *intelligent* relationship with the show. Acknowledging this, I ask Nimoy for his sense of what *Star Trek* is—and what it could be.

"For me, it always goes back to the basic ideas we were dealing with when I was very active with the show. The *Enterprise* crew was a professional team of people solving problems. Those problems had relevance in this culture, even though they were placed in the 23rd century. And it was always a very *humanistic* show; one that celebrated the potential strengths of mankind, of our civilization, with great respect for all kinds of life, and a great hope that there be communication between civilizations and cultures.

"Stories that grow out of that kind of an ethos are what *Star Trek* should always be about," he concludes. "And I think that resonates throughout the world."

■ *Jeff Greenwald, noted travel and science writer, has written for the San Francisco Examiner,* The Los Angeles Times, Wired, *and* Details. *He is the editor of GNN's "Big World" room on the Internet, http://gnn.com, writes a monthly column for HotWired, and has an extensive website at www.jeffgreenwald.com. In this selection, Greenwald asks* Star Trek *cast members what they see as* Trek's *appeal.*

MAKING SURE OF THE TEXT

1. How do each of the cast members interviewed see the function of *Star Trek*? For instance, Michael Dorn sees the series as entertainment; Gates McFadden does not. Summarize the responses.
2. How are Leonard Nimoy's ears (as part of the Spock costume) significant to the *Trek* concept? Think in terms of indexical signs and connotations; if you are a *Trek* fan, consider McCoy's frequent insults about Spock's ears to help you answer this question.
3. Executive producer Ron Moore suggests a clear difference between the images of the 1960s *Star Trek* and the 1990s *Star Trek*. What do the differences reflect?
4. How does *Star Trek* provide us with images of curiosity, which Joe Menosky points out is key to the series? That is, what images in *Trek* stand for "curiosity" to you?

CONSIDERING THE CONTEXT

1. Contrast the image of the African-American hero of *Star Trek*, Captain Benjamin Sisko, with the image of the African-American hero of Nelson George's article. What similarities do the two share? How do their differences reflect their different contexts?
2. What other images in *Star Trek* do you see that represent your perspective on "America"?
3. Contrast the function of *Star Trek* with the function of other science fiction shows, for instance *Lost in Space, Quantum Leap,* or *Babylon 5*. What differences and similarities do you find?
4. What is the effect of Greenwald's various references, from the Bible Belt, to the Italian boxer, to Bushmen of the Kalahari? What do you know about those references that adds to your understanding of Greenwald's article?

■ ■ ■

"When Screen Violence is Not Attractive," from *Why We Watch: The Attractions of Violent Entertainment* (1998)

Clark McCauley

Screen violence is not always attractive. In a volume focusing on the attractions of symbolic violence, it is useful to consider some of the limits of such attraction. In this chapter, I begin with research on disgust that found three documentary films of blood and violence that undergraduate students, at least, do not want to watch. After trying out some simple explanations of the unattractiveness of these films, I turn to theory and research aimed at understanding the genre of commercial film violence that should be most disgusting—horror films. This literature does not provide much help in understanding the unattractiveness of the disgusting films, but it leads to two new studies with results that suggest that viewers can enjoy the experience of negative emotions such as disgust and fear. I conclude by examining two possible theories of how negative emotions can be experienced as positive; both theories point to the importance of dramatic distance—framing violence as fiction—if screen violence is to be attractive.

REACTIONS TO VIOLENCE IN RESEARCH ON DISGUST

In their research on sensitivity to disgust, Haidt, Rozin, and McCauley (1994) put individual college students in front of a TV set to watch three documentary-style videotapes involving violence and gore. The first film shows a dinner party at a large table in which the centerpiece is a live monkey; the monkey is hammered unconscious on camera, its skull opened, and its still-pulsing brains served onto platters for the epicure diners. The second film shows a slaughterhouse; the camera follows steers as they are stunned, have their throats cut, and are hung up to be butchered. The third film shows head surgery conducted on a young girl; surgeons pull the child's face inside out away from her skull.

The student subjects in this research were given a control with which they could shut off the videotape whenever they did not want to watch anymore. (Students were told that this was a control condition for a hypnotism experiment, and that the investigators needed to find out what normal and awake subjects are willing to put up with.) The students did not find these films attractive. They turned them off, on the average, a little more than halfway into them. The expected gender differences were found: female students turned off the films at about the halfway mark, whereas male students typically endured about three-quarters before turning them off. And the expected correlation with sensitivity to disgust was found: students scoring higher on our pencil-and-paper disgust scale turned the three disgust tapes off sooner.

If undergraduate students are any indication, our three videotapes do not have much commercial appeal. Only about 10 percent of students watched these films all the way to the end, and even these few rated the films as somewhat disturbing and disgusting. Although we did not ask our students about their film- or TV-viewing habits, we are confident from other results with student populations that most of our subjects have paid to see a Rambo film, a Schwarzenegger film, or some equivalent of the *Texas Chainsaw Massacre*. Why isn't our violence as attractive as Hollywood's violence?

The difference cannot be that our violence is against animals and Hollywood violence is against people. Our facial-surgery film shows a startling violation of the features of a human child, and the results are about the same as for the films with violence against a monkey or a steer. Nor can the difference be that our violence is senseless whereas Hollywood violence is understandable and motivated. Killing to eat and disfiguring to cure are, if anything, more easily understood than the exaggerated violence of the good-guy-versus-bad-guy conflicts featured in Hollywood productions.

Perhaps the distinction between instrumental and impulsive violence can say something about our results. Instrumental violence is violence for some goal other than inflicting harm on another. Impulsive violence is violence for the pleasure of hurting another, a violence often associated with anger and revenge (Berkowitz, 1989). This distinction might suggest that instrumental violence is understandable and attractive, whereas impulsive violence is not understandable and unattractive. The immediate difficulty with this suggestion is that our films represent violence that is clearly more instrumental than impulsive. Indeed, the facial-surgery film shows surgeons doing violence to a child with the explicit intention of helping her.

At this point one might try turning the suggestion around. Perhaps it is impulsive violence that is attractive on-screen and instrumental violence that is not. But even cursory experience of screen violence contradicts this hypothesis as well. Hollywood violence is full of crazies, androids, extraterrestrials, and monsters from out of id or slime. These are typically frightening, attacking, killing, enslaving, devouring, or taking over the brains of innocent victims for reasons that have more to do with their inhuman goals (instrumental violence) than with any special reward from seeing their victims suffer (impulsive violence). Monsters are not usually seeking anything like revenge or experiencing anything like anger; anger is a moral emotion alien to an Alien, Predator, Godzilla, Mothra, Body Snatcher, Critter, or Dracula.

It appears, then, that the unattractiveness of our disgusting videotapes is not easily explained. Violence in our videotapes is not unattractive because it involves animals rather than humans, or because it is senseless, or because it involves instrumental rather than impulsive violence. Perhaps our violence is unappealing because it is real—documentary—rather than fictional. This obvious possibility is at most the starting point for an explanation, because it is not obvious why viewing fictional violence should be attractive when viewing real violence is not.

The comparison of our disgusting videotapes with Hollywood violence must now become more explicit and more detailed, and the comparison is best advanced by focusing on that genre of Hollywood film violence that contains the most obviously disgusting material—horror films. Horror films are full of representations that are known to elicit disgust (Haidt, Rozin, & McCauley, 1994): death and body-envelope violations, especially piercings and dismemberments with plenty of blood and guts on the screen. What does the literature have to say about the appeal of horror films? What can this literature suggest about why documentary violence should be unappealing?

THE APPEAL OF HORROR FILMS

Societal Fears

Stephen King (1981) suggests that horror films "often serve as an extraordinarily accurate barometer of those things which trouble the night-thoughts of a whole society" (p. 131). In *The Monster Show: A Cultural History of Horror* (1993), David J. Skal traces the societal fears that have been exploited in horror films. For example, Skal characterizes horror films of the 1950s as "responding uneasily to new and almost incomprehensible developments in science and the anxious challenges they posed to the familiar structures of society, religion, psychology, and perception" (p. 114). Films such as *Godzilla* and *Them,* both released in 1954, featured animals (a reptile and ants, respectively) transformed into large, destructive monsters by radiation accidents.

The underlying themes of horror films have changed with the times, and today Skal (1993) sees an underlying fear of the AIDS virus in the renewed interest in vampires. He believes that "the vampire serves a coping function, symbolically representing a dreaded plague death while at the same time triumphantly transcending it" (pp. 346–47).

Of course, horror films can also play upon fears that are chronic in the human condition. Beyond secular trends in fear, King (1981) suggests that horror films have the ability to "[point] even further inward, looking for those deep-seated personal fears—those pressure points—we all must cope with" (p. 131). Examples of such fears are fears of death and aging: "the most obvious psychological pressure point is the fact of our own mortality" (p. 68). Even types of horror that appear to lack a meaningful subtext, "slasher" films, such as *Friday the 13th,* can at least appeal to our fear of death.

Probably most horror films work on both the specific fears of a society and the universal fears of human beings. If these films are so good at finding exactly what scares us, why are they so appealing?

Catharsis

King (1981) suggests that "we make up horrors to help us cope with the real ones" (p. 13); he characterizes horror films as "barber's leeches of the psyche, drawing not bad blood but anxiety" (p. 198), "the tough mind's way of coping with terrible problems" (p. 316), and "an invitation to indulge in deviant, antisocial behavior by proxy" (p. 31). Here King is drawing upon Aristotle's conception of *catharsis,* which, as Mills (1993) points out, includes ideas of clarification and purification as well as purgation. The usual literary interpretation of catharsis emphasizes the idea of purgation, as King does (see also Carroll, 1990). As purgatives, horror films can draw out negative emotions, such as fear, rage, and disgust, to render the mind more healthy and to protect the social order by providing a safe outlet for "unsafe" emotions.

This conception of catharsis leads to three hypotheses. The first is an individual-differences hypothesis: a drama eliciting a particular emotion will be more appealing to viewers who come to the drama with more of that emotion. If there is no emotion to be purged, there should be no attraction to the drama.

The second catharsis hypothesis is that viewers will leave a successful drama with less of the elicited emotion than they came with. This is the controversial heart of catharsis theory. It is by no means obvious why dramatic instigation of anger, for instance, should decrease rather than increase the viewer's anger (cf. Mills, 1993, p. 256). The purgation hypothesis is problematic especially in light of evidence that anger is decreased by affective experience inconsistent with anger—for instance, the experience produced by exposure to humor or erotica (Baron & Ball, 1974; Baron, 1974; Ramirez, Bryant, & Zillmann, 1982).

The third catharsis hypothesis is that the greater the reduction in viewer emotion, the more appealing the drama should be. Of course, a drama may be attractive for reasons other than catharsis, but, if catharsis is a major source of attraction to drama, then any drama that fails to produce catharsis should be relatively unappealing.

A little-noted complexity of catharsis theory is that it seems to predict that drama should purge positive emotions as well as negative. That is, dramatic instigation of sympathy, or love, or triumph, should leave viewers with less of these emotions than they came in with. This prediction seems never to have been taken seriously.

With regard to negative emotions, the catharsis hypothesis has been most investigated in research aimed at assessing the effects of TV violence on viewer aggression. This literature does offer some support for the first catharsis hypothesis, the predicted link between viewer emotion and dramatic appeal. Males are more aggressive than females, and males like violent TV shows more than females do. Similarly, among males, those who are more aggressive watch more violent TV shows (Freedman, 1984).

But research on TV violence has not shown the purgation of emotion that is the central hypothesis of catharsis theory. In general, viewer aggression is reported to be increased rather than deceased by exposure to film violence (Zillmann, 1979). It is worth noting, however, that this research may not have adequately tested the catharsis prediction. The great majority of experiments on the effects of TV violence have made the dramatic experience unnatural at least to the extent of having one subject at a time exposed to either violent or nonviolent TV programming. Aristotle may never have imagined catharsis occurring with a drama staged for an audience of one.

The measure of viewer aggression used in most experiments on TV violence can also be faulted. Giving (supposed) shocks to a (supposed) other subject in a (supposed) learning experiment, for instance, does not cleanly distinguish instrumental from impulsive aggression; it may be that only impulsive aggression is purged by dramatic instigation of anger (cf. Berkowitz, 1989). Finally, TV-violence research has commonly exposed subjects to excerpts of violent films rather than showing entire films; it may be that the instigation of viewer emotion depends upon knowing more about the protagonists than is conveyed in a few minutes of fighting ripped out of context. Purgation of anger and hostility cannot be expected if dramatic violence does not succeed in instigating these emotions in the experimental subjects.

Thus, although it is correct to say that research on the effects of TV violence has found little evidence of catharsis effects, it must also be said that this research was not animated by much concern for clean tests of catharsis theory. Occasional reports of catharsis effects (e.g., Feshbach & Singer, 1971) may turn out to be only the tip of a phenomenon that deserves more careful attention.

In the research on horror films, there is some evidence that can be cited for the catharsis hypothesis. Tamborini and Stiff (1987) interviewed young people (70 percent were 18–21 years of age) who were leaving a theater after viewing a popular horror film, *Halloween II*. The interview assessed general liking for horror films and reasons for liking such films. The reasons that had the highest correlation with liking for horror films were "because they are exciting" and "because they are scary" (both $r = .67$). Although catharsis means more than just emotional stimulation, these reasons are consistent with catharsis at least in suggesting that people go to horror films in order to experience in safety emotions that are usually associated with danger.

Similarly, Tamborini, Stiff, and Zillmann (1987) found in male subjects a strong relationship ($r = .73$) between liking pornographic films and preference for graphic horror featuring a female victim. The authors' interpretation was that men who feel hostility toward women may find gratification not only in pornographic depictions of women but also in graphic horror films with female victims. This interpretation is also consistent with catharsis theory insofar as attraction to both horror films and pornographic films may depend upon the match between viewer emotion and the expression of that emotion on-screen.

Finally, it has often been noted that males report more interest in and liking for horror films than females do (Tamborini & Stiff, 1987; Tamborini, Stiff, & Zillmann, 1987; Zillmann & Weaver, 1995). Popular belief holds that male adolescents are the main consumers of the horror genre (King, 1981), although Clover (1992) points out the difficulties in trying to identify the main audience for horror when most of the revenue for horror films these days comes from videocassette rentals. Greater male than female preference for horror films is of course consistent with catharsis theory if males feel more anger and hostility than females. As noted above in considering research on TV violence, males are certainly more physically aggressive and more violent than females.

Curiosity/Fascination Theory

Carroll (1990) suggests that horror films do not so much purge negative emotions as appeal to our curiosity: "horror attracts because anomalies command attention and elicit curiosity" (p. 195). Horror movies present society's norms only to violate them. This violation of norms, which King (1981, see above) also recognized, holds a fascination for people to the extent that they rarely see these violations in everyday experience. Curiosity/fascination theory suggests that a horror film is immediately and directly enjoyed as it satisfies our curiosity, whereas catharsis theory, as already noted, suggests that the film is enjoyed only for the relief from negative emotions that it leaves in its wake.

This distinction is perhaps not so clear as it first appears, however. According to Carroll (1990), "the condition that permits this transgression of the norm is that, when . . . the narrative achieves closure, the norm has been reconstituted . . . so the norm emerges stronger than before" (p. 201). Now curiosity/fascination theory begins to sound like a form of catharsis theory: norm violation can be experienced safely in the film precisely because the film does not in the end challenge the norm. It seems possible that those more desirous of challenging the norm would find horror films more attractive, just as those with more hostility or fear or disgust may find horror more attractive.

Consistent with this version of curiosity/fascination theory, Tamborini, Stiff, and Zillmann (1987) found that the deceit subscale of the personality trait of Machiavellianism was a strong predictor ($r = .39$) of preference for films with graphic horror. The deceit scale measures approval of the use of dishonesty to achieve goals. Tamborini et al. suggest that willingness to use deceit may be associated with liking for horror because both imply "a desire to violate the norms of socially acceptable behavior, or to see them violated by others" (p. 548). Those who like horror are likely to favor another kind of norm violation—deceit.

Sensation Seeking

Another individual-differences variable that has been related to liking for horror films is the personality trait identified by Zuckerman's (1979)

Sensation Seeking Scale. This scale includes four subscales that measure tendencies toward disinhibition, boredom susceptibility, experience seeking, and thrill and adventure seeking. High sensation seekers are characterized as searching for intense stimulation, such as can be found performing thrilling activities, like skydiving. It is possible that horror films provide the kind of intense stimulation and arousal that will appeal particularly to high sensation seekers (Rickey, 1982).

As reviewed by Tamborini et al. (1987), there is considerable evidence linking scores on Zuckerman's Sensation-Seeking Scale with liking for horror films. Sparks (1984) found Sensation-Seeking scores positively correlated with his own scale of Enjoyment of Frightening Films ($r = .22$ for males, .28 for females). Tamborini and Stiff (1987) found liking for horror films positively correlated ($r = .21$) with a combination of Zuckerman's disinhibition, experience-seeking, and thrill-and-adventure-seeking subscales. Edwards (1984) found interest in horror movies strongly correlated ($r = .51$) with the total Sensation-Seeking Scale. Finally, Tamborini et al. themselves found the disinhibition, experience-seeking, and boredom-susceptibility subscales correlated with preference for films with graphic horror (rs of .29, .17, .18 for male and female subjects combined; rs of .29, .28, .29 for male subjects separately; correlation of total Sensation-Seeking Scale not presented).

There is little doubt, on the basis of this evidence, that high sensation seekers like horror movies more than low sensation seekers do. The relationship is not always strong, but it is consistent.

Sex-Role Reinforcement: The Snuggle Theory

Zillmann, Weaver, Mundorf, and Aust (1986) have suggested that one source of attraction to horror films is that these films provide the occasion for men and women to practice and fortify traditional gender roles. While watching horror films, men can prove their fearlessness and competence by remaining stoic in the face of blood and dismemberment, and women can show their sensitivity and need for protection by expressing fear. This suggestion, often called the snuggle theory of horror, entails that "enjoyment of horror derives in part from successfully behaving, under emotionally taxing circumstances, in accordance with societal precepts" (Zillmann & Gibson, 1995, p. 12).

To test this theory, Zillmann et al. (1986) showed a clip from *Friday the 13th, Part III* to undergraduate subjects who watched the film with an opposite-sex undergraduate who was a confederate of the experimenters. During the film, the confederate behaved in a manner that expressed either indifference, distress, or mastery. After the film, the subjects completed a questionnaire that assessed their affective reactions to the film. Zillmann et al. found that male subjects enjoyed the film more when they were with a woman expressing distress than when they were with a woman expressing mastery, whereas female subjects enjoyed the film more with a man showing mastery than with a man showing distress. The typical difference between males and females was also found: across conditions, males enjoyed the film more than females did.

These results support the snuggle theory in showing that both males and females like the horror film more when they can reinforce their gender roles in the watching of it. More generally, these results point to the importance of social context in affecting response to drama. As suggested earlier in connection with catharsis theory, watching a film alone may be a very different experience from watching as part of a group.

Mood Management

Zillmann's (1988) theory of mood management suggests that people choose their entertainment to create the mood they wish to experience, or to cure the mood they are in. Although Zillmann has not specifically applied his theory to liking for horror films, he has marshaled considerable evidence that different kinds of entertainment have consistently different effects on arousal and hedonic experience, and that individuals can and do take advantage of these effects in choosing among forms of entertainment.

Mood-management theory predicts that boredom should lead to a desire for arousing entertainment, including horror films. The evidence linking sensation seeking (including susceptibility to boredom) with liking for horror films is generally consistent with this prediction. Also consistent with mood-management theory are the reasons for liking horror movies that Tamborini and Stiff (1987) found to be best correlated with liking for horror: because it's exciting and because it's scary. Mood-management theory cannot work unless individuals can anticipate the effects of the entertainment they choose, and those who like horror most are evidently those who most like its arousal value.

The paradox of horror's appeal is not, however, resolved in mood-management theory. A little bit of fear or disgust may be better than boredom, but it is not clear why a massive dose of fear or disgust should be appealing. A potential answer to this quandary is suggested by the relief hypothesis.

The Relief Hypothesis

Rickey (1982) suggests that it is particularly the successful resolution of a horror film that is enjoyable. King (1981) calls this "the magic moment of reintegration and safety at the end . . . that makes the danse macabre so rewarding and magical" (p. 14). If horror movies are society's worst fears realized on-screen, it makes sense that seeing these fears resolved would be relieving, and thus enjoyable. On this account, horror films offer a kind of negative reinforcement; the removal of an unpleasant stimulus proves to be rewarding (Skinner, 1969). When the movie ends, the "monster" having been defeated, the relief is rewarding.

One difficulty with the relief hypothesis is the definition of "successful ending." Many horror films end with the threat unresolved. For example, films in the *Friday the 13th* horror series often end with a suggestion that the killer is not dead, such as a camera shot of the empty space where his dead body should be. Perhaps any ending is satisfactory because, regardless of whether the characters are still in danger, the audience is no longer threatened (Tamborini and Stiff, 1987). This idea is doubtful, because it is highly improbable that the audience truly believes itself to be threatened.

Although Samuel Coleridge (1951) suggested that it is possible to experience fiction with a "willing suspension of disbelief," it is unlikely that anyone attending to drama or literature comes to believe that the fictional is real. Carroll (1990) notes that "in order to respond appropriately to something like a horror film . . . we must believe we are confronted with a fictional spectacle" (pp. 67–68). If the audience were to believe itself in real danger, the experience of a horror movie would not be enjoyable at all; rather, viewers would be "calling out the army" (p. 67).

Despite some uncertainty about what makes a successful ending, de Wied, Zillmann, and Ordman (1994) have used relief theory to explain the appeal of tragedy. These investigators had undergraduate subjects view a shortened version of the film *Steel Magnolias*. The film was interrupted three times to ask subjects about physical and emotional reactions of sympathy and sadness. After the film, subjects were asked about how much they enjoyed it. The major result was that subjects who were the most sad during the film were the subjects who rated the film most enjoyable ($r = .55$). High empathizers were more sad during the film and reported more enjoyment after the film. De Wied et al. interpret these results in terms of relief theory: the subjects most disturbed by the tragedy are most relieved by the end of the film, and some of the arousal value of the sadness during the film is transferred to the positive emotional experience of the ending.

De Wied et al. believe that the ending of *Steel Magnolias* is successful in offering some meaning for human suffering, but they recognize that not all tragedies have so satisfying a conclusion: "The greatest remaining challenge . . . concerns the explanation of the enjoyment of tragedy that is simply devoid of concluding events that could be construed as inducers of positive affect or as something that gives human suffering redeeming value" (1994, p. 103).

Samuel [Taylor] Coleridge (1772–1834) · English Romantic critic who posited the notion that we are likelier to believe the unbelievable if we are not reminded about it by inconsistencies in the fiction.

HORROR THEORY INTERROGATED

It is time to return to our three disgusting films—the epicures and the monkey, the slaughterhouse, and the facial surgery. Why are these films so much less attractive than Hollywood horror? This question can now be raised in the light of the preceding review of theory and research on the attractions of horror.

The first point to note is that the violence in the three films is not exceptional in comparison with the violence of horror films. The focus on death and dismemberment in our films is a common theme in horror films, and presumably this focus can disturb all who are conscious of their own mortality. So it is not the nature of the violence that makes the films unappealing.

As noted earlier, the catharsis hypothesis has been more popular in literary than in psychological analyses of horror. But in any case, catharsis theory does not suggest why the three disgusting films are unappealing. The fact that more disgust-sensitive individuals turn off the films faster implies that these films are indeed eliciting disgust. If horror films appeal by eliciting and purging negative emotions, such as fear and disgust, then the three disgust films should likewise appeal.

The curiosity-fascination theory of horror's appeal is likewise unhelpful. The content of the three films is certainly anomalous, at least in the sense that few of our subjects had ever seen in everyday life anything like what they saw on-screen. Subjects should have been fascinated to see something so unusual and curious to see the end of these films. All three films were norm breaking in the descriptive sense of making public on-screen what is usually private, and the monkey epicures, at least, were breaking a moral norm, against eating a live animal. Despite all this foundation for curiosity and fascination, the disgust films were not generally appealing.

High sensation seekers, in particular, should have been attracted to an opportunity to escape boredom in an unusual and arousing experience. Although the 10 percent of our subjects who did not turn off the films may have been the high sensation seekers (we did not have sensation-seeking scores for our subjects), it is difficult to see how an individual-differences theory can explain why the average reaction to our films fell short of the broad appeal of horror films.

According to Zillmann's snuggle theory, our subjects should have been attracted to the three disgust films to the extent that the social setting gave subjects the opportunity to practice their gender roles. Our subjects, male and female undergraduates, did have some opportunity of this kind. Although only one subject at a time watched the films, each subject was observed and directed through the study by two research assistants—one male and one female undergraduate. Thus each subject watched the films in the presence of one same-sex and one opposite-sex undergraduate, in front of whom the subject should have been able to practice either mastery (male subjects) or distress (female subjects). This opportunity for gender-role reinforcement was evidently not enough to make the disgust films attractive.

Mood-management theory can be applied to the situation of our disgust subjects, but two uncertainties make the application tentative. First, we do not know how many of our subjects were bored. Second, our subjects were facing unusual and unknown content, whereas people choosing to see a horror film know enough to expect excitement and scariness. Still, to the extent that horror is an antidote to boredom, our films should have had the value of reducing boredom; apparently this value was not enough to make them attractive. Indeed, from the point of view of mood management, our subjects turned off the disgusting films because they anticipated feeling better with them off.

The last theory reviewed, relief theory, is also difficult to apply to our disgust study. Our subjects probably did feel some sense of relief when they turned off the disgust films, and this negative reinforcement may well have been multiplied by the transfer of unresolved arousal elicited by the violence they had just seen. Why didn't subjects wait for the pleasure of still greater relief by letting the films go on to their conclusions? Perhaps our subjects turned off the films because they could not anticipate the kind of satisfying resolution of the violence that they expect in at least some horror films.

It is worth noting that some viewers of horror films also "turn off" the film, at least briefly, by self-distraction and looking away from the screen. Tamborini, Stiff, and Heidel (1990) report that this kind of avoidance during a film is associated with not liking the film ($r = -.43$ with index of how appealing, pleasing, and interesting subjects found a film). Thus, although subjects were probably turning off the disgust films in search of relief, this relief was probably associated with disliking the films rather than with liking them.

The conclusion of this section must be that theories and research about the appeal of horror have not been very helpful in understanding why the three disgust films were not appealing. Notably, none of these theories offers any insight into why viewing fictional violence should be attractive when viewing real violence is not. In general, our documentary films did offer what the literature suggests will make horror films attractive: vivid death and dismemberment that should elicit and purge fear and disgust, appeal to curiosity and sensation seeking, give viewers the opportunity to practice their gender roles, increase arousal and reduce boredom, and set up a powerful sense of relief when the film is over. Nevertheless, subjects turned off the disgust films.

The question remains, when is horrific violence attractive and when is it not? Together with my student and colleague Jenny Stein, I undertook two studies aimed at learning more about this question.

TWO STUDIES AND SOME SURPRISING RESULTS

Film Sound

One striking difference between our films and commercial horror films is the quality of the sound track. Our films had the kind of sound typical of inexpensive documentary productions: no music, no special effects, and dialogue or voice-over without the vibrancy and diction that trained actors produce with the help of a good sound lab. It seemed possible that unappealing sound tracks made our films unappealing.

The importance of the sound track to a horror film's appeal is an issue that has not often been addressed. Clover (1992) has noted that "some viewers claim that they are more disturbed by the 'music' of horror movies than the images," but that "sound in cinema in general has been undertheorized, and horror sound scarcely theorized at all" (p. 204). In her review of musical sound tracks, Cohen (1990) suggests that "music serves a narrative role" (p. 113) by providing extra information about characters' emotions and that "associations generated by music influence the interpretation of the subject" (p. 114). Similarly, Pudovkin (1985) argues that "just as the image is an objective perception of events, so the music expresses the subjective appreciation of this objectivity" (p. 91). Belton (1985) agrees: "The sound track corresponds not, like the image track, directly to 'objective reality' but rather to a secondary representation of it" (p. 66). Cavalcanti (1985) puts this popular observation most succinctly: "While the picture is the medium of statement, the sound is the medium of suggestion" (p. 109).

There seems little doubt that film sound can be important in determining the emotional impact of a film, but the impact of sound is likely to be complex. Cohen (1990) highlights the paradox of film sound tracks: "Music makes the film more real but the very presence of the music contradicts reality" (p. 118). The same can be said of film sound effects, which long ago left fidelity behind in favor of surrealism. Gunshots, auto wrecks, and footfalls in the hallway are represented in film sound as ideal types, more vivid than the reality they signal.

If film sound is a cue for unreality, perhaps our documentary films were unappealing because they were too obviously what they were: records of reality. Of course the sound quality was not the only cue that our films were documentaries rather than fictional drama, but sound quality might be important in this regard. This possibility suggested an experiment to assess the impact of a commercial sound track by showing subjects a film clip from *Friday the 13th, Part III.*

The experiment compared the reactions of subjects who were exposed to the intact film clip (both video and audio) with the reactions of subjects exposed to the same video but with the audio turned off. If the film sound track is an important cue for unreality, and if assurance of unreality is important for enjoying film horror, then subjects watching the video without audio should be more disgusted, disturbed, and distressed by the screen violence than subjects watching the same video with audio.

Enjoyment during a Horror Film and the Relief Hypothesis

Above it was noted that the relief hypothesis was not easily applied to understanding why subjects did not like the three disgusting films. The theory suggests that viewers who are most distressed during a horror film should be those who most enjoy the film after it is over. This was indeed the pattern of results reported by de Wied et al. (1994) for the appeal of a tragic film: those most distressed and emphatic during the film were those who rated it afterward as most enjoyable. But subjects watching our disgust films turned them off, a behavior suggesting that they are not enjoying them (Tamborini et al., 1987).

What if subjects like being sad or scared, even as they are feeling sad or scared? Perhaps those most distressed by dramatic tragedy are also those who most enjoy it, not just in relief after the film, but even as they are watching it. And perhaps those who are most disturbed by horror (short of turning it off) are also those who most enjoy watching it, not just in relief after the film, but even as they are watching it.

These possibilities led to a study in which subjects watched the same clip from *Friday the 13th, Part III* and gave two ratings of their enjoyment of the film. One rating was during a brief pause in the middle of the film clip, the other after the film was over. If subjects enjoy being scared and disgusted, then the first rating should be as high as the second. If relief theory is correct, enjoyment of the film should be rated higher when the attacker is subdued and the film is over.

Three Measures of Affective Reaction to Horror

For both studies, the film clip used was a segment of *Friday the 13th, Part III* previously employed by Zillmann et al. (1986). This 14-minute clip offers a relatively complete episode of violence in which a young woman is repeatedly attacked by a masked killer; the woman finally escapes her attacker, leaving him covered in blood with an ax stuck in his skull. For both studies, the affective-reaction measures (0–10 scales, "not at all" to "extremely") were again taken from Zillmann et al., except that some of their positive adjectives were dropped to make room for three negative adjectives: "disgusting," "disturbing," and "distressing."

Combining subjects from the two studies, 63 female and 2 male undergraduates from Bryn Mawr and Haverford Colleges completed affective ratings of the film clip. Factor analysis of these ratings produced three dimensions that were represented by three indexes: involving (mean of involving, exciting, and not-boring scales), disturbing (mean of disturbing, disgusting, and depressing scales), and amusing (mean of amusing, not-believable, and entertaining scales). (A similar three-dimensional structure has been found in follow-up research by Susan Burggraf with students at Bowdoin College.)

These results have some interest in their own right. Tentatively, the involving index may be interpreted as assessing general arousal or excitation, whereas the disturbing and amusing indices seem to assess, respectively, negative and positive affective tone. The amusing index implies some distancing and unreality (not-believable) in addition to positive tone; it cannot be interpreted as equivalent to the more global rating of "enjoyment" that was included only in the second study. The scale that is most commonly associated with horror, "frightening," was not included in any of the indices because it correlated with both the involving and disturbing indices.

The three indices were essentially uncorrelated, indicating that arousal can vary independently of affective tone and that positive and negative affect can vary independently. The same kind of result is found in the literature on subjective quality of life (Bradburn, 1969; Warr, Barter, & Brownbridge, 1983; McCauley & Bremer, 1991), where positive and negative affect have been found to vary independently as a function of good and bad things happening to an individual during a given period of time. Overall subjective quality of life is usually assessed as some kind of balance or average of positive and negative affect. Thus, the simplest interpretation of the independence of positive and negative affective reactions to a horror film is that some aspects of the film produce amusement, some aspects produce disturbance, and overall enjoyment of the film should be related to the balance or average of these two indices.

This simple interpretation is denied, however, by the results of the second study. Subjects' ratings of enjoyment during and after the film clip were highly correlated (rs of .71 and .63) with the involving index, but not significantly correlated with either the disturbing or amusing index. The clear implication is that what subjects enjoyed about the film had little to do with the balance of positive and negative affect; rather, enjoyment was associated with finding the film involving, exciting, and not boring.

This pattern of results offers support for previous research that has found liking for horror associated with sensation seeking, including susceptibility to boredom and inclination for the thrill of new experiences. The results are also broadly consistent with mood-management theory; viewers expect horror films to be exciting and scary (Tamborini & Stiff, 1987), and our subjects are telling us they find involvement and excitement enjoyable regardless of whether viewing makes them feel good or bad.

The Impact of Film Sound

Using the involving, disturbing, and amusing indices just described, the first study compared subjects who got both video and audio tracks with subjects who got only the video. Contrary to prediction, the subjects receiving only the video were not higher on the disturbing index than subjects who got both video and audio. The two groups did not differ on the disturbing index, and there was if anything a trend toward more disturbance for subjects who got both video and audio. Nor did the two groups of subjects differ on the amusing index. On the involving index, however, the video-with-audio subjects were significantly higher than the video-only subjects. The impact of the sound track—music, special effects, a dialogue little more than exclamations—was to increase involvement. If the sound track did provide cues for unreality, these cues were either unimportant or redundant in limiting how disturbing the film was to our subjects.

Enjoyment During and After the Film

Subjects rated their enjoyment of the film significantly higher during the film than after. This result challenges relief theory, which assumes that negative emotions during a horror film are not enjoyable and predicts that the enjoyment of the film after it is over depends upon the positive emotion associated with the end of the film. Not only are subjects saying that they enjoy the film before any kind of resolution has occurred, they say that they actually like it more while involved in it than they do looking back on it. Putting this result together with the association of enjoyment with the involving index but not with the disturbing or amusing index, the implication is that many viewers enjoy their involvement in the film in a way that dos not depend upon either the positive or negative affective tone of the involvement.

Summary of Results

The results of two small studies of female undergraduates can at most point the way to further inquiries. With all due caution, then, the results seem to suggest two tentative conclusions. The first is that enjoyment of horror depends not upon the balance of positive and negative emotions elicited but rather upon excitement and involvement that can be associated with either positive or negative emotions. The second is that the enjoyment of horror is in the watching, not in the relief associated with the end of watching. These conclusions do not resolve the paradox of the appeal of horror, but make the paradox more acute. Scores on the disturbing index show that viewers do feel disturbed, disgusted, and depressed by horrific violence, but they enjoy their involvement in the film anyway. How can the paradox be resolved?

A TENTATIVE RESOLUTION

It is worth examining the possibility that human beings are capable of enjoying being frightened, disgusted, and saddened (Brosnan, 1976). The radical quality of this possibility becomes clear when it is held up against the alternatives that have been advanced, early and late, in order to avoid it. Catharsis is one such alternative; the catharsis hypothesis suggests that what is enjoyable in drama is not the experience of fright, disgust, or sadness but the purging of these emotions. The relief hypothesis is another evasion of the same sort; like catharsis it holds that the experience of negative emotions is noxious but holds out the reward value of relief from these emotions as the source of attraction to dramatic instigation of such emotions. These alternatives are a priori unlikely to the extent that human beings are notably weak in undertaking immediate losses for long-term gains (Rachlin, 1995). Now, tentatively, the evidence of two small studies makes these alternatives look even less likely.

If we face the possibility that human beings sometimes can enjoy what are usually accounted negative emotions, there seem to be basically two ways of understanding how the negative becomes positive. One way is to assume that the dramatic distance of fiction can moderate negative emotional reactions such that they provide an enjoyable arousal jag at small cost in negative hedonic tone. The other way is to assume that emotions instigated by fiction and drama are qualitatively different emotions from their everyday counterparts, and that the dramatically instigated emotions are always enjoyable.

The first theory amounts to saying that dramatically instigated emotions are simply weaker versions of everyday emotions. Assume that, for many individuals and under many circumstances, an increase in arousal is enjoyable. Assume that the cues for unreality in any dramatic or fictional representation can reduce the negative quality of emotions such as fear, disgust, and pity more than these cues reduce the arousal value of these emotions. Then dramatically instigated emotions offer good value of arousal increase for small cost in negative affect, and the net experience during the drama is positive. Viewers feel negative emotions that are moderately arousing but only slightly negative—and they enjoy the drama.

This understanding of the dramatic instigation of negative emotions has been urged by Apter (1992). Apter's theory encompasses the attractions of drama but goes beyond the appeal of drama and fiction to a general theory of "psychological reversals" in which dangers of many kinds become attractive when the arousal associated with danger can be experienced within the safety of a protective frame. Skydiving and mountain climbing are dangerous and arousing but self-confidence provides the protective frame that makes these activities exciting rather than anxiety provoking. Identification with others who take risks can provide arousal within the protective frame of "spectator." Dramatic productions, along with fantasy and recollection of past experience, are similarly enjoyable for providing access to arousal with the reassurance of present safety.

A second theory of how the negative becomes positive is that the emotions experienced in drama are qualitatively different from everyday experience of the same emotions. Indeed, this theory would assert that we err in calling dramatic emotions by the same names as everyday emotions; the dramatic emotions are a parallel but different reality.

This theory has ancient precedent in the *Natyasastra* of Bharata, a Sanskrit treatise on drama dating from 200–300 A.D. (Masson & Patwardhan, 1970). The *Natyasastra* focuses on the nature of the *rasa*, defined as "aesthetic or imaginative experience" (p. 1). The emotions that a character in a drama experiences are in turn experienced by an observer, but in a different manner. "The spectator can go further, and in a sense deeper. For when 'love' is awakened in him, it is not like the love that the original character felt . . . the [state of mind] is transformed into an extraworldly state" (p. 23). The emotion of the character is adopted by the observer and transformed to fit the observer, yet it is not an earthly state of mind; it exists "outside both time and space altogether" (p. 32). In the *Natyasastra,* the distinction between real and savored emotion is emphasized by having two names for each of the major emotions: one name for the everyday experience of the emotion and a different name for its dramatic counterpart.

Although the *Natyasastra* does not deal with horror, it offers an interesting account of the appeal of tragedy. "Sensitive readers become more and more deeply attracted towards this aesthetic of grief whereas they tend to shun the real experience" (Masson & Patwardhan, 1970, p. 31). "Anything that takes us away from preoccupations with ourselves is considered useful" (p. 34). In short, this account of the appeal of tragedy emphasizes the extent to which dramatically induced grief transcends the personal and individual problems of viewers. One result of this transcendence might be to make individual pains and problems seem smaller and less important. Just this kind of result has been reported by Zillmann, Rockwell, Schweitzer, and Sundar (1993), who were surprised to find that subjects tolerated more discomfort after exposure to film tragedy.

This interpretation resonates with one version of catharsis theory. As Mills (1993) has noted, catharsis may better be interpreted as purification than as purgation. The experience of fear and pity in response to dramatic tragedy can be attractive because the emotions are purified of self-interest and of the necessity to act—and to pay the costs of acting—in a complex and ambiguous world.

Applied to horror films, the perspective of the *Natyasastra* suggests that the experience of fear and disgust in reaction to a horror film is qualitatively different from everyday fear and disgust. Purified of self-interest, fear and disgust can be enjoyed as marks and qualifications of humanity, just as Mills's (1993) subjects valued their experience of empathy in responding to a film tragedy. But the key to enjoying these dramatically instigated emotions is the framing of the film as drama and unreal. In Apter's (1992) terms, the cues for unreality provide the protective frame in which dramatic rather than everyday emotions can be experienced.

It is time to return one last time to the three disgusting films. The answer to the question with which we began may after all be as simple as the difference between fact and fiction: these three films were disgusting rather than enjoyable because they were loaded with cues for reality and were lacking the frame of dramatic fiction. They were unappealing because they were documentaries, too brief and unrevealing about the people in them to support identification with any of these people. Thus Apter (1992) and the *Natyasastra* can suggest why documentary violence is unattractive, whereas the literature on the attractions of horror films leads all too easily to the prediction that our documentary violence should also be attractive.

Of course documentaries and news reports of violence, even real dismemberment by the side of the highway, can be enjoyable to some people. There are reports of whole families bringing picnic lunches to watch a hanging. But enjoying real violence may require some other form of distancing or protective framing to take the place of dramatic distance. As Apter (1992) would argue, the context of drama is only one of the frames in which negative emotion can offer a positive experience.

NOTES

My thanks to the Harry Frank Guggenheim Foundation for supporting the two studies reported in this chapter. Thanks also to Jenny Stein, who carried out these studies and wrote them up in a report from which I borrowed shamelessly for this chapter. And thanks to Dolf Zillmann, whose kindness in sharing with me many of his recent papers, both published and unpublished, should not implicate him in any errors of mine in the use of these papers. Finally, my special thanks to Joel Wallman, whose comments on a draft of this chapter were most helpful.

■ *Clark McCauley is a professor of psychology at Bryn Mawr College. He has co-edited the book* Stereotype Accuracy: Toward an Appreciation of Group Differences *and notes that it's important to recognize that extreme behavior is not something distant from ourselves, but rather a part of normal social psychology.*

MAKING SURE OF THE TEXT

1. How does the genre of horror films appeal to us? You might find it useful to paraphrase McCauley's answers in some depth as you respond to this question.
2. What does McCauley identify as "the catharsis hypothesis"? Try to explain it completely.
3. What are the distinctions between "instrumental" and "impulsive" violence, and how does McCauley follow through on his initial mention of them?
4. McCauley does not, except briefly, mention the constructed nature of the horror film; would examining the movie's use of the five channels of communication (from the Seiter article) defuse its power to horrify us?

CONSIDERING THE CONTEXT

1. How might McCauley's theories apply to violent images in music videos? Refer to Gary Burns' article, or Nelson George's, to help build your answer.
2. What effect is achieved by McCauley's use of headings and subheadings? How might you be able to use headings and subheadings in your own writing?
3. McCauley suggests, at the conclusion, that a dramatic context is "only one of the frames" through which negative emotion becomes transformed. What other "frames" might offer a positive experience from a negative emotion?
4. What arrangement pattern has McCauley used as he relates the various theories? Are they presented in a particular order, or are they randomly arranged?

■ ■ ■

Images: *Trek* Captains

MAKING SURE OF THE TEXT

1. The captains of *Trek* vessels must represent certain qualities to the viewers in order to be credible. Captain Kirk, for instance, might appear scientific and serious, but he might also be read as arrogant. Do the images of these *Trek* captains suggest certain qualities to you? What are they?
2. The images here are presented in chronological order. Rearrange them to reflect a different ordering system. For instance, you might rearrange them in order of personal favorite, or in order of "leadership style."
3. Notice the differences in uniform styles, even though each of the characters is wearing a captain's uniform. How might you explain the differences?

CONSIDERING CONTEXT

1. The original *Star Trek* series aired during the 1960s; *Star Trek: The Next Generation* aired during the 1980s, *Deep Space Nine* spanned the mid-1990s, and *Star Trek: Voyager* lasted throughout the late 1990s and 2000. How would you expect each series to represent its time frame? That is, if the original series is representative of its time, as Moore and Menosky point out, how do the spinoff series reflect cultural themes and trends?
2. We have often seen women in authority on *Trek* episodes and films; Kathryn Janeway is, however, the only continuing female *Trek* captain. Looking at her image, describe her "command" image as different from, for example, Kirk's. Be sure to include a discussion of lighting, camera angle, and other elements in Seiter's article.
3. What other images of space are so well known that they are, in effect, iconic?

■ ■ ■

Violent Movies: Why We Watch (Student Essay)

Lauren Mooney

The hows and whys of watching violent movies vary greatly from person to person. In his article, "When Screen Violence is Not Attractive," Clark McCauley compares the two genres of documentary and horror films and develops theories ranging from examining societal fears to the curiosity/fascination theory to explain the fascination with watching violence. Specifically, McCauley's theories regarding the different types of violence and their attractive qualities provide reasons for why someone might watch *The Matrix* and *The Cube*, representatives from the genres of action/sci-fi and suspense/horror.

The Matrix focuses on a character named Neo and his quest to become "the chosen one" who will lead enslaved humans to freedom. Morpheus, the resistance leader, seeks out Neo and trains him to fight the creators of the matrix, known as the agents. According to Morpheus, the matrix is a "computer generated dream world...the wool that has been pulled over your eyes to hide you from the truth." The truth that he speaks of is that the "real world" is only a small colony of pure humans that have survived the purges by the agents. The rest of the human species is cultivated like an unconscious crop to generate energy. One violent and gruesome scene involves the "birth" of Neo into the real world. Attached to a womb-like pod, the plugs and wires that secure him in his unconscious state link to a main plug in the back of his skull. When a robotic creature unplugs him, the other wires snap off of his body, spraying embryonic fluid everywhere and making a real mess. Among the other disgusting scenes is an early shot of Neo being "bugged" by the Matrix's agents: A very large mechanical device is placed on his stomach, where it begins to drive into his body through his belly button while Neo writhes and screams. The scene in which the bug is pulled out by fellow "pure human" Trinity is nearly as gruesome, but it has to happen before he can become the chosen one. After Neo accepts his role, he undergoes various training exercises in both the matrix and the real world. Many fight scenes between the group and the agents, who will stop at nothing, are naturally rich with shootouts, stabbing, and other acts of violence.

The Cube has fewer acts of violence, but is equally gruesome. The movie is basically about a group of seven people who wake up in a cube maze with over 17,000 rooms that periodically rotate. The cube has thousands of extremely violent traps designed to kill whoever enters the room. For example, the opening scene shows a man who has entered a room with a trap. The trap involves a razor sharp mesh that swings down over whoever enters the room, slicing their body into hundreds of tiny pieces. Afterwards, the pieces fall to the floor with a loud plopping noise. Other unsuccessful attempts to avoid the traps have resulted in acid burning one man's face or dozens of swords to slice and dice. The movie focuses on the attempts of the characters to escape the cube, alive and breathing. Throughout the movie, each character (a doctor, a cop, a math nerd, an escape artist, an architect, and a mentally retarded boy) offers theories about how they got there and what purpose the cube holds.

The key element in how we watch the movie *The Matrix* is the undeniable fiction of the story. Before even stepping into the movie theater or pressing "play" on the VCR, we are prepared to enter a world of fiction and fantasy. We expect the unexpected and do not question the reality of the film. We are much more accepting when we watch *The Matrix* because it is so unbelievable. According to Apter's theory of "psychological reversals," danger can be attractive when experienced in a protected environment known as "the frame of dramatic fiction" (161). A violent movie can elicit feelings of excitement because the viewer is only a spectator, safe from the violence (McCauley 160). Cues for unreality create the protective frame of fiction that allows the viewer to enjoy the violence (McCauley 161). *The Matrix* is a perfect example of this theory. Not only do the characters engage in extraordinary situations, but virtual reality is also used extensively. During Neo's training sessions and throughout the rest of the movie, he can bend all of the rules of reality. For example, he can climb walls, move faster than humanly possible, jump extremely long distances, and withstand an unbelievable amount of pain. The world is also not real; it is only the matrix. Other cues for unreality include the excessive use of special effects. These intriguing special effects were often the very reason people went to the movie, but since the violence is accomplished by means of the special effects, we are watching more gruesome violence than we might see in real life. It's just covered by the computer generated imagery.

Each film offers a different kind of violence. In *The Cube*, there are two main sources of violence: one stemming from the traps within the cube and the other created by the characters in the movie. In the violence created by the traps, a machine, without an identifiable source or reason, produces the violence. Even though the violence is sickening, we are not disgusted as easily because no known motive or source is present. The characters have a hard time grasping this idea and search for someone or something to blame. This blameless violence has no known human source and is therefore thought of only in terms of a machine. Machines cannot think or have morals, the qualities needed for placing blame or considering the action inhumane.

On the other hand, the human violence causes the viewer more discomfort. The character Quinton is a very violent man and ends up killing most of the other characters by the end of the movie. He stabs both Leaven and Worth and drops Holloway down the side of the cube, plunging to her death. This type of violence stems from anger and revenge, or what McCauley describes as impulsive violence.

Whereas *The Cube* has two main types of violence, most of the violence within *The Matrix* is impulsive violence produced by the characters. Neo seeks revenge on the agents to overthrow their power and save the humans. The violence present in this movie represents the ultimate battle between good vs. evil. Neo's motivation is to kill the agents, instead of helping them. Despite this overwhelming display of impulsive violence, instrumental violence also plays a major role. According to McCauley, instrumental violence has a goal other than inflicting harm on another (145). For example, Neo's debugging is extremely violent, but the scenes are not used to inflict harm on Neo; they simply display the technology present in the world that Neo now lives. Further adding to this type of violence, Morpheus tells Neo only his body makes him believe that pain is real. Because pain is not attached to the violent acts, the viewer is less likely to be disturbed by the violence.

The Matrix holds true to McCauley's curiosity/fascination theory. According to this theory, horror movies violate norms in the society to attract attention. Carroll argues, "horror attracts because anomalies command attention and elicit curiosity" (McCauley 149). This is also true for a variety of genres. The Matrix violates many norms that are rarely violated. The world in which we live is turned upside down and inside out, explained away by a computer program. The "real" is only "electrical signals interpreted by your brain" and nothing more. The theme of the movie is also quite captivating by its ability to cause the viewers to question everything around them. The technology presented in the movie is beyond any existing technology, which captures the viewer's attention by imagining a futuristic world in which knowledge can be transmitted in a matter of seconds and life can be used as a source of energy. In one scene involving the escape from the agents, Trinity must know how to fly a helicopter, but she lacks the knowledge. To solve this problem, she simply calls up Cypher and has him insert the training program for flying a helicopter. In seconds she has the ability to escape from the agents using the helicopter.

Another reason for watching The Matrix is the level of action and stimulation. This is especially attractive to those individuals who are high sensation seekers. According to McCauley's article, a movie that provides intense stimulation will attract many viewers who are sensation seekers. The rescue mission at the end of the movie is nothing but action. Trinity and Neo go on a shooting spree, killing close to a hundred men while showing off their gravity defying moves. Even more fascinating is Neo's ability to stop bullets in mid air or lazily fighting the superhuman agents who spell out suicide for the other members of the group.

Zillmann's mood management theory in McCauleys' article applies to The Matrix more than The Cube. According to the mood management theory, people choose the movie they want to watch based upon the mood they are in or the mood they wish to get out of (151). This is especially true for high sensation seekers, who wish to cure their state of boredom. Most viewers were well aware of the action level of The Matrix and chose the movie for this very reason. On the other hand, The Cube lacks action and most of the movie is spent solving the mystery of the cube. The plot focuses on the theories presented by the characters for the reason behind the cube and how to escape from it. This also supports McCauley's curiosity/fascination theory.

One of the major reasons for watching either of the films involves how societal fears and the human condition are played upon within the film.

Stephen King claims that horror films "often serve as an extraordinary barometer of those things which trouble the night thoughts of the whole society" (McCauley 146). The best example of the two movies is *The Cube*. This movie plays upon the question of staying humane in extreme circumstances. Each character is pushed to their limits and tested to see if they are able to keep their cool. Quinton obviously fails this test and murders several of the other characters in order to survive the situation. This is especially disturbing because Quinton is a cop, a commanding role associated with orderliness and justice. *The Matrix* also plays upon the societal fears involving deception and the manipulation of life. The deceptive nature of the matrix is very upsetting because it causes us to wonder how accurate our perceptions of our surroundings really are. We like to imagine ourselves as independent individuals, whereas the matrix undermines the intelligence of the human race, defining us as a mass of easily deceived people.

Moving away from theory, I have to say that I watched *The Matrix* with more interest than I did with *The Cube*. The violence in *The Cube* seemed gratuitous: it was there, but the degree of it seemed too much considering the plot. Killing people is all well and good, but the degree of blood and gore seemed like more than was necessary. But in contrast, *The Matrix's* violence seemed very real and very unreal at the same time, because of the sophisticated special effects employed by the director. Because the film was set in the frame of fiction, we knew the violence wasn't real—even though we also knew, at the same time, that the whole film wasn't real. Because the film played with our perceptions of reality, we were never sure if what we were watching was real or not, so we didn't know how to respond. McCauley's article doesn't really address the theories as they might apply to a movie that renders reality suspect; it might be interesting to see what he'd say about it.

■ ■ ■

■ **Works Cited** ■

The Cube. Dir. Natali Vencenzo. Perf. Nicole DeBoer, Julian Richings, and Nicky Guadagni. Videocassette. Trimark, 1998.

The Matrix. Dir. Larry and Andy Wachowski. Perf. Keanu Reeves, Laurence Fishburne, and Carrie-Anne Moss. Videocassette. Warner Brothers, 1999.

McCauley, Clark. "When Screen Violence is Not Attractive." *Why We Watch: The Attractions of Violent Entertainment*. London Oxford, 1998. 145–162.

■ **Ideas for Writing** ■

Journal

1. What cartoons did you watch as a child? How might you read them now, as Seiter does *Fangface*?

2. Take a famous figure and identify what the person stands for. Tom Hanks, for example, often stands for "good man confronted with bad events." Compare this with someone else's response toward the same famous figure.
3. Choose any one of the several images in this textbook and "read" it. Is anything hidden? Did you have to dig for meaning?

Response
1. Ward writes that several representations of the male body, "stripped and exposed to the erotic gaze," express "not its potency but its vulnerability," suggesting that these "representations critique phallocentrism." In what ways have you seen the female body, historically "stripped and exposed to the erotic gaze," used to critique feminism?
2. In what ways does Gary Burns's article from Chapter 1 identify images that stand for particular generational beliefs or tendencies? For instance, do you have a connection to those dancing raisins, to the Marvin Gaye tune, or to the countless other covers of the song?
3. How could you examine the spiritual artifacts in Chapter 4 with the tools offered in this chapter? For instance, can you find a way to use Seiter's article to read the still photo from *Smoke Signals*?

Argument
1. McCauley notes in his essay that sound tracks played a vital role in attracting viewers to horror films; Seiter notes also that sound is a vital factor to consider in our analysis of television. Drawing on both sources, examine a genre of television or film (that the authors do *not* address) and argue for a specific use of its music, both within the frame—as part of the story being told—and outside the frame—as cues for the viewer.
2. Using Seiter's analytical method, choose a music video to examine. For instance, identify the roles of the editing cuts, the music, the camera angles, and the faces and figures in the video. Develop an argument that is then supported by your analysis.
3. In what ways do the images of the dolls in Chapter 2 represent something else? For instance, you might argue that Barbie stands for marketing and advertising, or that the Hispanic Day of the Dead skeletons represent life instead of death.

Analysis
1. Sieter's article defines a typical starting point in television criticism and analysis as the gathering of "a small, manageable, and synchronic (contemporaneous) text or set of texts for analysis and, using the texts as a basis, try[ing] to establish the conventions governing the larger system." Following this pattern, choose a topic (such as one episode of *Friends*, *Star Trek*, or *NYPD Blue*) and apply a semiotic analysis that attempts to find the conventions governing "the larger system." You might find it helpful to closely examine the examples Seiter gives of this sort of analysis to identify a pattern.
2. Using Abt and Mustazza'a "Rules of Play" for talk TV, analyze one of the several

daytime or nighttime talk shows to measure the extent of the show's adherence to the formula. If you find discrepancies, discuss what they might mean.

3. In what ways do you see the images of spirituality from Chapter 4 as representative of American beliefs? Identify two or three images (from this book or other books) that represent spirituality to you, and then analyze their relationship to the culture.

4. Each of these articles and images represents something specific in the image culture. Reading this chapter as you would a collection of artifacts, develop an interpretation of the "image" in American pop culture.

Research

1. Conduct independent research among friends, classmates, and family members by asking for opinions about the appeal of horror films. You might also ask which theories your respondents tend to find credible. In your writing, summarize and synthesize the results, developing a coherent, reasoned answer that takes into account McCauley's review of the theories.

2. To practice some demographic research, look for information about the viewership of talk shows: Who watches them? Are the audiences for nighttime and daytime talk shows different, and if so, how? As you do your research, try to develop a sense of why people respond to talk shows.

3. Search through newspaper sports sections and sports publications to get an idea of the public and journalistic response to Michael Jordan's brief gambling troubles. From the coverage provided, how would you add to Nelson George's perception of Jordan?

CHAPTER 4

"I BELIEVE": PERSPECTIVES ON SPIRITUALITY IN POP CULTURE

Congress shall make no law respecting an establishment of religion, or prohibiting the free exercise thereof . . .

One of the stories that came out of the 1999 massacre at Columbine High School involved young Cassie Bernall, who was asked by the two shooters, Eric Harris and Dylan Klebold, if she believed in God. She said "yes." Then she was killed.

When this story was first told on national news, the intense response from the American public was quickly apparent, probably because Bernall's religious belief seemed to be the reason she had been shot. The news media covered the story widely; Bernall's mother wrote a best-selling book about her daughter's faith; her father took to the road to deliver inspirational sermons; and dozens of magazine covers, newspaper articles, and Web sites were devoted to Cassie Bernall's story. Because the shooters were presumed to be amoral, sociopathic, and possibly racist, Cassie Bernall's death was presumed to be the result of her Christian beliefs. In short, her murder recalled the martyring of Jesus Christ. (Later, the news media reported that in fact this exchange between Bernall and her killers had not happened. One of the survivors of the massacre had apparently been so rattled that in retelling his story, he'd gotten some of his facts wrong. He maintains, however, that his memory is clear on this point.)

Regardless of its veracity, the fact that the story got such widespread media coverage speaks to the functions of religion and spiritual practice in America. As an artifact of American religious belief, the public reaction to the story of Cassie Bernall's death suggests a deep identification with the need to believe, a need these particular circumstances seemed to magnify.

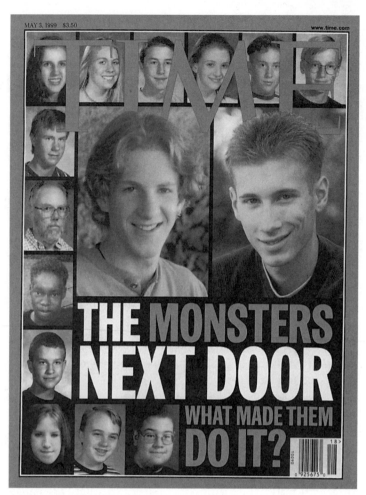

What do monsters look like?

The crosses in the photo stand for more than Christianity; what else do they suggest?

Writing About Spirituality

The demand for angels, for instance, can be seen everywhere, and a writer could cite many examples of the demand: angel bumper stickers, small gold figures that pin to your collar, greeting cards and wrapping paper with angels as decorations, and the ongoing Home Shopping Network collectible angel series are only a few of the examples an observant writer might find. The writer might also wonder, after seeing such a variety of angels, why so many people in our culture seem to have adopted the angel symbol. Collecting those angels might be read as collecting protective amulets, talismans against harm, and evidence for this reading could be the small figurines, decorative objects, and other representations of angels.

There's more than one reading to be seen in the angel culture, of course; a writer might also look elsewhere, perhaps at the symbolism inherent in angels as guardian figures. If an essay focused on that context, angels might be read as an artifact of our collective desire to believe in divine guidance and protection; an artifact supporting this particular reading is the popular bumper sticker that reads, "Drive no faster than your guardian angel can fly." What other artifacts might support this reading? A writer might pick and choose from dozens: television programs that discuss miraculous rescues, amazing stories of survival against the odds, and so on. Each of these examples might be used as evidence in the argument that we want to believe in *Something* protecting us. Artist Keith Mallett's "Earth Angel" series, one of which appears in this chapter, depicts a guardian angel for each season on Earth. In an interview with the author, Mallet notes that people often buy his paintings to give a guardian angel to a child born in a particular season.

(Box continues on following page)

Pop culture and spirituality—matters of faith and belief—might not automatically seem to go together. And yet, pop culture is one place where our collective spiritual interests (our way of life) develop into artifacts we can examine, forming texts we can read. Anthropologists years from now will be able to examine a rich array of religious and spiritual signs, from movies (e.g., *The Exorcist, Dogma, Witness, The Craft, Practical Magic, City of Angels*), to cartoons and cartoon characters (e.g., *God, the Devil, and Bob; Satan* on *South Park;* God's appearances on *The Simpsons*), to comic strips (e.g., *Peanuts, Family Circus, Rose is Rose*). American television's take on religion and spirituality ranges from *Touched by an Angel* to *Buffy the Vampire Slayer* and *Bewitched*. Apu on *The Simpsons* demonstrates Hindu beliefs and practices. Certainly the enormous culture in collectible angel figurines, books, and posters is an important text. American pop culture is clearly a rich stew of our beliefs and practices.

Writing About Spirituality *(continued)*

If a writer wanted to analyze the angel culture more specifically, she could take note of the fact that angels are representative of Christianity, so that the intense interest in collecting angels of any sort could be seen as a reflection of Christianity's popularity (as opposed, for instance, to religion as a whole), renewed and reformed for a new generation. It might add support to such an argument to look at other cultural elements that would be in context with this perspective: for example, a writer might discuss television shows such as *Touched by an Angel* and *Miracles,* or the film *Michael,* which brought the Archangel Michael to earth. Each of these programs, a writer might point out, could be read as a renewal of sorts. Especially when they're contrasted with programming such as *COPS* and *Hard Copy,* programs like *Miracles* could easily be argued to be refreshing, renewing, or simply providing relief from the depressing programming we often see on television.

And when the writer put all these readings together, the reader would probably be able to see that angels are significant in more than one way; even non-Christians might collect angels, for example, just as a collectible to put next to thimbles, Coke bottle caps, or baseball cards. In other words, a writer might point out that angels need not carry any particular religious significance, although that's probably the most obvious interpretation of the text of the angel culture. In what other ways could the collectibles culture in angels be read? What is your own perspective on the artifact angels?

Americans follow a great variety of faiths and practices, and so our popular culture reflects that variety: Baptist, Amish, Jewish, Buddhist, Catholic, Church of Latter-Day Saints, *santeria,* Jehovah's Witness, Scientology, Native American, and Wiccan perspectives and images appear on soap operas, in movies, parodied on *The Simpsons,* and on the covers of *Time* and *Newsweek.* We saw the Amish in *Witness,* Navajo purification ceremonies on *The X-Files,* witchcraft in *Practical Magic* and *Charmed,* John Travolta's leering alien in L. Ron Hubbard's Scientology parable *Battlefield Earth,* and Hasidic Jews in New York City preparing for the end of the world in *Independence Day.* Real life, too, takes a cue from pop culture's diversity: in the 2000 race for President of the United States, a practicing Orthodox Jew was, for the first time in American history, a vice presidential candidate.

To reflect American values about religious tolerance, the anchor article in this section encourages religious pluralism. The U.S. Constitution ensures that the government will not persecute anyone for his or her religious beliefs, and this tolerance encourages a plethora of spiritual practices. Many of us would agree with the Dalai Lama that each belief system offers something uniquely suited to its followers, and yet it is obvious—despite the claims inherent in many faiths that it is the one true faith—that one person's religious practice may not be right for someone else. The Lama metaphorically describes religion as medicine, suggesting that a specific medicine might be more effective for one individual than for another, even if both have the same illness. In this perspective, arguing about which medicine is "the best choice" for everyone is pointless. Identifying the similarities and differences, however, is a healthy and intelligent approach. The Lama points out that "it is essential to have a single-pointed commitment to one's own faith." He goes on to say:

> But at the same time, we have to find some means of reconciling this belief with the reality of a multiplicity of similar claims. In practical terms, this involves individual practitioners finding a way at least to accept the validity of the teachings of other religions while maintaining a whole-hearted commitment to their own. (225)

This balancing act appears to enact the U.S. Constitutional guarantee of religious freedom in many ways, and it helps us to realize—and to practice—a religious plurality, in which each individual believes firmly in his or her own faith while simultaneously acknowledging the equal validity of another's faith practice. Continued immigration spurs our subsequent ethnic and cultural diversity to grow exponentially; this country cannot insist on one religion, nor would it want to. This tolerant approach governs the rest of this chapter; without sacrificing your own perspective, examine (through the lens of pop culture) the texts of American spirituality. Keep in mind, too, that this is just one set of spiritual artifacts; were you compiling "artifacts of American religious practice," you might select entirely different items. The plurality, in other words, works on many levels at once. In the spirit of the Lama's article, the other selections in this chapter offer a cross section of spiritual perspectives in American pop culture.

Christianity is perhaps the most "popular" religion that Americans practice. Pop culture, then, often focuses on the Christian set of beliefs. Charles Schulz's immortal comic strip *Peanuts,* for instance, often paraphrases Biblical verses while Charlie Brown learns life lessons (usually from the philosopher Linus). Schulz was one of the first cartoonists to deal with religion in a comic strip, but the influence of this religious artifact extends beyond the funny pages: each December, millions of Americans watch the classic cartoon *A Charlie Brown Christmas.* First aired in 1965, the cartoon shows Charlie Brown disheartened by the relentless emphasis on glittery aluminum trees and shiny ornaments, the greedy desire for presents, and the ruthless commercialization of the season. Finally, he questions what it's all about—and Linus explains the gospel of Luke:

> And the angel said unto them, Fear not: for behold, I bring you good tidings of great joy, which shall be to all people. For unto you is born this day in the city of David a savior, which is Christ the Lord. (Luke 2:8)

"That's the true meaning of Christmas, Charlie Brown," Linus says. We might see the cartoon as an artifact of childhood; we might take the philosophy without the message. But we can't deny the basic Christian perspective, told gently through the voices of the children who never grow up.

In some ways, *A Charlie Brown Christmas* reveals the humorous underbelly to the crass consumerism Charlie Brown complains about: even Snoopy, for instance, indulges in the spirit of competition by decorating his dog house with lights and tinsel. Moreover, he wins the neighborhood contest, much to Charlie Brown's dismay. Humor, then, can be the lesson—as in the example of the satirical practices of Matt Groening. Homer Simpson's response to a persistent knocking on the front door is typical: when he sees three young people in suits standing on the front step, he groans, "Oh, great—Mormons!" Groening's satirical work in both his long-running series *The Simpsons* and the alternative comic strip *Life in Hell* offers the flip side of the religious cartooning we find in *Family Circus;* that is, instead of proselytizing, *Life in Hell* poses spiritual dilemmas. Questioning the existence of God, asking for proof, and so on are tricky matters. And yet, Groening asks real questions in the shape of a lighthearted art form, the comic. Why, for instance, does God allow suffering in a world he created? In the cartoon presented later in the chapter, Bongo realizes that "the theological implications are staggering."

The depiction of deity—a god figure—is not sanctioned by Christian beliefs, so pop culture's idea of what God looks like is important. That is, because God is said to have created humans in His own image, what we look like might influence how we imagine God. In *Star Trek 5: The Final Frontier,* Captain Kirk, Commander Spock, and Dr. McCoy meet "God," who is Caucasian, male, bearded, white-haired, deep voiced, and not unlike Charlton Heston; this image reflects a common representation of God. In contrast to this traditional God is the sometimes humorous but always pointed depiction of God as a woman; the film *Dogma*, starring Matt Damon and Ben Affleck, also stars God, played by singer Alanis Morrissette.

A religious symbol in this chapter goes somewhat further afield as it questions race: depictions of a brown-skinned guardian angel offer points of identification for groups who might feel slighted—or less welcomed— by religious imagery that focuses on the Caucasian. Artist Keith Mallett points out that this "Earth Angel" series of paintings is "more real" than just angels. They are "grounded in reality" and in fact blend the cultural themes of Western and African traditions as well as pagan. From yet another perspective, could a black angel (and, by extension, God) be seen as sacrilegious? What about liberating? Your own expectations and ingrained habits will help you answer this question. An interesting essay might arise from a comparison of various depictions of deity in gender, race, and species. Try to see each variation as an artifact itself. What do they tell you? Is the appearance of religious figures important? What significance might it have?

One significant religious artifact comes from a television show that premiered on NBC in the spring of 2000, the animated primetime series called *God, the Devil, and Bob.* The sitcom's premise was that the fate of the world rests on one person, Bob, whose task is to restore God's faith in humanity.

How would you depict a modern God?

If Bob can't restore God's faith in humanity, God will wipe out the entire population and start fresh. Particularly interesting in this sitcom is the way God appears: often shown wearing a tie-dyed shirt, tennis shoes, sunglasses, and white cotton drawstring pants, he looks much more like the late Jerry Garcia, leader of the cult band The Grateful Dead, than the grave and sober Yahweh we may be more familiar with. This God even drinks beer. It's light beer, but it's still beer. Such a depiction gives us some interesting material for analyzing pop culture's treatment of religious authority. (It may also be significant to our analysis that the series was canceled after only three episodes aired.) How might such a depiction of God function in our culture, especially given the Christian prohibition about images of God? From some perspectives, drawing God to resemble a man legendary for drug excesses might be highly offensive, but this hipper, more modern God might entice viewers who would reject a traditional God figure.

How we understand the Christian God is the subject of Joan Osborne's pop hit "One of Us," one song from an album peppered with religious references. In addition to questioning what God might look like, Osborne also wonders if God might be lonely as he tries to "make His way home / Back up to Heaven all alone." "One of Us" wonders out loud the questions many Christians—and non-Christians—ask themselves.

> If God had a name, what would it be
> And would you call it to His face?
> If you were faced with Him in all His glory
> What would you ask if you had just one question?
> —Joan Osborne

From wristbands that ask "What Would Jesus Do?" to bumper stickers reading "Born Again Pagan," religion is openly popular again. In some ways, this kind of popularity is surprising; for years, one's spiritual practice was not necessarily appropriate for public conversation. It wasn't hidden or secret, but it was personal and private. For many people, the experience of faith is so deeply individualized that public discussion of it is just not done. But God has lately been globalized and popularized; as one college professor puts it, "It's Wal-Mart God." From some traditional perspectives, a Wal-Mart God might be a highly offensive concept, whereas from the perspective of someone searching for Christian fulfillment, such an easily accessible God might be the perfect solution. Looking like Jerry Garcia might make God even more appealing.

Non-Christian faith practices (paganism, for instance) also appear in pop culture. *Paganism is* a spiritual path rooted in earthy, everyday practices, not a belief system reserved for an elite or educated few. Paganism can be an umbrella term for earth-centered, non-Christian practices, including Native American beliefs, witchcraft, and animism (the belief that every object has a spiritual essence). Often known as the Old Religion, witchcraft is perhaps the most recently popular of the pagan practices, and as this spiritual practice (which is often incorrectly assumed to be Satanic) becomes better understood, the representations of witches appear in more and more of our cultural texts: Tabitha on the soap opera *Passions* is a stereotypical "bad witch" who nonetheless offers a funny and welcome change from the melodramatic soap opera genre. Willow, the young witch on *Buffy the Vampire Slayer*, is often unnerved by her considerable and sometimes unreliable abilities; for instance, she manages to turn a school friend into a rat, but she can't reverse the spell. The films *Practical Magic* and *The Craft* and the television series *Charmed* also focus on the practice of earth magic. And while the image of witchcraft is notoriously associated with brooms and pointed black hats, Rose Morrigan points out in her article in this chapter that the witches she first met "don't look like the warty hags of childhood stories. They look like mothers and fathers, professionals and working folk; in short, they look like me."

In the context of spiritual practices, a reemergence of witchcraft might suggest a growing cultural tolerance; from Christian perspectives, witchcraft is often seen as Satanic and would thus be a negative force in pop culture. How shall we read the text of the growing popular interest in witchcraft?

Growing almost as rapidly as interest in the Old Religion is the interest in and attention to the diverse religious practices of the American Indians, whose spiritual mythologies also tend to emphasize an appeal to the forces of nature rather than deity. Just as witches with hooked noses and broomsticks are artifacts of our popular conception of Wicca, so are the chants, rain dances, and vision quests of the Native American. As in the case of witchcraft, however, these popular conceptions are not necessarily accurate representations. In the 1999 film *Smoke Signals*, Thomas and Victor, two young Spokane Indians, go on a quest to find Victor's father. Produced, written, and acted by Native Americans, the film offers a

Is evil the same from all religious perspectives?

depiction of reservation life that may be unfamiliar to you. The reservation's radio station, for example, celebrates the morning by saying, "It's a good day to be indigenous!" Certainly the film's characters are not "Indian braves." Thomas Builds-the-Fire is described by his author, Sherman Alexie, as "an Indian geek": "Thomas explodes the myth and stereotype about the huge, stoic, warrior Indian." His friend Victor, however, still subscribes to certain societal expectations: when two whites harass Thomas, Victor tells him to "get stoic, man." Thomas's faith is in incessant storytelling; Victor's faith is in the legend he has built up around his absent father.

In most religious traditions, faith means believing without proof: one does not question deity or ask for evidence to substantiate belief. (As Dr. McCoy says when Captain Kirk challenges the God they meet, "Jim, you don't ask the Almighty for his I.D.") Faith takes many forms—faith that the sun will rise in the morning, faith in the infallibility of a given deity, faith in a spouse's or partner's fidelity, faith in the simplicities and complexities of scientific belief, and so on. Not every expression of faith is spiritual or religious, but every experience of faith requires us to suspend skepticism and to believe that whatever it is you have faith in will continue unchanged. Alexie, a member of the Spokane Indian tribe, plays on the conceptions of faith in his poem "Water." Is his faith in the simple combination of hydrogen and oxygen molecules any different from a Christian's faith in God's mercy or a witch's faith in the earth? The Dalai Lama would probably say there is no difference.

How does Thomas's appearance violate Victor's expectations?

Religious and spiritual practices are, of course, deeply personal—and yet, as artifacts of culture, they speak to us at large. The point is, within the definition of "belief system" are dozens and dozens of possibilities. Even within the same religion there can be variations. Although you may have a clear conception of your own spiritual practices (and even if you don't), you can learn a good deal by examining, as the Lama suggests, the practices of those around you. Writing about those practices, and learning how they relate to the collective text of pop culture, will enable you to understand them much better, even if you're just learning about your own path.

"The Role of Religion in Modern Society," from *Ethics for the New Millennium* (1999)

His Holiness the Dalai Lama

It is a sad fact of human history that religion has been a major source of conflict. Even today, individuals are killed, communities destroyed, and societies destabilized as a result of religious bigotry and hatred. It is no wonder that many question the place of religion in human society. Yet when we think carefully, we find that conflict in the name of religion arises from two principal sources. There is that which arises simply as a result of religious diversity—the doctrinal, cultural, and practical differences between one religion and another. Then there is the conflict that arises in the context of political, economic, and other factors, mainly at the institutional level. Interreligious harmony is the key to overcoming conflict of the first sort. In the case of the second, some other solution must be found. Secularization and in particular the separation of the religious hierarchy from the institutions of the state may go some way to reducing such institutional problems. Our concern in this chapter is with interreligious harmony, however.

This is an important aspect of what I have called universal responsibility. But before examining the matter in detail, it is perhaps worth considering the question of whether religion is really relevant in the modern world. Many people argue that it is not. Now I have observed that religious belief is not a precondition either of ethical conduct or of happiness itself. I have also suggested that whether a person practices religion or not, the spiritual qualities of love and compassion, patience, tolerance, forgiveness, humility, and so on are indispensable. At the same time, I should make it clear that I believe that these are most easily and effectively developed within the context of religious practice. I also believe that when an individual sincerely practices religion, that individual will benefit enormously. People who have developed a firm faith, grounded in understanding and rooted in daily practice, are in general much better at coping with adversity than those who have not. I am convinced, therefore, that religion has enormous potential to benefit humanity. Properly employed, it is an extremely effective instrument for establishing human happiness. In particular, it can play a leading role in encouraging people to develop a sense of responsibility toward others and of the need to be ethically disciplined.

On these grounds, therefore, I believe that religion is still relevant today. But consider this too: some years ago, the body of a Stone Age man was recovered from the ice of the European Alps. Despite being more than five thousand years old, it was perfectly preserved. Even its clothes were largely intact. I remember thinking at the time that were it possible to bring this individual back to life for a day, we would find that we have much in common with him. No doubt we would find that he too was concerned for his family and loved ones, for his health and so on. Differences of culture and expression notwithstanding, we would still be able to identify with one another on the level of feeling. And there could be no reason to suppose any less concern with finding happiness and avoiding suffering on his part than on ours. If religion, with its emphasis on overcoming suffering through the practice of ethical discipline and cultivation of love and compassion, can be conceived of as relevant in the past, it is hard to see why it should not be equally so today. Granted that in the past the value of religion may have been more obvious, in that human suffering was more explicit due to the lack of modern facilities. But because we humans still suffer, albeit today this is experienced more internally as mental and emotional affliction, and because religion in addition to its salvific truth claims is concerned to help us overcome suffering, surely it must still be relevant.

How then might we bring about the harmony that is necessary to overcome interreligious conflict? As in the case of individuals engaged in the discipline of restraining their response to negative thoughts and emotions and cultivating spiritual qualities, the key lies in developing understanding. We must first identify the factors that obstruct it. Then we must find ways to overcome them.

Perhaps the most significant obstruction to interreligious harmony is lack of appreciation of the value of others' faith traditions. Until comparatively recently, communication between different cultures, even different communities, was slow or nonexistent. For this reason, sympathy for other faith traditions was not necessarily very important—except of course where members of different religions lived side by side. But this attitude is no longer viable. In today's increasingly complex and interdependent world, we are compelled to acknowledge the existence of other cultures, different ethnic groups, and, of course, other religious faiths. Whether we like it or not, most of us now experience this diversity on a daily basis.

I believe that the best way to overcome ignorance and bring about understanding is through dialogue with members of other faith traditions. This I see occurring in a number of different ways. Discussions among scholars in which the convergence and perhaps more importantly the divergence between different faith traditions are explored and appreciated are very valuable. On another level, it is helpful when there are encounters between ordinary but practicing followers of different religions in which each shares their experiences. This is perhaps the most effective way of appreciating others' teachings. In my own case, for example, my meetings with the late Thomas Merton, a Catholic monk of the Cistercian order, were deeply inspiring. They helped me develop a profound admiration for the teachings of Christianity. I also feel that occasional meetings between religious leaders joining together to pray for a common cause are extremely useful. The gathering at Assisi in Italy in 1986, when representatives of the world's major religions gathered to pray for peace, was, I believe, tremendously beneficial to many religious believers insofar as it symbolized the solidarity and a commitment to peace of all those taking part.

Finally, I feel that the practice of members of different faith traditions going on joint pilgrimages together can be very helpful. It was in this spirit that in 1993 I went to Lourdes, and then to Jerusalem, a site holy to three of the world's great religions. I have also paid visits to various Hindu, Islamic, Jain, and Sikh shrines both in India and abroad. More recently, following a seminar devoted to discussing and practicing meditation in the Christian and Buddhist traditions, I joined an historic pilgrimage of practitioners of both traditions in a program of prayers, meditation, and dialogue under the Bodhi tree at Bodh Gaya in India. This is one of Buddhism's most important shrines.

When exchanges like these occur, followers of one tradition will find that, just as in the case of their own, the teachings of others' faiths are a source both of spiritual inspiration and of ethical guidance to their followers. It will also become clear that irrespective of doctrinal and other differences, all the major world religions are concerned with helping individuals to become good human beings. All emphasize love and compassion, patience, tolerance, forgiveness, humility, and so on, and all are capable of helping individuals to develop these. Moreover, the example given by the founders of each major religion clearly demonstrates a concern for helping others find happiness through developing these qualities. So far as their own lives were concerned, each conducted themselves with great simplicity. Ethical discipline and love for all others was the hallmark of their lives. They did not live luxuriously like emperors and kings. Instead, they voluntarily accepted suffering—without consideration of the hardships involved—in order to benefit humanity as a whole. In their teachings, all placed special emphasis on developing love and compassion and renouncing selfish desires. And each of them called on us to transform our hearts and minds. Indeed, whether we have faith or not, all are worthy of our profound admiration.

At the same time as engaging in dialogue with followers of other religions, we must, of course, implement in our daily life the teachings of our own religion. Once we have experienced the benefit of love and compassion, and of ethical discipline, we will easily recognize the value of other's teachings. But for this, it is essential to realize that religious practice entails a lot more than merely saying, "I believe" or, as in Buddhism, "I take refuge." There is also more to it than just visiting temples, or shrines, or churches. And taking religious teachings is of little benefit if they do not enter the heart but remain at the level of intellect alone. Simply relying on faith without understanding and without implementation is of limited value. I often tell Tibetans that carrying a *mala* (something like a rosary) does not make a person a genuine religious practitioner. The efforts we make sincerely to transform ourselves spiritually are what make us genuine religious practitioners.

We come to see the overriding importance of genuine practice when we recognize that, along with ignorance, individuals' unhealthy relationships with their beliefs is the other major factor in religious disharmony. Far from applying the teachings of their religion in our personal lives, we have a tendency to use them to reinforce our self-centered attitudes. We relate to our religion as something we own or as a label that separates us from others. Surely this is misguided? Instead of using the nectar of religion to purify the poisonous elements of our hearts and minds, there is a danger when we think like this of using these negative elements to poison the nectar of religion.

Yet we must acknowledge that this reflects another problem, one which is implicit in all religions. I refer to the claims each has of being the one "true" religion. How are we to resolve this difficulty? It is true that from the point of view of the individual practitioner, it is essential to have a single-pointed commitment to one's own faith. It is also true that this depends on the deep conviction that one's own path is the sole mediator of truth. But at the same time, we have to find some means of reconciling this belief with the reality of a multiplicity of similar claims. In practical terms, this involves individual practitioners finding a way at least to accept the validity of the teachings of other religions while maintaining a wholehearted commitment to their own. As far as the validity of the metaphysical truth claims of a given religion is concerned, that is of course the internal business of that particular tradition.

In my own case, I am convinced that Buddhism provides me with the most effective framework within which to situate my efforts to develop spiritually through cultivating love and compassion. At the same time, I must acknowledge that while Buddhism represents the best path for me—that is, it suits my character, my temperament, my inclinations, and my cultural background—the same will be true of Christianity for Christians. For them, Christianity is the best way. On the basis of my conviction, I cannot, therefore, say that Buddhism is best for everyone.

I sometimes think of religion in terms of medicine for the human spirit. Independent of its usage and suitability to a particular individual in a particular condition, we really cannot judge a medicine's efficacy. We are not justified in saying this medicine is very good because of such and such ingredients. If you take the patient and the medicine's effect on that person out of the equation, it hardly makes sense. What is relevant is to say that in the case of this particular patient with its particular illness, this medicine is the most effective. Similarly with different religious traditions, we can say that this one is most effective for this particular individual. But it is unhelpful to try to argue on the basis of philosophy or metaphysics that one religion is better than another. The important thing is surely its effectiveness in individual cases.

My way to resolve the seeming contradiction between each religion's claim to "one truth and one religion" and the reality of the multiplicity of faiths is thus to understand that in the case of a single individual, there can indeed be only one truth, one religion. However, from the perspective of human society at large, we must accept the concept of "many truths, many religions." To continue with our medical analogy, in the case of one particular patient, the suitable medicine is in fact the one medicine. But clearly that does not mean that there may not be other medicines suitable to other patients.

To my way of thinking, the diversity that exists among the various religious traditions is enormously enriching. There is thus no need to try to find ways of saying that ultimately all religions are the same. They are similar in that they all emphasize the indispensability of love and compassion in the context of ethical discipline. But to say this is not to say that they are all essentially one. The contradictory understanding of creation and beginninglessness articulated by Buddhism, Christianity, and Hinduism, for example, means that in the end we have to part company when it comes to metaphysical claims, in spite of the many practical similarities that undoubtedly exist. These contradictions may not be very important in the beginning stages of religious practice. But as we advance along the path of one tradition or another, we are compelled at some point to acknowledge fundamental differences. For example, the concept of rebirth in Buddhism and various other ancient Indian traditions may turn out to be incompatible with the Christian idea of salvation. This need not be a cause for dismay, however. Even within Buddhism itself, in the realm of metaphysics there are diametrically opposing views. At the very least, such diversity means that we have different frameworks within which to locate ethical discipline and the development of spiritual values. That is why I do not advocate a super or a new world religion. It would mean that we would lose the unique characteristics of the different faith traditions.

Some people, it is true, hold that the Buddhist concept of *shunyata*, or emptiness, is ultimately the same as certain approaches to understanding the concept of God. Nevertheless, there remain difficulties with this. The first is that while of course we can interpret these concepts, to what extent can we be faithful to the original teachings if we do so? There are compelling similarities between the Mahayana Buddhist concept of *Dharmakaya, Sambogakaya,* and *Nirmanakaya* and the Christian trinity of God as Father, Son, and Holy Spirit. But to say, on the basis of this, that Buddhism and Christianity are ultimately the same is to go a bit far, I think! As an old Tibetan saying goes, we must beware of trying to put a yak's head on a sheep's body—or vice versa.

What is required instead is that we develop a genuine sense of religious pluralism in spite of the different claims of different faith traditions. This is especially true if we are serious in our respect for human rights as a universal principle. In this regard, I find the concept of a world parliament of religions very appealing. To begin with, the word "parliament" conveys a sense of democracy, while the plural "religions" underlines the importance of the principle of a multiplicity of faith traditions. The truly pluralist perspective on religion which the idea of such a parliament suggests could, I believe be, of great help. It would avoid the extremes of religious bigotry on the one hand, and the urge toward unnecessary syncretism on the other.

Connected with this issue of interreligious harmony, I should perhaps say something about religious conversion. This is a question which must be taken extremely seriously. It is essential to realize that the mere fact of conversion alone will not make an individual a better person, that is to say, a more disciplined, a more compassionate, and a warm-hearted person. Much more helpful, therefore, is for the individual to concentrate on transforming themselves spiritually through the practice of restraint, virtue, and compassion. To the extent that the insights or practices of other religions are useful or relevant to our own faith, it is valuable to learn from others. In some cases, it may even be helpful to adopt certain of them. Yet when this is done wisely, we can remain firmly committed to our own faith. This way is best because it carries with it no danger of confusion, especially with respect to the different ways of life that tend to go with different faith traditions.

Given the diversity to be found among individual human beings, it is of course bound to be the case that out of many millions of practitioners of a particular religion, a handful will find that another religion's approach to ethics and spiritual development is more satisfactory. For some, the concept of rebirth and karma will seem highly effective in inspiring the aspiration to develop love and compassion within the context of responsibility. For others, the concept of a transcendent, loving creator will come to seem more so. In such circumstances, it is crucial for those individuals to question themselves again and again. They must ask, "Am I attracted to this other religion for the right reasons? Is it merely the cultural and ritual aspects that are appealing? Or is it the essential teachings? Do I suppose that if I convert to this new religion it will be less demanding than my present one?" I say this because it has often struck me that when people do convert to a religion outside their own heritage, quite often they adopt certain superficial aspects of the culture to which their new faith belongs. But their practice may not go very much deeper than that.

In the case of a person who decides after a process of long and mature reflection to adopt a different religion, it is very important that they remember the positive contribution to humanity of each religious tradition. The danger is that the individual may, in seeking to justify their decision to others, criticize their previous faith. It is essential to avoid this. Just because that tradition is no longer effective in the case of one individual does not mean it is no longer of benefit to humanity. On the contrary, we can be certain that it has been an inspiration to millions of people in the past, that it inspires millions today, and that it will inspire millions in the path of love and compassion in the future.

The important point to keep in mind is that ultimately the whole purpose of religion is to facilitate love and compassion, patience, tolerance, humility, forgiveness, and so on. If we neglect these, changing our religion will be of no help. In the same way, even if we are fervent believers in our own faith, it will avail us nothing if we neglect to implement these qualities in our daily lives. Such a believer is no better off than a patient with some fatal illness who merely reads a medical treatise but fails to undertake the treatment prescribed.

Moreover, if we who are practitioners of religion are not compassionate and disciplined, how can we expect it of others? If we can establish genuine harmony derived from mutual respect and understanding, religion has enormous potential to speak with authority on such vital moral questions as peace and disarmament, social and political justice, the natural environment, and many other matters affecting all humanity. But until we put our own spiritual teachings into practice, we will never be taken seriously. And this means, among other things, setting a good example through developing good relations with other faith traditions.

■ *Tibetan spiritual leader Tenzin Gyatso, the fourteenth Dalai Lama, went into religious exile when he was 16 years old. Since then, he has written, taught, and lived Buddhism before a worldwide audience. Awarded the Nobel Peace Prize in 1989, the Dalai Lama currently lives in Dharamsala, India.*

MAKING SURE OF THE TEXT

1. How does the Lama suggest we begin developing interreligious harmony?
2. What distinctions does the Lama make between saying "I believe" and the "genuine practice" of religious faith?
3. Some religions rely on "witnessing," or reaching out to members of other paths, as part of their faith practice; the Lama, however, suggests that "it is unhelpful to try to argue [. . .] that one religion is better than another." How does the Lama resolve the contradiction of each religion's claim to be the one true religion?
4. What is the Lama's perspective on conversion from one faith to another? How does this explanation help to support his ideas about interreligious harmony?

CONSIDERING THE CONTEXT

1. Buddhism's popularity in America might help explain the success of *Ethics for the New Millennium* on the best-seller lists. What else might explain its popularity in this country?
2. Is it unusual to consider religion to be "an instrument"? In what perspectives could religious and spiritual practices be social "instruments"?
3. The Lama uses a medical analogy to make a point about individual spiritual practices; what other metaphors does he use to help make his perspective clear to us? What effect do they have?

■ ■ ■

"Drawing on the Divine," *The Orlando Sentinel* (2000)

Mark I. Pinsky

For the past half century, cartoonist Charles Schulz has demonstrated in a light-hearted and light-handed way that you can find faith in the funniest places.

The "Peanuts" gang takes their final bow next Sunday, and when they do, Charlie Brown, Linus and Snoopy also will be leaving a pen-and-ink pulpit with a worldwide congregation of more than 300 million.

"Have you noticed that I do a lot of spiritual things?" Schulz asked in a recent *Newsweek* interview.

Actually, a great many people have noticed, beginning with the Rev. Robert Short, who wrote *The Gospel According to Peanuts* in 1965. The paperback, which is still in print, has sold 10 million copies, according to the book's publisher. As a young graduate student, Short observed the comic's "unusual juxtaposition of humor and serious theology," which "often assumes the form of a modern-day Christian parable" paralleling those of the New Testament.

In one strip, for example, Jesus' warning not to build a house on sand is illustrated by a strip showing Linus sculpting an elaborate sandcastle that is washed away by a rainstorm. In another, Linus paraphrases the gospel of Matthew: "It rains on the just and the unjust, Charlie Brown."

There has always been a wistful, melancholy undercurrent to "Peanuts," whose characters sometimes quote the Book of Job and the prophet Isaiah. As Charlie Brown observes, "adversity is what makes you mature. The growing soul is watered best by tears of sadness."

But there is also joy. Each December, Linus reads the Christmas story from the gospel of Luke, in both the newspaper strip and on the 1965 CBS television special. Schulz told *Newsweek* that he told the network that the television show could not air without the passage from Luke.

Short, now a Presbyterian minister in Monticello, Ark., said in an interview that Schulz was not always in such a commanding position. Several early strips were rejected by his syndicate for including Bible quotations.

"I have been told that quotations from the Bible should never be used in such a lowly thing as a comic strip," Schulz wrote. But as the feature became more popular, the editors at his syndicate relented, starting with the Christmas strip.

"He was the first cartoonist who could openly quote scripture in a strip," Short said, which made him a trailblazer. "Since he's been doing it for such a long time, now everybody can get away with it."

At least half a dozen syndicated strips, old and new, incorporate religious themes and characters. There's a chaplain, a benign clergyman in Mort Walker's "Beetle Bailey." In Doug Marlette's "Kudzu," the buffoonish Rev. Will B. Dunn is lampooned. Marlette, who was raised a Southern

Baptist and lectures at seminaries, said that using a minister as a central character is natural, since "religion is about life." Dunn is featured in several of Marlette's collections, including one called *There's No Business Like Soul Business.*

Angels appear regularly in Pat Brady's "Rose is Rose." Bil Keane in "The Family Circus" portrays children praying, angels, heaven and the shades of the dead moving among the living. At the extreme end of the spectrum is a one-panel feature, "Facts About the Bible" by John Lehti, which urges readers to "Save this for your Sunday school scrapbook."

Short sometimes lectures at churches on "Meditations on Calvin and Hobbes and Christ," exploring religious themes in "Calvin and Hobbes," a once popular strip drawn by Bill Watterson from 1986 to 1995. In the feature, a young boy and his friend—an imaginary tiger—discuss profound theological and philosophical questions in charming and whimsical ways.

But there is still resistance to using the comics as a venue to discussing religion, according to Lucy Shelton Caswell, professor of journalism at Ohio State University and curator of the college's cartoon research library. A young cartoonist appearing in 75 to 100 newspapers might have religion-themed strips rejected by the syndicate, which distributes the feature.

"A lot of editors would be timid today," she said. Whether a particular strip would be accepted is "dependent on the thoughtfulness and creativity of the cartoonist."

For some reason, the underworld and its denizens are less controversial subjects for cartoonists. The first syndicated strip by Matt Groening, the creator of "The Simpsons" and someone who cited Schulz as an early influence, was (and is) the angst-ridden "Life in Hell," which runs in many alternative weeklies. Hell and the devil are frequently portrayed in Joe Martin's absurdist "Mr. Boffo." Martin said that when one newspaper complained about his "Life in Hell" strips and yanked them, several ministers called and demanded that they be reinstated.

Even the devilish "Dennis the Menace" attends church and says grace at the table with his family, and prays before bed—often with the back flap of his pajamas drooping. In 1993, Hank Ketcham published *Dennis the Menace: Prayers and Graces,* dedicated to his Seattle Sunday school teachers and with a brief foreword by Ruth and Billy Graham.

As the book illustrates, religion in the strip is gentle and entirely consistent with the characters, and never preachy. Kneeling by his bedside in one panel, Dennis looks up and says, "About this afternoon. If you'll take a look at the instant replay, you'll see it wasn't all my fault."

The Rev. Jimmie Lancaster, of Westminster Presbyterian Church in Hot Springs, Ark., often uses "Peanuts" and "Family Circus" to illustrate his sermons, later posting the strips outside his office on a bulletin board that reads, "A Cheerful Heart is Good Medicine."

"There's a therapeutic use for humor," he said "I'm a story teller, and a cartoon may fit into a story I'm telling."

"Peanuts" is still the cartoon venue most likely to talk about religion, and Charles Schulz is aware of the responsibility that entails. "I am always amazed that Charlie Brown and Snoopy can prompt some good theological discussions," he wrote recently.

A lay minister in the Indiana-based Church of God, Schulz wrote in 1963 that "I must exercise care in the way I go about expressing things. I have a message that I want to present, but I would rather bend a little to put over a point than to have the whole strip dropped because it's too obvious." As a result of this soft sell, Schulz wrote in the essay cited in Short's book, "all kinds of people in religious work have written to thank me for preaching in my own way through the strips. That is one of the things that keeps me going."

But a lot can change in 35 years, including the American people's attitude toward religion and their idea of what is an acceptable expression of faith. Short said that in recent decades Schulz has tended to "use religion themes more explicitly than when he first started out. His approach has shifted from the indirect to the more direct approach."

Still, Short said, "genuine religious concern" appears only in about 10 percent of Schulz's strips. This light touch to religion and theology in Peanuts contrasts with the more up-front approach of Johnny Hart, who does the "B.C." strip and co-authors "The Wizard of Id." Hart requested (and received) an autographed, original of an early "Peanuts" quoting the Bible, but he thinks Schulz may have played it too safe with his faith.

Hart said he experienced a religious conversion in the early 1980s, one that had a profound impact on his work and his life. "It all happened when I began to think more about the Bible," he said. "It was what I thought about all the time, so it began to work its way in my strips."

Soon, the cave men characters in "B.C." began to grapple with questions like the existence of God, the crucifixion of Jesus and Resurrection—the title of the strip notwithstanding. In one, a cave man rolls a stone away from a cave on Easter morning, looks in and, finding it empty, raises his fist and shouts, "Yes!"

Before long, Hart began to butt heads with his clients when he got into religion, especially explicit references to Christianity on Good Friday, Easter and Christmas. In recent years, major newspapers in Los Angeles, Chicago, Washington, D.C., and Denver have pulled individual strips. Several dropped it permanently because it offended non-Christian readers, or because the religious messages were jarring and out of context with the strip's humor.

Hart, whose strips reach nearly 100 million readers in 1,200 newspapers, is unabashed by controversy, and said he would bring religion into his strip every day, if he could: "God gave me my gift, my platform and my station."

A Presbyterian Sunday school teacher who once dabbled in the occult, Hart is planning a 20-foot cartoon illustrating the story of the Bible. Hart does not accept evolution; he said Noah's Ark could not accommodate the dinosaurs that often appear in his strip. He thinks America should be a Christian nation and believes that only those who believe in Jesus will go to heaven.

There are limits to how much he can use the strip to proselytize, Hart acknowledges, before the effort becomes counterproductive. "I don't want to beat people over the head with it," he said. "It's not easy to bring them over. I know how uneasy people get when they think someone is preaching at them. They resent your trying to force feed them."

Hart's approach has made him a hero among Christian conservatives—he was recently profiled in James Dobson's *Focus on the Family* magazine—yet it makes some of his natural allies uneasy.

"If there had to be a cartoonist to write about religion, it would be Johnny Hart," said Joe Martin, who draws "Mr. Boffo" and two other daily strips. "I've never had more respect for a humorist than Johnny Hart."

But sometimes, Martin said, Hart seems to be trying to make a religious point at the expense of a more universal approach to humor. "I don't think the comics are the place to editorialize," he said. "I'm one of the silly cartoonists. I think we should all be more silly."

In many ways, the debate over Hart's strips mirrors the larger dialogue between the evangelical and fundamentalist wing of Christianity, and the moderate, mainline wing, over the best way to share faith. Robert Short, for one, finds Hart "far too conservative for my tastes. He really has become ultraconservative, and the strip has gotten a little heavy-handed. He has to be antagonizing a lot of people."

Some cartoonists, even those with a strong religious faith, tend to eschew religion in their strips. *Orlando Sentinel* editorial cartoonists Ralph Dunagin and Dana Summers collaborate on a daily strip called "The Middletons." Dunagin calls Hart's use of religion "kind of an obsession. I never have felt comfortable doing that, preaching to anybody else."

Summers said that, while he and his partner will occasionally show characters in church, "we use situations to show moral lessons: family togetherness, a racially diverse neighborhood, that sort of thing."

The irony, Summers said, is that other strips get away with an array of material that makes many readers uncomfortable, including everything from homosexuality to bathroom humor. "Mention God in a strip, and sometimes you get in trouble."

■ *Mark I. Pinsky is a staff writer for the* Orlando (FL) Sentinel. *This article appeared days before* Peanuts *cartoonist Charles Schulz died on February 13, 2000.*

MAKING SURE OF THE TEXT

1. How do the religious cartoonists Pinsky mentions incorporate religious faith into their cartoons? Summarize.
2. Why is there resistance to using comics as a venue for discussing religion, and how do the cartoonists mentioned in the article overcome that resistance? (Be sure to include the cartoons about "the underworld" as well.)

3. If you've seen the other religious cartoon strips Pinsky mentions, how would you compare them with *Peanuts*?

CONSIDERING THE CONTEXT

1. Considering the religious perspectives in the United States, can you explain why cartoons mentioning homosexuality or "bathroom humor" are more acceptable than religious cartooning?
2. Pinsky quotes Reverend Lancaster saying, "There's a therapeutic use for humor" in religious cartooning. The Dalai Lama uses a similar medical metaphor to describe the benefits of religious practice. What would other metaphors imply?
3. Contrast Johnny Hart's perspective on preaching through his cartoons with the Lama's perspective on religious plurality. What might each say to the other?

■ ■ ■

Life in Hell cartoon (1986)

Matt Groening

■ *Matt Groening is the creator and writer of* The Simpsons, Life in Hell, *and* Futurama. *A cartoonist from a young age, Groening says that "Most grown-ups forget what it was like to be a kid. I vowed I would never forget." Life in Hell, from which this cartoon was drawn, was originally an ongoing "postcard" of sorts about his experiences in Los Angeles, where he now lives.*

MAKING SURE OF THE TEXT

1. Bongo's first test of faith is to remain by the dead squirrel until it comes back to life. What is the result of this test?
2. How is Bongo's single ear significant?
3. What are we supposed to infer from the context in which Bongo asks for a sign of divine wisdom and mercy?
4. What other depictions of this particular religious issue can you think of?

CONSIDERING THE CONTEXT

1. Bongo seems to give up rather easily on this testing ground for faith, once he's called to dinner. How, then, should we read his final comment that the "theological implications are staggering"?
2. As an artifact of American spirituality, how might we read the existence of a rabbit who prays to God?
3. The dead squirrel seems to be a significant artifact. What might it represent? In other words, why does Groening choose to draw a squirrel instead of, say, a pigeon or a cat?
4. Contrast this sort of cartooning with other religious cartoons, such as *B.C.* or *Family Circus*. What are the similarities? The differences?

■ ■ ■

Image from *God, the Devil, and Bob*

MAKING SURE OF THE TEXT

1. How would you characterize this depiction of God? Think, for example, how this image contrasts with images you might be more accustomed to.
2. God is generally presented as having white hair, beard, and mustache; how does this image of God present those expected attributes?
3. What do the sunglasses add to your understanding of this image? What might they represent?
4. God appears to be wearing sneakers, or tennis shoes, which contrasts with the more traditional sandals. What does the difference suggest to you?

CONSIDERING THE CONTEXT

1. Imagine God wearing a tie-dyed t-shirt, as the series usually depicted him. What do you associate with tie-dye, and what would that association bring to your reading of this image?
2. Could this image of God be understood as "the Wal-Mart God"? In what contexts might this particular God be most comfortable?
3. In the series, God makes a deal with the Devil. Knowing that, how does God's appearance take on significance? In other words, what patterns do you see being set up?

"Spring"

Keith Mallett

■ *Artist Keith Mallett was born in 1948 in Pennsylvania. He studied fine art at the Art Students League and Hunter College in New York City. Many of his paintings depict African-American relationships, specifically those between parents and children. As he puts it in conversation with the author, "I believe that life is sacred and that there is nothing more important than the link between mother and child. All mothers are guardian angels to their children. So all my paintings are the Madonna and Child."*

MAKING SURE OF THE TEXT

1. In what ways does this image of the guardian angel of spring reinforce or echo traditional religious themes? What are the differences? Consider elements of arm positioning, dress, posture, background, and so forth, as you read this text.
2. From what perspectives might this image be important? Offensive? Inspiring?
3. What artifacts in this painting help to reinforce the African-American theme?
4. What other "nontraditional" depictions of the Madonna and Child have you seen? In which contexts did you see them, and how do you read those texts?

CONSIDERING THE CONTEXT

1. Go online to the artist's Web site (www.keithmallett.com) and look at the complete series of the seasons' angels. How does "Spring" fit into this context?
2. What effect is provided by Mallett's choice of clothing fabric? That is, why has the artist chosen these patterns?
3. One obvious context for this portrait is "religious imagery." Where else might you see such religious imagery, and does the race of the subjects make a difference in the meaning?

"One of Us" (1995)

Joan Osborne

If God had a name, what would it be
And would you call it to His face.
If you were faced with Him in all His glory
What would you ask if you had just one question

Yeah, yeah, God is great
Yeah, yeah, God is good
Yeah, yeah, yeah, yeah, yeah

What if God was one of us
Just a slob like one of us
Just a stranger on the bus
Trying to make His way home

If God had a face, what would it look like
And would you want to see
If seeing meant that you would have to believe
In things like Heaven and in Jesus and the Saints
And all the Prophets and . . .

Yeah, yeah, God is great . . .

Tryin' to make His way home
Back up to Heaven all alone
Nobody callin' on the phone
'Cept for the Pope maybe in Rome

Yeah, yeah, God is great . . .

Just tryin' to make his way home
Like a holy rolling stone
Back up to Heaven all alone
Just tryin' to make his way home
Nobody callin' on the phone
'Cept for the Pope maybe in Rome

■ *Joan Osborne, pop singer and Generation Xer, "manifests an almost mystical grasp of a culture in spiritual disarray," according to* Billboard. *Her debut album's mu-*

sic combines spirit, body, mind, and faith in earthy lyrics and angelic voice. "Sexuality and spirituality are so closely related to me that to put the two right next to each other in the same song isn't a contradiction," notes Osborne.

MAKING SURE OF THE TEXT

1. Why are the questions Osborne asks important?
2. Osborne suggests a certain skepticism with the lyric "yeah, yeah, God is great." What is the origin of such skepticism?
3. Osborne's lyrics raise the issue of whether God might be lonely. How does she approach the question?

CONSIDERING THE CONTEXT

1. Study the words to a psalm or other religious tune. In what ways are Osborne's lyrics a restatement of the emotion in those words?
2. Contrast Osborne's lyrics with Sherman Alexie's poem "Water" in this chapter. How does each deal with the issues of faith?
3. Osborne offers commentary on the adage that seeing is believing. Considering the context of these lyrics, do you see contradiction in this statement of scientific reasoning?
4. Compare the religious references in this tune to Osborne's other tunes from *Relish*. Is her portrayal of the spiritual elements consistent? Does she focus on one element in each different tune? Do you see a pattern to her lyrics?

■ ■ ■

"Religion and Jesus are Popular Now," *Toronto Globe and Mail* (1999)

Stephanie Nolen

He is being silk-screened on gowns from Gaultier and Dolce & Gabanna, He has a board game, He is setting the publishing industry on fire. Jesus is the icon of choice on T-shirts and tote bags sold in trendy shops on Toronto's Queen Street West, and He pops up in the lyrics of some of rap music's biggest acts.

A controversial pocketbook version of the King James Bible, with introductions to each book written by the likes of rocker Nick Cave, tops the British bestseller list. And Jesus will soon have a starring role in "God: A Biography," a National Film Board documentary by Toronto's Nick Sheehan.

"Jesus is big," said Peter Emberley, a philosopher at work on a book titled *Suspended Disbelief: The Spiritual Searches of Canada's Baby Boomers.*

"He's really big."

As Jesus is lovingly embraced by pop culture, all things religious are being hustled back in from the cold. A rash of recent Hollywood movies—"Meet Joe Black," "City of Angels," "What Dreams May Come"—ponder the afterlife.

Trend-wise Americans are hiring spiritual personal trainers (much like psychiatrists, except they pray), and the church social is back as a great place to meet dates.

A revival is under way, but for a phenomenon with Jesus at its center, it has surprisingly little to do with mainstream religion.

"People aren't really going back to church," said Professor Emberley, who teaches at Carleton University in Ottawa. "They're circling on the edges."

There is no question that readers are interested. Lorraine Symmes, director of sales in the trade division for Random House, said books about religion and spirituality are growing more popular all the time. "Ten years ago, there was very little of this genre on the lists at mainstream publishing houses, but it's increased steadily."

She pointed to the persistent presence of such books as *Care of the Soul* and *A History of God* on the bestseller lists, and she predicted the forthcoming *The New Spirituality* (which she described as the *Our Bodies, Ourselves* of religion) is a sure-fire hit.

Pamela Dickey-Young, head of the religious studies department at Queen's University in Kingston, Canada, said she is pleased to report that business is booming. "I do see people interested in religion in a new kind of way—it's trendy. Our courses are full. People want to know

Gaultier and Dolce & Gabanna ·
upper-echelon clothing designers.

about Buddhism, Islam. People want to know about religion. We have to turn people away."

This renewed interest does not, however, translate into more warm bodies in the pews on Sunday morning. The statistics on church attendance are pretty much flat for the past two decades.

"The activity is on the fringes of the mainstream," Emberley said, citing such signs as the explosion in popularity of retreats, corporate spirituality seminars and lunch-time prayer-group meetings.

The most popular spiritual exercises today, he said, are either deeply charismatic and emotional, such as retreats, or hyper-traditional, such as a rising interest in Hassidic Judaism and old-school Prayerbook Society Anglicanism.

At her publishing house, Ms. Symmes said, the top sellers are about Buddhism, Jungian philosophy, Judaism and Sufism—books people use in their efforts to put together what she calls an "amalgam religion." She offered the example of cultural Christians who want to meditate or chant.

Theologians offer a similar explanation for the sudden hipness of Jesus.

"In a highly individual society, religion is very private," said Rev. Harry Maier, a Lutheran pastor and professor of the New Testament at the Vancouver School of Theology. "People want a personal experience with God. They want an easier, faster, no-fuss, microwavable God."

Maier said he marvels each week at the array of Jesus books in the racks at his supermarket, such as *Jesus at Thirty,* or the best-selling works of early Christian scholar John Dominic Crossan—books about Jesus the Guy.

The Nazarene preacher, he said, is today's "growth industry" because He lends himself so agreeably to nineties values. "He's a pluralist, He welcomes outsiders, He welcomes women, He is against organized religion, He's for economic justice. Jesus comes dressed up in the clothes of our own culture."

This is the Jesus of the Jesus Seminar, a group of New Testament scholars whose work has attracted wide popular interest. Since 1985, they have met twice yearly in the United States to debate the historical accuracy of the words and deeds of Jesus.

This is religion free of any institutional tie-in. In the increasingly popular evangelical model, people let Jesus into their hearts directly, with church in between. The other key factor in the popularity of the evangelical churches, Maier said, is the sort of fundamentalist diet of truths they can offer. "The mainstream is in the business of ambiguities," he said. "But the evangelicals have the corner on the market in certainties."

Maier also detects the influence of globalization in the Jesus boom. "In a capitalist world, in a world economy, people want an easily translatable God," he said. "They want it tradition free, context free—it's Wal-Mart God, it's generic."

All of this raises the question of what has sparked this flurry of spiritual shopping, and why it's happening now. Two reasons seem apparent:

a culture-wide malaise that has people seeking a metaphysical hot-water bottle, and the approach of 2000.

"The people who threw off the mantle of organized religion in the 1960s are now older with kids, in an ambiguous world," Maier said. "They want stability. It's a solution both for your current problems and for where you might go when you die."

■ *Stephanie Nolen is a staff writer for the Canadian newspaper* Toronto Globe and Mail. *She often covers world news events, but in this article her interest in the continuing popularization of religion takes priority.*

MAKING SURE OF THE TEXT

1. What sort of evidence does Nolen present in support of her claim that Jesus is being "lovingly embraced by pop culture"?
2. How does Nolen reconcile the growing popularity of Jesus with decreased church attendance figures?
3. Reverend Maier suggests that Jesus "lends himself [. . .] agreeably to nineties values." In what ways do contemporary religious practices reflect the liberal nineties?
4. What other forms of belief are increasingly popular, according to this article? For instance, what are the best-selling books and merchandise?

CONSIDERING THE CONTEXT

1. Research the titles that appear on the lists of best-selling books. Is it true that books about spirituality are a "persistent presence"? In the titles of other best-selling books, are there clues to spirituality's popularity?
2. If you read this article in a publication other than a newspaper, where would you expect to see it? What artifacts can you identify that would give your "reading" additional credibility?
3. If, as Maier suggests, people want a "context-free" God, what might that suggest? How would you present God to someone without a context for such a concept?

■ ■ ■

"Now, I Am a Witch: A Tale of Balance and Beginnings"

Rose Morrigan

The full moon rises high over the beach. The waves are rhythmic and powerful, echoed by the sound of drums. The intoxicating scent of incense wafts over black-robed figures dancing an endless spiral. "Isis, Astarte, Dionne, Hecate, Demeter, Kali, Inanna," the chant swells and rises as if to the moon herself. "Isis, Astarte, Dionne, Hecate, Demeter, Kali, Inanna . . ."

Some exotic island ritual? A scene from ages past? No. This is today, the United States, now. I am one of the dancers. I am a witch.

October 31

It's Halloween. I suppose it's almost painfully cliché, but I begin my journey as a Witch this night. The Witches call it Samhain. It's the night when the veil between the physical and spiritual, the living and the dead, is the thinnest. It is a time that belongs neither to the past nor the present nor the future, neither to this world nor the next. It is the Witches New Year's Eve. There is no better night to begin the year and a day that will mark my passage from being merely curious to being a Witch-in-training, a Witchling.

On this night, as I join the circle for the first time, I feel self-conscious, but curiosity wins out. I wonder about these other people with whom I have joined hands. They certainly don't look like the warty hags of childhood stories. They look like mothers and fathers, professionals and working folk; in short, they look like me. I watch with rapt attention as the ritual unfolds.

The Priestess speaks of the Ancestors, both our physical ancestors that have gone before, and our spiritual ancestors, those who show us the path, and those who died for their beliefs, or merely for being accused of them. She tells us how, on this night, they join us as we dance the ages-old Spiral Dance, hand in hand, laughing and celebrating their presence. As we file out of the sacred circle we pass the List of the Dead, the names of just some of the thousands put to death during the Burning Times, and we each light a candle in remembrance. Then we "ground" ourselves again to the physical world by feasting.

Isis · Egyptian deity.

Astarte · the Phoenician predecessor to the Greek Aphrodite, the goddess of war.

Hecate · traditionally, the goddess of witchcraft.

Demeter · Greek Goddess of the harvest.

Kali · Indian goddess.

Inanna · the Sumerian name for Astarte.

Tonight, in my bed, I remember all that I saw and I realize that I have indeed begun a journey.

December 22

It is Yule, a time of death and rebirth. In Wiccan mythology, this time of Winter Solstice is the time the Sun God dies. It is the shortest day of the year, and the time of light is brief. But this is a celebration, for although the God has died, on this day he will also be re-born of the Goddess, to re-fertilize her and bring back the light. The days will begin to get longer. Life will be reborn from death, light from darkness.

The Yule Log is burned, as the Priestess speaks of renewal in all aspects of our lives. Death, for the Witch, is not an end, but merely an opportunity for a new beginning. When we die, we return to the Summerland for a time of peace and rest before beginning again. When things die in our life, it is to make room for new things. Death is not evil and dark. It is only a change. We mourn the passing of the light and celebrate its return.

I have been studying. There is much to learn in order to be able to call oneself a Witch. The more I learn, it seems, the more I need to know. I have found these people most willing to share of themselves and their wisdom. I have learned that there are many Traditions in Witchcraft, similar to Denominations in Christianity. There are many paths from which to choose, and none are wrong. I like this freedom to discover what works and does not work for me.

I reflect that this is a good time to take inventory in my life and decide what needs to "die" to make way for what needs to come to life in me. I fall asleep this night with a renewed sense of discovery.

February 2

Candlemas, also known as Imbolc, is upon us. The Mother Goddess has recovered from her labors in giving birth to the God. The first stirrings of Spring are like the child's first tentative steps. The God begins to mature and Earth begins to become fertile again. This is a cleansing time. We begin the "Spring cleaning" of our homes, both physical and spiritual. We let go of the past and look to the future. I realize that I am still holding on to some of my old ideas and prejudices. I need to let go of these if I am to move forward. It is time to choose my name, my magickal name, by which I will be known inside the circle.

I think back to all I've learned so far. Of course, I've learned about Traditions and herbs and Sabbats, but there's so much more than that. I've learned to seek Deity in everything around me, and in myself. I've learned that when I think I know all there is to know about something, just looking at it in a slightly different way changes everything I thought I knew. But more important than that, the single biggest lesson I've learned is about balance. This is a concept I've never given much thought to before, but it seems to be the crux of everything I'm learning now. By nature, all things seek balance. There are the obvious things, like light and dark, cold and hot, even life and death. For all things, there is a balance. No thing is *truly* entirely good or bad. Look at life and death. We think of death as being a bad thing. Certainly, there is pain at the loss of a loved one. But, beyond the pain, we see that death makes way for new life. Without death, there could be no life, just as without sorrow, we'd never know joy. I think most difficulties in life are from things getting out of balance. Being out of balance is a very uncomfortable thing, and I've learned to see Witchcraft as a way of restoring that balance. Witchcraft is a very nature-oriented path, and this is needed now, more than ever, in an Earth that is getting more and more out of balance every day.

Such are my ramblings and musings at Imbolc.

March 31

It's Ostara, and Spring is in the air! Celebration is the order of the day! The God is maturing, the Earth is fertile, life is full of the promise of renewal. This is the Spring Equinox, when day and night are in perfect balance. There's that word again, balance. I've learned even more about it than before.

I've found my Magickal or Craft name. I think the Gods have a sense of humor. It's all about balance. Let me explain. I searched for my name. I meditated, lit incense, stared into scrying mirrors, all to no avail. Friends kept telling me to wait, that my name would come in good time. And, of course, it did, out of the blue. A Magickal name is commonly the name of a God or Goddess with which one has an affinity, or a sacred tree, or even an animal. I had considered many names, names I found pretty, or feminine, but none of them seemed right. I had in mind something like Rhianon (a musical name) or some variation on my birth name, Rose. What I got was quite a surprise. While scanning through a book one afternoon, a name just seemed to jump off the page, and a voice inside me told me this was to be my name. I knew nothing about this name, so I did some reading. What I found made me think I was mistaken. This couldn't be right! The name was Morrigan. Morrigan was a pre-Celtic Goddess of death, war, and passionate love. This was *not* what I had in mind. These things weren't "me" at all! I'd forgotten all about the issue of balance.

My Priestess told me that when something grabs you and won't let go, it's meant to be yours. I began to realize that all of what I had learned about balance was being called into play here. Death makes room for life. Death is also symbolic of change. War was the part I really had difficulty with. I consider myself a pacifist. War is a terrible thing, isn't it? Balance . . . Yes, war is a terrible thing, but sometimes a necessary thing. Would I not go to war to defend and protect those that I love? Of course I would. But beyond that, I began to see that a little war might be a necessary thing for ME! All my life, I have allowed others to walk all over me. I have seen injustice in the world around me, and felt powerless to change it. A little Morrigan is needed in my life. Balance.

It's Spring, and I, like the Earth, am springing to life.

April 30

Beltane has arrived. The God has matured to manhood and today impregnates the Great Mother Goddess! The cycle of life continues! This is the celebration of fertility, and indeed, of life itself. The Beltane fire is lit, and we dance around it joyously.

In days of old, couples would slip away from the fire to continue this celebration of fertility. A child born of this union was said to be a child of the Gods, and was blessed. Our Beltane fire is slightly less sexually liberating, but no less joyful. The Priestess and Priest symbolically perform the Great Rite, using his athame and her chalice, and we celebrate the conception of the God.

This is one of the things I love about the Craft, this lack of shame and guilt about our sexual selves, this outright celebration of the act of sexual pleasure. I am learning to get in touch with my body in ways I never did before. I am learning that it is not only ok, but essential, to appreciate my body, to listen to it, to enjoy it. There is a deeper sense of connection to self and to the Divine within. I dance at this Beltane celebration with joyous abandon, letting my body move, feeling the energy as it swirls through and around me, celebrating life itself.

June 22

And then the moon, like to a silver bow
New-bent in heaven, shall behold the night
    William Shakespeare - *A Midsummer Night's Dream*

It is Midsummer. The God is at his most powerful, the Earth is in abundance. The day has been spent in simple enjoyment of these bounties, and tonight I sit on the beach, watching the moon rise over the ocean, feeling only awe. How much of this abundance have I missed in my life, living from day to day, never stopping to notice the generosity of Mother Earth? It is an amazing thing merely to sit quietly and observe that which surrounds me. I have learned a bit more of balance today, as well. After a day full of joyful revelry, celebrating the Sun God in all his strength and might . . . I have a sunburn.

July 31

A busy day is Lammas. It is the day of the first harvest. I have spent it gathering herbs to be dried and used for winter rituals. On a much larger scale, farmers are beginning to take in the crops that have nurtured in the Mother all throughout the Summer. In a way, it is a time of birth, as well as death. The God is weakening, and soon will die. The Goddess, Great Mother, feels sorrow at his weakening, watching her powerful son begin to die, but also joy because she knows that he lives on in her belly, waiting to be reborn.

I am struck anew with amazement at the cycles, the ebb and flow, that have gone on around me my entire life, without my noticing. I think perhaps the greatest gift that Witchcraft has given me is eyes and ears and spirit that are wide open.

September 21

Mabon, the second harvest. The God is further weakening, the blended joy and sorrow of the Goddess more poignant. By now the fields are cleared, leaving only stubble awaiting the reanimation of Spring. I have brought in the last of the fresh herbs to adorn my altar as a sacrifice of thanks for the bounties of Nature. I adore the sights and smells of autumn.

I have been thinking of all the changes I've experienced in the past few months. I have learned a lot about Witchcraft, and much more about myself. When I first began this journey, I was terrified that people would somehow know that I am a Witch, and feared their rejection. Now, less than a year later, I walk down the street wearing my new pentacle with pride. It's not that I'm necessarily more comfortable with *their* thoughts of me but am more comfortable with my own.

Someone did approach me last week to ask me if I knew that I was wearing "the devil's star" on my necklace. Prejudice and misunderstanding still run deep. I wanted to stop right there and explain to her how, far from being a symbol of evil, my pentacle is a symbol of the very Elements of life itself; fire, water, air, earth, and spirit. I wanted to tell her how things came to be so very misunderstood, how in olden times the Witch was the village healing woman who knew the very best herbs to use to help ease the pain of childbirth, and how to make a potion to help ease your arthritis in the long cold winter months, and the right spells to help the crops grow strong and healthy to keep the village fed for another year. I wanted to explain how we came to be seen as evil persons in cahoots with the devil only after the Christian church condemned us for not swapping in our ages-old beliefs in favor of this newcomer religion, and that the devil with horns we were accused of worshipping was none other than the Horned God, the Green Man, the Lord of Nature, and not some evil creature at all. I wanted her to understand that I had nothing against her religious beliefs, and am certainly not anti-christian.

But, knowing how long-held beliefs are deeply ingrained, I simply smiled and walked on. I wish her well.

October 31

Where has the year gone? How has it flown by so quickly? Tonight, when the veil between the living and the dead is the thinnest, I will ask the Ancestors to witness as I take my initiation, as I become a Witch.

The full moon rises high over the beach. The waves are rhythmic and powerful, echoed by the sound of drums. The intoxicating scent of incense wafts over black-robed figures dancing an endless spiral. "Isis, Astarte, Dionne, Hecate, Demeter, Kali, Inanna," the chant swells and rises as if to the moon herself. "Isis, Astarte, Dionne, Hecate, Demeter, Kali, Inanna . . ."

■ *Rose Morrigan is a practicing witch. A member of the Cauldron of Fire, a pagan spiritual organization in Florida, Morrigan is also a mother, a girlfriend, a daughter, and an ex-wife; she wrote this essay especially for this book, saying it helped her to articulate her own spiritual journey.*

MAKING SURE OF THE TEXT

1. What significance do the names at the beginning and end of the essay hold?
2. How does Morrigan's description of witchcraft contrast with your own perspective on witchcraft?
3. Summarize the Wiccan (or Pagan) mythology Morrigan provides.
4. How does the arrangement pattern reflect the content of the essay?

CONSIDERING THE CONTEXT

1. How does Morrigan's description of balance echo the notion of religious tolerance mentioned by the Dalai Lama?
2. Research what Morrigan calls "the Burning Times," the period of several hundred years when witches, usually women, were systematically exterminated. What do you find as the "clues" to a person's witchcraft? In other words, on what evidence were witches burned?
3. The open acceptance of sexuality in pagan traditions may seem at odds with other religions' teachings about sex. How is sexuality reconciled with divinity?

■ ■ ■

Interview with Sherman Alexie, denversidewalk.com (1999)

Sherman Alexie was the geek of his Indian reservation: the misfit kid who marched to a different drummer.

But the 31-year-old writer has since turned that skewed perspective into one of the most unique and creative voices in American literature. Absent from the award-winning poet and novelist's writings are the hackneyed portrayals of Indians as loincloth-clad, befeathered warriors or disillusioned drunks. They've been replaced, by funny and flawed contemporary people who bear little resemblance to the caricatures we've come to expect.

Fueled by his literary success and the impact his writings have had on perceptions of Indians, Alexie is now shifting his art to the big screen. His first feature film, "Smoke Signals," which follows the stoic Victor and his nerdy sidekick Thomas on their road trip to recover Victor's estranged father's ashes, is one of the most notable films of the season. And as the first film ever produced, directed and written by Native Americans, it's also a cinematic milestone.

We caught up with Alexie at the Nantucket Film Festival, where "Smoke Signals" was screening to a rapt audience. Here's what he had to tell us about himself, his career and the impact of his ground-breaking debut film.

> **SIDEWALK:** Thomas Builds-the-Fire seems so at odds with the kinds of stereotypical Indian film roles we've come to expect. He's a garrulous geek, and annoys the hell out of everyone. Why create such a surprising character?
>
> **ALEXIE:** Because Thomas explodes the myth and stereotype about the huge, stoic, warrior Indian. He's the exact opposite of what people have come to expect the idea of an Indian geek just doesn't happen. He's something of a trickster figure, sort of a coyote figure, and he's mythological in that sense. He's always subverting conventions, not only Indian conventions about Indians but white conventions about Indians.
>
> The funny thing is that while he's over the top in many ways, he's a recognizable cultural character for Indians, because there's two or three of those guys on every reservation. I was the one on mine. He's very much like me, or like I was. I've since learned to hide my geekiness. Well, a little bit.
>
> **SIDEWALK:** When you were a boy, did you dream of writing poetry and making films?
>
> **ALEXIE:** I never dreamed of either thing. Growing up on a reservation, nobody tells you you can do this. I never read a book written by an Indian until I was 21 years old and in college. So the idea of creating art in that way was completely outside

my realm of possibility, beyond anything I ever imagined. I was going to be a pediatrician, but I kept fainting in human anatomy class.

SIDEWALK: Practicing medicine on the reservation is one way to give back to your people. Is making movies another?

ALEXIE: In a different sort of way. The thing is, being a good artist and being a good member of a tribe are often mutually exclusive. Being an artist is all about being iconoclastic and rebellious and questioning the status quo at all times. But being a good member of a tribe is about filling and accepting your role. So I'm often at odds with members of my tribe simply because of what I do as an artist. That's been the case forever.

SIDEWALK: What kind of reception did you get during the filming?

ALEXIE: It was a huge event on the Coeur d'Alene reservation. Although our actors may not be all that well-known in the outside world, Adam Beach is Elvis on the reservation. No matter what time we were filming, there would be big crowds watching. On the night we did the fire, it was freezing and rainy and horrible, and there were 40 people watching the filming. Our assistant directors had to keep shushing everybody because they were so excited.

SIDEWALK: Writing is a silent and lonely project. Making a film involves collaboration. Was the adjustment difficult?

ALEXIE: In writing books, I am the Fidel Castro of my world. I determine everything. In the filmmaking project, I'm more like the senator from Wyoming. So getting used to that took some doing. Making this film was like being on a basketball team. There are certainly stars and people who take the last shot of the game, but also people who pass the ball—everybody's a part of the team. Once I started thinking of it that way, then it got to be fun.

SIDEWALK: Why is this the first major film ever to be written, directed and produced by Indians?

ALEXIE: First of all, I don't think movie producers in general think there's an economic audience for these kind of films. There are only a million and a half Indians in the country, so the built-in audience isn't as large as it is for a Chicano or a black filmmaker. So they didn't think they'd make their money back, which is already wrong—without even selling a ticket [to "Smoke Signals"] we've already made all the money back twofold.

Secondly, most Indian filmmakers who've been making Indian feature films have been so didactic and political that the art suffers. This film doesn't work that way. It's highly political, highly politically aware, but we do it in ways that are very artful and funny and interesting. This film is subtle enough and clever enough to get its political messages across without hammering people over the head with it.

People have never clamored to get Indian directors or writers to work on their projects. But with this movie, things are changing. Already I've seen eight different Trail of Tears screenplays. I need to get a T-shirt that says "no loincloth movies."

SIDEWALK: What kind of impact do you think this film is going to have on Indians?

ALEXIE: I've already seen that impact. At a special screening at Sundance for the Indian community in Utah, there was a 70-year-old Indian man sitting next to me. He chuckled through the whole movie. Just rubbing his belly kind of chuckling. He was so delighted. And that was so wonderful to see him so happy with something I'd helped create. Another time, an Indian woman walked up to me, and she'd had serious issues with her father. And she said, 'Now I know how to talk to him.'

SIDEWALK: Why do Indian stereotypes continue to persist?

ALEXIE: It's part of the national consciousness. If people start dealing with Indian culture and Indian peoples truthfully in this country, we're going to have to start dealing with the genocide that happened here. In order to start dealing truthfully with our cultures, they have to start dealing truthfully with that great sin, the original sin of this country, and that's not going to happen.

Just look at the sports teams. You couldn't have a team called the Washington Kikes or the Washington Micks. But yet you can have the Washington Redskins and this Indian with a big nose and big lips running around. How would you feel if it was the Washington Rabbis and you had a guy with braids running around throwing bagels? Or the Washington Jesuits with some guy handing out communion wafers. It wouldn't happen. So, it's an insult. It's proof of the ways in which we get ignored.

■ *Sherman Alexie is a Spokane/Coeur d'Alene Indian who lives in Washington. Originally intending to be a pediatrician on the reservation, Alexie found himself unsuited for medical work and made the move to artistic expression, specifically writing. Alexie has won several poetry awards and in 1999 earned critical and popular praise for his film* Smoke Signals.

MAKING SURE OF THE TEXT

1. Alexie describes Thomas Builds-the-Fire as "the exact opposite of what people have come to expect" of Native Americans. What are the traditional stereotypes he refers to? How has this perspective come to be so pervasive?

2. Victor, the film's protagonist, seems concerned that Thomas is not "Indian" enough; what does that seem to mean to him?
3. What information does Alexie give you about his own spirituality? In what ways does this information reinforce or contradict your perspective on American Indian religious beliefs?
4. The introduction to this interview with Alexie suggests that we have come to expect "caricatures" of Native Americans when portrayed on film. What examples can you think of to support this claim?

CONSIDERING THE CONTEXT

1. This interview takes place at a film festival. What elements of such an atmosphere might color the interview? In other words, what information would you expect such a publicity interview to cover? Are your expectations met?
2. Alexie describes himself as "the Fidel Castro of my world" and characterizes *Smoke Signals* star Adam Beach as "Elvis on the reservation." What do such allusions add to your understanding of Alexie's work?
3. Alexie's final comments are about the continued racist depictions of Native Americans, yet earlier he suggests that his film makes its political statement in "subtle" and "clever" ways. Do you see any contradiction in his statements?

■ ■ ■

"Water," www.fallsapart.com

Sherman Alexie

1.
I know a woman
who swims naked
in the ocean
no matter the season.

I don't have a reason
for telling you this (I never
witnessed her early morning
dips into the salt) other than
to let you know that I once found
the thought of her nudity erotic

but now can only imagine
the incredible cold, how I would want
to cover her body with my coat
and tell her how crazy she is
for having so much faith
in two parts hydrogen, one part oxygen.

2.
While reading a mystery novel (I
don't remember the title), I

dropped a cup of hot tea
into my lap. Third degree burns

on my thighs, penis, and scrotum. I
still have the scars and once told

a white woman they were the result
of a highly sacred Spokane Indian adulthood ceremony.

3.
I knew a man
who drowned in three inches of water.

Rain collected
in a tire track.

His family and friends accuse me
of making light

of his death, but I insist
on my innocence. Lord, I think

his death is tragic, possibly epic
the first and last act

of a reservation opera, and I wish
I could use his name here, make him

remembered, but I am forbidden
from doing so by tribal laws

that are more important than any poem.
But I want to give him a name

that means what I say, and I so I name him
Hamlet, King Lear, Othello, Noah, Adam.

4.
Boo tells me, "Whenever I feel depressed or lonely
I drink a glass of water and immediately feel better."

5.
In the unlikely event of a water landing
you can use your seat cushion as a flotation device.

I worry about this.

I wonder if the puny cushion can possibly support
my weight. I am a large man. In the unlikely event

of a water landing, you can use your seat cushion
as a flotation device. Of course, we don't crash.
We land safely. We always land safely. And Ha! Ha!
the flight attendant tells the disembarking passengers
to drive safely away from the airport because driving is
so much more dangerous, statistically speaking, than flying.

I want to slap her across the mouth, statistically speaking.

In the unlikely event of a water landing, you can use
your seat cushion as a flotation device. I am suddenly
    afraid
of gravity so I take my seat cushion off the plane. I steal
the damn thing and run through the airport, chased
by an ever increasing number of security people,

men and women, so I'm glad this airport has progressed
beyond an antiquated notion of gender roles. But wait,

I have no time to be liberal, I have to run fast, so I do run fast
with that seat cushion pressed tightly against my chest.
I cannot run fast enough in such an awkward position
as I am a large man with large hands. I cannot easily hide.
I cannot blend into the crowd. I cannot duck behind
the counter of the Burger King and ask for your order, your order,
   your order.

Oh, in the event of a water landing, you can use your seat
   cushion
as a flotation device, and here I am, running, and praying as I
   run,
every step shouting Lord, Lord, Lord, every other step whispering

amen, amen, amen.

6.
At the restaurant, I ask the waiter to leave the pitcher of water
because I drink lots of water.

I can't do that, he says.

Why not? I ask.

Because we never leave the pitcher, he says.

Not once? I ask.

Never, he says, have we ever left a whole pitcher of water, not
   once
in the entire history of this restaurant. It is impossible for us to
   do so.
It is inconceivable for us to even consider such a thing. Who
   knows
what would happen if we set such a precedent?

7.
When I was seven, I took swim lessons at the YMCA
from three beautiful teenagers who all seemed like women to me.

They hugged me when they saw me waiting in line
to see JAWS at the Fox Theater in downtown Spokane.

Where are those girls now? Somewhere, they are being women.

Do they remember teaching me how to swim? Do they
recognize my face when they pick up the local newspaper
or see my photograph on the back of my latest book?

Oh, strange, strange ego.

Here, I've decided I want them to love me from afar. I want them
to regret their whole lives because they were once sixteen year old
swimmers who never stopped to passionately kiss
the seven year old me, as I floated
from the deep end of the pool back to the shallow.

8.
My brother, the big one, says, "It ain't water
unless it's got some Kool-aid in it."

9.
My wife, the Hidatsa Indian, grew up in Southern California
with a swimming pool. Wow!

Her father, the trickster, called relatives back home
in North Dakota. Called them in late December
when trees were exploding in the high plains cold.
Called them and said, "Hey, it's December

and the kids are swimming in the pool. Can you hear them
splashing the water?" He held the phone up to the air, toward
the empty pool, because it was too cold to swim in December,
even in Southern California, but the North Dakota Indians
    didn't know
any better, so they were jealous and happy at the same time.

My wife, just a child then or five or ten or eighteen years old,
heard the slurred laughter of her father, the drunk, and
maybe he would laugh and get off the phone and be
    charming
or maybe he would be the cruel bastard, but there was no way
of knowing until he got off the phone, so she'd sit in her room
with a glass of water on the windowsill, oh, she'd be praying
to that glass of water, oh, she'd be praying
like everything was two parts broken heart and one part hope.

MAKING SURE OF THE TEXT

1. Identify the contexts within which faith appears in this poem; how are they different from each other?
2. How does the poem's organization pattern reinforce or reject its content?
3. The poem's American Indian speaker explains to a white woman that he bears scars as the result of a sacred ceremony; in what way has the speaker reinforced a stereotype? How does his audience's race affect your answer?

CONSIDERING THE CONTEXT

1. What is the connection between faith and water? That is, how does the title of the poem reflect its subject?
2. What is the significance of the scene at the restaurant with the waiter and the pitcher of water? How is this a perspective on faith?
3. How does the last scene help to bring conclusion to the poem's examination of faith?

■ ■ ■

Religious Belief Stew (Student Response Essay, 2000)

Bill Powers

Religion is a belief that helps someone make sense of the world. Since not everyone thinks the same way, it would not make sense to have only one religion. And yet, some religions insist that their religion is the only one, and that anyone who doesn't believe in it is doomed. Other religions respect the beliefs of different religions. All these religions, those who accept others and those who don't, exist separately but all on the same planet. In a world full of so many religions, how can someone know what to believe, and how do they know whether they have made the right choice? In my case, I put together parts and pieces of a few different religions. Now, what I believe makes the most sense to me, and I am comfortable with my choice.

I grew up as a Presbyterian. I attended church every so often; my mom didn't go every Sunday, usually only when we went to visit my grandparents. Growing up in the Presbyterian environment was good. Yet, while it instilled a lot of good values, I never really took to it the way other Presbyterians did. It wasn't really until freshman year in high school that I realized how I felt about my religious beliefs. We took a course that studied the religions of different parts of the world. A lot of these seemed to make sense to me. So I started thinking about what I really believe, and I adapted what the religions taught to how I feel. In the end I came up with a mixture of different religions, something like a stew, in which each piece is saturated with the essence of the other parts, but is still its own piece.

The first religion that really intrigued me was Buddhism. I still don't totally understand it, but the idea of enlightenment makes sense to me. I have this drive inside me to understand, and that's what the Buddhist's enlightenment is—complete understanding. It didn't make sense to me that you could only reach it through meditation, though, because so much happens outside of meditation. Meditation is a good technique to understand yourself, but for me, understanding comes from interactions with people and my environment and then interpretation of those interactions. Reincarnation also plays a big role in the Buddhist religion, and it makes sense to me that we are reincarnated. It would take more than one life to reach enlightenment, and there are things that I just seem to know so well—a heightened knowledge that reincarnation explains.

Buddhists believe that there is life force in everything in nature. Wiccans also feel that nature has its own internal power. I myself tend to lean more toward the Wiccan perspective. I do not believe, however that everything in nature was or will be a human at some point in its ongoing life, but I do accept the idea that nature has a life force that needs to be respected so that people can live in harmony with it. I believe that nature has a life force; for me there are times that nature has a feeling—that majestic mountain you see after days of climbing, the sunsets and sunrises, that moment you see one of nature's creatures. In those moments everything seems at peace. Such moments to me are very real, and nature's life force would explain my feeling. Once, on a trip in Europe, I was at an estate where there was a leafless but not dead tree, whose branches were twisted and creeping. It looked almost alive to me; I went and sat under it. While under the tree I was at peace. Nothing bothered me, and I felt something between the tree and I. People might be able to explain it other ways, but for me the Wiccan idea that nature has a life force explains it best.

Wiccans live in the present. But for me the past still plays a big role. In my life the creation of this enormous and intriguing universe is unexplainable and encourages me to believe in the Christian god. My belief is closer to the Deist point of view, in which "God the Watchmaker" put together this universe and is now just watching. Some people, however, claim that God is involved with life because of all the miracles that we experience. My roommate last year thought so. His dad had a large baseball-sized tumor in his leg. One night the elders of the church came and prayed for my ex-roommate's dad, and the next time he went to the hospital, the tumor was gone. I can't disprove that God caused this, but I can give my alternative. In holistic medicine, which Wiccans use, there is a technique of healing with positive auras, an area of positive energy generated by the healers. As many people pray and focus positive energy on one area, they encourage the body to perform at its optimum performance. Even if the people that cause the aura don't believe in the ability to create the aura, the aura is created. The aura generated by the prayers helped my roommate's dad's body take care of the tumor. Then there is the story of the miracle where the mother lifts the car off her son. Outside of the simple adrenaline explanation, there is the Buddhist "Chi", or also known as "Ki". Chi is an energy that comes from deep within the body. This energy can be manipulated to help you achieve things that normally couldn't be achieved. Shao-Lin monks, for example, achieve amazing things with just the simple manipulation of Chi. They have been known to survive sleeping outside in freezing cold temperature with just a sheet, because of how they manipulate their Chi.

In my view of right and wrong, many choices come into play. Imagine a tree laid down on its side, and divide the branches down the trunk. All the branches above the middle line represent good paths achieved by good or overall good decision making. The branches below indicate bad decision-making. No, this tree isn't everyone's life, but it represents the large number of possible paths we can choose to follow. We start neutral, neither good nor bad, and depending on our decisions, we follow a path along that tree of our life. Eventually we reach a point of absolute good and absolute evil. Absolute good represents the Buddhist's idea of enlightenment, a point where everything is in harmony. Absolute bad is just a point of no return, where you have reached such a negative point that you can't imagine anything good. Between these absolutes there are many different degrees between good and bad. All the choices we make determine the level of good or bad we are at. This is my idea of good and bad.

You might ask, "what is the point of knowing how good or bad we are?" We don't know, but some eternal collective of life force does know. This life force judges how good or bad we are. And judging how far up or down we are on the scales tells us where we will be on the scale when we start our new life. When our life-entity is first created, we start neutral, neither good nor bad, and throughout life we move up and down. We don't continue on forever, and we don't have a limited number of lives to live. We choose to be reincarnated. If our entity wants to keep living, it will; if it doesn't, we end. Now when our life ends, there is no heaven or hell; there is just mental enjoyment or anguish, which serve as heaven and hell. At that last moment of consciousness, we have our last thoughts. If they are good and peaceful, then we will be in eternal mental enjoyment after we die. If we feel guilty for what we have done or other such negative feelings, we will be in mental anguish. Since it's our last thought, it will last forever. I'm not saying we all know when we are going to die, because it is unknown. What I am saying is that our unconscious is always contemplating and evaluating our life. When we die, it is our unconscious that takes over at last moment and depending how we feel at that moment determines whether we will be in mental enjoyment or anguish. Those people who reach the absolutes still have a choice about reincarnation. If they have reached absolute bad, even though they can choose to be reincarnated they would most likely see only pain and no hope for change in the future and end their existence. The absolute good might decide to end their life, or continue with another to teach others what they have learned.

As I said, my beliefs are like a stew. One thing about it, I find new things to add all the time, so this idea is ever changing. In fact, it changed as I wrote the paper, because I was more easily able to explain how I feel. So my beliefs became clearer. But one thing I feel strongly about is not trying to force others to believe what I believe. So please, if you don't agree with me, I'm fine with that. I'm not saying this how the world is; it's just my interpretation. All religion is, it seems to me, is our interpretation of how the world works.

■ ■ ■

■ Ideas for Writing ■

Journal
1. What would you say is the function of spirituality or religion, whether in your life or the world at large?
2. What representations of spirituality have you seen in pop culture? What have your reactions been? Try to give at least four examples.
3. The Lama might say that it's impossible to separate one's sense of identity from one's practice of faith. What part does spirituality play in your sense of yourself?

Response

1. After giving a brief summary or paraphrase of the Dalai Lama's perspective, contrast it with your own: what is your response to his suggestions for achieving interreligious harmony? How do they parallel with Chapter 5's Holdren, who suggests achieving planetary balance?
2. What might Robert Knight, from Chapter 1, say about using the cartoon format for religious purposes? Identify passages in his article that support your answer.
3. How do you perceive deity? For instance, some people think of deity as only male, or only female, whereas others think of deity as incorporating elements of both genders. Still others refuse to consider aspects of gender. What is your perspective? Draw on the article by Culbertson in Chapter 2 as you develop your answer.

Argument

1. Take the Lama's perspective on achieving harmony as an argument and construct a counter-argument; for instance, is it really necessary to practice interreligious harmony? Is it always valuable to share the practices of one faith with another?
2. Build an argumentative thesis about the way religion and matters of the spirit are recontextualized in pop culture (in comic strips, TV series, movies, and so on). To get you started, what religious perspectives are not usually addressed? Should they be?
3. Matters of faith and sexuality often create conflict for people. For instance, Philip Culbertson, Robert Knight, Rose Morrigan, and Joan Osborne all appear to have different perspectives on this relationship. After re-reading the selections by these four people, develop your own stance on the relationship between sex and spirit.

Analysis

1. What are the foundations of your spiritual practice? For instance, what are its beliefs in deity, life on earth, and life afterward? What does it say about the human soul? What do its tenets require, and how is one supposed to follow these requirements? Compare your faith with one that practices differently; what do the texts of these two faith practices suggest?
2. Find several images or religious icons and examine their place in spiritual practice. For instance, you might look at Romantic poet William Blake's etchings and relate them to the state of religion in nineteenth-century England; you might also consider how a Jerry Garcia-ish representation of God reflects a twentieth-century approach to religion.
3. How does the concept of religious faith influence scientific development? Examine, for instance, Chapter 5's Brave, who discusses genetic engineering; Shostak, who suggests alien intelligence in machine form; and the film *Contact*, which presents the conflict between reason and faith in visual terms.
4. Choose one of the readings in this section to read closely. As you read, consider these points: What is the author's position? What are the author's

qualifications for writing about this subject? How does the author signal transitions between ideas? From these questions, develop an analysis of one of the following: the author's perspective on the issue; the way the author has structured the article for the reader; the intended audience for the reading.

Research

1. On the Web or in your library, find an interview with a scholar (religious or academic) that deals with a movie such as *The Exorcist, Dogma,* or *Stigmata.* Then, interview a faculty member from your college's Religion or Sociology department about the same movie. What contrasts and agreements do you notice? How do the different perspectives result in different readings of the same text?
2. Collect from the Web, your library, and several art books at least ten depictions of God, Buddha, or other deity or divine figure. Compare the portrayals. How does the religious figure seem to be presented? How are such images constructed for the viewer?
3. How has cartooning about spiritual matters been received by the general public? Conduct interviews with several classmates, your parents, other adults, and/or members of the clergy.
4. Find the news coverage of the Dalai Lama's flight from Tibet and compile a summary of the context surrounding his exile. What was Tibet's political position? What factors played a part in Tibet's religious practices after the Lama left for the West?

CHAPTER 5

THE FUTURE: PERSPECTIVES ON WHAT COMES NEXT

"Make Yourselves at Home!"
—SIGN HELD BY WELCOMING HUMAN IN *INDEPENDENCE DAY*

One of the most haunting artifacts of the future came from noted director James Cameron in his hugely successful 1984 film *The Terminator*. As the time-traveling hero, Reese, falls into an uneasy and exhausted sleep, the sounds of a nearby construction crane induce a nightmare of his life in 2029. It's a bleak existence. Humans scrabble to survive a computer revolt in a radioactive scrap metal waste-land, where they hide from intelligent ma-chines by day and try to hunt them down at night. What remains of the human race has been driven underground to live in dark, crowded, dank tunnels, where grubby chil-dren lethargically watch flames flickering in an old, burned-out television set to the sound of persistent sobbing. Little food and less hope make human existence a relentless prison: dirt and disease—and heartbreak—add layers of desperation to the harsh metal-lic sounds of a race being systematically exterminated by a superior machine intelli-gence. Explaining this inhuman intelligence to a skeptical Sarah Connor, Reese says sim-ply, "they say it got smart."

In our conception of pop culture—*the texts and practices of a particular people or group, which signify or otherwise intend meaning*—the future is written in what seems like a library

How smart is "too smart"?

of our collective societal concerns, hopes, and desires. For instance, many of us worry about the ultimate intelligence of machines, fearing, perhaps, that they'll "get smart" and take over; *The Terminator* resolves the issue by finding a way to terminate the unstoppable terminator. In the film *Gattaca,* our concerns about the dangers inherent in the genetic revolution are reinforced by the film's depiction of a new, privileged race of "perfected" people. In Ridley Scott's classic film *Blade Runner,* advances in robotics have led to the creation (and rebellion, and subsequent execution) of a race of highly intelligent androids known as "replicants"; *A.I.* uses the same themes to explore the role of emotions in artificial intelligence. Carl Sagan's novel *Contact,* made into a 1998 movie with Jodie Foster, questions the confrontation of faith and science, whereas Ridley Scott's *Alien* films tell us that the extraterrestrials we meet will be even worse than we'd suspected. The 1999 hit *The Matrix,* starring Keanu Reeves, challenges our version of reality by suggesting that what we see isn't real, that it is created for us by aliens who are, in essence, growing humans like a crop of wheat. The cult classic (and its 2001 remake) *Planet of the Apes* warn us that Darwinian evolution could just as easily have privileged the other primates. How shall we read these artifacts of the future?

As a culture, we collectively ask the questions as well as produce the texts; when we read them back to ourselves, we see ourselves mirrored. The text of pop culture's future is written in our answers to the big question: What comes next? Science fiction—the premiere vehicle for speculation about the future—has defined many of the important issues in pop culture. The anchor article for this chapter, by noted science fiction author Samuel R. Delaney, describes what might happen to New York City by the year 3000 as "future shock." Discussing the development of genetic engineering technology, the resolution of the social problem of homelessness, and the final answers to the ongoing concerns about equity among races and genders, Delaney demonstrates that science fiction has answered nearly all the problems we can think of: from this imaginative perspective, every issue can be resolved with technology. Although science fiction is not the only form in which our future is presented to us, it's clearly the dominant form of our pop culture's predictive vision; it is the primary artistic text through which groups of people record their imaginings and pass them on to others. Intellectual texts that also speak to the future, however, are clearly part of pop culture, so this chapter offers readings from the artifacts of artistic and intellectual activity.

As the anchor reading, Delaney's text combines the artistic and the intellectual. He uses what's real—the ongoing social problem of homelessness, for instance—to illuminate both current science (developments in nanotechnology) and future scientific speculation (developments in "a new plastic or ceramic, notably cheaper and stronger than steel"). This technique, writing about the future by extrapolating from the past, combines both the intellect and the imagination.

We see this pattern in much of pop culture's texts about the future. Because we don't know what's coming yet, we speculate about the future using the past

Writing About the Future

One reading a student writer might identify is that we humans will bring about our own downfall. The artifacts of self-destruction are easy to see if we look around; most of us have heard the predictions that humanity will destroy itself long before it can leave the planet. After all, a writer might argue, based on our history of environmental damage, we'll wreck what's left of the ozone layer, melt the polar ice caps, destroy the rainforests that produce our planet's oxygen, launch nuclear warheads and biochemical weapons at each other, and overpopulate the planet beyond recovery. The subtext of "what will happen next?" often seems to be that we're doomed, so a writer could suggest that pop culture's take on the future echoes that feeling, supporting it with the readings of these particular films.

For instance, a writer might describe how human arrogance is at the heart of the original *Planet of the Apes* series of films, in which humans have ruined Earth with atomic weapons, thus giving apes the chance to evolve to the highest life form on the planet. Another possibility is for the writer to take the warning of the films *Blade Runner* and *A.I.* seriously: should we continue to develop artificial intelligence technology, we will run into serious ethical problems when our creations become independent of us. A student writer might also, after watching the film *Gattaca*, describe its portrayal of genetically perfected humans as "better" than normal humans and offer a reading that suggests that in this future, technology is in control, not the people themselves. All three films, then, would be evidence, artifacts of our collective suspicion that the future will see us destroying ourselves with technological know-how.

If a writer wanted to add depth and perspective to this essay, however, it might be good to include another reading of the pop culture artifacts of the future. A writer might, after seeing the film *Contact,* notice that it avoids stories about alien creatures intent on harvesting humans in favor of a story praising scientific endeavor and the value of international collaboration. Similarly, Arthur C. Clarke's classic *2001: A Space Odyssey* refuses to try to scare the audience about aliens. The writer might then contrast this reading of *2001* with the films about scaly monsters: *2001* suggests that the true mystery is the one within ourselves, that perhaps within our DNA lie the seeds for the next flowering of human evolution.

Clearly, this sort of reading is a more complex vision than the stereotypical "aliens come to eat our brains" scenarios that Hollywood continues to promote, and this complexity is a good thing for college writers; the topic demands careful analysis and explanation because it discusses what *might* be. An essay suggesting that science fiction really depicts human appreciation of the mysteries of science and the stars will probably challenge a reader, which will be welcomed by most of your college audience. If a writer provides enough evidence, enough artifacts to make this reading credible, the challenge will be welcomed and probably rewarded.

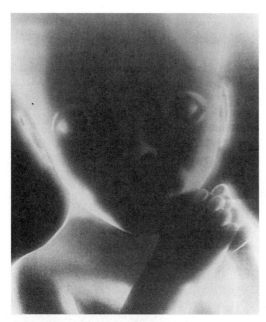

Are humans still infants?

and the present as building blocks. Reading the past helps us read the future. Thus, real-world concerns, such as the outcomes of genetic engineering and listening for radio signals from "outer space," take shape in various intellectual and artistic forums and help form our readings of the future.

Clearly, science fiction is an artifact of pop culture; in a more intellectual way than in the previous chapters, however, we see that a physicist's concerns and the concerns of songwriters are not that different.

Our collective concerns about the environment take many pop culture forms; for instance, in *Blade Runner* the world's biodiversity has been so decimated that owning a "real" owl—rather than a clone—is a mark of fabulous wealth and power. The atmosphere in 2019 Los Angeles is so filthy that only the poorest people live close to the ground; in another revealing artifact of socioeconomic class, the very rich live literally above the pollution levels. Other environmental concerns involve the effects of global warming: In the Kevin Costner epic *Waterworld*, the polar ice caps have melted and flooded the known world, turning humans into boaters and rafters and rendering simple vegetation so valuable that people murder each other for it.

Planetary health, however, is intricately tied to big industry, without which we cannot continue to develop the technology necessary to heal the planet. At the same time, the results of such efforts are often even more pollution. This sort of interconnection is reflected in a physicist's recommendations for the next fifty years. Rather than making a prediction, John Holdren offers four intertwined challenges that he says must be met in order to create, over the next half century, "an environmentally sustainable and politically stabilizing prosperity for all the world's inhabitants." The real challenge is that all these challenges must be met simultaneously in order for any of them to succeed. Without such efforts, he says, we risk depriving our descendants of life as we know it.

In yet another example of "real-life" issues being reflected in pop culture's mirror, our current work on cloning and genetic engineering leads to questions about the ultimate nature and value of the human genome. For instance, in the film *Gattaca*, the norm was to be genetically perfect;

fetuses are examined and genetically corrected to avoid the dangers of alcoholism and attention deficit disorder, to say nothing of exercising preferences about height, weight, and eye color. People who do not meet rigorous genetic standards are assigned to menial labor, whereas those with the "right" genetic makeup are placed in high-prestige positions, thus earning opportunities not available to the "invalid" humans.

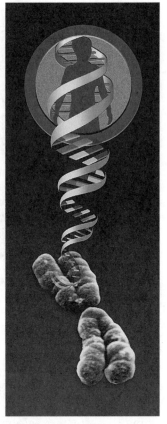

The sort of bigotry and prejudice depicted in the film mirrors the concerns of more than one scientist involved in cloning and other genetic engineering technology; as *Salon* writer Ralph Brave puts it, "Once we figure out how to safely manipulate our genes, people will start adding and deleting them to their perceived advantage." Imagine, for instance, that you could alter your DNA to ensure that you would not be at risk for cancer, heart disease, or even the common cold. Once that sort of genetic alteration became common and accepted, would we then begin to make more changes? Would we select for height if it meant that the child would have a good basketball career? Since people with blue eyes are more susceptible to sunstroke than people with brown eyes, might we begin to choose brown-eyed children? There'd be no need to risk any sort of unpleasantness, when a simple tweak of genetic material could prevent it, and as

How much knowledge is enough?

James Doraz, the student writer in this section, points out in his response essay, films like *Gattaca* are all too realistic. The danger from some scientific perspectives is that by tampering with more and more of our DNA, sooner or later we'll create a different race of people. And yet, if we place genetic engineering in context not with "dangerous inventions" but "life-extending technology," making those sorts of changes is a positive thing. In what context (religious? medical?) shall we view this kind of development?

Closely allied with the effect of technology on our cultural and international development is the effect of computer communications on our personal development. As more and more people go online and make contact with others, we hear more stories about the dangers inherent in spending "too much" time online. Fears of increasing isolation in a country already perceived as fragmented lead to worries about people who completely shut themselves away from "real life" to live online, through the windows of role-playing games, instant messaging, and chat rooms.

Artifacts such as the films *The Net* and *The Matrix* suggest the horrors of living online, but the reality, according to a writer for *Business Week*, is that some software lets us form online communities that are far more specialized than simple chat rooms. The 150 million people known as Netizens include only a handful who share your specific interests and goals; the software helps us to find them and not just the people looking for a "place" to hang out. If you've gone into chat rooms, you probably know that despite titles like "teen talk" or "looking for romance," people in chats rarely restrict themselves to those subjects. You might be in a chat where nobody addresses the topic at all. Instead of just locating chat rooms, then, the software identifies places where you might actually find like-minded people. Therefore, as Neil Gross puts it, we can actually find *more* intellectual community on the Web, not less. What sort of artifact is this software? If you joined with others in your individual context, what artifacts might you produce?

Because "the present" is always now, we are anchored here. When we talk about "the future," however, we have a lot of options: thirty-five years from "now," or five hundred years from "now," or ten thousand years from "now." George Orwell's *1984*, for instance, was written in 1949 and warned of a negative utopia, or a *dystopia*, developing a mere thirty-five years later. When we reached 1984, we didn't have Big Brother or the Thought Police, but we had the beginnings of the sort of computer technology that would allow such developments. (Some would argue that in the early years of the 2000s, we do indeed have something eerily similar to Big Brother: the Internet, which watches our movements and records them.) Samuel Delaney's article itself aims at 3000. *The Terminator*, released in 1984, suggests that in 2029, not only will nuclear war have devastated the planet, but machine intelligence will also have "gotten smart" enough to decide that humans are the enemies.

Two readings in this chapter also offer timelines. "In the Year 2525," a classic rock tune written by Zager and Evans, describes the development of test tube children (in 6565) and Judgment Day (in 8510). Rarely has science fiction looked that far forward, except for series like Frank Herbert's *Dune* and Isaac Asimov's *Foundation* trilogy. Most of the artifacts of the future suggest stories and developments within imaginable time limits: for instance, a children's magazine usually found in dentists' offices, *Highlights for Children*, uses the cartoon twins Goofus and Gallant to offer lessons on good behavior and manners. In the context of the future, these characters show us that tolerance and cleanliness are still valued. After all, if nuclear disaster happens, we'll need to know how to behave with a limited oxygen allotment, to say nothing of the etiquette needed when radioactive mutants try to enter the house in 2085.

When *Star Trek* debuted in 1966, the small computer data disks used were remarkably similar in concept and design to CDs; the communication devices were clearly the predecessors of cellular phones. *Star Trek* takes place in the twenty-third century, yet cell phones are everywhere in the twenty-first century. There's a lag, then, between our perceived futures and when those future developments might come to pass. Such differences are perhaps not relevant

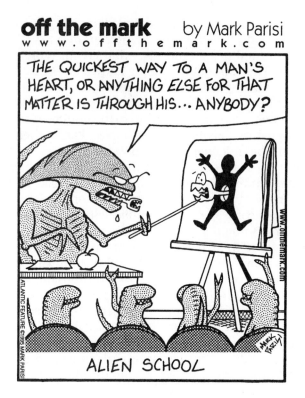

to you because they involve futuristic depictions; however, one relevant artifact of the future included in this chapter is a reliable timeline from an authoritative source.

In his book *Visions*, renowned physicist Michio Kaku sketches out a timeline for scientific developments that spans the present to the year 2100. Kaku writes from the perspective that "any advanced civilization in space will eventually find three sources of energy at their disposal: their planet, their star, and their galaxy. There is no other choice." He suggests that if the formula holds, we'll be ready to master terrestrial weather and extract energy from the core of the earth within a century or two; the time we need to truly reach out into space, however, exceeds ten thousand years or more. It seems like a long time from the human perspective—none of us will be around to see our species in space, if Kaku is right. And yet, from a cosmological perspective, ten thousand years is less than the blink of an eye. The estimated age of the universe is twelve billion years, give or take a few million; in that context, ten thousand years might not seem like long enough.

Of all the possible pop culture artifacts of the future, perhaps the most intriguing is our collective interest in the inevitable first contact with off-world species. We've talked about aliens since long before the legendary 1947 crash in Roswell, but it was that crash that truly sparked pop culture's fascination with the issue of first contact. Most scientists agree that life "out there" is inevitable,

although there's still debate about when and how that life might make contact with us.

In the absence of concrete information, we speculate: What will those species look like? The only real model we have to go by is ourselves, after all, and by definition, "alien" will mean another model altogether. The "alien" artifacts in pop culture take on different forms: attacks by Moon Men in the early days of science fiction became attacks by Martians. Soon after, the adorable and homeless *E.T.: The Extraterrestrial* suggested that aliens might be benevolent, even cute, and not evil at all. Contrasting sharply with the inexorable destruction of the planet in the classic film *War of the Worlds* is the welcome arrival of aliens and our joyful union with them in *Close Encounters of the Third Kind*. In a more paranoid (or realistic, depending on your perspective) approach, aliens have been visiting us—and abducting us—since the 1940s.

Aliens look just like us (in *Contact*), are reptilian (in *Alien*), or are small and gray with large black eyes, images immortalized by *The X-Files* and countless retellings of that mysterious incident in Roswell, New Mexico. *Star Trek*'s Borg are a combination of flesh and machine, however, echoing our current conceptions of *cyborgs*—cybernetic organisms. The Borg are an artistic artifact that Seth Shostak, head of the Search for Extraterrestrial Intelligence (SETI), finds significant. After all, as he says, we're already implanting mechanical parts in humans; from this perspective, we might well expect an alien intelligence to have humanized its machines. "Robots designed to do the tasks that humans would rather avoid—picking strawberries, mining coal, or servicing nuclear reactors—are not far in our future," Shostak says. Assuming that intelligence progresses at more or less the same rate throughout the known cosmos, it's entirely feasible that the first alien "life" we meet will be mechanical, not biological. It may be, he suggests, that "the ultimate achievement of biological intelligence is to get the silicon sentients underway." This perspective may scare you—certainly it alarms many people concerned about going "too far" with artificial intelligence—but it's an intriguing idea. As an artifact of pop culture, what does it tell you?

To recall our definition of pop culture's artifacts, they are the *works and practices of intellectual and artistic activity*, often transmitted to a large audience through the mass and popular media. In no other forum does our imagination get such a workout as when we project what the future might be like; the perspectives are often curious, but as you know from the overhyped and ulti-mately groundless worries about the Y2K bug (remember the fears about computers being unable to handle the number 2000?), sometimes we dread our own accomplishments. These questions and uncertainties are part of the everyday experience for most of us—and the broad panorama of pop culture allows us to collectively speculate, wonder, dream, worry, and hope for and about the future. The authors in this chapter are thinkers, dreamers, and cyn-ics. Some of their perspectives will probably shock you, and some will proba-bly seem pretty unlikely when you read them in depth. Remember that this text is about perspectives. You probably won't share all of them. And that's the point.

"Future Shock," *Village Voice* (2000)

Samuel R. Delaney

The first scene of "The Graveyard Heart," by the late science-fiction writer Roger Zelazny, takes place at a party on New Year's Eve of the year 2000. It's a tale of fabulous wealth, beautiful women, and tiny ceramic dogs; of people who behave like vampires, and love that spans the centuries. It's a story I plan to reread on the big evening, as I wait to see if the lights stay on past midnight or if my word processor still works the next morning. It's hard to believe that story was written almost 40 years ago. But it's a tale to send the mind ahead to contemplate what science fiction suggests the future might actually hold, once it gets here—as, with or without us, it inevitably does.

But what might happen along the way? Science fiction of the last 25 or so years has a number of standby scenarios that, now and again, one writer or another has brought to bear on the prospects of tomorrow.

When the author of *2001: A Space Odyssey*, Arthur C. Clarke, said, so many years ago, "Any truly advanced technology will look to us like magic," he could have had nanotechnology in mind—that "very small" technology where computer science meets microbiology. Imagine tiny, very simple computers, each no larger than a molecule, each of which can perform only the simplest tasks, like turning off and on and letting the molecule next to it know which state it's in. Now imagine billions of these molecular-sized computers working together to solve problems of internal physical chemistry far more complicated than any we can solve alone, including the problem of their own reproduction—that is, imagine computers built on the model of the growing, organic brain, rather than on the model of the fixed and limited electronic diode.

In science fiction, nanotechnology suggests scenarios such as: You spray a mess of properly programmed computer foam over a junked car lot near Coney Island, say, and the whole thing begins to hiss, bubble, and steam. Twenty-four hours later, the hundreds of junked chassis have been transformed into a 50-story office building, standing firm on the site, complete with functioning doors and windows. Or you get a bit of the stuff on your hand; as it enters through the skin, it turns you into a dog or a dolphin or a pig—or into a writhing blob of sentient computer foam yourself. Or . . . it kills you.

With or without nanotechnology, I suspect, a new plastic or ceramic, notably cheaper and stronger than steel, will come along to change architecture and the look of urban dwellings and work spaces entirely. (Science fiction writer Joanna Russ once called the stuff "Gleepsite.") Will this result in more people living in smaller spaces or more people being able to spread out? Helped along with a little nanotech, dwellings could easily spread down into the earth the way they once towered into the sky. At any rate, it will create a difference in "urban life" notably greater than the difference between life in, say, 10th-century Paris—a walled is-land in the middle of the Seine where wolves sometimes broke in and roamed the streets at night—and life in New York now.

Back in 1984 Greg Bear, whose novel *Blood Music* is still the best in-troduction to the subject, suggested nanotech was not 300 or 400 years away, but a mere generation or two. Well, the Big Industrial Technology of today often becomes the domestic technology of to-morrow. Imagine, a few decades after the big changes, say, in the 2090s, when ordinary people have access to nanotech (the way today every fourth or fifth homeless guy wears a Walkman with sound qual-ity that would have blasted a 1950s "Hi-Fi" enthusiast right out of his rumpus room). Suppose you could carry in a toothpaste tube the nan-otech stuff to build a pretty decent one or two room house out of whatever junk happened to be lying around. And suppose that, after you were finished with it, the stuff went back into the toothpaste tube of its own accord so that you could use it again. Press, squeeze, and you're a little less homeless—at least for the night. As ever, though, I imagine the police will still come by early in the morning with tooth-paste tubes of their own, full of foam specially programmed to disas-semble the hastily constructed shelters back into junk; and the again-homeless will be told to move on.

What about inequality? Enough people have been thinking about the problems of racial and gender oppression over the last 200 years that I wouldn't be surprised if those were finally done away with, and rela-tively soon (in another 150 years or so). The solutions, though, when they come, would be as hard for many of us alive today to understand as the solution to the problem of witchcraft and demonic possession would have been for, say, witch-hunting minister Cotton Mather. Imag-ine old Cotton, fresh from the Salem trials of the 1790s, asking today's New York lawyer: "How did you finally solve the problem of witchcraft and demonic possession?"

Our present-day lawyer scratches his head: "Well, finally we realized there weren't any such things as witches and demons. They were just misperceptions and personal projections—often about real estate, so his-tory tells us—egged on by superstition." Cotton would rack him and the entire postmodern world up as nut cases.

Well, if one of us were to ask a New Yorker of a few centuries hence, "How did you solve the problem of race hostility and gender oppres-sion?" I'm pretty sure the answer will be much the same: "We finally re-alized there weren't any such things as races or genders either. . . ."

Cheek by jowl with nanotechnology is science fiction's notion of cy-berspace as an abstract space, a giant planetary storehouse for informa-tion. (The idea comes from William Gibson's 1984 novel, *Neuromancer.*) Is it possible that some part of the Web might become so complicated that it comes to life? Might it be hostile to us? Suppose it's clever enough to take over machines and build *Terminator*-like creatures to do us battle?

Personally I don't think that's very likely, but I do think the problem by the 21st century is going to be the problem of misinformation. And we'd better solve it by the 22nd century, or we will have another reason not to entertain much hope for cities—or, indeed, any kind of civilization a millennium hence.

Why is this? In the same way bad money drives out good, misinformation drives out information. (Every six months or so, a friend will sweep the Net and print 20 or 30 pages of this "information" about me. Inevitably about a fifth of it is wrong, from the spelling of my name to the sex of my child to the publication dates and titles of my books.) Unless information is stabilized by a strong evaluative filter, such as science, with its controlled experiments and repeatable results, it gets swamped by simpler, stabler misinformation. If the people who design and run the Web don't develop reliable ways to evaluate and stabilize information, the Internet may become the agent of social chaos.

Carefully evaluated, accurate information may indeed become so precious that gangs will "roam" around in cyberspace, stealing it from one stronghold or another, plotting to hijack it, hoarding and selling it, while data saboteurs hoarding and selling good information and replacing it with bad—in order to drive up the price of the good stuff—eat up the scientific legacy of the last 300 years the way the oil-based economy has eaten up nature's reserve of hydrocarbon fuels. As the pundits of the 26th century will constantly reiterate, while the store of accurate information is indeed being replaced, it is being replaced at nowhere near the rate at which it's being erased, forgotten, and eroded.

Genetic engineering is another of science fiction's favorite solutions to pretty much all problems. If progress had left the world notably harsher than it is today, genetic dispositions from diabetes and osteoporosis to dyslexia and color blindness might have bred themselves out of the gene pool by now through natural selection. On the upside, however, our increased population and the greater ease of survival in developed countries means there's likely to be more random genetic advancement. Because positive factors may be connected (that is, fall on the same chromosome) with negative ones, it may take genetic engineers to collect the good stuff and separate it out from the bad. The problem, of course, is how to tell which is which. Nature's gross way (what survives is good; what doesn't, isn't) turns out to be pretty complicated after all—which is the major lesson of ecology.

Suppose, for example, that the rate of appearance of new genetic anomalies, good or bad, has been fixed by evolution at the optimum level for species survival and that either increasing or decreasing that number may be lethal for our species. Genetic engineering might give us circus rides with real unicorns and giraffes with wings, as well as new antibiotics produced by genetically engineered molds. But it could also give us a worldwide epidemic to make the Black Death or influenza look like the sniffles.

Which brings us to what might lead to New York City's decline. In a few hundred years, perhaps an epidemic or a nuclear strike in some war we haven't even imagined might finally force people to decide that the risks of living in such close proximity to one another are just greater than the benefits. And there is always that Armageddon-style asteroid that could give the world a thump. But don't you think it's even more likely that it might start with some nut case—say on a New Year's Eve, 300 or 400 years from now—who goes down to Times Square (torn down, rebuilt, torn down, then rebuilt by some historically minded antiquarians) to stand around and watch the ball fall—only he shows up in the crowd of 20,000 with 12 sticks of very old-fashioned dynamite strapped to his body (it's so primitive no one even thinks of it much: but then, the 26th century is a retro age) and sets himself off at midnight in the crowd and the world watches 500 or 700 people killed and another few thousand maimed in the confusion.

We've seen people desert the city before. But give us the right catastrophe, and people will start leaving as fast as the new "mag-lev" train (that's magnetic levitation: they're already zipping around in Japan at twice the speeds of Amtrak) can carry them!

As much of a city lover as I am, I still suspect that, whatever brings its end about, the Great City as we have it today—an enclave of two million to 10 million inhabitants embroiled in culture, commerce, and capital—just can't hang together for an entire thousand years. It's too large and unwieldy, too likely to break up after a few centuries or so and disperse in general sprawl or what sociologists call "edge cities." Consider: There were no cities of more than a million inhabitants before 1800. In 1850 the population of Manhattan was only 500 thousand people with another 200 thousand scattered among the other four boroughs. The population passed the million mark only around 1875. The mega-population center is entirely the result of 19th century industrialization. Only with the advent of steam, iron, glass, electricity, and concomitant transportation advances could those river-and-market communities that had attracted folks around them into a growing township import enough food and materials for life and manufacture and export its growing number of goods—and get rid of a million or so people's garbage. The really big city may just be a 200-to-500-year historical flash-in-the-pan.

The late French historian Fernand Braudel estimated the economic moorings holding New York to its position as the capital of the 20th century started to slip in 1974. All over the world great cities will probably start to break up when our oil-based energy system is depleted in another 75 to 125 years. There's only a limited amount of oil under the ground and we've already used up a good deal of it. It's historical arrogance to expect the entire structure of the Great City to persevere intact like the pyramids or the Parthenon.

Meanwhile, out at the what once was LaGuardia Airport, on the cracked and abandoned runways, those jerry-rigged nanotech homes of the homeless go up and down, up and down, day after day, because air travel as we know it today will no longer exist. Virtual travel will be cheaper and will use no oil-based fuel. In effect, people will scan themselves into their computers and then e-mail themselves wherever they want to go, or else hop onto a browser and, well, browse through space. Actual movement of people over long distances will become more and more restricted to the very rich who wish it for more and more eccentric reasons.

And Times Square? Well, the big movie industry will have folded for good. That's because your home computer will create Hollywood-style movies from scratch if you simply type in the topic and the kind of story you want to see (I actually saw demonstrations of some prototype programs for this the last time I was up at MIT's media lab.) These films can star anyone you like—any movie star, or, indeed, yourself or your friends, if you just feed in a few pictures. So with only an art film market, the 13 theaters in the now dilapidated, 100-year-old E-Walk have become the site of Live Sex Shows, their names changed from the Majestic, the Imperial, and the Crown to the Anthony Comstock, the Mary Baker Eddy, and the Rudolph Giuliani.

By the time we get to 3000, I suspect even the United States itself will have long since been absorbed by other national configurations. (Historically, national boundaries are even less stable than the cities within them.) The most widely spoken language not only on Earth but in the several interplanetary colonies that will have grown up on Mars, Venus, and the moons of Saturn and Jupiter (and a dozen more on the moons of the gas giants circling a few of the nearer stars) will be some dialect of (I pick one out of a hat: we just know it won't be English) Tagalog. The history of its rise to prominence over 150 years will be at least as complex and intricate as the history of France's rise once was when it became, for a century or so, the lingua franca of the world—before it gave way to English. Finally, allowed to dig along the rim of that island in whatever they're calling the Hudson River in those distant days, a few archaeologists may look curiously at all those ancient nanotech toothpaste tubes turning up in their excavations as reminders of a long-since superseded technology. And, hunting in the ruins of cyberspace for accurate accounts of the English language and accurate examples of texts written in it, a few scholars will, I hope, now and again retrieve some notion of the glory that was Brooklyn, the marvel that was Staten Island, and the grandeur that was the Bronx as well as the wonder that once flourished on that island in their midst.

■ *Samuel R. Delaney is a highly respected science fiction novelist. An English professor at the State University of New York at Buffalo, Delaney has published eighteen works of fiction, three memoirs, and seven books of literary and cultural criticism. He is the winner of the top literary awards in his field and was a National Book Award nominee; his work has been the subject of many scholarly studies. In this short essay, Delaney speculates on the future of his favorite city, New York.*

MAKING SURE OF THE TEXT

1. Aside from nanotechnology, what ideas about the future does Delaney offer that might "look to us like magic"?
2. Summarize the process of "misinformation driving out information" that Delaney describes.
3. What present-day examples of Delaney's warning about genetic engineering can you think of? What developments might make "the Black Death [. . .] look like the sniffles"?
4. Using New York City as an example, what do Delaney's suggestions imply about the growth of large cities? How does Brave's article help to answer his concerns?

CONSIDERING THE CONTEXT

1. Does Delaney's notion of "virtual travel," in essence e-mailing ourselves somewhere else, make sense to you? That is, can you imagine it happening? What uses might we have for this technology?
2. What techniques does Delaney use to present his speculations as credible? Look closely at the construction of paragraphs, for instance. What effect do these techniques have for you?
3. Do some research. What sort of publication is *The Village Voice*? What perspective does it offer, and how does Delaney's article fit this context?

■ ■ ■

"Thoughts on Science, Technology, and Human Well-Being in the Next Fifty Years," American Physicists Society (1998)

John P. Holdren

Rather than trying to predict what the world will be like in 2048, I want to focus on what I think society ought to be STRIVING FOR, over the next 50 years, in terms of four threats to human well-being on which current science sheds light and to which future science and technology, intelligently applied, can help provide the answers. Posed as challenges, the four issues I want to address are:

1. Eliminating weapons of mass destruction;
2. Meeting global energy needs while limiting the atmospheric concentration of carbon dioxide to less than twice its preindustrial value;
3. Sharply reducing the global rate of loss of biodiversity; and
4. Preventing the population of the planet from exceeding 9 billion people.

These challenges are interrelated (in more ways than there is space here to discuss); and they are all essential parts of the larger agenda of fashioning, over the next half century, an environmentally sustainable and politically stabilizing prosperity for all of the world's inhabitants. Failure in meeting any one of the four challenges is likely to put at risk that larger agenda and, in so doing, to risk denying to large numbers of our descendants the life-enhancing benefits that the advance of science and technology along other fronts would otherwise be bringing.

WEAPONS OF MASS DESTRUCTION

The end of the Cold War has brought with it a widespread but alas wholly unwarranted complacency about the dangers still posed to the human condition by chemical, biological, and nuclear weapons.

To be sure, a global ban on chemical weapons has recently been agreed, joining a similar ban on biological weapons agreed 25 years earlier; more than 180 nations are parties to the recently indefinitely extended Nuclear Non-Proliferation Treaty; a comprehensive ban on nuclear weapons testing has been signed by most of the world's nations; and the United States and Russia are embarked on nuclear-force reductions that—assuming implementation of the START II agreement—will reduce the number of nuclear weapons in these two nations' stockpiles to between one-third and one-fourth of their respective peak Cold War values.

But, the world does not yet have in place either the technology or the institutions for reliable monitoring and verification of compliance of either the chemical or the biological weapons convention; the safeguards on nuclear facilities that could be used to violate the Nuclear Non-Proliferation Treaty are far from comprehensive; it is quite clear that a number of countries have violated these agreements or intend to do so (and, of course, some others never signed them); even after START II the

United States and Russia may retain something in the range of 10,000 nuclear weapons each; and the danger of "leakage" of nuclear bombs or bomb-usable materials into the hands of terrorists or black marketeers has quite clearly GROWN in the post-Cold-War era, largely because of reduced reliability of the protection for these deadly commodities under current conditions in Russia.

Meanwhile, the United States—while it denounces the aspirations of potential proliferator states to acquire weapons of mass destruction of any kind—continues to assert its own need and right to retain a nuclear arsenal of some size indefinitely, and so far has refused to renounce even the option of first use of its nuclear weapons against nonnuclear threats or attacks. We do not seem to be much troubled by the inconsistencies of asserting a need and right for the United States to wield weapons of mass destruction while denying that any nation besides us and the four other officially certified nuclear-weapon states has reason or right to possess such weapons—whether nuclear, chemical, or biological—including the reason of wanting them as a counter to ours.

I am not asserting here that there is no political or military advantage to the United States from being able to threaten to use nuclear weapons against a country that does not have them, as we have implicitly threatened Iraq more than once. I am simply asserting that those advantages come at too high a cost. The cost of ANY country's insisting on retaining weapons of mass destruction of ANY kind is the provision of a continuing incentive to MANY countries to acquire weapons of mass destruction of one kind or another.

I believe the logic of this is implacable. In the long run, we are either going to have a world in which NO nations have weapons of mass destruction, or a world in which MANY nations do. And, in a world in which many nations have these weapons, the probability that some of the weapons will be set off (whether by accident or by design, by nations or by terrorists) becomes much too large. If we cannot get rid of weapons of mass destruction in the next fifty years, there will be too high a chance that they will get rid of altogether too many of us.

Of course, to confidently verify a prohibition of nuclear weapons will require large improvements in the science and technology of verification, as well as a general increase in transparency and openness in scientific, industrial, and governmental activities around the world. The most painstaking protection and monitoring of all nuclear-weapon-usable materials, including those in use in civilian energy systems, will be an essential part of the elimination effort. These ingredients of an adequate verification regime for elimination of nuclear weapons will not materialize overnight, but we are already moving in these directions in connection with the cuts in nuclear weaponry already achieved or under negotiation, and another half century should not be too little to accomplish all that is required.

GREENHOUSE GASES, CLIMATE CHANGE, AND SUSTAINABLE ENERGY SUPPLY

The greenhouse gas most responsible for the growing threat of human-induced disruption of climate is carbon dioxide, some of it emitted by deforestation but mostly coming from the combustion of fossil fuels. Before the industrial revolution, when no fossil fuels were being burned, the concentration of carbon dioxide in the global atmosphere was about 280 parts per million (ppm).

In 1998 civilization's fossil fuel burning will release about 6.3 billion tons of carbon, and the atmospheric concentration will reach 365 parts per million, 30 percent above the preindustrial level. Under "business as usual", annual emissions from fossil-fuel burning in 2048 would total around 15 billion tons of carbon per year, and the atmospheric concentration of carbon dioxide would reach 500 to 550 parts per million. The momentum of the business-as-usual trajectory, moreover, would be carrying us rapidly toward a tripling or more of the preindustrial concentration in the second half of the next century.

Growth of this magnitude in carbon-dioxide concentrations, combined with hard-to-avoid increases in other greenhouse gases such as methane and nitrous oxide, is likely to entail severely disruptive changes in climate in many regions, including the United States. The productivity of farms and forests, the patterns of disease, the magnitude of damages from storms and floods, and the livability of our cities in summer are all likely to be adversely affected.

In the decades ahead we need simultaneously to try to better understand these climate-change liabilities, through increased investments in the science of climate and climate-change impacts, and to reduce the probability of intolerable outcomes by using advanced technologies to move off of the "business as usual" emissions trajectory to a much lower one. It will be extremely difficult to do much better than holding atmospheric carbon dioxide to a doubling of its preindustrial concentration; but it will be extremely dangerous to do much worse.

The needed technological improvements can be brought about through a combination of R&D to expand and improve the array of available emissions-reducing technologies plus incentives to deploy the best ones available. These technologies will sharply lower the energy intensity of economic activity by increasing the efficiencies with which energy is transformed and used, as well as lowering the carbon intensity of energy supply through use of lower-carbon and zero-carbon energy sources (renewables, fusion if we can make it work, and fission if we can fix the problems that have afflicted it) and through capture and sequestration of the carbon dioxide (from the fossil fuels that continue to be used).

R&D · Research and Development.

BIODIVERSITY

We do not even know the number of species on the planet to within a factor of three—it is thought that there are between 10 million and 30 million, of which fewer than two million have been identified and named. There is reason to believe that the rate of extinction of species is in the range of 1,000 times (give or take maybe a factor of 10) the average extinction rate prior to major human influence. The Global Biodiversity Assessment estimated that up to a third of the species in tropical forests—the largest reservoir of biodiversity on the planet—may be lost over the next several decades.

The species making up the biota are the indispensable foundation of the environmental goods and services on which, no less than on economic goods and services, the well-being of every person on the planet depends: the cycling of nutrients, the building and maintenance of soils, the purification of air and water, the natural control of many agents and vectors of human disease, and much more. This biodiversity also constitutes a vast library of genetic information, from which new food crops, drugs, vaccines, and other valuable products could come.

But since most of this genetic information has not even been cataloged, much less analyzed, it should be apparent that the current epidemic of extinctions amounts to burning down a unique and irreplaceable library without ever having read the books. I say "irreplaceable" because, notwithstanding the wonders of biotechnology, there is no reason now to think that we will be able to reconstruct the genetic information in species lost before they have been discovered, not to mention the information residing in the co-evolved complexity of the ecosystems of which these species were a part.

There is a tremendous task ahead for science—in building understanding of what the biodiversity of the planet is, how it works, and what it does—and a tremendous task for our technology and our institutions in arranging to meet human needs and aspirations for increased economic prosperity without destroying the indispensable foundation of well-being provided by the biota.

POPULATION

In mid-1998 there will be about 5.9 billion people on the planet, nearly two and a half times as many as in 1948. Because the rate of population growth has been falling, we will not see the same 2.5-fold growth in the next 50 years we saw in the last 50. Instead, barring nuclear war or global pandemic, the figure in 2048 will probably be between 8 billion and 10 billion people . . . and by 2098 between 9 and 12 billion. Most of the challenges that civilization will need to overcome in the next century— particularly the challenges of supplying sustainably the food, water, energy, housing, health care, education, employment opportunities, and other ingredients of a fulfilling life for all of the world's people—will be considerably more difficult if the 2048 population is at the high end of this range than if it is at the low end.

Accordingly, as part of our strategy for addressing all of these other challenges, we should strive for the lower end of the range of mid-21st century population possibilities . . . and for a peak population thereafter that does not exceed 9 billion. In doing so, we should bring to bear both the relevant insights of social science (about, for example, the effects on desired family size of economic and social development, including especially improvements in the status and education of women) and the capabilities of modern—and doubtless still improvable—contraceptive technologies to avoid unwanted births.

CONCLUSION

The sluggishness with which society is today addressing these problems, notwithstanding abundant information about their character and consequences, says something about the effectiveness (or, more accurately, the lack of it) of those who have long been laboring at the intersection of science, technology, and policy. It also says something about the inertia of the institutions of public-policy formation that would need to be energized in order to mount a serious attack on these problems. And it says something, finally, about our educational system, which clearly needs to do better in developing the skills of the populace in relation to numeracy, earth-system science, interdisciplinary thinking, and envisioning both the consequences of a "business as usual" future and pathways toward more promising alternatives.

■ *Dr. John P. Holdren, Professor of Environmental Policy at Harvard University, has been a member of the President's Committee of Advisors on Science and Technology, has authored several books, and was trained in aeronautics/astronautics and plasma physics at the Massachusetts Institute of Technology and Stanford University. This piece, appearing in the publication of the American Physicists Society, marks a public address to the needs of the global enviropolitical economy.*

MAKING SURE OF THE TEXT

1. What problem is posed by carbon dioxide, and why does Holdren name it as one of the four challenges critical to our continued health and well-being on this planet?
2. If we can't even count the "number of species on the planet to within a factor of three," why should it matter to Holdren if biodiversity is reduced? What perspectives can you identify that would support Holdren's position?
3. In what ways might we improve our educational system so that interdisciplinary thinking can be encouraged? Why is it important to be able to think in this way?
4. Given that we continue to do "business as usual," in Holdren's phrase, what futuristic film do you think most accurately captures the result? In other words, have we already seen the results of failing to meet these four challenges?

CONSIDERING THE CONTEXT

1. In what ways might the genetic technology involved in Brave's article be applied to one of Holden's challenges?
2. Holdren's audience would appear to be other physicists, who can (arguably) be assumed to agree with him. What effect does it have on you as a nontechnical reader? What changes might Holdren make in his article for this different readership?
3. How does Holdren use current statistics to make predictions that are credible?
4. Holdren's article might well be considered a political stance, a feminist stance, or an environmental stance. Given his subject matter and references, in what other perspectives might this article appear convincing?

■ ■ ■

"Building Better Humans: The Sci-Fi Possibilities of Genetic Tampering," Salon.com (2000)

Ralph Brave

A young couple having difficulty conceiving a child undergoes tests to pinpoint the problem. As they sit in the doctor's office, awaiting the results, each wonders whose reproductive system has failed.

"There's nothing wrong with either of you," the doctor tells them, at last.

"So what's the problem?" they ask.

"You're two different species. You can't interbreed."

Science fiction? Perhaps for now. But according to the eminent physicist Freeman Dyson, this is where the human genome project will inevitably lead us. He and his Princeton colleague, molecular biologist Lee Silver, say that rapidly emerging genetic technology will ultimately split humanity into many species.

They draw their conclusion from cold, complex science, but their point is simple, and frightening: Once we figure out how to safely manipulate our genes, people will start adding and deleting them to their perceived advantage. Different sorts of humans will emerge. And it's safe to assume that each will decide that it is superior.

While anyone who watched even a minute of "Britney in Hawaii" might believe that this has already occurred, rest assured it has not.

But the development and use of genetic engineering are the subject of ferocious debate among the scientific elite. Some influential scientists, notably James D. Watson, the father of DNA research, are pushing for experiments that were once unthinkable: tampering with the human germline—sperm and egg cells. In other words, genetically altering not only an individual, but future generations.

"Some people are going to have some guts and try germline therapy without completely knowing that it's going to work," Watson said at a UCLA conference in 1998. "And the other thing, because no one has the guts to say it, if we could make better human beings by knowing how to add genes (from plants or animals), why shouldn't we do it? What's wrong with it?"

Human germline engineering is prohibited in federally funded research. But there is no ban on such experiments in the private sector. Last weekend, a coalition of activisits and organizations met in San Francisco to form the Exploratory Initiative on New Genetic Technologies. On Wednesday, the group will announce efforts to develop a broad movement to push for limitations on genetic technologies, including statutory bans on germline genetic engineering and human cloning.

"A ban," says Watson, "would be a disaster."

To get a glimpse of what might very well be our future, it helps to understand some boring science. All current human genetic therapy trials are called somatic: they involve genes in various parts of the body, but not the sex cells, which produce eggs and sperm. Tampering with sex cells—producing genetic alterations that will be passed to your offspring, and their descendents—takes genetic engineering into an entirely new technological and ethical realm.

While many experts believe that germline engineering is at least a decade away, Hamilton Smith, a Nobel laureate biochemist, sees the technology developing much more rapidly. "It might come pretty quickly," he says.

Smith knows something about the speed of technological advance. He is the director of DNA Resources for Celera Genomics Corp., which, in just nine months, produced a rough map of the human genome—a feat that most scientists said would take years.

The pressure for germline engineering is also likely to come from another direction—you and me. We want children better than ourselves. We certainly don't want them to suffer unnecessarily. David Baltimore, a Nobel laureate who heads CalTech, believes that consumer demand will encourage the rapid development and utilization of germline engineering.

Genetic screening is already standard in prenatal care. It is not far-fetched to imagine that prospective parents will one day turn to clinics to produce embryos that can not only be tested for genetic defects, but also "corrected." And is there any reason to think people will stop at fixing disease-causing defects? Is it such a stretch to imagine people demanding genetic enhancements—mental, physical, behavioral?

■ *Brave, a freelance writer for Salon.com, covers biotechnology, genetics, reproductive technology, and biology for the online 'zine. Founded in November 1995 by David Talbot, Salon.com has been called "intriguing and intelligent" (Washington Post), "truly compelling" (Time), and "smart and provocative" (Forbes).*

MAKING SURE OF THE TEXT

1. In what ways have humans already developed new species? For instance, do we consider genetically enhanced plant species to be new species?
2. Summarize the concept of human germline engineering. Why is there such debate over it?
3. How does Brave seem to be defining "safe" manipulation of the genes? That is, what changes would be less threatening than others?
4. What are the similarities and differences between human germline engineering and nanotechnology?

CONSIDERING THE CONTEXT

1. With others in a group, create a prioritized list of which genetic traits we might collectively work on weeding out. How do you prioritize the traits? Are they artifacts of negativity? Self-protection? Materialism?
2. Watson's blunt comment that a ban on genetic engineering and cloning "would be a disaster" is set off in a paragraph of its own. What impact is achieved by such a technique?

3. This selection is not the complete article. Read it online, and afterward, discuss what information is developed further or downplayed from the first section. In other words, how might the entire article present the issue differently than this short selection from it?

■ ■ ■

"Choreographers of Matter, Life, and Intelligence," *Visions: How Science Will Revolutionize the 21st Century* (1998)

Michio Kaku

TIME FRAMES FOR THE FUTURE

In making predictions about the future, it is crucial to understand the time frame being discussed, for, obviously, different technologies will mature at different times. The time frames of the predictions made in *Visions* fall into three categories: those breakthroughs and technologies that will evolve between now and the year 2020, those that will evolve from 2020 to 2050, and those that will emerge from 2050 to the end of the twenty-first century. (These are not absolute time frames; they represent only the general period in which certain technologies and sciences will reach fruition.)

To the Year 2020

From now to the year 2020, scientists foresee an explosion in scientific activity such as the world has never seen before. In two key technologies, computer power and DNA sequencing, we will see entire industries rise and fall on the basis of breathtaking scientific advances. Since the 1950s, the power of our computers has advanced by a factor of roughly *ten billion*. In fact, because both computer power and DNA sequencing double roughly every two years, one can compute the rough time frame over which any scientific breakthroughs will take place. This means that predictions about the future of computers and biotechnology can be quantified with reasonable statistical accuracy through the year 2020.

For computers, this staggering growth rate is quantified by Moore's law, which states that computer power doubles roughly every eighteen months. (This was first stated in 1965 by Gordon Moore, co-founder of the Intel Corp. It is not a scientific law, in the sense of Newton's laws, but a rule-of-thumb which has uncannily predicted the evolution of computer power for several decades.) Moore's law, in turn, determines the fate of multibillion-dollar computer corporations, which base their future projections and product lines on the expectation of continued growth. By 2020, microprocessors will likely be as cheap and plentiful as scrap paper, scattered by the millions into the environment, allowing us to place intelligent systems everywhere. This will change everything around us, including the nature of commerce, the wealth of nations, and the way we communicate, work, play, and live. This will give us smart homes, cars, TVs, clothes, jewelry, and money. We will speak to our appliances, and they will speak back. Scientists also expect the Internet will wire up the entire planet and evolve into a membrane consisting of millions of computer networks, creating an "intelligent planet." The Internet will eventually become a "Magic Mirror" that appears in fairy tales, able to speak with the wisdom of the human race.

Because of revolutionary advances in our ability to etch ever-smaller transistors onto silicon wafers, scientists expect this relentless drive to continue to generate newer and more powerful computers up to 2020, when the iron laws of quantum physics eventually take over once again. By then, the size of microchip components will be so small—roughly on the scale of molecules—that quantum effects will necessarily dominate and the fabled Age of Silicon will end.

The growth curve for biotechnology will be equally spectacular in this period. In biomolecular research, what is driving the remarkable ability to decode the secret of life is the introduction of computers and robots to automate the process of DNA sequencing. This process will continue unabated until roughly 2020, until literally thousands of organisms will have their complete DNA code unraveled. By then, it may be possible for anyone on earth to have their personal DNA code stored on a CD. We will then have the Encyclopedia of Life.

This will have profound implications for biology and medicine. Many genetic diseases will be eliminated by injecting people's cells with the correct gene. Because cancer is now being revealed to be a series of genetic mutations, large classes of cancers may be curable at last, without invasive surgery or chemotherapy. Similarly, many of the microorganisms involved in infectious diseases will be conquered in virtual reality by locating the molecular weak spots in their armor and creating agents to attack those weak spots. Our molecular knowledge of cell development will be so advanced that we will be able to grow entire organs in the laboratory, including livers and kidneys.

From 2020 to 2050

The prediction of explosive growth of computer power and DNA sequencing from now through 2020 is somewhat deceptive, in that both are driven by known technologies. Computer power is driven by packing more and more transistors onto microprocessors, while DNA sequencing is driven by computerization. Obviously, these technologies cannot indefinitely continue to grow exponentially. Sooner or later, a bottleneck will be hit.

By around 2020, both will encounter large obstacles. Because of the limits of silicon chip technology, eventually we will be forced to invent new technologies whose potentials are largely unexplored and untested, from optical computers, molecular computers, and DNA computers to quantum computers. Radically new designs must be developed, based on the quantum theory, which will likely disrupt progress in computer science. Eventually, the reign of the microprocessor will end, and new types of quantum devices will take over.

If these difficulties in computer technology can be overcome, then the period 2020 to 2050 may mark the entrance into the marketplace of an entirely new kind of technology: true robot automatons that have common sense, can understand human language, can recognize and manipulate objects in their environment, and can learn from their mistakes. It is a development that will likely alter our relationship with machines forever.

Similarly, biotechnology will face a new set of problems by 2020. The field will be flooded with millions upon millions of genes whose basic functions are largely unknown. Even before 2020, the focus will shift away from DNA sequencing to understanding the basic functions of these genes, a process which cannot be computerized, and to understand polygenic diseases and traits—i.e., those involving the complex interaction of multiple genes. The shift to polygenic diseases may prove to be the key to solving some of the most pressing chronic diseases facing humanity, including heart disease, arthritis, autoimmune diseases, schizophrenia, and the like. It may also lead to cloning humans and to isolating the fabled "age genes" which control our aging process, allowing us to extend the human life span.

Beyond 2020, we also expect some amazing new technologies germinating in physics laboratories to come to fruition, from new generations of lasers and holographic three-dimensional TV to nuclear fusion. Room-temperature superconductors may find commercial applications and generate a "second industrial revolution." The quantum theory will give us the ability to manufacture machines the size of molecules, thereby opening up an entirely new class of machines with unheard-of properties called nanotechnology. Eventually, we may be able to build ionic rocket engines that may ultimately make interplanetary travel commonplace.

From 2050 to 2100 and Beyond

Last, *Visions* makes predictions about breakthroughs in science and technology from 2050 to the dawn of the twenty-second century. Although any predictions this far into the future are necessarily vague, it is a period that will likely be dominated by several new developments. Robots may gradually attain a degree of "self-awareness" and consciousness of their own. This could greatly increase their utility in society, as they are able to make independent decisions and act as secretaries, butlers, assistants, and aides. Similarly, the DNA revolution will have advanced to the point where biogeneticists are able to create new types of organisms involving the transfer of not just a few but even hundreds of genes, allowing us to increase our food supply and improve our medicines and our health. It may also give us the ability to design new life forms and to orchestrate the physical and perhaps even the mental makeup of our children, which raises a host of ethical questions.

The quantum theory, too, will exert a powerful influence in the next century, especially in the area of energy production. We may also see the beginnings of rockets that can reach the nearby stars and plans to form the first colonies in space.

Beyond 2100, some scientists see a further convergence of all three revolutions, as the quantum theory gives us transistor circuits and entire machines the size of molecules, allowing us to duplicate the neural patterns of the brain on a computer. In this era, some scientists have given serious thought to extending life by growing new organs and bodies, by manipulating our genetic makeup, or even by ultimately merging with our computerized creations.

Toward a Planetary Civilization

When confronted with dizzying scientific and technological upheaval on this scale, there are some voices that say we are going too far, too fast, that unforeseen social consequences will be unleashed by these scientific revolutions.

I will try to address these legitimate questions and concerns by carefully exploring the sensitive social implications of these powerful revolutions, especially if they aggravate existing fault lines within society.

In addition, we will address an even more far-reaching question: to where are we rushing? If one era of science is ending and another is just beginning, then where is this all leading to?

This is exactly the question asked by astrophysicists who scan the heavens searching for signs of extraterrestrial civilizations which may be far more advanced than ours. There are about 200 billion stars in our galaxy, and trillions of galaxies in outer space. Instead of wasting millions of dollars randomly searching all the stars in the heavens for signs of extraterrestrial life, astrophysicists engaged in this search have tried to focus their efforts by theorizing about the energy characteristics and signatures of civilizations several centuries to millennia more advanced than ours.

Applying the laws of thermodynamics and energy, astrophysicists who scan the heavens have been able to classify hypothetical extraterrestrial civilizations into three types, based on the ways they utilize energy. Russian astronomer Nikolai Kardashev and Princeton physicist Freeman Dyson label them Type I, II, and III civilizations.

Assuming a modest yearly increase in energy consumption, one can extrapolate centuries into the future when certain energy supplies will be exhausted, forcing society to advance to the next level.

A Type I civilization is one that has mastered all forms of terrestrial energy. Such a civilization can modify the weather, mine the oceans, or extract energy from the center of their planet. Their energy needs are so large that they must harness the potential resources of the entire planet. Harnessing and managing resources on this gigantic scale requires a sophisticated degree of cooperation among their individuals with elaborate planetary communication. This necessarily means that they have attained a truly planetary civilization, one that has put to rest most of the factional, religious, sectarian, and nationalistic struggles that typify their origin.

Type II civilizations have mastered stellar energy. Their energy needs are so great that they have exhausted planetary sources and must use their sun itself to drive their machines. Dyson has speculated that, by building a giant sphere around their sun, such a civilization might be able to harness their sun's total energy output. They have also begun the exploration and possible colonization of nearby star systems.

Type III civilizations have exhausted the energy output of a single star. They must reach out to neighboring star systems and clusters, and eventually evolve into a galactic civilization. They obtain their energy by harnessing collections of star systems throughout the galaxy.

(To give a sense of scale, the United Federation of Planets described in *Star Trek* probably qualifies for an emerging Type II status, as they have just attained the ability to ignite stars and have colonized a few nearby star systems.)

This system of classifying civilizations is a reasonable one because it relies on the available supply of energy. Any advanced civilization in space will eventually find three sources of energy at their disposal: their planet, their star, and their galaxy. There is no other choice.

With a modest growth rate of 3 percent per year—the growth rate typically found on earth—one can calculate when our planet might make the transition to a higher status in the galaxy. For example, astrophysicists estimate that, based on energy considerations, a factor of ten billion may separate the energy demands between the various types of civilizations. Although this staggering number at first seems like an insurmountable obstacle, a steady 3 percent growth rate can overcome even this factor. In fact, we can expect to reach Type I status within a century or two. To reach Type II status may require no more than about 800 years. But attaining Type III status may take on the order of 10,000 years or more (depending on the physics of interstellar travel). But even this is nothing but the twinkling of an eye from the perspective of the universe.

Where are we now? you might ask. At present, we are a Type 0 civilization. Essentially, we use dead plants (coal and oil) to energize our machines. On this planetary scale, we are like children, taking our first hesitant and clumsy steps into space. But by the close of the twenty-first century, the sheer power of the three scientific revolutions will force the nations of the earth to cooperate on a scale never seen before in history. By the twenty-second century, we will have laid the groundwork of a Type I civilization, and humanity will have taken the first step toward the stars.

Already the information revolution is creating global links on a scale unparalleled in human history, tearing down petty, parochial interests while creating a global culture. Just as the Gutenberg printing press made people aware of worlds beyond their village or hamlet, the information revolution is building and forging a common planetary culture out of thousands of smaller ones.

What this means is that our headlong journey into science and technology will one day lead us to evolve into a true Type I civilization—a planetary civilization which harnesses truly planetary forces. The march to a planetary civilization will be slow, accomplished in fits and starts, undoubtedly full of unexpected twists and setbacks. In the background always lurks the possibility of a nuclear war, the outbreak of a deadly pandemic, or a collapse of the environment. Barring such a collapse, however, I think it is safe to say that the progress of science has the potential to create forces which will bind the human race into a Type I civilization.

Far from witnessing the end of science, we see that the three scientific revolutions are unleashing powerful forces which may eventually elevate our civilization to Type I status. So when Newton first gazed alone at the vast, uncharted ocean of knowledge, he probably never realized that the chain reaction of events that he and others initiated would one day affect all of modern society, eventually forging a planetary civilization and propelling it on its way to the stars.

■ *Michio Kaku is an internationally recognized authority in theoretical physics and the environment. He holds the Henry Semat Professorship in Theoretical Physics at the City College and the Graduate Center of the City University of New York. He has published more than seventy articles in physics journals and earned "popular" status when* Visions *appeared on the* New York Times *best-seller list. As a result of his work, he is often considered Carl Sagan's successor. In this excerpted chapter from* Visions, *Kaku provides a quantifiable timeline for technological development.*

MAKING SURE OF THE TEXT

1. What are the key developments Kaku predicts for the next hundred years?
2. How, according to Kaku, will the Internet become a "magic mirror" of the sort in fairy tales?
3. What are the differences between the "true robot automaton" and the development of nanotechnology?
4. What are the distinctions between the types of civilization? Define Type I, Type II, and Type III.

CONSIDERING THE CONTEXT

1. Compare Kaku's description of machine intelligence with Shostak's. What similarities do you find? Differences?
2. What does the "Choreographer" of the title suggest to you? Why has Kaku chosen this metaphor instead of another?
3. From this scientific perspective, the development of the future seems fairly linear. What, from your viewpoint, might throw this development off its track? In other words, from what other perspectives might this scientific approach be too simple or too unrealistic?

■ ■ ■

"The Etiquette Lesson," *New York Times Magazine* (1996)

Bruce Handy and Ross MacDonald

Highlights for Children *began publication in 1946 and has been a staple in doctors' offices ever since. Goofus and Gallant, the twin boys through whom lessons in courtesy and kindness are taught, are two of the favorite characters in the magazine. This satire of the cartoon appeared in a special "100 years from now" issue of the* New York Times Magazine.

MAKING SURE OF THE TEXT

1. This humorous look at *Highlights For Children* in 2096 suggests that while some things change, others never do. What errors does Goofus make that parallel the mistakes our own younger generation make?
2. What cultural and global developments would lead to the cartoon from 2034, or from 2072?
3. The last cartoon, placed in 2096, offers a gruesome look at the future of humanity and reminds the reader of an old joke about who might survive a nuclear holocaust. In this case, the lesson is not one of etiquette but of survival. Are the other cartoons similarly doubled in intent?

CONSIDERING THE CONTEXT

1. What other lessons about etiquette might need to be taught in the future? List some examples and explain what cultural changes would have brought about the need.
2. Compare the events in this cartoon strip to the events in "In the Year 2525." What parallels do you find?
3. As an artifact of the future, how does this cartoon compare with, for instance, the cartoons such as *The Jetsons* or *Futurama*? In what contexts (e.g., humorous, religious, technological) could both cartoons appear?

■ ■ ■

"In the Year 2525" (1969)

Zager and Evans

In the year 2525
if man is still alive
if woman can survive
They may find

In the year 3535
Ain't gonna need to tell the truth, tell no lie
Everything you think, do and say
Is in the pill you took today

In the year 4545
You ain't gonna need your teeth, won't need
    your eyes
You won't find a thing to chew
Nobody's gonna look at you

In the year 5555
Your arms hangin' limp at your sides
Your legs got nothin' to do
Some machine's doin' that for you

In the year 6565
You won't need no husband, won't need
    no wife
You'll pick your son, pick your daughter too
From the bottom of a long glass tube

In the year 7510
If God's a-coming, He oughta make it by then
Maybe He'll look around Himself and say
"Guess it's time for the judgement day"

In the year 8510
God is gonna shake His mighty head
He'll either say "I'm pleased where man has been"
Or tear it down, and start again

In the year 9595
I'm kinda wonderin' if man is gonna be alive
He's taken everything this old earth can give
And he ain't put back nothing

Now it's been ten thousand years
Man has cried a billion tears
For what, he never knew
Now man's reign is through

But through eternal night
The twinkling of starlight
So very far away
Maybe it's only yesterday

■ *First released in August 1969, "In the Year 2525" depicts projections of social ills and religious developments between 2525 and 9595. The song stayed at the Number One position on the Top Ten list for nearly four weeks.*

MAKING SURE OF THE TEXT

1. Are the dates meant to be humorous, realistic, or rhythmic?
2. Identify the social progressions this song refers to: What events lead to the next ones?
3. The last stanza of the song could refer to the current example of looking simultaneously into the heavens and back into time. Summarize (if you can) the concept of lightyears.
4. Is this a cheerful future, a depressing future, or somewhere in between? What is your reading of the lyrics?

CONSIDERING THE CONTEXT

1. Leaving aside the strict accuracy of the dates, compare the developments in this song to the developments Kaku provides in his article. Do the artifacts seem to agree or disagree? How do they enlighten each other?
2. Research the social events in 1969; to which of them does this song seem to respond? Can you read these lyrics in context with current events?
3. What clues in the lyrics could provide you with information about the date of composition?

■ ■ ■

"Home Sweet Virtual Home," *Business Week* **(1999)**

Neil Gross

Toward the end of the 1990s, a loose-knit community of programmers with limited financial resources took on the world's most powerful software companies—and triumphed. Known as the open-source movement, this freewheeling confederacy grew up on the Internet. Unbound by geography or time, it has used the new communications medium as both a laboratory and a launchpad for high-quality programs such as Linux, Apache, and Perl that compete head on with Microsoft, IBM, and Sun Microsystems. The movement has spawned a whole new set of rules for the world's $150 billion software industry. And it has established a new model of how people can live and work online.

It's fitting that a band of programmers should blaze trails for online communities. Teams of engineers designed the Net to transcend crass physical limitations. Once this ethereal infrastructure was laid, waves of homesteaders arrived: physicists chasing data on quarks and black holes, religious fanatics, revolutionaries waving every known political banner, children looking for cyber playmates on the other side of the planet. With traditional communities weakening in a fast-paced world, the Net offered a potent way to form new bonds based on pure intellectual affinity.

But the Net's early pioneers learned a painful lesson: In a world of infinite electronic choices, it can be extremely difficult to connect. How do you find a handful of like-minded souls in a global pool of 150 million Netizens? Facts and data are readily available. But today's best search engines can't sift through a thousand news groups and message boards for a discussion thread that will inspire you or guide you to a community of your peers.

STILL CAVE DWELLERS

Fortunately, dozens of research labs and Internet startups, stretching from the Massachusetts Institute of Technology Media Laboratory to the University of Tokyo, are on a mission to improve life on the Internet. Within five years, software will take much more accurate soundings of who you are and what you seek. New programs will let strangers on the Net appraise one another—whether they are looking for expert advice or buying and selling goods. Other software tools will make it easier for members of a group to wander the Web together, untethered to a particular portal, mailing list, or message board. Human voices are already augmenting text in chat rooms. Next, for Netizens who seek intimacy—not anonymity—video will provide human faces for online personas. Until these tools reach maturity, however, Net communities will remain in the Stone Age. Says Steve Larsen senior vice-president of Minneapolis-based Net Perceptions, which pioneered the first wave of software that recommends books and music at

Amazon.com and CDNOW: "At this stage, we're all still sitting around the fire in loincloths holding clubs."

The new tools can't come soon enough for Michal Plume, a mother of four who runs a small business from her home in Palo Alto, Calif. Worried about declining standards in the local school system, she spent much of the mid-1990s debating issues in education news groups, organizing mailing lists, and struggling to find or forge a community that could influence haughty high school administrators. "For the longest time, the kids saw only the back of my head," she says. After many frustrating months, she concluded that "real people who have the information you need don't join these groups."

Nor does she expect to find soulmates in the random and repetitive cyberstreets of Geocities, Tripod, Xoom, TheGlobe, and other virtual metropolises. For every lively chat room debate about hot stocks or hunger in Africa, there are hundreds of dead discussion areas, dreary or abandoned home pages, threads that go nowhere, lonely voices in the darkness. "The sense of community has been lost on these sites," says Emily Meehan, an analyst who covers online communities for Yankee Group in Boston.

Yet the raw material for vibrant communities exists on the Net in spades. There are astounding repositories of poetry and pop culture and expertly moderated bulletin boards. Side by side with abject quackery are superb e-mail forums like that of the British Medical Journal, where physicians from around the world debate everything from organ transplants to euthanasia (www.bmj.com).

In life-and-death matters, virtual communities—for all their flaws—can be a godsend. Parents of dying children sustain one another in hope and grief. Cancer patients become wise partners to their physicians. "Many of my patients who spend time on the Net are extremely well informed and ask astute questions," says Dr. Hiram S. Cody III, a breast cancer specialist and surgeon at Memorial Sloan-Kettering Cancer Center in New York.

The trouble is, finding jewels on the Net today depends far too much on luck. That's why so many experts in online communities are studying the experience of the open-source movement. This community, which has roots in the early '70s and comprises thousands of hackers worldwide, swears allegiance to no central portal. Instead, teams of programmers collaborate via dozens of decentralized mailing lists and message boards.

INFORMED CRITICS

They find one another because they understand an emerging set of shortcuts and secret passageways that will one day be common through cyberspace. "What serious geeks do is a predictor for what larger groups do," says Tim O'Reilly, open-source evangelist and president of publishers O'Reilly & Associates. Out of sheer necessity, such programmers have built some of the best tools to locate high-level discussion and to refine useful information from all the random noise on the Net.

To watch this in action, visit a bustling technology hub called Slashdot (www.slashdot.org), a unit of technology news site Andover.Net in Acton, Mass. Created by open-source hackers in their early twenties, the site is "required reading," says Raghu Ramakrishnan, professor of computer science at the University of Wisconsin at Madison. Thanks to a process of continuous peer review, the hottest tidbits from technology mailing lists and discussion boards around the world show up on Slashdot's main menu. "This is an organic community that shapes itself, a place where you can discover not just what people claim to be but what others think of their claims," says Ramakrishnan.

Slashdot's band of editors deserves credit. But they also depend on homegrown computer code to help rank input from the message boards. The higher a participant is rated by his peers at Slashdot, the greater clout he or she will get as a judge of others who post comments. "Slashdot's software is all open source, and now a lot of other Web sites are using it," says Christine Peterson, the executive director of the nonprofit Foresight Institute in Palo Alto and the one credited with coining the term "open source."

INVISIBLE INK

Hypertext is another trademark of the open-source community—and it's not just those blue highlighted links among static documents. To cut communities loose from portals and news groups, programmers developed software, available for free at www.crit.org, that lets gangs of Netizens annotate any other Web site they visit with the electronic equivalent of sticky notes that only group members can read. Crit.org hasn't tried to popularize its free software, but similar tools and support are available from a startup in Redwood City, Calif., called Third Voice Inc. "The successes of open source will be part of everyone's background culture," says Eric S. Raymond, author of the open-source manifesto, *The Cathedral and the Bazaar* (www.tuxedo.org).

The open-source gang doesn't have a lock on communitarian technology. At online auctioneer eBay Inc., you can post details—good and bad—about your experience with vendors, who are free to respond. The credibility this feedback loop inspires may explain how eBay and other auction sites attracted a cool $1 billion in transactions last year.

All these software advances, however, carry the seeds of their own corruption. If continual peer review is the crux of online credibility, there can be strong incentives to stuff the ballot box. A crooked vendor at eBay, for example, could load the message boards with spurious testimony. To avoid such outcomes, "we're putting a lot of effort into how people develop reputations online and how they can manage complex, long-term identities," says Judith S. Donath, an assistant professor and

community expert at MIT's Media Lab, which pioneered product rec-
ommendation software in the early 1990s.

The emergence of sensually rich media on the Net could help resolve
some of these issues. Voice-based chat will be followed by video, virtual
reality, and simulated touch. These formats could help foster trust
among cybernauts by linking online personas more tightly to flesh-and-
blood individuals.

Trust, indeed, has been a factor in the open-source community's success. Because the movement draws volunteers from hundreds of organizations, members are forced to juggle conflicting loyalties. They must
learn to let others tinker with their code and help debug it. Few get rich
off the resulting programs, which are mostly distributed free on the Net.
But there are other rewards, says analyst Dan Kusnetzky at International
Data Corp.—like watching the market share for Linux server software
soar from zip in 1995 to nearly 16% worldwide last year.

That's just a glimmer of what online communities can accomplish. As
social beings, humans have an irrepressible drive to connect and collaborate. Once upon a time, connection meant church suppers, street fairs,
and committee meetings. Now, online groups breach all physical boundaries to share the sorrows of illness, the wisdom of age, the wonder of
art. Tomorrow, we'll talk and touch with levels of intimacy that we select from an ever-richer palette. The dream is that this enrichment will
make online communities less random. And a rendezvous with friends
or colleagues in cyberspace will be as satisfying as any encounter you
treasure in the real world. This may well be the ultimate promise of the
Internet.

■ *Neil Gross is senior editor in charge of science and technology for* Business Week,
*a publication covering all aspects of medicine, life sciences, communications and
consumer technology, new materials, the environment, and Internet culture. Gross
has written for the journal since 1987.*

MAKING SURE OF THE TEXT

1. What is the "open-source" movement Gross describes? Why is it relevant?
2. What is the advantage of being able to "annotate" a Web site with the equivalent of a sticky note? Why does Gross think it's important?
3. What are the qualities we treasure in real-time contacts that we might be able
   to transfer to virtual time?
4. How will adding video to chat rooms increase accountability?

CONSIDERING THE CONTEXT

1. Whereas Brave suggests the negative outcomes of increased genetic engineering, Gross focuses on the positive outcomes of increased software engineering. What are some of the drawbacks to the developments he suggests?
2. From some perspectives, "virtual homes" might seem to be contributing to a
   perceived decline in American culture; from other perspectives, such software

increases community. What are some of the artifacts of each perspective? In other words, what evidence could you bring to support these viewpoints?

3. What organization pattern has Gross used for this article? How does it reflect the content?

4. Gross concludes with a reference to a cyberspace *rendezvous*, a term that might suggest sexual encounters. Could his article be read for a subtext supporting "virtual sex" encounters?

■ ■ ■

"Machine Intelligence," from *Sharing the Universe* (1998)

Seth Shostak

Our view of E.T. is heavily predicated on what *we* are: the first thinking beings to occupy the planet. We assume that if the human species can figure a way to survive its own destructive tendencies, then perhaps an extraterrestrial species has managed to do the same. The result would be the establishment of a long-lived, technological civilization. Such societies may exist elsewhere in the Galaxy, and we might either overhear or meet them. But note that we have subtly assumed that our contact will be with the *first* sentients to appear on the planet they occupy. In fact, our quest is not so restrictive. We're only looking for cosmic company. We don't insist that any aliens we discover are the original thinking critters from their own star system. All that counts is that they be around now.[1]

This is an intriguing point simply because the universe is old and the Earth is young. Other worlds will have started down the tricky paths of life billions of years ago. They may have spawned intelligent beings long before our planet came into existence. But species come, and species go. As unpleasant as the thought may be, even *thinking* species might come and go. A commonplace scenario, as we've already noted, might be one in which intelligent creatures spring up on a planet, strut their brief stuff, and are forthwith extinguished by external circumstance, or more plausibly by their own hand. Many editorial writers have postulated such a dismal end for *Homo sapiens,* after all.

If this dystopian view of alien nature is accurate, then self-destruction could frequently bring quick and ugly ends to technological species (a point we will return to later). In that case, our efforts to locate intelligent neighbors might be stymied. Shortly after the aliens become sophisticated enough to build radio transmitters and rockets, they will suddenly expire in a mushroom-shaped cloud of smoke.

But if, as we have emphasized, intelligence has real survival value, it will come back like a bad penny. It will arise Phoenix-like from the ashes of its prior destruction, undoubtedly in new form. Imagine being on such a world when civilization erupts for a second time, and the archaeologists begin to dig up the ruins of a long-gone, intelligent species on their own planet! This phenomenon could be encouraging news for those seeking cosmic company. If intelligence is persistent, if sentient species routinely have successors, then the outlook for finding them brightens considerably.

Another possibility is that thinking beings can manage to avoid any such break in the reign of intelligence. They might do this by finding a

---

[1]In the case that we find the aliens by, say, overhearing a radio broadcast, "around now" means that they were around at the time the transmission was sent.

cure for the built-in aggression that is an inevitable by-product of evolution in a competitive world. A civilization whose members were content to contemplate their navels or play harmless video games might last a long time. But another, less insipid approach is possible. A sentient society might be able to short-circuit biological evolution, and deliberately engineer its own successors. This seems plausible simply because we see signs of it on our own technological horizon. We may be unwittingly taking the first steps toward producing the next thinking inhabitants of this planet.

Consider the medical practice of transplanting body parts, such as hearts or knee joints. (Whether the parts come from other humans or from other species, for example by using a pig heart instead of a human one, may be of great interest to moralists, animal activists, and the pig community. It is not particularly relevant to our argument here, however.) Success with these biological transplants will create a strong drive to develop artificial replacements. Manufactured parts will, in the long run, be cheaper and more readily available when required. The recipients' bodies will also be less prone to reject them.

Dialysis machines (artificial kidneys) are a contemporary example, although today's models are too large for comfortable implantation. But there is little doubt that the next half-century will witness the development of a greater variety of both artificial body parts and synthetic bodily fluids, such as blood. At some point in the next century, we may, indeed, have the technology for the *Six Million Dollar Man*.

Parallel with this partial mechanization of humans will be the humanization of machines—the production of sophisticated robots. These devices will be outfitted with computing horsepower that will allow them to take on far more challenging work than today's models, such as those that put together the family car. Robots designed to do the tasks that humans would rather avoid—picking strawberries, mining coal, or servicing nuclear reactors—are not far in our future.

These easily-foreseen co-minglings of machine and protoplasm are, in a broader sense, simply hi-tech tool use. For thousands of years we have been constructing devices that facilitate our existence, that free us from the infirmities and unpleasant labor that interfere with what we like to do most: contemplating new physics, chasing one another around the desk, or dozing in front of the TV. We can confidently expect that within our lifetimes, the rude chipped flints of our forefathers will evolve into sophisticated household robots and implantable spare parts.

This is all but a modest extrapolation of current capability. The situation changes radically, however, if we take one more step and produce a stand-in for our brains. This would go far beyond tool use, for now we have replaced the guy using the tool. We will have engineered our successors.

Is this possible? Everyone knows that machines can't think. The best among them can play a depressingly good game of chess, but none can, say, write a book on the Zen of Chess. For years, researchers toiling away in the optimistically-named field of Artificial Intelligence have tried to build machines that could successfully tackle such relatively simple problems as stacking tin cans or diagnosing illnesses. Their success so far is modest. But the researchers involved remain upbeat in their belief in the possibility of thinking machines, although the idea is not without naysayers. Among those who are not so sanguine about the possibility of synthetic sentients is the British physicist Roger Penrose. He has argued that consciousness and creativity may depend upon unpredictable quantum mechanical processes, and would therefore be beyond the capabilities of a deliberately constructed device. However, most scientists subscribe to a more mundane and mechanistic view of our thinking apparatus. MIT physicist Philip Morrison has described brains as merely "slow-speed bit processors operating in salt water." If so, it is quite possible, in principle, to replicate their functioning in dry hardware. The detailed construction of such a machine might be somewhat different than that of the human brain, in the same way that airplanes don't imitate birds by flapping their wings. But the functional behavior could be the same.

Science fiction long ago mastered the production of such cybernetic cerebellums. A contemporary example is the android Data, a favorite character on *Star Trek: The Next Generation.* Data is human-shaped, presumably for ease of accommodation aboard the U.S.S. Enterprise-E, a ship built, and largely crewed, by hominids. He has landed the job of Operations Manager, showing that even in the 24th century, machines are still putting humans out of work. Even more perplexing, Data has been accorded full civil rights as a sentient being. This is enlightenment of a curious sort, for it suggests that if enough citizen androids were constructed, they might vote themselves into office and take over civilization via the ballot box.

Data was programmed without emotions, although an emotion upgrade chip was made, and even inserted into the android's socket. Lamentably, the chip burned up due to a power problem, and Data remains saddled with a Pinocchio complex: he wants to be human. Data longs to understand us, and even develop a sense of humor. He wants to be a good primate.

Data is like many aliens of both fiction and the popular imagination: he suffers an emotion gap. And because of this, we feel a bit sorry for him. Poor Data; he's got all the equipment any red-blooded male has, and is programmed in multiple unspecified 'techniques,' but he can't quite muster love. Naturally, this gives the android some reassuring vulnerability. But emotions, as we've noted, are useful survival tools for a biological being in a competitive environment. They could be less beneficial for a machine, and as Mr. Spock might remark, could lead to behavior that (from a machine's point of view) is "not logical." Androids don't have to get mad to defend their turf or fall in love to ensure their progeny. They might be as cool as chipped ice.

However, it is Data's intellectual prowess that is of interest here. He claims to have a mental storage capacity of 100 quadrillion bytes, which is about a hundred times as much information as you'll find in the Library of Congress. Despite this impressive total, the android doesn't shame his fellow (human) crew members with overwhelming intellectual insight and brilliant deduction. Data's just another guy on the ship's bridge (except that his jokes tend to fall flat).

But imagine a real thinking device, able to react to new situations, plan ahead, and evaluate strategies. It could be fed the world's accumulated knowledge and not forget a thing. One of the first tasks we might put before this super savant is to design its own successor—a machine more capable than itself. And that machine would be asked to do the same. In short order, we could produce a device that the slow and uncertain processes of biological evolution might never bring forth.

The consequences of silicon smarts for our own society would no doubt be revolutionary. But for the purpose of finding the extraterrestrials, the important point is that truly capable machines would be able to do something that is quite hard for biological intelligence: they could journey to the stars. Biology is fragile, and complex organisms live only a short time. Interstellar travel for biological aliens will only be practical if enormous velocities, close to the speed of light, can be attained. Machines, on the other hand, are less likely to be in a hurry. Cheaper and safer slow-speed rocketry might be an acceptable travel mode for a machine.

Why would a machine leave the planet of its birth? One obvious attraction would be the fact that its natal neighborhood might, like Earth, be in a relatively dull part of the Galaxy. When asked what the truly interesting and important things in the universe are, most humans would probably answer "sex and money." In fact, a more global answer is matter and energy (which we manage to convert to sex and money on Earth). Matter and energy can be found in far greater abundance elsewhere. For example, in the central regions of our Galaxy, the density of stars is more than a million times higher than in the fringe areas we inhabit. We are in the galactic boondocks, and a machine capable of leaving home might naturally hanker to go where the action is.

So one possibility is that machines developed billions of years ago by a distant, alien civilization have spread through the star fields of the Milky Way, perhaps producing occasional duplicates as back-ups, and are now cruising the interstellar voids like a flotilla of insects. They could rapidly adapt to the harsh environments of the Galaxy, since machines can improve themselves. This ability doesn't extend to living species, despite beliefs to the contrary by early researchers. At the beginning of the 19th century, the French biologist Jean Baptiste Lamarck proposed that creatures could influence the characteristics of their offspring by their own behavior. In straining to reach leaves on high branches, giraffes would stretch their necks, and this modification would be passed on to their progeny. In fact, acquired traits like a stretched neck are not inherited. Biological evolution, as Darwin showed, is a slow and haphazard process of pruning for comparative advantage.

But machine improvement wouldn't proceed at Darwin's languorous pace. The machines could rapidly refine themselves, and adapt to existence in the rarefied bath of starlight and gas that fills the vastness of space. Their evolution would be Lamarckian and speedy. Their ability to think might earn for them the honor of being the true intelligentsia of the Galaxy.

In characterizing the aliens, we can make plausible arguments as long as they are biological. Our description of E.T.'s cultural level, cranial capability, and moral bent are all based on traits and behaviors that have clear survival value in a competitive, life-filled environment. They obviously apply to us, and, one assumes, to any biological aliens that inhabit a planet not enormously dissimilar to Earth. But if E.T. is a machine, and possibly a lonely machine with very little daily interaction with others, then his attitude and behavior will be strange beyond our imaginings.

It may be that the ultimate achievement of biological intelligence is to get the silicon sentients underway. Biology is a nice, necessary first step, and a creature like *Homo sapiens* is an example of a simple foray by life into the realm of thinking entities. But the next big step, the truly dramatic step, is the start of machine intelligence. You might regard this scenario as both arguable and depressing. Nonetheless, if sentient machines do exist, then their obvious advantages could make them an important, if not the dominant, intelligence in the Galaxy. Should SETI scientists succeed in picking up a signal from the cosmos, no one will be surprised to learn that the signal comes from a machine, a radio transmitter. But we should also be prepared for the possibility that *that* machine is in the service of another machine.

■ *Seth Shostak is an astronomer with a BA in physics from Princeton University and a PhD in astronomy from California Polytechnic Institute. He edits the newsletter, oversees the Web site, gives talks, and writes magazine articles (and books) about the Search for Extraterrestrial Intelligence (SETI). He also teaches a half-dozen informal education classes on astronomy and other topics in the Bay Area.*

MAKING SURE OF THE TEXT

1. In what ways does Shostak suggest that we are perhaps "producing the next thinking inhabitants of this planet"?
2. In what contexts have you seen "mechanized humans" produced? Shostak mentions *The Six Million Dollar Man*. What other contexts can you identify?
3. What are the arguments for and against being able to replicate intelligence in a machine?
4. Why wouldn't machine evolution mimic Darwinian processes, according to Shostak?

CONSIDERING THE CONTEXT

1. How do the sentient machines Shostak mentions resemble the nanotechnology discussed by Kaku?
2. What artifacts of machine intelligence can you identify? For instance, what about "smart classrooms" or other "intuitive" software?
3. Shostak concludes by mentioning that we see alien life largely from biological perspectives because "they obviously apply to us, and, one assumes, to any biological aliens." Is the mechanical perspective the only other option? In other words, must aliens be either biological or mechanical? What artifacts, or evidence, can you supply for this shift in perspective?

■ ■ ■

Realistic Future Depictions (Student Response Essay, 2000)

James Doraz

Los Angeles has become even more of a filthy and disgusting metropolis. The air has become so thick from pollution that it's hard to see the sun. The city has been abandoned except for the small space vehicles flying high above the skyscrapers. This smog city incorporates humans and aliens from different galaxies into an uneasy community. Robots, created by humans, now rule over the city and vaporize any life forms that get in their way. Most futuristic sci-fi movies are all similar with either scary aliens or killer robots. They never show real life or how humans will really be living in the next fifty or hundred years. Taking advantage of the recent interest in genetics, and showcasing sophisticated technology, the movie *Gattaca* is the best depiction of what the future will be like.

The movie *Gattaca* provides a realistic and eerie view of how human lives might change through harnessing the power of genetics. The movie begins with a couple having a baby boy named Vincent. Vincent is born too early to take advantage of new procedures to genetically alter babies. The cost of the procedures to make people stronger, more intelligent, and more beautiful than ever before splits society into two distinct classes. The families who can't afford it and the children born before the new procedures are called invalids, relegated to the bottom of society and given low-paying, labor-intensive jobs. The valids, genetically altered humans, are the wealthier, perfect humans. They are born stronger and smarter because their genes are chosen for them.

In the movie *Gattaca*, the costumes and scenery lend a realistic, yet futuristic look to the picture. Unlike most science fiction movies, the sets show a simple design lacking the normal high technology covered with electronics. The furniture and building are all rounded with no sharp edges, suggesting a modern look. The costumes in the movie help depict the two social classes: The "valids" dress very well, in classy, simple fashions, but the "invalids" wear plain clothes and look very ordinary. The distinctions in clothing mimic our own society. At the present time there are two social classes here in America. The upper class who are the celebrities, politicians and the extremely wealthy are just like the "valids," because they are privileged and can achieve whatever they want. The "invalids" resemble the present day middle and lower classes who have big dreams but no way to realize them. The only difference between the present and the movie's future is that in the present you can change which class you want to live in. In *Gattaca*, however, your social class is determined at birth. Genetic engineering as it's shown in the film serves to broaden the divide between the social classes.

Genetic development has been in the news recently for the great advancements in this field. Scientists right now are researching people's DNA to find out which chromosomes affect people's behavior, personality, and looks.

Gattaca shows what a world would be like if people could decide what hair color their child was to have, or how smart their child would be. Using genetics, we could also cure alcoholism, heart problems, and vision problems. Using the research that is going on right now with genetics, a gene altering world doesn't seem too far away. *Gattaca* seems real.

The movie's technology projected realistically what our future will look like. The use of solar power, for example, was evident in many outdoor scenes, suggesting that the population changed to a cleaner form of energy. Daily space shuttle launches to Titan, the newly founded colony, showed a realistic view of what space travel and planetary colonization will be like. *Gattaca* showed the audience a realistic view of what technology can do to a civilization. The movie's modern look gave the audience the idea that this could happen at any time. It also showed an original conception of the future. Since there are no clichéd space aliens from Mars killing humans, the film had time to explore how current research could change people's lives in the future.

■ ■ ■

■ Ideas for Writing ■

Journal

1. What does your future hold? Write from several perspectives: your personal future, your family's, your chosen profession's, your planet's. How do you come up with your answers?
2. What do you think are the most important issues to be resolved in the next century? Start with Holdren's article and work from there. Do you agree with his priorities? What would you change if you were the one writing the article?
3. If you could change some of your genetic makeup (for instance, the human germline cells), knowing that your descendants would also carry these changes, would you? Use Brave's article to help you speculate.

Response

1. In your perspective, and taking into account Kaku's descriptions of Type I, II, and III civilizations, what do you think is the most important element in bringing human culture to Type I status? How will this be accomplished?
2. What futuristic pop culture depictions do you think are most valid or realistic? For instance, consider *A.I., Star Trek, Blade Runner, 1984, Gattaca, The Matrix, The Running Man, Fahrenheit 451, The Martian Chronicles*, and so on. Be sure to explain your choices. What does "valid" or "realistic" mean to you?
3. Draw on Chapter 4's essay from the Dalai Lama, the poem by Sherman Alexie, and Chapter 3's *Star Trek* photo essay to identify the similarities you find between scientific belief and religious faith.

Argument

1. Take a slightly more local approach to Holdren's global argument: argue for the four most important issues to resolve in the United States in the next fifty years, or the four most important issues in your hometown. Be sure to consider the different answers encouraged by a shift from a global to a local perspective.
2. James Watson, quoted in Ralph Brave's article, asks "if we could make better human beings by knowing how to add genes [. . .] why shouldn't we do it?" Develop a stance on this issue and support it with examples of current genetic engineering practices on plants and animals and current gene therapy techniques. How does Chapter 1's concept of recontextualizing factor into your answer?
3. How might each of the chapter readings thus far change over the next ten years? For instance, how will pop music, perceptions of sexuality, or the popularity of religion shift in response to a changing popular culture? Remember to provide historical perspectives to support your answers.

Analysis

1. Compare the artifacts of the future for what they suggest about humanity's ultimate fate. For instance, you might look at films, books, TV series, or a combination of these media. How does the human race further itself, and what might stop it?
2. Choose one of the readings in this section to read closely. As you read, consider these points: What is the author's position? What are the author's qualifications for writing about this subject? How does the author signal transitions in ideas? From these questions, develop an analysis of one of the following: the author's perspective on the issue; the way the author has structured the article for the reader; the reading's intended audience.
3. Shostak suggests that "the obvious advantages" of machine intelligence would lead to their being an "important, if not the dominant," galactic intelligence. What are these advantages, and how would they elevate machine above biological intelligence?

Research

1. In your school library and on the Internet, find and evaluate several Web sites devoted to UFOs or the possibilities of life on other planets. Identify the strengths and weaknesses of each site, and explain, in your paper, how each site is effective or ineffective in its context.
2. In your school library, find a text that speculates about the future of the human species (its population, its technological developments, its dangers, its encounters with other species, etc.) and examine it for its realism. Be sure you explain what your criteria are for assigning value; your perspective and the context of the text will help determine its realism.
3. Using your library and the Internet, find depictions of the future from 1920, 1950, and 1980. You might consider researching scientific projections or reading literature. What do you find? What changes in perspective do you notice from these earlier times?

INDEX

CREDITS

This page constitutes an extension of the copyright page. We have made every effort to trace the ownership of all copyrighted material and to secure permissions from the copyright holders. In the event of any question arising regarding the use of any material, we will be pleased to make the necessary corrections in future printings. Thanks are due to the following for granting permission.

LITERARY CREDITS

Chapter 1: 35: "Popular Music, Television, and Generational Identity," *Journal of Popular Culture,* 30:3, Winter, 1996, pp. 121–141. Reprinted by permission. **44:** From Robert H. Knight, *The Age of Consent: The Rise of Relativism and the Corruption of Popular Culture,* 1998. Spence Publishing Company, Dallas, Tex. **52:** N. George, "Da Joint! and Beyond," from *Hip Hop America,* pp. 208-212. Copyright © 1998. Used by permission of Viking Penguin, a division of Penguin Putnam Inc. **57:** © 1997 Perfect Sound Forever. Reprinted with permission. **67:** "Society's Mixed Messages: How Popular Music Influences Alcohol and Other Drug Use," webpage, 1998, copyright © 1885-1998 William J. Bailey, Indiana University. **69:** *Lucy in the Sky with Diamonds* by John Lennon & Paul McCartney. Copyright © 1967 (/renewed) SONY/ATV Tunes LLC. All rights administered by Sony/ATV Music Publishing, 8 Music Square West, Nashville, TN 37203. All rights reserved. Used by permission.

Chapter 2: 89: "Portrait of my Body," copyright © 1996 by Philip Lopate. First appeared in the *Michigan Quarterly,* from *Portrait of My Body* by Philip Lopate. Used by permission of Doubleday, a division of Random House, Inc. **98:** "Designing Men: Reading the Male Body as Text," from *Textual Reasoning.* Copyright © 1998 Philip Culbertson. Reprinted with permission from *Textual Reasoning.* **107:** "Open Letter to *MS,*" *MS Magazine,* January, 1998. Copyright © 1998, Ms. Magazine. Reprinted by permission of Ms. Magazine. **113:** "The Female Body" from *Michigan Quarterly Review,* 1998, pp. 39–46. © 1998 by Margaret Atwood. Reprinted with permission. **117:** "Men, Women See Themselves Differently," Miami Herald, February 1, 1998. Copyright © 1998 Dave Barry, the Miami Herald, Miami, FL. **120:** "Lumbar Thought" from *Travels in Hyperreality,* by Umberto Eco, copyright © 1983, 1976, 1973 by Gruppos

Evans. Reprinted by permission of Zerlad Music Enterprises, Ltd. **300:** "Home Sweet Virtual Home" from *Business Week*, 10/04/99, Issue 3649. Reprinted with permission of McGraw-Hill, New York. **305:** Selections from "Machine Intelligence" from *Sharing the Universe*. Copyright © 1998 by Seth Shostak. Reprinted by permission of Berkley Hills Press.

PHOTO CREDITS

Chapter 1: 2: (top right) © SYGMA/CORBIS; **2:** (bottom right) © 1998 Lyons Partnership, L.P./The Everett Collection; **2:** (bottom left) © 2000 Kraig Geiger/The Everett Collection; **3:** © SYGMA/CORBIS; **5:** The Everett Collection, NY; **16:** Copyright 2002 Columbia Broadcasting System; **20:** © Mike Salsbury/AP Photo/AP/Wide World Photos; **25:** Copyright © 2001 Robert Altman; **27:** (top left) © AP Photo/Suzanne Plunkett/AP/Wide World Photos, NY; **27:** (top right) The Everett Collection, Inc., NY; **27:** (bottom right) Cover Photo by Annie Liebovitz, from *Rolling Stone*, February 1, 1973. Copyright © by Rolling Stone LLC 1973. All rights reserved. Reprinted by permission; **27:** (bottom left) © AP Photo/Adam Nadel/AP/Wide World Photos, NY; **29:** The Everett Collection, NY; **30:** (left) © Kraig Geiger/The Everett Collection, NY; **30:** (right) Copyright © 1998 Bad Boy Records, Mkt.; **31:** The Everett Collection, NY; **32:** (top) © Bettmann/Corbis; **32:** (bottom) Jim Cornfield/CORBIS; **33:** © CBS/The Everett Collection, NY.

Chapter 2: 81: (left) The Everett Collection, NY; **81:** (right) © PhotoEdit; **83:** (top left) © PhotoEdit; **83:** (top right) © PhotoEdit; 83: (center left) © PhotoEdit; **83:** (center right) © PhotoEdit; **83:** (bottom left) © PhotoEdit; **83:** (bottom right)© PhotoEdit; **84:** © Reuters Newsmedia, Inc./CORBIS; **87:** © AP Photo/Gail Oskin/AP/Wide World Photos, NY; **110:** (top left) © Laura Dwight/CORBIS; **110:** (top right)© Bettmann Archive/CORBIS; **110:** (bottom left) © Lynn Goldsmith/CORBIS; **110:** (bottom right) © Hanah Gal/CORBIS; **111:** (top left) © Ali Meyer/CORBIS; **111:** (top right) © Ann Purcell/CORBIS; **111:** (bottom)© Richard Cummins/CORBIS.

Chapter 3: 129: © 20th Century Fox/The Everett Collection, NY; **131:** (top left) © Gary Brasch/CORBIS; **131:** (top right) The Everett Collection, NY; **131:** (center left) © Reuters Newsmedia, Inc./CORBIS; **131:** (center right) The Everett Collection, NY; **131:** (bottom) The Everett Collection, NY; **133:** (left) © 1997 Fox Broadcasting Company/The Everett Collection, NY; **133:** (right) © AP Photo/Charles Tasnadi/AP/Wide World Photos, NY; **134:** (bottom) © 1997 20th Century Fox/The Everett Collection, NY; **136:** © 1989 Paramount Picture Corp./The Everett Collection, NY; **206:** (top) The Everett Collection, NY; **206:** (bottom) © 1990 Paramount Picture Corp./The Everett Collection, NY; **207:** (top) © Paramount Picture Corp./The Everett Collection, NY; **207:** (bottom) © 1996 Paramount Picture Corp./The Everett Collection, NY.